Nación Genízara

Querencias Series

Miguel A. Gandert and Enrique R. Lamadrid | SERIES EDITORS

Querencia is a popular term in the Spanish-speaking world that is used to express a deeply rooted love of place and people. This series promotes a transnational, humanistic, and creative vision of the US-Mexico borderlands based on all aspects of expressive culture, both material and intangible.

ALSO AVAILABLE IN THE QUERENCIAS SERIES:

El Camino Real de California: A History
by Joseph P. Sánchez

Imagine a City That Remembers: The Albuquerque Rephotography Project
by Anthony Anella and Mark C. Childs

The Latino Christ in Art, Literature, and Liberation Theology
by Michael R. Candelaria

Sisters in Blue/Hermanas de azul: Sor María de Ágreda Comes to New Mexico/Sor María de Ágreda viene a Nuevo México
by Enrique R. Lamadrid and Anna M. Nogar

Aztlán: Essays on the Chicano Homeland,
Revised and Expanded Edition, edited by Francisco A. Lomelí,
Rudolfo Anaya, and Enrique R. Lamadrid

Río: A Photographic Journey on the Old Río Grande / Río Bravo
edited by Melissa Savage

Coyota in the Kitchen: A Memoir of New and Old Mexico, with Recipes
by Anita Rodríguez

Chasing Dichos through Chimayó by Don J. Usner

Enduring Acequias: Wisdom of the Land, Knowledge of the Water
by Juan Estevan Arellano

Hotel Mariachi: Urban Space and Cultural Heritage in Los Angeles
by Catherine López Kurland, Enrique R. Lamadrid,
and Miguel A. Gandert

Sagrado: A Photopoetics Across the Chicano Homeland
by Spencer R. Herrera and Levi Romero

Nación Genízara

ETHNOGENESIS, PLACE, AND
IDENTITY IN NEW MEXICO

Edited by Moises Gonzales and Enrique R. Lamadrid

University of New Mexico Press | Albuquerque

© 2019 by the University of New Mexico Press
All rights reserved. Published 2019
First paperback edition, 2021
Printed in the United States of America

ISBN 978-0-8263-6107-3 (cloth)
ISBN 978-0-8263-6330-5 (paperback)
ISBN 978-0-8263-6108-0 (e-book)

Library of Congress Control Number: 2019951207

Cover photograph: Niño de los Guajolotes, "Turkey Boy."
Talpa, New Mexico, 1996. Courtesy of Miguel A. Gandert.

Designed by Mindy Basinger Hill

Composed in 10.2/14pt. x 26 picas Adobe Caslon Pro

DEDICATED TO ALL THE GENÍZARO ANCESTORS, AND OF LATE:

Gilberto Benito Córdova (1943–2011), Lucero de Abiquiú, first Genízaro anthropologist, historian, novelist, community scholar.

José Antonio "Galento" Martínez (1938–2017), jinete extraordinario, Gran Comanche de Alcalde, aka Cuerno Verde.

Floriano "Floyd" Eudoro Trujillo (1934–2019), Hermano de La Morada de Nuestra Señora de los Dolores del Alto, Pueblo de Abiquiú.

CONTENTS

List of Illustrations
xi

Foreword
Recordando el Futuro /
Remembering the Future:
Mal-Criados, Memory,
and Memorials
ESTEVAN RAEL-GÁLVEZ
xv

Estrellita Reluciente del Pueblo de Abiquiú: Coplas de Entrada /
Little Shining Star of the Pueblo of Abiquiú: Verses of Entry
DAVID F. GARCÍA
xxv

Acknowledgments
xxvii

Abbreviations
xxix

Introduction
Nación Genízara:
Ethnogenesis, Place, and
Identity in New Mexico
ENRIQUE R. LAMADRID AND
MOISES GONZALES
1

Chapter One
Visualizing Genízaro Cultural
Memory and Ritual Celebration
MIGUEL A. GANDERT
19

Chapter Two
Mexican Indians and Genízaros:
Soldier-Farmer Allies in the
Defense and Agricultural
Development of New Mexico
TOMÁS MARTÍNEZ SALDAÑA,
ENRIQUE R. LAMADRID,
AND JOSÉ A. RIVERA
27

Chapter Three
Genízaros and Cultural
Systems of Slavery in the
Hispanic Southwest
WILLIAM S. KISER
47

Chapter Four
Genízara Self-Advocacy
in Eighteenth-Century
New Mexico
CRISTINA DURÁN
63

Chapter Five
The Genízaro Origins of the
Hermanos Penitentes
RAMÓN A. GUTIÉRREZ
80

Chapter Six
The Colonial Genízaro
Mission Pueblo of Belén
SAMUEL E. SISNEROS
118

Chapter Seven
Genízaro Ethnogenesis and
the Archaeological Record
CHARLES M. CARRILLO
165

Chapter Eight
Survival of Captivity:
Hybrid Identities, Gender, and
Culture in Territorial Colorado
VIRGINIA SÁNCHEZ
173

Chapter Nine
Genízaro Settlements of the Sierra
Sandía: Resilience and Identity in
the Land Grants of San Miguel del
Cañón de Carnué and San Antonio
de las Huertas
MOISES GONZALES
225

Chapter Ten
*Huellas de Sangre, Amor, y Lágrimas:
Rescatando a Mis Cautivas*
Trails of Blood, Love, and Tears:
Rescuing My Captives
SUSAN M. GANDERT
250

Chapter Eleven
Genízaro Salvation:
The Poetics of G. Benito
Córdova's *Genízaro Nation*
MICHAEL L. TRUJILLO
261

Chapter Twelve
*Sangre de Indio que Corre en
Mis Venas: Nativo* Poetics and
Nuevomexicano Identity
LEVI ROMERO
288

Chapter Thirteen
Genízaro Identity and
DNA: The Helix of
Our Native American
Genetic History
MIGUEL A. TÓRREZ
305

Chapter Fourteen
Epilogue: Persistence
and Resistance
in Genízaro Identity
TERESA CÓRDOVA
326

Contributors
345

Index
351

ILLUSTRATIONS

Map 1 Indo-Hispano *querencia* or homeland from the mid-eighteenth to mid-nineteenth centuries xxx

Figure 0.1 "A Memorial Recognizing the Role of Genízaros in New Mexico History and Their Legacy," House Memorial 40, Senate Memorial 59 xx

Figure 0.2 "A Memorial Recognizing the Role of Genízaros in New Mexico History and Their Legacy," House Memorial 40, Senate Memorial 59 xx

Figure 0.3 Musical score by David F. García xxiv

Figure 1.1 Captive children of the Nanillé dance 18

Figure 1.2 Dancing for Santo Tomás 18

Figure 1.3 La Perijundia rests, surrounded by Matachines dancers 20

Figure 1.4 "La Rueda del Cautivo" (Circle Dance of the Captives) 20

Figure 1.5 "Guerrera de 'Desert Storm'" 21

Figure 1.6 "Last Stand of Cuerno Verde, September 3, 1779" 22

Figure 1.7 "Ya Se Va, Ya Se La Llevan" (She Goes, They Are Taking Her), captive song 22

Figure 1.8 "Galento en Su Plaza" (Galento in His Plaza) 23

Figure 1.9 "Esclavos de Jesús" (Slaves of Jesus) 24

Figure 1.10 "Corazón de la Sierra" (Heart of the Mountains) 24

Figure 1.11 "Danza de las Generaciones" (Dance of the Generations) 24

Figure 1.12 "Comanchita del Alma" (Little Comanche of My Soul) 25

Figure 1.13 "Niño de la Flecha" (Arrow Boy) 25

Figure 6.1 "Los Genízaros" signature 120

Figure 6.2 Detail of 1778 map by Bernardo Miera y Pacheco 131

Figure 6.3 Detail of 1779 map by Bernardo Miera y Pacheco 133

Figure 6.4 José Isidoro García seated outside his home in Belén, undated 146

Figure 6.5 Delfinia "Virginia" García with Charles O'Neal, undated 146

Figure 6.6 Manuel García O'Neal and Antonia Rael and family, undated 149

Figure 8.1 Detail of 1778 map by Bernardo Miera y Pacheco *174*
Figure 8.2 Trade bond of Celedonio Valdez, February 21, 1858 *178*
Figure 8.3 Doll, tanned hide, glass beads; Ute, Colorado or Utah, ca. 1875–1890 *181*
Figure 8.4 Gabriel Woodson, ca. 1880s *184*
Figure 8.5 Peonage contract between Juan Antonio González and Theodore D. Wheaton, March 22, 1851 *190*
Figure 8.6 Conejos County captives enumerated by Indian agent Lafayette Head, 1865 *194*
Figure 8.7 Navajo captive boy, undated *195*
Figure 9.1 Plazas de la Sierra Sandía *226*
Figure 9.2 Detail of 1779 map by Bernardo Miera y Pacheco *228*
Figure 9.3 Military Census of Las Huertas, 1806 *233*
Figure 9.4 Los Matachines, San Antonio feast day, June 14, 1935 *242*
Figure 9.5 Comanchitos de la Sierra, La Madera, December 17, 2016 *246*
Figure 10.1 Lillian P. Mondragón de Gandert, 1949 *252*
Figure 10.2 Gertrudis Gallegos de Valdez, ca. 1951 *254*
Figure 10.3 Josie Valdez, ca. 1931 *254*
Figure 10.4 William Frederick Gandert, ca. 1863 *255*
Figure 11.1 De Genízaro y Mulata, Gíbaro, ca. 1775, *casta* painting *260*
Figure 13.1 MtDNA haplogroup distributions in New Mexico genetic genealogy *312*
Figure 13.2 MtDNA SNP (single nucleotide polymorphism) "snip" haplogroup mutations *313*
Figure 13.3 María Magdalena Leyba *315*
Figure 13.4 Amelia George *315*
Figure 13.5 Y-DNA haplogroup distributions in New Mexico genetic genealogy *316*
Figure 13.6 Y-DNA SNP distributions in New Mexico genetic genealogy *316*
Figure 13.7 Juan Felipe García, born July 1, 1907 *319*
Figure 13.8 Juan Felipe García, later in life *319*
Figure 13.9 Sample set of fifty randomly chosen participants with atDNA results that can be defined as classic Nuevomexicano *320*
Figure 14.1 Teresa Córdova, Nora Hawks Córdova, and Gertrudes González, 1987 *329*

TABLES

Table 2.1 Colonization of Northern New Spain by the End of the Sixteenth Century *30*

Table 6.1 Population Data of Belén, from the Spanish Census of 1790 *136*

Table 6.2 Members of the Confraternity of the Blessed Souls of Purgatory, Plaza de los Genízaros de Belén, 1802 *140*

Table 8.1 Raiders of the Moqui Pueblos at Oraibi, 1867 *183*

Table 8.2 Captives Reported by Indian Agent Lafayette Head, 1865 *197*

Table 8.3 Captive Indians by Owner Surname, 1860–1880 *206*

FOREWORD

Recordando el Futuro / Remembering the Future
Mal-Criados, Memory, and Memorials

ESTEVAN RAEL-GÁLVEZ

Memory sits in places and people, and even if believed to have disappeared, it endures through the generations. Sometimes it resembles a precious seed that has lain for centuries in sacred spaces, shut up airtight and yet still retaining its germinative power.

The ancient and sovereign landscape of the region known now as the American Southwest is one of these sacred spaces, which holds a tremendous repository of memories, including those thought to be long since vanished. They are manifest in the physical and social landscape, both resonant and silent. They are recalled in the names of mountains and trails, held in the contours of the plazas, and reside in those houses that remain standing and those long since melted into the ground. Memory is also revealed in the intangible, in dust rising from dances that have persisted for ages, in stories that are passed down from one teller to the next, and in language that holds words, one inside the other, like nesting dolls.

While ethereal, even words that carry the legacy of a story can sometimes hurt. Although I was a young child, I remember the first time I heard someone speak such a word—*genízaro*. Although whispered, it carried a sting and was used to pronounce upon, define, and chastise a child for acting out of place. The actual phrase used was *malcriado genízaro*, which essentially carried a double reproach, which I first wrote about and reinscribed in my own doctoral work on the subject (2002). On the one hand, the word "genízaro" conveyed a derogatory racial epithet—of being Indian-like, which indicated a deep-seated racism. The combination with the word "malcriado," however, although also used as an admonishment, was linguistically entwined within the foothold of colonialism. The word *criado* derives from the Spanish verb *criar*, to rear, educate, and bring up in one's family's home. In the Spanish vocabulary, it has also come to mean a "servant," adapted, however, as a euphemism to avoid the use of the word "slave." What this combined term revealed, then and now, are the relations of rule created, manifested, and maintained in the unequal positions implicit in that relationship of master and slave as well as precisely what words attempted to conceal, a memory, fragmented, yet palpable still in a community's consciousness.

The articulation also embodied a resonant burden that I would not understand for many years, until I realized that the weight it carried was not only about the past but how it remained present, not only in me but in all those around me. Although Genízaro now belongs to the social and physical landscape of New Mexico, the word actually originated in the fourteenth century as a marker given to captives, evolving over time into a distinct identity. They were the *yeniçeri*, Janissaries—children who were once forcibly abducted, traded, and trained as soldiers of the Ottoman Empire. But over the ages, the name traveled, translating people and places beyond its own origin. It was carried from Turkey to Spain, and with those who came to colonize, it flowed across the Atlantic Ocean to Mexico. There, it was Hispanicized, as Genízaro, where it first streamed into the intricacies of the caste system that dictated people's place in the Spanish colonial world. From there, it moved north to what would become New Mexico, over six thousand miles from the place where it was first used in Turkey, naming the silence.

More than a temporal and spatial meaning, the experiences of captivity and enslavement can be traced in the Southwest through three distinct governments: the Spanish, Mexican, and American. My own work, particularly in the last of these eras, reveals that even if this slavery, present in the territories, was considerably different from that of the American South, and even if it was of Indians—still then considered significant obstacles and threats to westward expansion—slavery of any kind, from an ideological standpoint, posed a significant problem for the nation, just then emerging from itself divided over the issue. Yet, indigenous captivities and enslavements would continue to take place well into the late nineteenth century in places like New Mexico and Colorado.

Like the marker attributed to a people on the other side of the world, in New Mexico, the word Genízaro, and an entire parallel vocabulary, was used as a euphemism for slavery. More than simply words spoken or inscribed on paper, thousands of indigenous women and children were captured and held in households across the southwestern part of the United States. Beyond the legally constructed national boundaries between the United States and Mexico and other countries in Central and South America, the numbers of indigenous enslaved across the entire continent reveal the enormous extent of this slavery and its consequences of displacement. There is no way, however, to fully measure the statistical impact and depth of the cultural wound left upon communities enduring these losses, which is at the heart of what it means to inherit this legacy.

Remembering the Past Forward

The challenges of recovering this story whole—as well as those individuals who passed through these experiences—are based on the fact that even while indigenous slavery was taking place, the details of these people's lives were not considered worth remembering, particularly by those who wrote the histories. This is true of any slavery, but certainly of one that is called by another name. This erasure was further compounded by the imperial transition that took place with the American conquest of northern Mexico. Here, even the stories of the elite in conquered territories were erased and obscured, let alone those of the marginalized people that they held. The specific stories of indigenous captivity and enslavement was and continues to be overshadowed by the narrative of slavery in the United States, in which the story of enslaved and emancipated Africans has largely defined nearly every aspect of our nation's history, including the various racial constructions that render nonwhites and nonblacks invisible to this day.

In the face of this obscured reality, and sometimes with nothing more than documentary fragments, the use of imagination as a decolonizing methodology remains a critical imperative in the historiography of any colonized people.[1] I have often contemplated the fact that there was a day in time when the last indigenous man and woman captured and held as enslaved persons in the American Southwest closed their eyes forever. The passing of these individuals was a gradual occurrence, made up of countless individual deaths. One such event took place as late as December 1942. Luis Valdez was a man who had been captured and held in the San Luis Valley of southern Colorado and who was among 149 enslaved individuals included in a listing compiled by

Lafayette Head, Indian agent for the US government, in 1865, a listing that I analyzed in great depth as part of my doctoral work. Luis was also the subject of a story later recorded in 1934 as part of an oral history project in Colorado. He died in Denver in the home of his original master's great-grandson. Other men and women spent these final moments in many places across a vast landscape, including in large cities like Albuquerque and Los Angeles as well as in Indian pueblos and Indo-Hispanic settlements alike. Some died destitute and alone, while others passed away surrounded by their own children and grandchildren.

Most of these deaths were set in the context of the early twentieth century, a particularly interesting moment in terms of the formation of identity in the Southwest. As a political and tourism-driven booster, a mythic narrative began to develop in these decades that characterized the descendants of Hispanic borderlands peoples as having an idealized and pure Spanish past, all at the expense of the actual and profound complexity of the population and their experiences. In time, and in response to Anglo-American domination in this region, even the most vocal Hispano proponents of this myth began to propagate it, imagining themselves "Spanish." Set in this context, being Indian held its own negative resonance, and when coupled with a former condition of captivity and servitude, the stigma was all the more heightened.

As a foundational legacy for New Mexicans, the story of enslaved Indians has been quieted over the years by whispers as much as by silence, hushed aside even by those who have inherited it—carrying if not its geography in their faces and hands, then certainly its memory in an aching consciousness. Particularly as a story perhaps never meant to be passed on, remembering these lives whole was not easy. Yet, the most telling aspects of any deep and sustained study of Nuevomexicano Indo-Hispano culture, in fact, reveals how the long story of the people themselves rises from beneath layers of histories formed somewhere in between erasure and memory—histories experienced, imagined, and passed down through story, *telling*, as it is, *identities*.

With the imperative of awaking these stories, I recall Ralph Ellison's memorable words about the importance of keeping "the painful details and episodes of a brutal experience alive in one's aching consciousness, to finger its jagged grain, and to transcend it" (1972, 78). Like many of the writers in this book, recovering these stories of slavery is more than a professional project but a personal one, and among all of my endeavors it has remained my life's project—to remember these stories and reveal the beauty of this complexity, locally and nationally. This endeavor is also at the heart of many efforts that have taken place over the past several decades to recover and recognize these narratives.

The Memorial

There are many ways to remember these stories. For most, they are secrets held closely in family lore, left in some generations as private matters only to be recovered in other generations by both curiosity and a consciousness of loss. Equally profound are the imaginary manifestations in which prose, poetry, and song reinscribe the subjects of these experiences. For some few, they have manifested in more visible, even public traditions that have encouraged the interest of a wide range of scholars and documentarians. Perhaps not unlike other efforts that evolved out of civil rights–era discourse and strategies to reframe and reclaim ethnic pride, the move by some New Mexicans to identify indigenous ancestors has been growing over the decades.

The motivations for recovering these histories are as diverse as those engaged in the process. Some individuals simply want to know more about their ancestry, while others seek to counter the amnesia and false narratives that have narrowly defined identity in the Southwest for over a century. Some are convinced that the discovery of an ancestor would result in individual tribal recognition. However, the reality of slavery anywhere, including in the Southwest, is that if recovery is possible at all, it often emerges with a great deal of ambivalence. This is the impact of colonialism and its foothold of slavery—it obscured names and origins. Yet, remembering is as much about recording absence and loss as it is about recovering and inscribing presence.

The global impact of colonialism upon indigenous peoples generally has been noted by many scholars, and in the United States, efforts to gain federal recognition have characterized many communities for decades. Set within this context, the New Mexico state legislature unanimously adopted two memorials in 2007 that recognize the role of Genízaros in New Mexico history and their legacy. House Memorial 40, carried by Speaker of the New Mexico House of Representatives Ben Luján, was sent to the Labor and Human Resources Committee, chaired by Representative Miguel P. García, where it received full support. It subsequently was passed in the House of Representatives with unanimous support, with sixty-three members voting affirmatively. New Mexico Senate Memorial 59 was carried by Senator Richard C.

 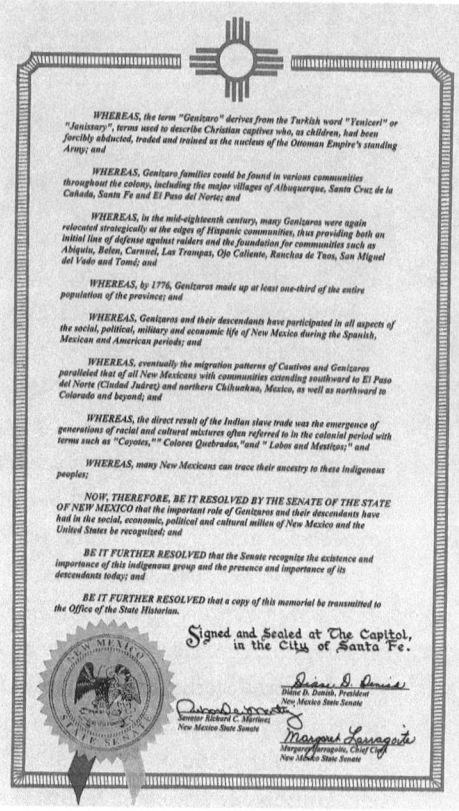

FIGURES 0.1 AND 0.2 "A Memorial Recognizing the Role of Genízaros in New Mexico History and Their Legacy," House Memorial 40, Senate Memorial 59, New Mexico state legislature, 2007. State Historian of New Mexico Estevan Rael-Gálvez, Regis Pecos, and others collaborated on the writing and passage of this historic memorial. Courtesy of Estevan Rael-Gálvez.

Martínez. It was sent to the Rules Committee, chaired by Senator Linda M. López, where it received full support. It passed in the full Senate, also with unanimous support, with thirty-three members voting affirmatively. While not embodying the force of law, the memorials defined a formal expression of the New Mexico legislature, thus conveying the importance of Genízaros to the history of the state.

As the state historian of New Mexico at the time, I personally authored the memorial, but its genesis and ultimate legislative enactment reveal the importance of intercultural dialogue and the core values of trust, friendship, and respect, as well as the strategies of relationship building and storytelling, to these types of initiatives. The champions were of course, Speaker Luján and Senator Martínez, as well as Senator López and Representative García, who recognized not only the requisite balance these memorials gave to history but, as New Mexicans, how this particular memorial was also personal. While my efforts were defined by working with many legislators during those years, the particular opportunity afforded by this initiative allowed me to sit with these leaders and countless others to both share stories and recover them from the legislators themselves.

The effort, however, began with a conversation between myself and Regis Pecos, a former governor of Cochití Pueblo. At the time, Regis served as chief of staff to Speaker Luján, and we had begun to develop a friendship that has lasted to this day. In recalling the story of the memorial, Regis reflected:

> Our discussions grew and grew [until] . . . the appreciation become very personal [such] that we [realized we] had an obligation to do something. . . . For us, at a time [when we were] in places of influence, [we] found the compassion to use the [legislative] process to bring this resilient people into a place of recognition. . . . [P]eople were amazed [by] the hidden stories and truth and admitted their ignorance. It was an enlightening experience and a rewarding one that was of little recognition but in retrospect was amazing and historic. (personal communication, 2017)

Utilizing Regis's experience, skill, and knowledge of both the federal recognition and the legislative processes, and my knowledge of the subject matter, we began a journey together that would involve innumerable conversations that felt more like storytelling, culminating in the memorial's adoption by the New Mexico state legislature. This historic effort reminds me of the words of one of the continent's greatest writers, whose efforts to recover the seeds of memory have served as an inspiration for many. "When it's truly alive," writes Eduardo Galeano, "memory doesn't contemplate history, it invites us to make it" (1998, 210).

Conclusion

This sentiment of a living memory and history is precisely what this book is about. It contains essays by writers—many who descend from indigenous men and women, whether they were specifically labeled Genízaros or not—

whose work takes the seeds planted generations before and replants them for the generations that follow. Although these memories may resemble precious seeds, their germinative power lies in their ability to make whole what was once broken.

I have argued that there is no contemporary New Mexican who cannot trace his or her roots back to these seeds, even if those memories have been disclaimed. I am fortunate to have been raised by individuals who encouraged me to find these seeds and to learn more about these narratives. There are several stories of indigenous slaves in my own ancestry, some mere fragments and others amazingly complete. Of these, I think of doña Inés, a Tano woman of the pueblo of San Cristóbal, who was captured in 1591 during the Gaspar Castaño de Sosa expedition and who would become the matriarch of the Martín-Serrano (Martínez) family in New Mexico, living the final years of her life in Santa Fe. There are many like doña Inés who enter into these histories, and for those of us who descend from them, it is important to remember these experiences and understand what meanings they carry for us.

Like the words Genízaro and malcriado, which are storied and translated across place and time, the word "remember" is likewise significant. The Spanish *recordar*, "to remember," is from the Latin *recordis*, the process of awakening and passing something back through the heart and mind, in order to make something or someone whole. The eyes of all of the descendants of those indigenous ancestors continue to awaken the possibility of remembering with each new birth of a New Mexican. *Nación Genízara* is about how individual and collective lives are remembered; how a community takes the memories, stories, and traditions of what has been passed down from one generation to the next and reimagines itself, now in the present and into the future.

Note

1. For more on the "decolonial imaginary" as a way of overcoming a colonial past, see Emma Pérez (1999).

References

Ellison, Ralph. 1972. *Shadow and Act*. New York: Vintage.

Galeano, Eduardo. 1998. *Upside Down: A Primer for the Looking-Glass World*. Translated by Mark Fried. New York: Picador.

Pérez, Emma. 1999. *The Decolonial Imaginary: Writing Chicanas into History*. Bloomington: Indiana University Press.

Rael-Gálvez, Estevan. 2002. "Identifying Captivity and Capturing Identity: Narratives of American Indian Slavery in Colorado and New Mexico, 1776–1934." PhD diss., University of Michigan.

———. 2007. "A Memorial Recognizing the Role of Genízaros in New Mexico History and Their Legacy." Forty-Eighth Legislature, House Memorial 40, Senate Memorial 59. Santa Fe: New Mexico State Legislature.

FIGURE 0.3 Musical score by David F. García. Used with permission.

Estrellita Reluciente del Pueblo de Abiquiú: Coplas de Entrada
Little Shining Star of the Pueblo of Abiquiú: Verses of Entry

DAVID F. GARCÍA

Arrivals, entrances, and departures from sacred spaces are ritualized in Nuevomexicano folk rituals. Permission must be asked and granted for the transition from outside to inside. Crossings of liminal boundaries and transitional thresholds like doorways are accompanied by verses, song, blessings, and even dance steps. If a sacred space like a chapel or a home where a prayer service is being held, visitors traditionally enter with the right foot first. If the space is secular, like a meeting hall, permission suffices. David F. García, "el poeta del Río Chama," composed and sang entradas for the Genízaro Nation advanced seminar at the School for Advanced Research in Santa Fe, and for the community symposium at the parish hall of the Pueblo de Abiquiú. The tune and texts of the latter are noted here.

ESTRELLITA RELUCIENTE
DEL PUEBLO DE ABIQUIÚ:
COPLAS DE ENTRADA

En el marco de esta puerta
el pie derecho pondré,
con licencia de esta gente
estas coplas cantaré.
Eres manantial profundo,

LITTLE SHINING STAR
OF THE PUEBLO OF ABIQUIÚ:
VERSES OF ENTRY

In the threshold of this door
I will place my right foot,
with the license of all these people
these verses will I sing.
You are a deep wellspring,

la fuente de nuestro río,	the source of our river,
del oriente pa'l poniente,	from the east to the west,
desde el sur al norte frío.	from the south to frigid north.
Eres linda, eres bonita,	You are beautiful, you are lovely,
el color de obsidiana	the color of obsidian
de ese Cerro Pedernal,	from that Flint Mountain,
La Virgen Guadalupana.	the Guadalupian Virgin.
De todas las lindas flores	Of all the pretty flowers
eres tú la más sublime,	you are the most sublime,
es por eso que te quiero	that is why I love you,
santa Rosita de Lima.	Saint Rosita of Lima.
Eres mi norte y mi guía	You are my north and my guide
en un cielo tan azul,	in a sky so blue,
estrellita reluciente	shining little star
del Pueblo de Abiquiú.	of the Pueblo of Abiquiú.
No lloro pero me acuerdo	I don't cry but do remember
y reflejo hoy en día,	and reflect on this day,
presenciando las historias	witnessing the histories
de la gran Genizaría.	of the great Genízaro Nation.
Yo no canto porque sé	I don't sing because I know how
ni porque mi voz sea buena,	or because my voice is good;
canto por estar alegre	I sing because I'm happy
en esta tierra y en la ajena.	in this land and in that of others.
Ya me voy, ya me despido,	I am going, I take my leave,
ya me voy a retirar,	I am going to go away,
a todita esta gente	to all of these people
las gracias les quiero dar.	I want to give my thanks.

ACKNOWLEDGMENTS

This endeavor emerges directly from the struggles and perseverance of the *antepasados*, those who came before, the many generations of indigenous and mestizo peoples in New Mexico, whose stories we bring into the light of our *resolana*. They are remembered in the prayers of our communities as *las ánimas benditas de los cautivos y criados*, the blessed souls of captives and slaves, who created the Genízaro legacy of New Mexico. Rooted in the twin concepts of *respeto y permiso* (respect and permission), we see our work as a tribute to our families and communities. We also pay homage to our antepasado scholars, Fray Angélico Chávez, and Doctors Gilberto Benito Córdova, Roberto Villalpando, and Tomás Atencio. We also remember Edward Dozier, Frances Swadesh Quintana, and Alfonso Ortiz. We appreciate the steadfast encouragement of James F. Brooks, and the example of Malcolm Ebright and state historian Rick Hendricks. Special recognition for the inspirational cultural leaders of Genízaro communities—Floyd, Dexter, Virgil, and Isabel Trujillo of Abiquiú; Francisco "El Comanche" Gonzales of Ranchos de Taos; and the late José Antonio "Galento" Martínez of Alcalde.

Our advanced seminar and community symposium were made possible by the Center for Regional Studies (CRS) at the University of New Mexico, and were graciously hosted by the School for Advanced Research (SAR) in Santa Fe, and the Pueblo de Abiquiú Library. The Gutiérrez-Hubbell House hosted the "Genízaro Identity and Continuance" exhibit and related events. The McCune Foundation generously supported our northern New Mexico field schools. Our own institutional support provided us the time to work, although several of our contributors are independent scholars. The list of universities is long, beginning with the University of New Mexico and including New Mexico Highlands University; the University of Chicago; Texas A&M University–San Antonio; Colegio de Postgraduados, Texcoco, Mexico; and the University of Illinois at Chicago. Strategic intramural support units include the University of New Mexico Press's Querencias Series; the Southwest Hispanic Research Institute (SHRI); the Office of the Vice President of

Research; Center for Southwest Research (CSWR) at the University of New Mexico's Zimmerman Library; the *New Mexico Historical Review*; the New Mexico Land Grant Studies Program; and the Community and Regional Planning Program at the School of Architecture and Planning.

Our significant community partners include the Pueblo de Abiquiú, and its library and cultural center and Nanillé dancers; the Cristóbal de la Serna Land Grant; the San Antonio de las Huertas Land Grant; the Cañón de Carnué Land Grant; Los Comanchitos and Matachines de la Sierra Sandía; Los Comanches y Matachines de Alcalde; and the Genízaro Federation of New Mexico.

The individuals to thank are so numerous that their names would fill several pages. *Perdonen las ausencias*. Generous donations from the Jane C. Sánchez Grant of the Historical Society of New Mexico, Ramón Gutiérrez, Virginia Sánchez, and Enrique Lamadrid provided support for the index, permissions, and additional production values. Others include Genízaro scholars Bernardo Gallegos, Gregorio Gonzales, Cynthia Gómez, Ana X. Gutiérrez Sisneros, and Patricia Trujillo; CRS directors Aracely Chapa and Gabriel Meléndez; UNM vice president for research Gabriel López; SAR president Michael Brown; Clark Whitehorn, the University of New Mexico Press's former executive editor, and his staff; and the editors' life partners, Lynn Velarde de Gonzales of Alcalde and Carlota Domínguez de Lamadrid of Taos. *¡Gracias a todos!*

ABBREVIATIONS

AASF
Archives of the Archdiocese
of Santa Fe

AGN
Archivo General
de la Nación (Mexico)

AHAD
Archivos Históricos del
Arzobispado de Durango

BANC
Bancroft Library

BLC
Bancroft Library Collections
Pertaining to New Mexico and New
Spain (Mexico), 1581–1904

CSWR
Center for Southwest Research
(Zimmerman Library,
University of New Mexico)

MANM
Mexican Archives
of New Mexico

NARA
National Archives and
Records Administration

NMGS
New Mexico
Genealogical Society

NMHR
*New Mexico
Historical Review*

NMSRA
New Mexico State Archives
and Records

PGPA
Palace of the Governors
Photo Archives

SANM
Spanish Archives
of New Mexico

SCRC
Spanish Colonial
Research Center

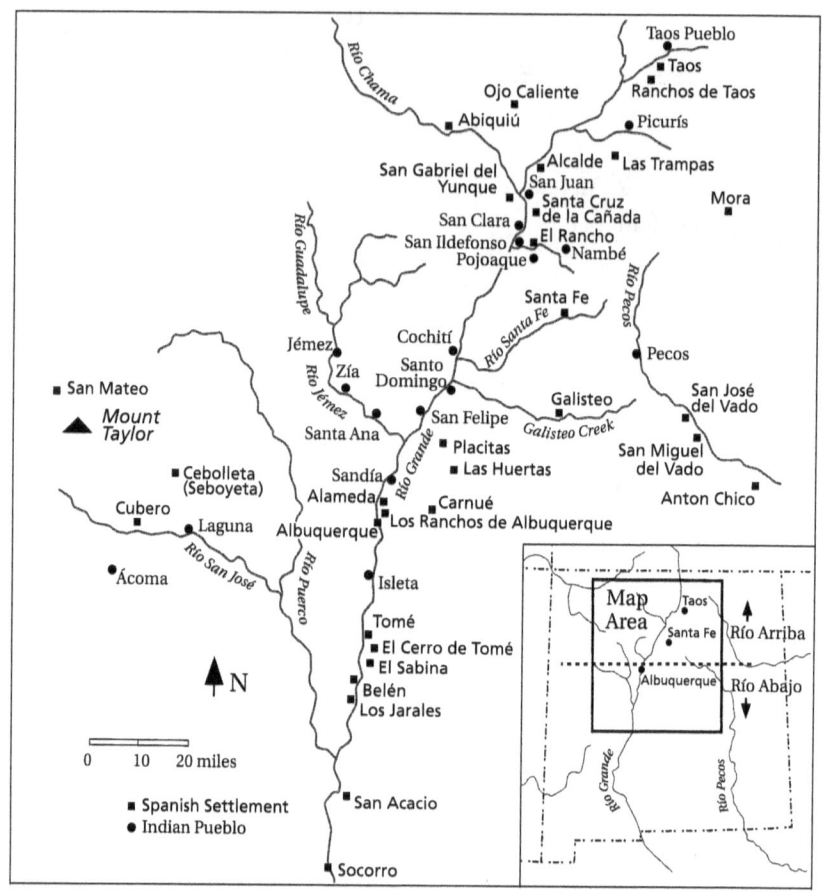

MAP 1 The Indo-Hispano *querencia* or homeland from the mid-eighteenth to mid-nineteenth centuries, with Tanoan and Keresan pueblos, Hispano plazas, and the villas of Santa Fe, Santa Cruz de la Cañada, and Alburquerque. Genízaro land grant settlements include Belén, Abiquiú, Ranchos de Taos, Carnué, and Las Huertas-Placitas, with Genízaro families and enclaves found throughout. Courtesy of the University of New Mexico Press.

INTRODUCTION

Nación Genízara
Ethnogenesis, Place,
and Identity in New Mexico

ENRIQUE R. LAMADRID AND MOISES GONZALES

In eighteenth-century New Mexico, the term *Genízaro*, "janissary," emerged as an ethnonym designating a sizeable sector of the indigenous population, whose descendants are still present in the region. Hispanicized from the Turkish word *yeniçeri*, (new troops), in Spain genízaros referred to the Ottoman sultan's elite guard composed of rigorously trained and fiercely loyal Christian captives. In New Spain and the rest of Latin America, genízaro became a generic low-caste synonym of mestizo (mixed race), the racially and culturally hybrid. With independence from Spain in 1821, the term was abolished.

In the far northern borderlands of the upper Río Grande, Genízaros were an ethnic assemblage of individuals and communities of Native peoples of mixed origins, mostly Apache, Navajo, Ute, Paiute, Kiowa, Comanche, and Pawnee. Groups with common bonds of language, culture, and family were called *naciones* (nations), similar to the modern usage of the word "tribe." Genízaros entered Spanish colonial society in the early eighteenth century as captives taken during frequent skirmishes with the numerous enemy "nations" that surrounded the upper Río Grande region (Brooks 2002). Some Pueblo groups such as the Hopi-Tewa of Abiquiú and others became Genízaro by displacement and relocation (Córdova 1979). Enemy nomads raided for what they wanted, often women and children, whom they valued for their labor and reproductive capacity. By then, the failed encomienda (assignment) system of forced labor, and the reformed repartimiento (distribution) system of tribute labor, had long been dismantled and slavery outlawed. But the doctrine of *guerra justa* (just war) enabled the taking of insurgents as captives, and the institution of the *rescate* (rescue) allowed the ransom of Native captives, notably children (Magnaghi 1990, 86). Large numbers of captives taken by the Spanish were sent far away to work the silver mines of northern Mexico, the henequen fields of Yucatán, and the sugarcane fields of Cuba.

Those who remained behind numbered about three thousand by the turn of the nineteenth century. Genízaros were euphemistically "rescued" from their captors, "adopted," Christianized, and assimilated. After a century of intergroup warfare and captive taking, those Genízaros specifically identified in the 1790 census, plus all those individuals whose servile occupations and lack of surnames indicated similar backgrounds, accounted for approximately one-third of the population (Schroeder 1975, 62; Magnaghi 1990, 89; Gutiérrez 1991, 171). Genízaros lived among Hispanos, using Spanish surnames taken from their masters, Christian baptismal names from godparents, speaking a distinctive form of Spanish as their tribal languages diminished, and residing together or dispersed in towns and ranchos (Chávez 1979, 198). Traces of their provisional, heavily accented Spanish appear on the lips of certain characters of folk plays like *Los Comanches* (Lamadrid 2003, 77). "Ladino Spanish" as used in New Mexico and other areas of colonial Latin America refers not to the language of Jewish settlers but rather the fluent Spanish acquired by some Native leaders and interpreters. Genízaros were put into the service of Hispano families as domestic servants, farmhands, and herders, or in group work settings or *obrajes* for the processing, weaving, and knitting of wool (Magnaghi 1990, 90). Genízaros occupied an ethnic, identifiable space between Spanish, Pueblo Natives, and mestizos. In the *diligencias matrimoniales* (prenuptial investigations), another significant registry of ethnic classifications, the proliferation of terms used from the 1760s to the 1780s was afterward streamlined into two—*indios* (Pueblo Indians) and *vecinos* (neighbors). By the end of the century, the latter term culturally conflated Spanish, mestizos, and Genízaros (Frank 1996, 777).

The same Laws of the Indies that outlawed slavery granted Genízaros their freedom after fifteen years or upon marriage. Many distinguished themselves in armed service as scouts and militia in frontier areas, another reason they were associated with the Ottoman Janissaries. With their geographical and cultural knowledge of the vast plains and mountains surrounding New

Mexico, Genízaros also served as guides for expeditions both large and small (Sánchez 1997). After ransomed individuals worked off the debt of their "rescue," their children were freeborn, but many Genízaros were reabsorbed into the servitude of debt peonage and into the extended families of their masters (Rael-Gálvez 2002). Sold or born into slavery and then partly or totally emancipated, Genízaros and Genízaras learned and earned their rights, sought redress from abuse, and successfully defended themselves, their honor, and their interests in courts. When the Genízaros of Belén faced outside encroachment and harassment by their Spanish/Mestizo neighbors, they sought and received an audience with the viceroy in Mexico City (Sisneros 2017, 462). As documentary evidence of Genízaro ethnogenesis, the emergence of this new cultural identity is repeatedly marked with terms like *nación genízara* (Genízaro nation), the ethnonym first used by officials and then adopted by the people themselves for self-designation, hence the title of this anthology.

Since the 1730s, Genízaros actively sought, received, and defended *mercedes* (land grants) given to them in frontier or buffer areas during the Apache, Ute, and Comanche wars. The first instance was an unsuccessful 1733 petition to occupy the abandoned Sandía Pueblo grant, since the Tiwas had taken refuge with the Hopis over half a century earlier after the 1680 Pueblo Revolt. Governor Gaspar Domínguez de Mendoza established the first Genízaro Land Grant of Belén in 1741. Two-term New Mexico governor Tomás Vélez Cachupín (1749–1754 and 1761–1767) was one of their most dedicated advocates. He deployed a plan for New Mexico whereby landless Genízaros and mixed Indian castes could assist in expanding a network of defensible buffer settlements to protect the primary population and administrative centers, the three villas (chartered towns) of Santa Fe, Santa Cruz, and Alburquerque. Vélez Cachupín encouraged Genízaro settlements and communities with enclaves of Genízaros at Belén, and issued land grants in Las Trampas (1751), Abiquiú (1754), Cañón de Carnué (1763), and San Antonio de las Huertas (1767) (M. Gonzales 2014). In addition to these land grant settlements, significant populations of Genízaros resided in Ranchos de Taos, Pueblo Quemado, Valencia, Tomé, Atrisco, Santa Fe's Barrio de Analco, and San Miguel del Vado. Genízaros were serving at official military posts at Cerro de Tomé and Valencia by 1740, and an entire detachment from Analco was stationed at San Miguel del Vado in 1794 on the Pecos River, at the edge of the Llano Estacado ("Staked Plains") (Chávez 1979, 199). This military community later became New Mexico's port of entry to American traders after 1821.

New Genízaro communities offered gainful employment and land ownership even as they discouraged and diminished attacks by enemy Indians that were threatening both Pueblo and Hispano communities in northern New Mexico (Swadesh 1974). The communities were established in compliance with the Laws of the Indies, which required the construction of compact, defensible settlements popularly known as *plazas* (plaza-centered villages) as well as a system of equitable distribution of land and water for both individual and communal use (Ebright 1994). Governor Vélez Cachupín believed that community land grants for Genízaros in frontier settlements was a way to move this landless and often unruly indigenous population into land ownership to serve a strategic military function for the province.

According to sociologist and philosopher Tomás Atencio, a distinct "Genízaro consciousness" emerged in the early nineteenth century as a political and cultural identity, even as the ethnonym itself disappeared from official documents (1985). Proclaimed six months before the victory over Spain and the Treaty of Córdova, the 1821 Plan of Iguala guaranteed the rights of all Mexicans and abolished the despised caste system and its race-based terminology. Every Mexican became a *ciudadana/o* (citizen) of the new republic and assumed the civil status as a title. But the cultural memory of Genízaros persisted in many communities.

After Mexican independence, New Mexico's economy grew along with the population, and Genízaros began to participate in their political future. In 1837, a coalition of Genízaros, Pueblo Indians, and Coyotes (a persistent caste term designating mixed ancestry) joined in an antifederalist rebellion that arose in many regions of the struggling Mexican Republic. In most regions, social elites fomented the rebellion to protest new taxes and the centralization of power, but in New Mexico they withdrew and left a ragtag group of insurgents to face the consequences of their actions. After they assassinated and beheaded Governor Albino Pérez and executed many of his supporters, the rebels installed a provisional government north of Santa Fe in Santa Cruz. El Cantón de la Villa de Santa Cruz de la Cañada (the District of the Holy Cross of the Drovers' Road), as it was called, seated José Ángel Gonzales, a Genízaro from Taos, as governor (Lecompte 1985). A poorly armed group of 1,500 to 2,000 rebels engaged a force of 200 trained militia soldiers, who prevailed. By January 1838, the liberal Mexican state regained full control and executed Governor Gonzales and other leaders. Genízaro resistance during the Mexican period failed politically, but strengthened Genízaro political consciousness.

After the signing of the Treaty of Guadalupe Hidalgo (1848), which ceded the northern half of Mexico to the United States, enterprising Americans allied themselves with elite New Mexican families and strengthened their grip on the economy. During the extended territorial period, the Santa Fe Ring, a cabal of lawyers and speculators, orchestrated a legalized theft of millions of acres of common lands from community land grants (Ebright 1994; Correia 2013). Sharp class differences emerged between Genízaro descendants and the Hispano elites who were part of the new order. In the final push for statehood, the complex ethnic mix of New Mexico was eclipsed by an Anglo-initiated campaign to emphasize "Spanish American" culture and identity, and distance New Mexico from Mexico (Nieto-Phillips 2008).

Genízaro consciousness reemerged in the latter half of the twentieth century with participation in the land grant movement and the Alianza Federal de Mercedes (Federal Alliance of Land Grants) with its leader, Reies López Tijerina, and in the Chicana/Chicano liberation movements. Fray Angélico Chávez made the astute observation that many enthusiastic participants in the revolutionary social movements of the 1960s were Genízaro descendants: "[T]he people of full or major Genízaro descent and upbringing are definitely more Indianic in their outlook than they are *castizo* [racially and culturally pure] by their Hispanic contact. Significantly, in the current revolutionary social movements, they are ones who join the agrarian and urban Mexicans or Mexican-Americans in the social protest, and consequently like to be called 'Chicanos' along with them" (Chávez 1974, 270). The hegemonic Spanish American identity was challenged by Mexican American, Chicana/Chicano, and Genízaro identities, which all acknowledge their mestizo and indigenous heritage (Gallegos 2017).

When he wrote the Genízaro chapter for volume 9 of the Smithsonian Institution's *Handbook of North American Indians* (1979), Chávez reminded the world who the Genízaros were and what their place was in New Mexico history. Since their ethnonym was stricken from official records after 1821, historians have assumed that this sizable colonial ethnic group somehow disappeared as well. Truly enough, many Genízaros attached to both Pueblo and Hispano communities merged with those groups from below. Subsequent historians have dutifully echoed Chávez's shorthand description of them as "detribalized, Hispanicized Indians" to the extent that "historical writing has become the tomb of Genízaro identity discourse" (G. Gonzales 2017, 6).

In his 1979 dissertation, historian-anthropologist Gilberto Benito Córdova proclaimed himself a Genízaro anthropologist as he reminded New Mexico that in Abiquiú, the original Hopi-Tewa core community, with additional settlers from more than ten other tribes, still know who they were and who they are as Genízaros. There and in several other communities in the Valle de Taos and Sierra Sandía, socially and geographically isolated in remote or mountainous areas by their land grants, Genízaro identity has persisted. Their original tribal languages and identities were lost and displaced, but Genízaros have been "retribalized" with a new lingua franca, traditions of self-governance, customs, and spirituality. A distinct style of folk Catholicism emerged, complete with a calendar of feast days and in many villages the Hermandad de Nuestro Padre Jesús Nazareno (Brotherhood of Our Father Jesus the Nazarene), a religious confraternity notably popular among Genízaros, dedicated to Lenten rituals and the well-being of their communities (Gutiérrez 1999).

This anthology recapitulates the work of successive generations of scholars, the awakening of what Atencio called "Genízaro Consciousness" (1985). Eighteen activist scholars, many Genízaro descended and several Genízaro identified, reflect and converse between disciplines including anthropology, archaeology, history, sociology, literature, folklore, and musicology. The more personal pursuits of genealogy, oral history, poetry, and genetic research are also expressed in these pages as *testimonio*, the testimonial narrative of family and community memoir. Former New Mexico state historian Estevan Rael-Gálvez notes in his foreword to this volume that "*Nación Genízara* is about how individual and collective lives are remembered; how a community takes the memories, stories, and traditions of what has been passed down from one generation to the next and reimagines itself, now in the present and into the future."

FOREWORD *Recordando el Futuro* / Remembering the Future: *Mal-Criados*, Memory, and Memorials, by Estevan Rael-Gálvez

The former New Mexico state historian reflects on the occasion of the tenth anniversary of the unprecedented and pivotal 2007 memorials passed by the two houses of the New Mexico legislature. He authored "Recognizing the Role of Genízaros in New Mexico History and Their Legacy," ending the post-1821 erasure of the group in the official record. He uses the Spanish adjective *malcriado* (badly raised, bad mannered, crude) as simile for Genízaros.

Estrellita Reluciente del Pueblo de Abiquiú: Coplas de Entrada /
Little Shining Star of the Pueblo of Abiquiú:
Verses of Entry, by David F. García

Passages over thresholds that link sacred with secular spaces in Nuevo México are traditionally observed with verse, prayer, and song. Permission is always requested to enter, and the insiders, present in body or spirit, are acknowledged. Crossings of liminal spaces and transitional thresholds like doorways are accompanied by verses, song, blessings, and even dance steps. "El poeta del Río Chama" composed and sang these to honor the activist scholars of the Nación Genízara project at their seminar and community symposium in Abiquiú in 2016.

CHAPTER ONE Visualizing Genízaro Cultural Memory and Ritual Celebration, Photo Essay by Miguel A. Gandert

The tricultural promotional narratives that underlie the modernization of New Mexico since 1848 have oversimplified a complex cultural landscape. Genízaros and the legacy of slavery were erased or relegated to a remote, irretrievable past. The antidote to oblivion involves our most primal senses of vision and hearing. The persistence of Genízaro identity can be most clearly seen and heard on the plazas of several land grant communities and urban enclaves. The Native and mestizo peoples of greater Mexico have always dramatized their political and cultural struggles in festival and ritual display. Gandert's lens and these photographs taken over a quarter-century period provide a glimpse of what the scholars of *Nación Genízara* recall, discuss, and theorize.

CHAPTER TWO Mexican Indians and Genízaros: Soldier-Farmer Allies in the Defense and Agricultural Development of New Mexico, by Tomás Martínez Saldaña, Enrique R. Lamadrid, and José A. Rivera

The entrada into New Mexico by don Juan de Oñate in 1598 expanded the colonial rule of New Spain into the present-day southwestern United States. Following the pattern of colonization into northern Mexico, the Spanish formed a political and military alliance with Mexicano Natives, notably the Tlaxcalans, to assist in the establishment of permanent settlements along "la

Ruta de la Plata" (the Silver Road) from Tlaxcala, Mexico, to the northern borderlands, where, from 1564 to 1598, they established agricultural colonies at strategic locations such as San Luis Potosí, Querétaro, Zacatecas, Guadalajara, Durango, Saltillo, Colotlán, Monterrey, Parras, and many others. Santa Fe was established around 1610, and some 150 years later the Tlaxcalans were credited with having founded their own pueblo on the south bank of the Río de Santa Fe, depicted in José de Urrutia's map of 1767 as the Pueblo o Barrio de Analco. Scholars continue to debate the presence of Tlaxcalans at Analco, but the hydraulic agricultural model they established at Saltillo and other settlements in the deserts of northern Mexico remains an important historical and cultural heritage present in New Mexican *acequias* (irrigation canals). Analco still exists as a barrio in Santa Fe today, with an *acequia madre* (mother ditch) that continues to run and is protected by state statute. The Analco district itself is a historic treasure for the role it played as the first clearly non-Pueblo Native district in New Mexico that assisted in the assimilation of Natives into Spanish culture and governing systems. Residents from Analco were recruited to establish other Genízaro communities elsewhere in the Río Arriba such as Belén, Santo Tomás de Abiquiú, San José de Las Trampas, and San Miguel del Vado. The purpose of this chapter is to discuss the origins and adaptation of Barrio de Analco, and its role in the assimilation of Genízaro identity.

CHAPTER THREE Genízaros and Cultural Systems of Slavery in the Hispanic Southwest, by William S. Kiser

The servile Genízaros who occupied New Mexico's northern settlements played important roles in local society and culture, and they also figured into America's national equation of emancipation in the mid-nineteenth century. The majority of slaves in the Southwest attained freedom through the ideological transformations that swept the nation during the age of emancipation. Also important to this evolution of American democracy, however, was the indirect role that peons, captives, and Genízaros played in promulgating the legal and political revolutions that helped to end most forms of coercive labor in the United States. Genízaros occupied an important place in the fabric of their local society and culture, but an equally significant aspect of their history was their contribution to the emergence of free labor ideology and the abolition of involuntary servitude in nineteenth-century America.

CHAPTER FOUR Genízara Self-Advocacy in
Eighteenth-Century New Mexico, by Cristina Durán

This chapter highlights the efforts of Genízaros and Genízaras to defend their rights during the eighteenth century in colonial New Mexico. Precious little has been written on them, and not much of what we know has come from Genízaros themselves. The Genízaro voice can be heard, however, in many instances when they accessed the Spanish-controlled courts to protect their rights. Colonial documents characterize them as unwanted, dependent, lost, and criminal, but good fighters. The fact that Genízaros took action to assert their rights is significant, even more so that women, the Genízaras, took such action on their own. The system of protection for the rights of Indians and Genízaros was established through the office of the Protector de Indios, and surviving legal records that chronicle court cases provide us with an opportunity to foreground the lives of Genízaros and view them as complex figures in the shaping of Indo-Hispano relations. A review of secondary sources, both ethnohistorical and anthropological, addresses the significance of Genízaros and Genízaras as subjugated peoples who managed to assert their identity and view themselves as worthy of protection under Spanish law.

CHAPTER FIVE The Genízaro Origins of
the Hermanos Penitentes, by Ramón A. Gutiérrez

The Franciscan friars who ministered to the indigenous peoples of the Kingdom of New Mexico focused their energies on the Pueblo Indians, finding the Genízaros too rude, crude, and poor; the friars complained that they did not speak the Spanish language well, and that they were interlopers and thieves. At best, Genízaro chapels were *visitas*, sanctuaries infrequently visited by priests. This chapter explores how the Genízaros employed the Catholic Church's confraternity system to attend to their own religious needs, forming the Cofradía (Hermandad) de Nuestro Padre Jesús Nazareno (Confraternity [Brotherhood] of Our Father Jesus the Nazarene), who in time became known as the *penitente* (penitent) brothers. After the secularization of the missions in 1818, their religious life was largely unsupervised by priests, and *moradas*, or penitente chapels, became part the civic-religious foundation of Genízaro towns. In the 1850s, Archbishop Jean-Baptiste Lamy acidly complained that although the origins of this confraternity had been religious, by 1850 it was primarily a political organization.

CHAPTER SIX The Colonial Genízaro Mission Pueblo of Belén, by Samuel E. Sisneros

The historical memory of Belén, New Mexico's Genízaro emergence, settlement, and identity, has been blurred by over two hundred years of environmental and political rupture and the silence of both popular and official histories. Modern civic identity narratives have resulted in historical erasure with a layering-over of pseudo-histories. These dominant and silencing narratives have disconnected contemporary Belén from its indigenous legacy. To begin a narrative recovery of Belén's colonial settlement requires an alternative perspective of origins, linking a current sense of place to the remnants of Native "blood memory" and regional family histories to those once called Genízaros de Belén. The chronology of census records, ecclesiastical reports, and sacramental registries validates the Genízaro origins and foundation of the Pueblo de Belén and its outpost plazas. With two original segregated settlements (1720s–1740s)—one "Genízaro" and one "Spanish"—within four or five decades Belén became an increasingly Spanish migratory destination, resulting in a growing mestizo population and eventually the loss of a Genízaro designation and identity. Within the Genízaro narrative is a connection to the Pueblo world, especially to the Tiwa Pueblo of Isleta and the mission communities of El Paso del Norte. These connections, along with the Genízaros' position as new Spanish Christians, were used by both the Genízaros and the Spanish authorities to imagine and construct Belén as a Pueblo Indian mission, which became a fast-merging and growing Río Abajo cultural hub.

CHAPTER SEVEN Genízaro Ethnogenesis and the Archaeological Record, by Charles M. Carrillo

Emerging interest in Genízaros and the archaeological inquiry about these people have caused Charles Carrillo to rethink his conceptual treatment of archaeological evidence gathered from Genízaro settlements. He argues that the historicity of material practices and material culture should be reconceptualized so that material culture is viewed as an active constitutive element of social practice. Carrillo, a student of "New Archaeology," was taught to view culture as an adaptive system with material outputs and specific archaeological correlates. He proposes to now view Genízaro material culture as an active fundamental element of social practice, challenging archaeologists and ethnographers to understand the context in which social/cultural experiences are activated as practice, rather than focusing on the identification of Genízaro material culture or the characterization of Genízaro material. Carrillo argues that research should focus on the dynamics of Genízaro culture and its mutability as embedded in contexts of social life and social relations.

CHAPTER EIGHT Survival of Captivity: Hybrid Identities, Gender, and Culture in Territorial Colorado, by Virginia Sánchez

In a few oral histories, indigenous captives witnessed the slaughter of their families during raiding expeditions and warfare. What they faced as "captured, captive, and enslaved" individuals in a new culture is almost unimaginable—the challenges of learning a new language, practicing a different religion and customs, and living and working among strangers. The histories documented here give voice to the unique lives of *cautivos*—indigenous captives. Hispano and Anglo families are now giving voice to their stories by openly discussing the turbulent times of frontier Colorado, when their ancestors captured, sold, or owned captives. For generations, this legacy remained behind closed doors, and family secrets were not shared outside the home. The trades some owners made and the purchase prices they paid confirm the demand for labor on southern Colorado sheep ranches. Documents record the names and identity of indigenous captives and their owners as a part of Colorado's southwestern history. One table compiled by Indian agent Lafayette Head in 1866 is full of information about captives and their owners. Another includes the names of 277 captives in southern Colorado newly found between 1860 and 1870, and identifies owner families. This research honors the survivors of captivity in southern Colorado.

CHAPTER NINE Genízaro Settlements of the Sierra Sandía: Resilience and Identity in the Land Grants of San Miguel del Cañón de Carnué and San Antonio de las Huertas, by Moises Gonzales

The cultural identity of the Genízaro descendant communities in the Sandía Mountains subtly exists in the material and cultural memory of the people who still occupy these lands. The communities of Carnué, San Antonio de Padua, and San Antonio de las Huertas situated along the Río Abajo's Sierra Madre share a similar story of being founded as buffer settlements to protect the Villa de Alburquerque from raids from the Comanche, Kiowa, and Apache Nations. Many Genízaro families participated in the formation of frontier settlements as well as the struggle to maintain them due to constant attack. These communities were often temporarily abandoned and reorganized as buffer towns well into the early nineteenth century. Francisco Ignacio de Madariaga, assessor for the Mexican government, noted that in order to maintain the necessary population at Carnué and San Antonio de las Huertas, he would cancel the rights of the settlers who refused to return, despite their objections. Many would stay and endure the constant threat of attack in order to maintain the status of landowner in a community land grant, to avoid servitude in the Río Abajo. Although raids would continue well into the 1860s, collective community building led to the resiliency of these communities today. This chapter describes the evolution of Genízaro settlements and identity through historical documents, oral histories, and analysis of contemporary cultural ritual such as the dances of the Comanchitos and Matachines.

CHAPTER TEN *Huellas de Sangre, Amor, y Lágrimas: Rescatando a Mis Cautivas* / Trails of Blood, Love, and Tears: Rescuing My Captives, by Susan M. Gandert

Following a colleague's encouragement to participate in a DNA study of New Mexico families, Susan Gandert explores the origins and stories behind her own *mestizaje* (mixed-race heritage) and the deeply rooted *querencia* she has for New Mexico. Relying on US census documents, and stories and resources provided by family and friends, she discovers how Indian slavery in New Mexico played a part in her family history. She rescues from oblivion the story of her *cautiva* great-great-grandmother on her mother's side and the cautiva owned by her great-great-grandfather on her father's side. Her discovery of Josephine M. Córdova's memoir *No Lloro Pero Me Acuerdo* also provides insight into the suffering and hardships endured by her great-great-grandparents and other Nuevomexicanos amid the Indian raids in nineteenth-century New Mexico Territory.

CHAPTER ELEVEN Genízaro Salvation: The Poetics of G. Benito Córdova's *Genízaro Nation*, by Michael L. Trujillo

Anthropologist and fiction writer G. Benito Córdova was among the first scholars to elaborate the ethnic/racial category of "Genízaro," and also among the first Native Nuevomexicanos to formally (re)claim this same identity. This chapter analyzes the Genízaro poetics of his final major work, the fictional novel *Big Dreams and Dark Secrets in Chimayó* (2006). Cordova employs, perhaps naïvely, a poststructural semiotics that addresses the complexities and contradictions of our fraught times. The novel's main character, Salvador Cascabel Natividad, and that character's mentor, Wilberto B. C. Ferrán, are self-identified Genízaros seeking to make their way in the troubled world. Salvador is depressed, abusive, absurdly masculine, and alcoholic. Moreover, Salvador stands in for a more general Nuevomexicano and/or Chicana/Chicano experience depicted in Córdova's own anthropological ethnography and broader social science literature. Despite the difficulties of his times and circumstances, Córdova's protagonist's case is not hopeless. Salvador's mentor Wilberto advises the younger man and chastises him with the purpose of teaching him the promise of a Genízaro way of being. Ultimately, Córdova's Salvador exemplifies a healing semiotics of salvation for those living in a time of, and embodied experience of, contradiction. In other words, Salvador is an example for Córdova's own home community, and Nuevomexicanos and Chicanas/Chicanos more generally as well as others who suffer the pain of social inequality. Salvador offers the possibility of a way to heal himself and heal others, and the possibility of a better way of life. Finally, this chapter elaborates Córdova's poetics in the context of his published oeuvre, biography, and archival materials. This author is a native of the Genízaro village of Abiquiú.

CHAPTER TWELVE *Sangre de Indio que Corre en Mis Venas: Nativo* Poetics and Nuevomexicano Identity, by Levi Romero

An intimate sense of Indo-Hispano consciousness motivates emergent Nuevomexicano narratives, poetry, song, and film after the Movimiento Chicano. What is it like to be and not be Xicanindio? Or Casindio, as New Mexico born poet-artist José Montoya named his Sacramento-based musical group? The movement was a *re-concientización*, a recognition of pride in mestizo and indigenous heritage. Hit songs from the 1970s on the radio included "Sangre de indio" and "Mi prieta linda." Filmmaker Moctesuma Esparza's 1977 documentary *Águeda Martínez: Our People, Our Country* celebrates the famous weaver, who acknowledges Navajo ancestors on both sides of her family. A newfound appreciation arose for traditional *indita* ballads and Indo-Hispano ritual dances like the Comanches, Comanchitos, Matachines, and Nanillé. Famed poet of the people Cleofes Vigil wrote a new indita for the 1976 Bicentennial to inform America what New Mexico was doing in 1776—negotiating a lasting peace with the Comanches. His "Himno de la Nacioncita de la Sangre de Cristo" (Hymn of the Little Nation of the Blood of Christ) praises a new people, in the register of what Tomás Atencio called "Genízaro Consciousness":

Raza buena y amorosa	A good and loving people
color bronce de mestizo	bronze-colored mestizos
mezcla del indio del pueblo	mixed with Pueblo Indians
donde salió un genízaro	born with the Genízaro
jeyá, jeyá, jeyá, ja . . .	heya, heya, heya, ha . . .

CHAPTER THIRTEEN Genízaro Identity and DNA: The Helix of Our Native American Genetic History, by Miguel A. Tórrez

Genetic testing for genealogical and anthropological research is a steadily growing science and pursuit, for scholars and laypersons alike. Genetic genealogy is a science that blends traditional genealogy with a scientific approach. The deep roots and migration patterns of population groups can be ascertained from Y-DNA and mtDNA (mitochondrial DNA) testing. Such testing in New Mexico has been an ongoing effort for over ten years. DNA testing has answered many questions regarding family lineages and surname links/distinctions and has given contemporary New Mexicans a view into their genetic ancestry. They can now trace themselves back to the early colonial settlers who came to La Nueva México in several waves, beginning with don Juan de Oñate and later with don Diego de Vargas. A diverse Native American supporting cast accompanied these colonists. Through the centuries, Native Americans became an integral part of the mestizaje that developed in Nuevomexicano culture and society. This chapter presents what genetic genealogy through DNA is uncovering among the Nuevomexicanos.

CHAPTER FOURTEEN Epilogue: Persistence and Resistance in Genízaro Identity, by Teresa Córdova

The power of Chicana/Chicano identity emerges from the recognition of indigenous roots. In the ongoing struggle to decolonize institutions, Chicanos and their movement realized early on that they needed to decolonize themselves through an exploration of their own mixed cultural origins, their mestizaje, and their transnational roots. But beyond family histories, very little historical detail on indigenous identity was available for Chicanas/Chicanos. The new generation of research on the persistence of Genízaro identity presented in this anthology fills in many historical gaps for Nuevomexicanos and documents the rise of what Tomás Atencio has called "Genízaro Consciousness." This epilogue is a comprehensive reflection on the process of discovery and self-discovery that emerged in the Nación Genízara seminar and community symposium in Abiquiú.

Today, the persistence of Genízaro identity blurs the lines of distinction between Native and Hispanic frameworks of race and cultural affiliation. It also interrogates and contests the hegemonic Hispanophile or "Spanish American" identity, so (in)famous beyond the borders of New Mexico, a fantasy heritage originally promoted by nineteenth-century Anglo-American political elites impatient with the much-delayed political process of statehood. This anthology creates an opportunity to broaden this dialogue in a new *resolana*, a collective forum on the plaza illuminated by the sun. It emerged from a 2016 advanced seminar sponsored by the University of New Mexico's Center for Regional Studies and hosted by the School for Advanced Research in Santa Fe, which was followed by a community symposium in the Pueblo of Abiquiú. Topics as diverse as Genízaro ethnogenesis, slavery, early settlements, expressive culture, poetics, religion, gender, and mestizo genetics are addressed. The resurgence of interest in Genízaro history and identity is what motivates each author to redefine the terminology of indigenous ethnicity. The multiplicity of definitions converges with singular purpose, and the editors invite readers to compare them and absolve the seeming redundancy. For some authors, Genízaro is about servitude, and for others it is about agency and freedom. Together, we invite a wider audience to explore the cultural legacy of what colonial documents call *La nación genízara*. This book is the first solely dedicated to the detribalized Native experience in New Mexico, a story of conquest, transculturation, and resilience.

References

Atencio, Tomás. 1985. "Social Change and Community Conflict in Old Albuquerque, New Mexico." PhD diss., University of New Mexico.

Brooks, James F. 2002. *Captives and Cousins: Slavery, Kinship, and Community in the Southwest Borderlands*. Chapel Hill: University of North Carolina Press.

Chávez, Fray Angélico. 1974. *My Penitente Land: The Soul Story of Spanish New Mexico*. Albuquerque: University of New Mexico Press.

———. 1979. "Genízaros." In *Handbook of North American Indians*, vol. 9, *Southwest*, edited by Alfonso Ortiz and William C. Sturtevant, 198–200. Washington, DC: Smithsonian Institution.

Córdova, Gilberto Benito. 1979. "Missionization and Hispanicization of Santo Tomás Apóstol de Abiquiú, 1750–1770." PhD diss., University of New Mexico.

Correia, David. 2013. *Properties of Violence: Law and Land Grant Struggle in Northern New Mexico*. Athens: University of Georgia Press.

Ebright, Malcolm. 1994. *Land Grants and Lawsuits in Northern New Mexico*. Albuquerque: University of New Mexico Press.

Frank, Ross. 1996. "Economic Growth and the Creation of the Vecino Homeland in New Mexico, 1780–1820." *Revista de Indias* 56, no. 208 (December): 744–82.

Gallegos, Bernardo. 2017. *Postcolonial Indigenous Performances: Coyote Musings on Genízaros, Hybridity, Education, and Slavery*. Rotterdam: Sense Publishers.

Gonzales, Gregorio P. 2017. "Si eres Genízaro: Race, Indigeneity, and Belonging in Northern New Mexico." PhD diss., University of Texas.

Gonzales, Moises. 2014. "The Genízaro Land Grant Settlements of New Mexico." *Journal of the Southwest* 56, no. 4 (Winter): 583–602.

Gutiérrez, Ramón A. 1991. *When Jesus Came, the Corn Mothers Went Away: Marriage, Sexuality, and Power in New Mexico, 1500–1846*. Stanford, CA: Stanford University Press.

———. 1999. "Crucifixion, Slavery, and Death: The Hermanos Penitentes of the Southwest." In *Over the Edge: Remapping the American West*, edited by Valerie J. Matsumoto and Blake Allmendinger, 253–71. Berkeley: University of California Press.

Lamadrid, Enrique R. 2003. *Hermanitos Comanchitos: Indo-Hispano Rituals of Captivity and Redemption*. Albuquerque: University of New Mexico Press.

Lecompte, Janet. 1985. *Rebellion in Río Arriba, 1837*. Albuquerque: University of New Mexico Press.

Magnaghi, Russell M. 1990. "Plains Indians in New Mexico: The Genízaro Experience." *Great Plains Quarterly* 10, no. 2 (Spring): 86–95.

Nieto-Phillips, John M. 2008. *The Language of Blood: The Making of Spanish-American Identity in New Mexico, 1880s–1930s*. Albuquerque: University of New Mexico Press.

Rael-Gálvez, Estevan. 2002. "Identifying Captivity and Capturing Identity: Narratives of American Indian Slavery in Colorado and New Mexico, 1776–1934." PhD diss., University of Michigan.

Sánchez, Joseph P. 1997. *Explorers, Traders, and Slavers: Forging the Old Spanish Trail, 1678–1850*. Salt Lake City: University of Utah Press.

Schroeder, Albert. 1975. "Río Grande Ethnohistory." In *New Perspectives on the Pueblos*, edited by Alfonso Ortiz, 41–70. Albuquerque: University of New Mexico Press.

Sisneros, Samuel E. 2017. "Los Genízaros and the Colonial Mission Pueblo of Belén, New Mexico." *New Mexico Historical Review* 92, no. 4 (Fall): 453–94.

Swadesh, Frances Leon. 1974. *Los Primeros Pobladores: Hispanic Americans of the Ute Frontier*. Notre Dame, IN: University of Notre Dame Press.

FIGURE I.1 Captive children of the Nanillé dance with Floyd Trujillo and his *tombé*. Abiquiú, New Mexico, 1999. Courtesy of Miguel A. Gandert.

FIGURE I.2 Dancing for Santo Tomás. Abiquiú, New Mexico, 1999, Miguel A. Gandert.

CHAPTER ONE

Visualizing Genízaro Cultural Memory and Ritual Celebration

MIGUEL A. GANDERT

The "tricultural" promotional narratives that underlie the modernization of New Mexico since 1848 oversimplified a complex cultural landscape. Genízaros and the legacy of slavery were erased or relegated to a remote, irretrievable past. The antidote to oblivion involves our most primal senses of vision and hearing. The persistence of Genízaro identity can be most clearly seen and heard on the plazas of several land grant communities and urban enclaves. The Native and mestizo peoples of greater Mexico have always dramatized their political and cultural struggles in festival and ritual display. Alterity, hybridity, and identity are negotiated on the plaza and in the cultural imagination. To read cultural narratives and metaphors more deeply, we must follow them beyond the documents of history and literature and into choreography, costume, ritual, and song.

The Pueblo de Abiquiú, descended from an amalgamation of over a dozen tribal groups, celebrates its own repertory of distinctive dances and songs, culminating in el Nanillé (the captive children's dance) and a series of pantomime captures and ransoms on the plaza. Genízaro traditions are celebrated for the feast of Santo Tomás Apóstol, just before the Advent season begins (Córdova 1979).

In other Genízaro communities, two traditions of Indo-Hispano ritual celebrated across New Mexico intertwine, the Matachines dance-drama and the Comanche dances and plays (Lamadrid 2003). Danced to the most ancient melodies in the land, the Matachines reconciles the spiritual conflicts of conquest and colonization. *Danzantes* (spirit dancers) wear *cupiles*

FIGURE 1.3 La Perijundia rests, surrounded by Matachines dancers. San Antonio, New Mexico. Courtesy of Miguel A. Gandert.

FIGURE 1.4 "La Rueda del Cautivo" (Circle Dance of the Captives). Talpa, New Mexico, 1995. Courtesy of Miguel A. Gandert.

FIGURE 1.5 "Guerrera de 'Desert Storm.'" Talpa, New Mexico, 1996, Miguel A. Gandert.

(Aztec-style fringed crowns), carry a rattle, and wave a three-pointed *palma* (palm) or lightning wand said to represent the Holy Trinity. The cast of characters includes the *monarca* (king), also known as Moctezuma; an angelic little girl dressed in white named Malinche (spiritual teacher); a *torito* (little bull); and *abuelos* (ancestral spirits). The choreography animates the dancers, often twelve in number, who form lines, exchange positions, and merge into a cross. They kneel in symbolic death and are revived by Malinche into a new spirituality. In a satirical pantomime, the totem bull of Spain is confronted by Malinche, defeated, and castrated by the outrageous abuelos, one of whom is la Perijundia (boogey-woman), a cross-dressed female who animates the fiestas of the Sandía Mountain villages. Postmortem castration symbolizes the end of empire and the defeat of its evils.

Comanche celebrations are cast in the historically updated mold of the Morismas, the festivals of the Christians and their archenemies, the Moors. The dances, nativity celebrations, and equestrian dramas referred to as los Comanches honor the historical struggles with enemy nomadic tribes, honoring victims, survivors, and captives, especially children—los Comanchitos (Lamadrid 2003, 80–134). Genízaro identity is ritually enacted in Ranchos de Taos and Talpa, with their own repertory of Hispano-Comanche dances and *vocable* (syllable singing): "El Águila" (The Eagle); "El Torito" (The Little Bull), which honors both bison and domestic bulls; "El Espanta'o" (The

FIGURE 1.6 "Last Stand of Cuerno Verde, September 3, 1779."
Alcalde, New Mexico, 1999. Courtesy of Miguel A. Gandert.

FIGURE 1.7 "Ya Se Va, Ya Se La Llevan" (She Goes,
They Are Taking Her), captive song. Alcalde, New Mexico,
2000. Courtesy of Miguel A. Gandert.

Frightened One), or the shield dance; and "El Cautivo" (The Captive), to honor captives taken in pantomime. An analysis of Hispano-Comanche melodies reveals that only the shield dance song can be identified by tribal Comanche, the Nuhmuhnuh (people). The others reveal their Kiowa, Apache, Navajo, Ute, and Pueblo musical roots, the same index of groups who became Genízaros (Lamadrid 2003, 135–78).

Just north of San Juan Ohkay Owingeh Pueblo, Alcalde was a colonial administrative center with a substantial population of Genízaros. Today, the village may not claim Genízaro identity but still celebrates both Matachines and the spectacular Comanches equestrian play that dramatizes the 1779 defeat of the powerful Comanche leader Cuerno Verde (Green Horn). At the edge of the fray, two *cautivas* await the outcome, hoping to return to their families.

The land grant communities of Carnué (Cañón de Carnué) and Placitas (San Antonio de las Huertas) and the other Hispano *plazas* (villages) of the Sandía Mountains have always celebrated Matachines, in a network of feast days that spans the calendar and unites the region. In recent years, many of these communities have revived the Comanchitos dance during Advent, which honors all the captives of the past. As these people migrated to more

FIGURE 1.8 "Galento en Su Plaza" (Galento Martínez in His Plaza). Alcalde, New Mexico, 2000. Courtesy of Miguel A. Gandert.

FIGURE 1.9 *below* "Esclavos de Jesús" (Slaves of Jesus). La Madera, New Mexico, 2016. Courtesy of Miguel A. Gandert.

FIGURE 1.10 *right* "Corazón de la Sierra" (Heart of the Mountains). La Madera, New Mexico, 2016. Courtesy of Miguel A. Gandert.

FIGURE 1.11 "Danza de las Generaciones" (Dance of the Generations). La Madera, New Mexico, 2016. Courtesy of Miguel A. Gandert.

FIGURE I.12 *above* "Comanchita del Alma" (Little Comanche of My Soul). La Madera, New Mexico, 2016. Courtesy of Miguel A. Gandert.

FIGURE I.13 *left* "Niño de la Flecha" (Arrow Boy). La Madera, New Mexico, 2016. Courtesy of Miguel A. Gandert.

urbanized areas like Bernalillo and Atrisco (near Albuquerque), they took their rituals with them (Lamadrid 2003, 120–27).

Dedicated to Santo Niño de Atocha and San Luis Gonzaga, a pilgrimage is celebrated to the old plaza and chapel of the abandoned outpost village of La Madera, deep in the Sandía Mountains above Placitas. Prayers, *alabado* hymns, and memories accompany the procession. The dance is measured by the beat of the *tombés* (single-headed hand drums) to the soothing lament of lullabies and the chants of the old *indita* songs, with the recitation of the names of the *antepasados* (ancestors), especially the cautivos.

References

Córdova, Gilberto Benito. 1979. "Missionization and Hispanicization of Santo Tomás Apóstol de Abiquiú, 1750–1770." PhD diss., University of New Mexico.

Lamadrid, Enrique R. 2003. *Hermanitos Comanchitos: Indo-Hispano Rituals of Captivity and Redemption*. Albuquerque: University of New Mexico Press.

CHAPTER TWO

Mexican Indians and Genízaros
Soldier-Farmer Allies in the Defense and Agricultural Development of New Mexico

TOMÁS MARTÍNEZ SALDAÑA,
ENRIQUE R. LAMADRID, AND JOSÉ A. RIVERA

Tlaxcalans to Genízaros: Politics of Cultural Hybridity

The Spanish conquest and colonization of Mexico and New Mexico never would have been possible without the collaboration of key indigenous allies. To understand the origins, culture, and political role of Genízaros in the defense of eighteenth-century New Mexico, the history of other Native allies from the two previous centuries must be considered. Free Mexican Indians participated in the exploration of northern New Spain in the sixteenth century and in its settlement thereafter. Highly motivated by their own origin myths and by the opportunity to return to the northern lands of Aztlán, they volunteered in large numbers to participate in these projects (Levin Rojo 2014). Spanish chroniclers refer to them only as *indios mexicanos* (Náhuatl-speaking Indians), for their lingua franca was called *mexicano*. They were from different city-states and regions and included Tlaxcalans, Tlatelolcos, Texcocanos, Caxcanes, Huachichiles, Mexicas, Tenochas, and Tarascos (Oster 2006).[1]

Continuously occupied since 1609, the Barrio de Analco de San Miguel began as a twin community settled by Mexican Indian allies right across the river from Santa Fe de San Francisco, the second capital of the kingdom.[2] Foundational documents are lacking, since Analco was not a commissioned settlement, as was the case in other twin towns in northern New Spain. Tlaxcalans gravitated to Analco at Santa Fe independently, or may have been recruited by the Oñate expedition of 1598 and later immigration projects. Like other Mexican Indians, they would be armed to also serve as soldiers. A few eighteenth-century documents suggest that the Tlaxcalans were indeed present from the beginning (Vélez de Escalante [1778] 1965; Urrutia 1766). In his 1630 Memorial Report on New Mexico, Fray Alonso de Benavides praised the loyalty and military prowess of the residents of Analco, who were about seven hundred in number, with two hundred Spanish and another one hundred servants and mestizos living in Santa Fe. Whenever needed, they all fought together with great valor and at their own expense to defend their *villa* (Benavides 1630, 27).

By 1750, Analco had become a Genízaro barrio in a process historically unique to New Mexico but similar to that of other settlements across the northlands, where, over the course of four or five generations, Indians became mestizos (Frye 1996). Genízaros were a sizable emerging class of Indians from a range of tribal backgrounds and languages, including Utes, Paiutes, Comanches, Kiowas, Navajos, Apaches, Pawnees, and even some Pueblo Natives. Their lingua franca was Spanish. Many were raised as captive children, taking the surnames of their adoptive families, and gained their liberty through marriage and military service. As with the Mexican Indians before them, Genízaros were also valued for their loyalty and skill as mounted soldiers. During his term as governor of New Mexico (1749–1754), Tomás Vélez Cachupín dispatched various groups from Analco to defend the frontier perimeters of the colony (Ebright 2014, 193–218). As a reward, they were provided with grants to the lands they defended with the water resources needed to engage in agriculture. They blended into Nuevomexicano society as citizens by the time of Mexican independence in 1821. In several historically Genízaro communities, strands of historical memory are still enacted in feast day celebrations, and aspects of Genízaro consciousness and identity persist (Gandert 2000).

Tlaxcalans: Exemplary Allies, Soldiers, Settlers

In central Mexico, in 1521, the military alliance of King Xicoténcatl and the city-state of Tlaxcala with Hernán Cortés and his band of conquistadores brought down the most powerful empire in the northern Americas, the Aztecs, based in the city-state of Tenochtitlán. In recognition of the alliance and their nominal acceptance of Christianity, the Tlaxcalans were granted many favors and privileges by the Spanish Crown. With the Capitulaciones de 1591, Viceroy Luis de Velasco II renewed these rights and responsibilities, which included minor nobility or hidalgo status, exemption from taxes and servitude, self-governance in distinct communities, and the right to own and ride horses with saddles, armed. They were invited and commissioned to be equal partners in the colonization of northern New Spain, the vast territory of frontier borderlands that now form the northern states of the Mexican Republic and the border states of the United States (Colegio de Historia de Tlaxcala 2009).

These semi-arid lands attracted settlers, who included a diverse array of soldiers, missionary brothers, prospectors and miners, cowboys, hunters, rustlers, and vagabonds. The region is drained by the Río Grande/Río Bravo and Río Conchos and extends along the colonial border between Nueva Vizcaya and Nuevo México. Priests founded missions, governors established presidios, and new settlers traveled to the north in hopes of acquiring land for ranches, farms, and haciendas. Over time, this process of migration resulted in an uncontrolled wave that generated conflict and ecological crises. For governance, the populations were organized into small towns, missions, and provincial capitals headed by local authorities.

The northlands were connected to Mexico City by the Camino Real de Tierra Adentro, which linked Zacatecas, Aguascalientes, Durango, Parral, and Chihuahua to El Paso del Norte and Santa Fe and continued to the terminus at San Juan Ohkay Owingeh. These towns were founded around mines and presidios, centers of wealth and power that became civil and religious administrative centers.[3] From 1590 onward, at the end of the Chichimeca War (1540s–1590), the Spanish Crown modified the process of conquest, turning it into a plan for colonization that granted authority to miners and landlords under the surveillance of officials and clergy. Farmer settlers arrived in several waves, first as part of the garrisons, posts, and provision centers along the road.

At the end of the sixteenth century, the government established two institutional colonization projects. One was commissioned by Viceroy Luis de Velasco II and financed by the state treasury to establish five towns in what is called the Tlaxcalan Diaspora as a strategy to end the Chichimeca War. The other project was organized and commanded by don Juan de Oñate, a wealthy miner from Zacatecas who intended to settle New Mexico as part of a royal contract. This process had an agricultural component, and settlers arrived at Nueva Vizcaya and New Mexico led by the church, the royal administration,

TABLE 2.1 Colonization of Northern New Spain
by the End of the Sixteenth Century

NEW SETTLEMENTS	COLONIZING EXPEDITIONS	DATES	COLONISTS
San Estevan de la Nueva Tlaxcala	Tlaxcalan Diaspora don Francisco de Urdiñola	1591	Españoles, Tlaxcalans, Tarascos, Huachihiles
San Luis de Colotlán	Tlaxcalan Diaspora Tlaxcalan Capitán Miguel Caldera	1591	Tlaxcalans, Nahuas, Huachichiles, Zacatecos, Españoles
San Andrés y Chalchihuites	Tlaxcalan Diaspora Capitán Miguel Caldera	1591–1592	Tlaxcalans, Nahuas, Huachichiles, Zacatecos, Españoles
San Miguel de Mezquitic	Tlaxcalan Diaspora Tlaxcala Capitán Miguel Caldera	1591	Tlaxcalans, Nahuas, Huachichiles, Españoles
Santa María de las Parras	Colonización de don Francisco de Urdiñola	1598	Tlaxcalans, Huachichiles, Españoles
San Gabriel Yungue Owingeh	Colonización del Adelantado don Juan de Oñate	1598	Españoles, Tlaxcalans, Mestizos

and private companies like that of Oñate. Indigenous and mestizo soldiers, farmers, and cowboys were recruited into these sorties, which originated in central New Spain. This process generated an even more varied and complex group of people, who mixed with other Indians already in the north. Local soldiers and farmers became part of the garrisons established for the military protection of the missions and towns.

The presence of Mesoamerican settlers in northern New Spain is fundamental for an understanding of the agricultural colonization that the government managed throughout the northern territory. The predominance of Tlaxcalan Indians during this period of expansion is due to the success they had as settlers, soldiers, cavalrymen, and technicians, and their expertise in horticulture, ranching, and the husbandry of cattle and horses. In addition, the hydraulic technology and intricate patterns of intensive agriculture practiced by the Tlaxcalans made them valuable in food production as colonization advanced north into marginal desert areas. These critical skills were deployed in the 1590s as part of the settlement program of the Tlaxcalan Diaspora at Saltillo, Colotlán, and Parras, and the colonization of New Mexico by Juan de Oñate.

After their first encounter with Cortés, the Tlaxcalans allied with the Spanish government in the process of imperial expansion because of their ability as soldiers; their military skills made them a defensive asset. In his 1766 Santa Fe map, José de Urrutia credits them as the founders of Barrio de Analco de San Miguel, located on the south bank of the Río de Santa Fe. This placed them in a strategic position to guard the government center on the other side of the river from any possible attacks on Santa Fe coming from the eastern plains. By the time of the Urrutia map, Genízaros from various tribal groups dominated the Barrio de Analco. Other Genízaro settlements were soon established to protect the other villas of New Mexico, Santa Cruz, and Alburquerque. Defensive plazas were established at Belén, Abiquiú, Ojo Caliente, Trampas, San Miguel del Vado, and other places to defend against Utes, Apaches, Comanches, Pawnees, and Navajos who conducted periodic raids on Spanish and Pueblo Indian villages. These were largely the same enemy groups into which the Genízaros had been born. As with the Tlaxcalans, the Genízaros became full partners in settlement and defense.

Processes of Colonization

The northern territories of New Spain were visited by a succession of expeditions led by explorers and missionaries in a quest for souls as well as for the mythical lands of Aztlán and the legendary cities of Cíbola and Quivira. By 1542, Francisco Vásquez de Coronado had scouted the vast region, but it was not until the latter half of the sixteenth century that permanent colonization was attempted. Little was achieved prior to 1590 because of the severe danger posed by a large population of hunter-gatherers who dominated the areas north of Querétaro, who since 1540 confronted Spanish power and later gave rise to the Chichimeca War. Roughly translated as "barbarian," the term *Chichimeca* was applied to a variety of nomadic cultures and languages. The fierce episode of the capture of the Mixtón mesa in New Galicia occurred in 1542. Some twenty years later, the colonized border was very limited and extended only to Querétaro, Guanajuato, San Luis Potosí, and Zacatecas.

Despite the inherent dangers of ventures into the frontier borderlands, with the discovery of the silver belt at Pachuca, Guanajuato, Zacatecas, and Parral, the north became a land of fabulous riches that attracted the great *señores*, silver tycoons, cattle and ranch barons, miners, and investors. The lure of discovering new deposits of silver ore was reason enough to muster military campaigns against the nomadic Indians who impeded them from advancing settlements further north. Miner soldiers succeeded in waging the fifty-year Chichimeca War, which also filled New Spain's borders with soldiers, missionaries, and settlers, who peopled garrisons, missions, and villages. This was a time of merciless war that nobody won, but the patience of friars, officials, and Indian caciques brought about a lasting peace that was bought and paid for by persistence and military force (Arnal 1995).

The agricultural settlement of northern New Spain took place after the Chichimeca War with the arrival of creoles, mestizos, Tlaxcalans, and other indigenous people from central New Spain who already possessed a robust farming and hydraulic culture. Thanks to the discoveries of Francisco de Ibarra, who established the road between Guadiana and Valle de San Bartolomé, the colonization policy founded a string of orchard towns irrigated by acequias north of Zacatecas, including Chalchihuites, Súchil Valley settlements, and Nombre de Dios, and from there to Guadiana, the capital of the kingdom of Nueva Vizcaya, continuing through Canatlán, San Juan del Río, and the garrisons of Cinco Señores, El Casco San Luis, El Gallo, Cerro Gordo, Valle de San Bartolomé, Parral, San Francisco de los Conchos, Namiquipa, San Buenaventura, and Janos Santo Niño in Chihuahua.

Following the road established by Ibarra, Juan de Oñate continued with the colonization of *el reino*, the kingdom of Nuevo México, along the route that became known as the Camino Real de Tierra Adentro (the Royal Road of the Interior). He and his group of settlers and families began the journey to New Mexico in 1596, departing from Zacatecas to Guadiana, then taking Ibarra's road and reaching the place known as El Casco in the modern state of Durango, where they camped for almost two years until they received official orders to proceed with the foundation of El Reino de Nuevo México. From there, he continued to San Bartolomé and then followed the foothills alongside the Sierra Madre, across deserts to the Río del Norte (now the

Río Grande) up to confluence of the Río Chama, where he established the temporary capital of San Gabriel Yungue Owingeh in 1598–1599, which was subsequently moved in 1610 to its permanent site at Santa Fe.

The Founding of Nuevo México

The Oñate family, the richest and most ambitious mining family in Zacatecas, realized and financed the founding of New Mexico. The wealth of this family supported don Juan de Oñate's quest for silver, power, and the establishment of a new kingdom based on the legitimacy of its ruling family. Oñate's son Cristóbal was not only Basque but through his mother, Isabel de Tolosa, had the blood of both the conquistador Cortés and the Aztec emperor Moctezuma in his veins.[4] After a number of delays, don Juan eventually received approval from the viceroy and the governor of Guadiana. Among the officials selected by Juan de Oñate to help organize the expedition was the protector captain of the town of Santa María de la Paz in Chalchihuites, royal ensign don Francisco Sosa Peñalosa. He became part of the colonizing expedition in 1598 and was commissioned to solicit farmers, teachers, master agriculturalists, and peasant soldiers. Chalchihuites became a major site for the recruitment of colonists to accompany the Oñate caravan and logically would have included a number of Tlaxcalans, as had been the case in prior expeditions (Sego 1998).[5]

Tlaxcalans were already established at Santa María de la Paz de la Nueva Tlaxcala in Chalchihuites, New Galicia Province, and were prepared to follow their former captain, Sosa Peñalosa. They had arrived from Tlaxcala in a "Great Caravan" of the four hundred families of the Diaspora. Sosa Peñalosa knew firsthand the skills and knowledge of the Tlaxcalans because he had been in Chalchihuites for six years when he recruited them to join the caravan and support Oñate's expedition to New Mexico. From there, he led a large contingent to El Casco, the gathering place for the Oñate caravan situated between Guadiana and Santa Bárbara (Sego 1998). Some twelve years after the families from Chalchihuites arrived at the Oñate colony at San Gabriel, they appear to have been relocated to help found the new capital, Villa de Santa Fe, as credited by Urrutia in his 1766 map. A special district was set aside for a group of colonists referred to as "Tlaxcalan" with its own "chapel of the Indians" dedicated to San Miguel (Swadesh 1974, 12). The settlement became known as Barrio de Analco de San Miguel. The hydraulic agricultural model established in the Tlaxcalan colonies began in various places, but its full-fledged development took place in San Esteban de la Nueva Tlaxcala–Saltillo, and it appears to have been replicated in Santa Fe. Urrutia's map depicts an irrigation system with two main *acequia madres*, one for the Spaniards and the other for Tlaxcalans, which he credits in the legend with helping to found the villa: "Pueblo o Barrio de Analco que debe su origen a los Tracaltecas [*sic*] que acompañaron a los primeros Españoles que entraron a la Conquista de este Reino" (Town or barrio of Analco that owes its origin to the Tracaltecas [*sic*] who accompanied the first Spaniards that entered to conquer this kingdom). The town plan at La Villa de Santa Fe appears to have followed or been influenced by the Tlaxcalan hydrologic model of irrigated agriculture. The place name "Barrio de Analco" was derived from the sixteenth-century practice of separating the civic centers of Spanish government from the area, usually across a river, designated for use by the indigenous people who provided the labor force in both craft industries and agriculture (Wroth 2010). Rivers were boundary markers denoting physical as well as social and economic separation between the Spanish classes and the Indians who accompanied them. Prototypes for Barrio de Analco de San Miguel, on the southern bank of the Río de Santa Fe, likely included Villa Alta in Oaxaca, the Barrio de Analco on the east side of the Río de San Juan de Dios across the river from the plaza of Guadalajara, and especially the still-existing Barrio de San Juan Bautista de Analco in the Spanish Villa de Guadiana, now named Durango (Wroth 2010).

The word "Analco" is of Náhuatl origin, meaning "on the other side of the river," which is appropriate given the location of the community (Simmons 1964, 108). In the Urrutia map, the north side of the river included the Iglesia y Convento de San Francisco, the Casa del Gobernador, la Capilla de Nuestra Señora de la Luz, the Camino de la Cañada (to Santa Cruz), and an Acequia para Regadío. The south side included the Iglesia de San Miguel and the Barrio de Analco. Roads shown by Urrutia include the Camino del Álamo (later Agua Fría), Camino de Galisteo, and Camino de Pecos, plus another Acequia para Regadío. Historical documentation of the presence of Tlaxcalans in Analco is scarce and is still debated by scholars. But their cultural and agricultural heritage is evident (Lamadrid 2016).

Recent scholars who doubt the presence of Tlaxcalans in New Mexico include José Antonio Esquibel (2010), William Wroth (2010), and Malcolm Ebright (2010, 2014). In his study of the Villa de Santa Fe in 1608–1610 prepared for the *cuartocentenario*, Esquibel claims that seventeenth-century records do not indicate the presence of Tlaxcalans, relying on the 1630 Fray Alonso de Benavides Santa Fe census, which didn't specify any. Wroth states that Oñate brought many Indian servants and laborers, as did other expeditions. They originated in the central valley of Mexico, especially the Mexica communities, and once in Santa Fe they were described as Indios Mexicanos or as being *de nación Mexicana* in occupations such as domestic servants, farm laborers, herders, cooks, blacksmiths, and master masons. Based on his sources, Wroth concludes that there is "no evidence of a formal government" organized for Tlaxcalan settlers in Santa Fe, as had been established in other northern provinces. The Mexican Indians residing at Analco also lacked an agreement or contract with the rights and autonomy that existed for the formal Tlaxcalan settlements elsewhere in northern Mexico. Wroth does concede, however, that some Tlaxcalans may have "made their way to Santa Fe" (Wroth 2010, 176–77).

Ebright (2014) references the work of historian Marc Simmons (1964) with respect to the Tlaxcalan presence at Analco, but in his own more recent account, he now agrees with other scholars and concludes that the Analco settlement included Mexican Indians of tribal groups besides the Tlaxcalans. Based on deeds and land grant records, Ebright constructed a map of early Santa Fe depicting property ownership on both sides of the Río Santa Fe, with the lands of the governor on the north and the "Tierras de los Mexicanos" (Lands of the Mexican Indians) at the Barrio de Analco on the south. He states that Mexican Indians and mestizos "may have lived in the Analco barrio" since around 1607 or before, a few years prior to the founding of the Villa de Santa Fe, when Santa Fe probably was a military post with presidio soldiers and Mexican Indians as auxiliaries occupying Analco. In this map, there is an Acequia Madre de Analco running through the area designated as "common agricultural lands farmed by the Analco Indians" (Ebright 2014, 56–58). As to the presence of Tlaxcalans, Ebright's map includes a landholding of the "Tlascalan [*sic*] Indian Juan de Leon Brito," who received a grant in 1742 confirming pre-revolt family holdings in the Analco area (55–56).

Tlaxcalan Agricultural Heritage

Spanish-irrigated agriculture in northern New Spain started with the arrival of the first settlers of Nueva Vizcaya at Nombre de Dios and Guadiana, under the command of Francisco de Ibarra, the first captain colonizer of the

Camino Real in the north, followed by Juan de Oñate. Many of the settlers were from Basque families, reputed to be the best miners in Spain. While they prospected for silver, Tlaxcalan farmers tilled and planted the land with orchards at Indé in 1580, Valle de San Bartolomé in 1580, and Chalchihuites by 1585. The departure of the four hundred families of the Tlaxcala Diaspora in June 1591 accelerated this process, and small irrigation systems were soon deployed at San Estevan de la Nueva Tlaxcala–Saltillo, Santa María de la Paz, Parras, and San Eleazario.

The Tlaxcalans were master farmers, skilled at designing, constructing, and managing gravity-fed irrigation diversions, dams, ditches, and drains, which watered small cultivated strips of land between the waterways with fruit trees and cereals. Their hybrid technology combined existing indigenous systems with European technology and governance first developed by the Moors in southern Spain. When confronted with new conditions as they advanced into the northern provinces, Tlaxcalan farmers improvised technologies that they had acquired from the Spanish and adapted them to suit their needs (Butzer 1999). Evidence of this amalgamation can be found as early as 1550. The efficacy of these systems enabled their spread up the Camino Real reaching the Río Grande/Río Bravo basin. Their success lay in their ability to handle weather-related changes and, above all, to preserve environmental humidity, which enabled optimal management. Also important in the early agricultural colonies of New Mexico was the melding of irrigation technologies and practices that converged from diverse sources, including antecedents from Moorish-Iberian traditions transferred to the New World; Puebloan agriculture as observed by Spanish explorers during the entradas of the late sixteenth century; and the irrigation horticulture of Mesoamerica brought by Mexican Indians who accompanied the Spanish caravans along the Camino Real de Tierra Adentro (Rivera 1998; Rivera et al. 2014).

Tlaxcalan skills in agricultural planning were evident in a vast array of systems in their original territory of Tlaxcala, where they were using complex water utilization systems even before the arrival of the Spaniards. Archaeology and ethnography of modern irrigation in contemporary Tlaxcala demonstrates a diverse utilization of water resources, evidenced by the continued use of flooding systems, drained fields, raised fields (*chimampas*), and canal irrigation. The systems transferred to the north included orchard gardens, the management of trenches, and anti-erosion terraces (*apantles* and *metlepantles*) on slopes, with irrigated strips sown on the edges with maguey agaves and fruit trees. These regions were irrigated by water diversions using channels, ditches, and trenches.

Hybrid irrigation agriculture and cultivars provided food for mines, settlements, forts, and missions. At the beginning of the northward expansion, local flora such as nopal (prickly pear), pecan trees, and mesquites, as well as European plants such as *membrillo* (quince bushes), were used to construct protective barriers or green fences for irrigation systems. In the acclimatization gardens of Tlaxcala, European and Mesoamerican plants were adapted for arid and semi-arid cultivation, protected from the desert in hydrological microsystems. In more northern climates, fruits from the temperate zones thrived, while tropical fruits such as zapotes, avocados, and guavas were not suitable. The Tlaxcalans are credited with introducing *nixtamalización* (the processing of corn with lime) from their own Mesoamerican traditions, as well as teaching Pueblo farmers the wheat cultivation they had recently learned from the Spanish.

The prototype for the hydraulic agricultural model established in Santa Fe can be seen in the fully developed systems of San Esteban de la Nueva Tlaxcala–Saltillo, in the region of Coahuila. The town plan from 1591 included two pueblos separated by a canal aqueduct for purposes of irrigation: the Villa de Saltillo for some twenty *vecinos españoles* and San Esteban for about eighty *guerreros tlaxcaltecas*. For the planting of crops and the raising of livestock, each pueblo was provided with sufficient land; as for water, the cabildo at Saltillo decreed that the San Esteban farmers should receive three-fourths of all water shares from the irrigation canal (Sego 1998). With an abundant supply of water and fertile land, the San Esteban community was built within two square kilometers—about two hundred hectares—and included a complex and intensive irrigation system surrounded by a thick layer of vegetative material native to the region, including palm and pecan trees, prickly pears, huisache (a type of acacia), mesquites, and others. This rectangle of land held five divisions that were a part of the San Esteban Administrative Center, and four districts, including the main ones of Santa Ana and San José. In turn, each district delineated its property with additional barriers of fruit trees along the main irrigation ditch and supply channels. The Tlaxcalan hydraulic model, with its ability to store the ever-scarce sources of water, was replicated in other Tlaxcalan settlements and in the establishment of the garrisons and missions of northern New Spain over the next two hundred years (Martínez Saldaña 1998).

Tlaxcalan Legacy: Expressive Culture and Traditions

Before the Spanish conquest, the religious practices, architecture, artistic traditions, dance, and ritual calendar of Tlaxcala were similar to those of other Nahua groups in central Mexico. Each city-state had its favorite tutelary deities, but all shared their devotion to the major gods, such as Tlaloc, the god of water and rain, and Quetzalcóatl, the plumed serpent deity. Since weather patterns that brought rain to the valley of Mexico originated in the mountain peaks and valleys to the east, where Tlaxcala was located, the devotion and sacrifices to Tlaloc were especially important.

Tlaxcala was the first Mesoamerican city-state to convert to Christianity. Hernán Cortés himself and his consort interpreter Malinche were at the baptism of King Xicoténcatl, a key scene in the *Lienzo de Tlaxcala*, a narrative canvas painted in the style of the ancient codices. Native historians realized the necessity of telling their own story, since Spanish chronicles did not distinguish between indigenous Mexicano groups. The *Lienzo* portrays the major events of the alliance with the Spanish Crown and the joint military campaigns that followed the demise of the Aztecs (Kranz 2010).

Tlaxcalan folk Catholicism did not exclude Native origin stories, such as the Seven Caves of Chicomóstoc, where the seven Nahua tribes emerged and began their migration from the land of Aztlán in the north down to central Mexico (Levin Rojo 2014). The desire to return to the place of origin remained a powerful spiritual motivation. The new devotions to the saints and their vocations was another especially syncretic element that allowed the transformation rather than the elimination of Native beliefs. The Tlaxcalans adored the supernatural *santos* even more than the human ones—like the four archangels, especially Miguel, who presided over the four gates of heaven as well as the four sacred directions of the earth. Not enough can be said about the Virgen de Guadalupe and her ability to cross cultural boundaries. Thirteen years after her original 1531 appearance on the Cerro de Tepeyac, in 1544 she appeared atop a cloud of dust over the Cerro de la Bufa in Zacatecas and put an end to a raging battle between the Zacateco Indians and the four Basque soldiers, Cristóbal de Oñate, Diego de Ibarra, Juan de Tolosa, and Baltazar de Bañuelos. The soldiers, who were also miners, examined the rocks the Indians were throwing down from the hill and were surprised to find the richest silver ore they had ever seen. They interpreted the bonanza of the silver mines of Zacatecas as a gift from Guadalupe, who showed them the "metal of the moon" that later financed the settlement of New Mexico for her greater glory (Terán Fuentes 2002).

One particular image tied to the Pueblo Revolt of 1680 and the attack on Analco and Santa Fe is the Virgen de la Macana. In her hand she holds a *macana*, the fearsome but fragile obsidian-edged wooden swords or clubs used in Mesoamerica before the Spanish brought in steel weapons. Before the first battle between the armies of Cortés and Tlaxcala, a warrior approached a soldier on horseback and cut off the horse's head with one clean blow. Macanas may have been kept as mementos by Mexican Indian families in Analco. The santo in question began as a small statue of the Virgen de la Sacristía de Toledo, which belonged to the family of Capitán Juan Durán de Miranda, governor of New Mexico from 1671 to 1675. In 1674, his ten-year-old daughter, who was gravely ill, reported to her father that the Virgin appeared and told her that New Mexico would be destroyed in six years, a prophecy that came to pass with the 1680 Pueblo Revolt. In the battle for Santa Fe, one of the rebel Indians with a macana, presumably from Analco, struck the statue with it, nicking its forehead. Fray Buenaventura de los Carros carried the statue back to Mexico City, where her name was changed to La Virgen de la Macana; she was placed in the Convento Grande de Francisco. In the eighteenth century, a devotion grew up around the image, which was believed to grant protection from Indian attacks to her devotees (Katzew 1998).

Typical of folk Catholicism, the ritual calendar was readily syncretized, combining Mesoamerican and Christian symbols and feast days. At the center of the fiesta is the table set with the same hybrid foodways introduced to the upper Río Grande, including chile and new varieties of corn as well as new fruits and vegetables from Europe, not to mention domestic animals like cattle, sheep, goats, pigs, and chickens (Carrillo 1998; Brokmann Haro 1996; González de la Vara 1996; Martínez Saldaña 1998). The new combinations of flavors were prodigious and exuberant. Wheat and corn tortillas, and tamales, were some of the everyday delicacies newly introduced to the north. The cornucopia is well documented by Padre Benavides in 1630:

> All this land is very fertile, it gives forth with great abundance everything which is sown in it: corn, wheat, beans, lentils, garbanzos, horse beans, peas, pumpkins, water melons, cantaloupes, cucumbers, every kind of vegetable:

cabbage, lettuce, carrots, thistles, garlic, onions, cactus fruit, pitahayas, apricots, peaches, nuts, acorns, blackberries and many others which I won't mention to avoid exaggeration. (Benavides 1630, 36)

A hybrid Mesoamerican-European pharmacopeia of medicinal plants also was taken north to supplement the regional remedies of the northlands (Curtin 1997; Martínez Saldaña 2002).

Besides agriculture and foodways, the aspect of Tlaxcalan material culture most directly tied to New Mexico is weaving. Sheep thrived in the grasslands, valleys, and mountains of the north, and raw wool as well as textiles were major exports in colonial times. Master weavers, notably the Bazán brothers from Puebla, were brought by the government to improve the quality of New Mexican production. The dissemination of design elements that left Tlaxcala and the valley of Puebla and were developed in Saltillo may be traced north, where they took root (Lucero and Baizerman 1999; Fisher 1994). Often called the "Eye of God," the brilliant central diamond design of these textiles keeps multiplying, watching over, and warming its people, in their places of origin as well as among new groups like the Diné (Navajo), who also embraced these textiles and began raising sheep that provided the wool for yarn.

Ritual dance and drama that originated in Tlaxcala are still celebrated on feast days across northern Mexico, notably a double cycle of Morismas and Matachines—traditional folk celebrations shared between indigenous, mestizo, and Spanish Mexican groups (Gandert 2000). The oldest is the Morisma, the famous and many-faceted dramatic plays of Christians and Moors that address themes of conquest and reconquest dating back to the eighth century on the Iberian Peninsula. The dances, skirmishes, harangues, and pitched battles remind the participants of their long cultural memory, as corporeal as it is cerebral. After the conquest of Mexico, Cortés organized pageants of Moors and Christians to celebrate great victories in Europe and to demonstrate the superiority of his arms and animals (Harris 2000, 118). Juan de Oñate did the same in his entrada into New Mexico eighty years later. From the first contacts between Spaniards and Tlaxcalans, historical events and cultural processes have been dramatized for political and ritual purposes. The official transcripts of triumph and evangelization are contested with hidden transcripts of resistance and redemption. In New Mexico, the Morismas were updated to substitute Moorish opponents with the new Comanche enemies of the eighteenth century, and the Genízaros who fought them subsequently represented them in the plays (Lamadrid 2003). In Hispano-Comanche dances, as in those of the Matachines, the texts of the harangues and battle speeches become choreography and a play of symbols with deep histories behind them.

The social nexus that connects cultural organization and agricultural production over the centuries are the *cofradías* (secular religious confraternities) and sodalities in which many community members participated. In northern Mexico, their responsibilities included ensuring the general spiritual and material well-being of the community, plus maintaining the devotions dedicated to their patron saints. Some cofradías in mining areas accumulated capital in silver. Other cofradías controlled farms, sources of water, orchards, livestock, and even property in urbanized areas. Besides economic resources, the cofradías also had political influence. *Hermanos* (brothers) often held political and administrative posts such as *alcalde* (mayor). They maintained civil order and participated in military defense. They also organized the ritual events of the religious calendar and the festivities of rites of passage—marriages, baptisms, and funerals (Lamadrid 2008, 437).

By the early eighteenth century, there was a proliferation of confraternities and sodalities in northern New Spain. The Bourbon reforms, which reorganized the economy and defenses of the region, also consolidated the confraternities. The most prominent is dedicated to and named for Nuestro Padre Jesús Nazareno (Our Father Jesus the Nazarene), which celebrates the aspects of the Passion that recall Ecce Homo (Jesus at his trial) and the Man of Sorrows (Jesus scourged, crowned, wounded, and humiliated). This suffering Jesus is supremely human, a man still standing with all the strength necessary to fulfill his transcendental burdens. As the Son of God, he takes on the role of his Father and exemplifies suffering humanity. In the Genízaro communities of New Mexico, this brotherhood was the principle religious and secular organization, the precursor of many others to come, including the *mutualistas* (mutual aid societies) and political parties of the nineteenth and twentieth centuries (Rivera 2010).

Independence and a New Border: Persistent Legacies and Cultural Complications

When Mexico gained its independence from Spain, the colonial hydraulic and legal heritage was in jeopardy. After 1821, individuality was favored as inherited from the French Revolution; the privileges of Tlaxcalan settlers were abolished in 1857, and the rights of communities, councils, and stewardships were cancelled. In the new Republic of Mexico, the local right to manage lands, irrigation, cemeteries, and churches was lost. A few decades later, however, Mexico no longer held all the territory inherited from Spain, because the towns beyond the Río Bravo and their lands came under the US flag. Through the Treaty of Guadalupe Hidalgo signed in 1848 by Mexico and the United States, the legal systems and irrigation rights north of the border remained just the way they had been under Spanish domination. On the contrary, the lands of the Chihuahuan towns all the way up to El Paso del Norte, later Ciudad Juárez, went through a process of destruction of their hydraulic and legal systems, which ended in 1904, when the towns lost their communal lands at the hands of the Chihuahuan landlords, who had become wealthy and powerful thanks to their manipulation of the Reform Laws and the disentitlement policy under the government of *Presidente* Porfirio Díaz. The lay brotherhoods lost their civil and community role, and they only played a secondary role in religious festivities.

The opposite happened in the United States, since the religious brotherhoods and other mutual aid societies, along with the acequia governments, had a prominent role in the formation of the social and political structure of New Mexico during the territorial period and somewhat into statehood in 1912. These lay brotherhoods, mutual aid societies, and their counterpart acequia associations did not experience the liberal reform, and for many generations have retained their decision-making capacity and autonomous management. The Hermanos de Nuestro Padre Jesús, popularly known as *penitentes* (penitent) brothers, north of the border became deeply involved in politics and supported cultural resistance to the American occupation and its project to subordinate the Nuevomexicano and Native population. Religion was a refuge and source of strength for the larger struggle at hand. With the political isolation that followed during the next fifty years, the social organization of mutual aid–based communities managed to survive more or less intact; most of these would continue, especially in the cases of the acequias that still controlled water, land, and culture. In the upper Río Grande, the hydraulic, agricultural, and legal traditions remain associated with the traditional organizations of the New Spain that no longer existed in Mexico after 1857, when Mexican irrigation communities were deprived of their water rights, and the Mexican Revolution failed to restore those rights.

More than four centuries after the foundation of New Mexico, traces of

Tlaxcalan and mestizo Mesoamerican cultural heritage abound. New Mexican Spanish overflows with hundreds of Náhuatlisms, mostly for plants and animals native to the northern Americas, plus Náhuatl place-names such as Analco and Atrisco. Agricultural traditions and institutions of water management still thrive. A hybrid gastronomy based on the plants and animals of the Columbian exchange provides an amazing new constellation of flavors, seasoned with favorite varieties of chile. In the artisanal weavings of the borderlands, the Eye of God is ever present. A colorful cycle of Indo-Hispano feasts and rituals still expresses themes of conquest and resistance that take on special meaning in our own times. A complex cultural heritage keeps evolving to accommodate the dreams and ambitions of the descendants of an Indo-Hispano legacy, enacted in the fields, the kitchens, the looms, and the plazas of the northlands, the places where it is memorialized.

Notes

1. The most recent excavations/stabilizations at San Miguel de Analco Church in Santa Fe revealed material culture remains from several of these groups of indios mexicanos. To this day, the Tarascos from Michoacán still speak their own language—Purépecha.

2. From the Latin, *barrio* originally referred to a neighborhood located outside the walls of a city. A more accurate Náhuatl term for this type of Native community is *altepetl*, which has no implication of marginality.

3. The early settlements were founded in Durango (1564), Saltillo (1575), San Esteban (1591), Monterrey (1594), Parras (1598), El Camino del Paso del Norte (1598), San Gabriel (1598), Santa Fe (1610), El Paso (1650), Alburquerque (1706), Chihuahua (1709), and Aguayo (1750). Each of these towns formed a cultural nucleus that influenced the surrounding areas as centers of cultural, technical, social, and political dissemination.

4. The legitimacy of the Oñate family to rule New Mexico was one of the themes of Gaspar Pérez de Villagrá's epic Renaissance poem, *Verdadera historia de la conquista de la Nueva México* (1610).

5. In a footnote, Eugene Sego (1998) points out that the *escribano* (scribe) of Nombre de Dios, a Spanish town with four Indian barrios located near the border between Nueva Vizcaya and Nueva Galicia, testified that the Juan de Oñate caravan included "una grande multitud de gente" (a great multitude of people) (114–15). Sego credits Sosa Peñalosa for recruiting colonists from Chalchihuites to join the expedition to New Mexico but does not identify how many were Tlaxcalans. For a project of this magnitude, he assumes that a large number would have been recruited, but he does

acknowledge that there is no definitive proof of Tlaxcalan participation. It should be noted that the absence of documents and records from that time has generated a debate that has led some historians to deny the presence of Tlaxcalans in the Oñate expedition to and settlement of New Mexico.

References

Arnal, Simón Luis. 1995. *El presidio en México en el siglo XVI*. México: Facultad de Arquitectura, Universidad Nacional Autónoma de México.

Benavides, Alonso de. 1630. *Memorial*. Madrid: Imprenta Real.

Brokmann Haro, Carlos. 1996. *La cocina mexicana a través de los siglos, III Mestizaje culinario*. México: Editorial Clío/Fundación Hérdez.

Butzer, Karl W. 1999. "Tecnologías de irrigación tlaxcalteca: ¿Mito o realidad?" In *Constructores de la nación: La migración tlaxcalteca en el norte de la Nueva España*, edited by Israel Cabazos Garza et al., 135–40. San Luis Potosí, Mexico: El Colegio de San Luis/Gobierno del Estado de Tlaxcala.

Carrillo, Ana María. 1998. *La cocina del tomate, frijol y calabaza*. México: Editorial Clío.

Colegio de Historia de Tlaxcala. 2009. *La participación tlaxcalteca en la colonización del norte novohispano*. Tlaxcala, Mexico: Colegio de Tlaxcala.

Curtin, Leonor S. M. 1997. *Healing Herbs of the Upper Rio Grande: Traditional Medicine of the Southwest*. Revised and edited by Michael Moore. Santa Fe: Western Edge Press.

Ebright, Malcolm. 2010. "A City Different Than We Thought: Land Grants in Early Santa Fe, 1598–1900." In *All Trails Lead to Santa Fe: An Anthology Commemorating the 400th Anniversary of the Founding of Santa Fe, New Mexico in 1610*, 65–96. Santa Fe: Sunstone Press.

———. 2014. *Advocates for the Oppressed: Hispanos, Indians, Genízaros, and Their Land in New Mexico*. Albuquerque: University of New Mexico Press.

Esquibel, José Antonio. 2010. "Thirty-Eight Adobe Houses: The Villa de Santa Fe in the Seventeenth Century, 1608–1610." In *All Trails Lead to Santa Fe: An Anthology Commemorating the 400th Anniversary of the Founding of Santa Fe, New Mexico in 1610*, 109–28. Santa Fe: Sunstone Press.

Fisher, Nora. 1994. *Rio Grande Textiles: Spanish Textile Tradition of New Mexico and Colorado*. Santa Fe: Museum of New Mexico Press.

Frye, David L. 1996. *Indians into Mexicans: History and Identity in a Mexican Town*. Austin: University of Texas Press.

Gandert, Miguel A., with Enrique R. Lamadrid. 2000. *Nuevo México Profundo: Rituals of an Indo-Hispano Homeland*. Santa Fe: Museum of New Mexico Press.

González de la Vara, Fernán. 1996. *La cocina mexicana a través de los siglos*. Vol. 2, *Época prehispánica*. México: Editorial Clío/Fundación Hérdez.

Harris, Max. 2000. *Aztecs, Moors, and Christians: Festivals of Reconquest in Mexico and Spain*. Austin: University of Texas Press.

Katzew, Ilona. 1998. "La Virgen de la Macana: Emblema de una coyuntura franciscana." *Anales del Instituto de Investigaciones Estéticas* 20, no. 72: 65–72.

Kranz, Travis Barton. 2010. "Visual Persuasion: Sixteenth-Century Tlaxcalan Pictorials in Response to the Conquest of Mexico." In *The Conquest All Over Again: Nahuas and Zapotecs Thinking, Writing, and Painting Spanish Colonialism*, edited by Susan Schroeder, 3–21. Eastbourne, East Sussex, England: Sussex Academic Press.

Lamadrid, Enrique R. 2003. *Hermanitos Comanchitos: Indo-Hispano Rituals of Captivity and Redemption*. Albuquerque: University of New Mexico Press.

———. 2008. "Rutas del Corazón: Pilgrimage and Cultural Commerce on the Camino Real de Tierra Adentro." *New Mexico Historical Review* 83, no. 4 (Fall): 423–49.

———. 2016. "Tlaxcalans in New Mexico: Fading Traces, Contested Legacies." *New Mexico Historical Review* 91, no. 2 (Spring): 147–62.

Levin Rojo, Danna. 2014. *Return to Aztlán: Indians, Spaniards, and the Invention of Nuevo México*. Norman: University of Oklahoma Press.

Lucero, Helen R., and Suzanne Baizerman. 1999. *Chimayó Weaving: The Transformation of a Tradition*. Albuquerque: University of New Mexico Press.

Magnus, Morner. 1967. *Race Mixture in the History of Latin America*. Boston: Little, Brown.

Martínez Saldaña, Tomás. 1998. *La diáspora tlaxcalteca: La expansión agrícola mesoamericana al norte de México*. México: Ediciones Tlaxcallan/Gobierno del Estado de Tlaxcala.

———. 2002. "La riqueza botánica del Río Grande: La herencia olvidada del Camino Real." *El Caminante*, edited by Juan Estevan Arellano, no. 1 (Fall): 10–12.

———. 2014. "La herencia hidraulica agrícola tlaxcalteca colonial: El caso del norte de México y suroeste de los Estados Unidos." In *Migración e identidad: Presencia de Tlaxcala en América*, edited by Silvia Aboytes Perete, 295–328. México: Universidad Autónoma de Tlaxcala.

Oster, Elizabeth. 2006. "San Miguel Excavation Report." Unpublished manuscript.

Rivera, José A. 1998. *Acequia Culture: Water, Land, and Community in the Southwest*. Albuquerque: University of New Mexico Press.

———. 2010. *La Sociedad: Guardians of Hispanic Culture along the Río Grande*. Albuquerque: University of New Mexico Press.

Rivera, José A., Juan Estevan Arellano, Enrique R. Lamadrid, and Tomás Martínez Saldaña. 2014. "Irrigation and Society in the Upper Río Grande Basin, U.S.A.: A Heritage of Mutualism." In *Irrigation, Society, Landscape: Tribute to Thomas F. Glick*, edited by Carles Sanchis-Ibor et al., 443–57. Valencia, Spain: Universitat Politècnica de València.

Sego, Eugene B. 1998. *Aliados y adversarios: Los colonos tlaxcaltecas en la frontera septentrional de Nueva España*. San Luis Potosí, Mexico: El Colegio de San Luis/Gobierno del Estado de Tlaxcala.

Simmons, Marc. 1964. "Tlascalans in the Spanish Borderlands." *New Mexico Historical Review* 39, no. 2 (April): 101–10.

Swadesh, Frances Leon. 1974. *Los Primeros Pobladores: Hispanic Americans of the Ute Frontier*. Notre Dame, IN: University of Notre Dame Press.

Terán Fuentes, Mariana. 2002. *El artificio de la fe: La vida pública de los hombres del poder en el Zacatecas del siglo XVIII*. Zacatecas, Mexico: Universidad Autónoma de Zacatecas/Instituto Zacatecano de la Cultura.

Urrutia, José de. 1766. *Plano de la Villa de Santa Fee, 1766*. British Library Add. Ms. 17662 M.

Vélez de Escalante, Fray Silvestre. (1778) 1965. *Letter of the Father Fray Silvestre Velez de Escalante, Written on the 2nd of April, in the Year 1778*. Albuquerque: University of New Mexico Press.

Wroth, William. 2010. "Barrio de Analco, Its Roots in Mexico and Role in Early Colonial Santa Fe, 1610–1780." In *All Trails Lead to Santa Fe: An Anthology Commemorating the 400th Anniversary of the Founding of Santa Fe, New Mexico in 1610*, 163–78. Santa Fe: Sunstone Press.

CHAPTER THREE

Genízaros and Cultural Systems of Slavery in the Hispanic Southwest

WILLIAM S. KISER

In 1776, while Americans on the Atlantic coast were declaring independence from an English overlord, a Franciscan friar named Francisco Atanasio Domínguez toured New Mexico, the most isolated province of colonial New Spain's northern frontier. As he visited each village, the clergyman made extensive notes that included, among other things, census data counting the Crown's subjects. In several places, Domínguez enumerated segregated communities of "Genízaros." He found 297 of them on the outskirts of the capital city of Santa Fe; another 209 at Los Jarales near Albuquerque; and 136 more residing at Abiquiú along the Chama River (Domínguez 1956, 42, 126, 208; Adams 1953, 205; Cutter 1975, 351). Throughout northern New Mexico's Río Grande Valley and its hinterlands, smaller contingents of this distinctive ethnic enclave could be found living together on the fringes of Hispanic hamlets like Belén, Cerro, Tomé, and Valencia (Hackett 1937, 395, 401–2; Kinniard 1958, 83, 89; Simmons 1977, 34–35). Domínguez discovered clusters of Genízaros in most northern New Mexico villages, but he explained that "they have no true home, because hunger and the enemy pursue them from every side" (Domínguez 1956, 119).

The men, women, and children whom the friar classified as Genízaros were in fact Indian captives and their offspring who, to varying degrees, had been acculturated and assimilated into New Mexico's Hispanic and Catholic society while remaining in a condition of servility and dependency. Servants and slaves made up a significant percentage of New Mexico's colonial-era population—historians have variously estimated that anywhere from 12 to 33 percent of the provincial inhabitants were enslaved in the late 1700s and early 1800s—and the servile Genízaros who occupied regional settlements played important roles in local society and culture (Brooks 2002, 145; Gutiérrez 1991, 171).[1] On an even broader level, Genízaros and other types of slaves in the Southwest also figured into America's national equation of emancipation in the mid-nineteenth century.[2]

Although the chattel system of slavery in the American South and elsewhere in the New World differed from the cultural form of slavery that developed around Indian captivity in northern New Mexico, some important similarities did exist. While Genízaros typically could not be converted to cash and did not constitute a monetary asset, they nonetheless experienced overt disempowerment and subjugation at the hands of their masters and overseers as they fulfilled menial tasks in either the household or the fields and pastures. Like black slaves on the sugar plantations of Cuba or the tobacco estates of Virginia, New Mexico's Genízaros lived under the thumb of the Hispano elites who held them in bondage, thus denying many of these human subjects their physical liberty and minimizing their social and political agency. And despite their differences in economic and cultural purpose, both systems of slavery objectified the victims and coerced them into a life of degrading, involuntary servitude. Over time, however, many Genízaros developed shared group identities around the stigmatization of enslavement as well as their shared spiritual and cultural consciousness. This helped them to resist the most violent forms of persecution and in some instances even promulgated slight degrees of political and judicial empowerment that other types of slaves, including unbaptized Indian captives and Hispanic debt peons, generally failed to attain.[3]

Several transitional periods influenced the development of the regional institutions of slavery that existed in New Mexico. Prior to the arrival of European imperialists in the 1500s, Native peoples frequently took captives when raiding enemy tribes, and many of those abductees were forced into servitude while being assimilated through fictive kinship, cultural ceremony, and other strategic mechanisms (Lawrence and Lawrence 2016, 3–20). When Spanish colonists began arriving in the seventeenth century, they implanted a modified form of this same slaving system, adding an economic component to the cultural and filial motivations that undergirded the preexisting indigenous methods of captivity. For more than two centuries, from Juan de Oñate's entrada of 1598 until Mexican independence in 1821, Euro-American settlers on New Spain's agricultural and pastoral frontier created the demand for manual labor that drove the multilateral system of Indian slavery (G. C. Anderson 1999, 3–8; Calloway 2003, 205).

As Spain hemorrhaged its Western Hemisphere possessions during the Age of Revolution, the rhetoric of emancipation gradually took hold in some of the emerging democratic nations, and newly independent Mexico abolished racial slavery by constitutional decree in 1824 and again by executive order in 1829 (Torget 2015, 77–80, 142–45, 150, 190). Not until New Mexico came under the legal jurisdiction of the United States in 1848, however, would any meaningful action be pursued in regard to Genízaros, debt peons, and other enslaved peoples in that region. During the turbulent American political crisis of the 1850s, Northern abolitionists advocated for the prohibition of the alternative forms of slavery that existed in the Hispanic Southwest, although laws banning peonage and Indian captivity would not be passed until the years of Radical Reconstruction after the Civil War (Kiser 2014, 169–89; Kiser 2017, 142–69). In this sense, Genízaros played an important role in the regional evolutions of slavery in North America during the eighteenth century, as well as the sweeping abolition of multiple forms of human bondage during the age of emancipation.

In New Mexico, Indian slavery originally targeted the Pueblo Indians following Oñate's colonization, although this early manifestation was largely predicated on Spain's encomienda (labor assignment) system and demanded that indigenous laborers pay tribute to their benefactors rather than live under them in complete subjectivity (Snow 1983, 347–57; H. A. Anderson 1985, 353–73). The Pueblo Revolt of 1680 helped to undermine the trend of coerced servitude among sedentary Puebloan peoples. Although New Mexico's more southerly tribes—particularly the Chiricahua Apaches—had already been targeted for enslavement in the mines of central Mexico prior to the 1680 uprising, Spanish colonists increasingly redirected their slave raids away from the Pueblos and toward neighboring nomadic groups following the *reconquista* in 1692 (John 1975, 70–71; Gutiérrez 1991, 150–52). The use of the term "Genízaro" emerged around that same time as an appellation to specifically describe Natives in Spanish New Mexico who had been abducted from their tribes of origin and placed in servile captivity (Brooks 2002, 127–29, 374).[4] Eventually, more than half a dozen different tribes fell into this cycle of slave raiding. At the village of Abiquiú—an epicenter of this vicious borderlands slave trade—an inventory of twenty-five Genízaros living there in the mid-1700s identified their tribal origins as six Pawnee, six Jumano, four Apache, three Kiowa, two Aa, one Tano, one Ute, and two unspecified (Ebright and Hendricks 2006, 29).[5] As this melting pot of tribal and ethnic identity stirred, it absorbed Hispanic folkways and religious traditions, producing a hybrid culture of Genízaros at the margins of many New Mexico villages.

Contemporaneously in other areas of North America, English and French settlers developed systems of captive slavery that similarly targeted Indians and forced them into exploitative bondage as servants. By the eighteenth century, Genízaros were not alone in their plight, as indigenous peoples throughout the New World faced the threat of capture and lifetime enslavement.[6] Indian captives in New Mexico, however, differed in at least one crucial area of their traumatic experiences, as the Hispanic captors often baptized abductees in an attempt to culturally and spiritually assimilate them into the settler society. The widespread religious indoctrination of "heathen" Indians differentiated the Spanish from other European colonizers and constituted one of the Crown's foremost purposes in colonizing the New World. Throughout New Mexico, Catholic clergymen recognized baptismal anointment as the most useful mechanism for converting Native peoples and instilling in them a reverence—often superficial and contrived—for the power of God and the church (Elliott 2006, 66–72). Between 1700 and 1849, New Mexico's parishes recorded over three thousand baptisms of captive Indian women and children, many of whom thereafter entered the Hispanic society as Christianized Genízaro subjects (Chávez 1957, 198–219; Brugge 1985, 30; Gutiérrez 1991, 200; Blackhawk 2005, 72–74).

Over the course of a century and a half beginning in the 1700s, the captive slave trade brought at least five thousand Genízaros into the Hispanic communities of northern New Mexico (Brooks 2002, 125). The segregated residential configurations that Fray Domínguez observed during his tour of the province developed around localized social and class structures, and Genízaro families often clustered on the fringes of each village as objectified outsiders and servile underlings. As baptized Indian captives, they constituted something of a hybrid group—biologically and ethnically Indian, but culturally and spiritually caught somewhere in the limbo between their natal indigenous civilizations and adoptive Spanish societies. Even after being baptized and symbolically converted to Catholicism, many Genízaros sustained an outwardly identifiable ethnic identity as Indians and, as evidenced by the perseverance of rituals and ceremonies that blended the old and the new, developed a shared sense of group consciousness around their plight as captives and servants (Córdova 1973, 63–67; Lamadrid 2003, 135–39; Gallegos 2010, 205–23).

The multitudinous roles that Genízaros played in New Mexican society reflected their servile group identity as well as their partial Hispanicization, because these detribalized men and women were sometimes treated as both slaves and citizens.[7] In addition to the various types of work that they performed as servants, Genízaros functioned as interpreters for Hispano residents when meeting with Indian leaders, a task that entailed significant diplomatic and political responsibilities (Worcester 1949, 240–41).[8] For many decades, Spanish governors also expected them to defend the New Mexico frontier from the hostile inroads of neighboring tribes, a requirement that effectively militarized a segment of the provincial slave population (Ferguson and Whitehead 1992, 21–23). The segregated positions that Genízaros occupied on the periphery of New Mexico's towns established a sort of buffer zone, allowing Hispano settlers to employ detribalized Indians as a protective shield against the raids of external Native enemies. Although this may seem like a cruel and cunning tactic on the part of Spanish leaders, it actually afforded Genízaros with a modicum of political agency that otherwise would have been unattainable for enslaved people. In 1733, for example, a group of Genízaros used their role of military defenders as leverage when petitioning Governor Gervasio Cruzat y Góngora for a land grant near Sandía Pueblo, pointing out rather bluntly that the Hispanic colonists would benefit from the establishment of a new community to block "the gateway of the Apache enemies" (NMSRCA, SANM I, Roll 4, #1208). Years later, when Governor Pedro Fermín de Mendinueta demanded that Genízaros reoccupy an abandoned frontier settlement at Ojo Caliente, he unwittingly admitted the extent to which settlers depended on slaves for protection. Without the Genízaros as a defensive bulwark, Mendinueta conceded, portions of New Mexico would be "exposed to total ruin" (NMSRCA, SANM I, Roll 2, #656; Simmons 1977, 35). This role actually expanded as time wore on. In the 1820s, as the regional population continued to grow, new settlements arose on the eastern slopes of the Sangre de Cristo Mountains, and exposed frontier villages like San Miguel del Vado, Anton Chico, and El Cerrito attracted Genízaro populations who acted as defensive cordons around their towns (Brooks 2009, 337–44; Nostrand 1992, 77–81; Nostrand 2003, 18–30).

To these ends, some statesmen recommended that full citizenship be granted to the baptized Indian population and that land grants be issued on their behalf to ensure continued cooperation (Simmons 1977, 34–35).[9] In a few rare instances, Genízaros even used the legal system to overcome oppressive conditions—a truly remarkable accomplishment for enslaved persons regardless of the time or place in world history. This served as a further testament to the social status implications of their religious and cultural adaptation, as well as the important place they occupied in New Mexico communities.[10] The same group of seventy-seven Genízaros who asked Governor Cruzat y Góngora for a land grant understood that religious status, cultural assimilation, and kinship association played critical roles in the way that Spanish citizens treated them. Realizing the benefits that might ensue if they embraced Catholicism, the petitioners openly praised "the very high Lord" and declared themselves grateful for "the waters of baptism" (NMSRCA, SANM I, Roll 4, #1208).[11] In many instances, detribalized Indians shed another element of their indigenous identity when accepting a new Christian surname after baptism. Juana Luján, an eighteenth-century resident of the northern New Mexico village of Santa Cruz, acted as a godmother to fourteen boys and girls, among whom several Genízaros could be counted. As part of the baptismal ceremony, each of these children took the Luján name and became an adopted member of the family (Ahlborn 1990, 326). Gilberto Benito Córdova, a scholar of Genízaro history and identity, has described this process of familial incorporation in relation to his own grandmother, an Indian girl who was captured and forced into concubinage with the family of Vicente Córdova at San Miguel de la Puente. At first a mere "domestic servant," the young woman underwent baptismal rights at a local parish, donned the Córdova family name, learned to speak Spanish, and filtered into New Mexican society as a Genízara of indigenous birth and Hispanic upbringing (Córdova 1999, 8).

By the time Mexico achieved independence from Spain in 1821, Genízaros had forged a distinct ethnic and cultural identity for themselves, acquired limited rights to judicial redress, and occupied an important place in local society in spite of their ongoing stigmatization as servile bondpeople. Although the realities of daily life remained much the same after Mexico became a republic, things began to change for Genízaros from the political and legal standpoints. In 1821, as one of the first acts of the new government, the Plan de Iguala eliminated the official basis for the caste system throughout Mexico, propagating an overarching liberalization of society that included the statutory abolition of racial slavery (Gómez 2007, 56–57). As a part of this process, the inegalitarian terminology of racial exclusivity that expressed itself in Spanish reports and censuses began to disappear, meaning that words like "mestizo," "Coyote," and even "Genízaro" fell out of daily use in many places (Swadesh 1974, 41–46; Nostrand 1992, 14–19; Bustamante 1991, 157).[12] These political proceedings had a mostly superficial impact, however, because the people who once bore these distinctions did not go away or in any way modify their religion, language, culture, or ethnicity simply because they suddenly owed allegiance to a different flag. Rather, these events symbolized a shift in political and social ideologies that accompanied a wave of democratic revolutions, which in turn liberated much of the New World from the throes of European dominion.

A landmark moment for Genízaros occurred in 1824, when the first Mexican constitution codified the new nation as a federal republic and reiterated the premises of the Plan de Iguala by granting citizenship to those living inside the country's borders (Gammel 1898, 73). Genízaros in New Mexico thus became citizens within their nation, another remarkable development for a population of veritable slaves. In the neighboring United States, by contrast, many politicians and judges worked assiduously to ensure that black slaves would never attain full citizenship, an objective that Chief Justice Roger Taney affirmed with his majority opinion in the Dred Scott case of 1857. As it turned out, however, citizenship would be about the only benefit that New Mexico's slave population derived from the liberalizing Mexican government, because the antislavery laws and decrees that the country issued in 1824 and 1829 had no discernible impact on the traditional forms of servitude practiced on the country's far northern frontier. As one historian has noted in reference to the toothless nature of these official abolitions, "law and custom did not coincide in New Mexico" (Brooks 2002, 240). Indeed, the twenty-five years during which Mexico held sovereignty over New Mexico actually saw an increase in the prevalence of alternative institutions of slavery like Indian captivity and debt peonage.

This seemingly anomalous development, wherein racial slavery became illegal and began to disappear throughout much of Mexico while cultural systems of slavery remained legal and grew in prominence, had roots in two distinctly New Mexican trends. The first involved the advent of the Santa Fe trade, which opened the province to legal foreign commerce with the United States and significantly impacted the local economy. This increased outside demand for New Mexico's exports, which in turn raised the need for manual labor and resulted in more and more impoverished Hispanos being subjected to servitude through indebtedness, meaning that peonage became more widespread in the years after Mexican independence.[13] The second development pertained to the nature and extent of warfare with neighboring Indian tribes, particularly the Navajos. After 1821, Mexican soldiers as well as independent New Mexican militias took the field against that tribe on numerous occasions, prosecuting a vicious war that claimed many lives and took scores of captives, most of whom became slaves in the Hispano villages.[14] Although the extent to which these Navajo captives underwent the modes of acculturation necessary to become Genízaros is not precisely known, this influx of Indian slaves certainly had a cultural and demographic impact on preexisting Genízaro communities. Thus, New Mexico's distinctive systems of servitude not only outlasted the multiple abolitions of slavery that Mexico enacted, but actually expanded and thrived under the auspices of the Mexican republic.

The prevalence of these cultural forms of bondage began to wane following the American occupation of New Mexico in 1846, although the transformation toward freedom would be slow in materializing. The conquest of the Southwest occurred as part of the Mexican-American War, which in turn invigorated sectional debates in the United States and served as one of many catalysts for the Civil War. The first indication of this arose with Article 11 of the 1848 Treaty of Guadalupe Hidalgo, which delegated to the US military the responsibility of preventing captive slave raiding across the new international boundary with Mexico. Officers and bureaucrats soon found this measure unenforceable for a variety of reasons and abrogated it five years later as a condition of ratifying the Gadsden Purchase (DeLay 2008). In the 1850s, as Northerners and Southerners engaged in verbal sparring contests over the future of slavery on American soil, New Mexico and the United States exerted reciprocal ideological influences over one another in regard to unfree labor. With the Hispanic Southwest added to the national domain, congressional deliberations that had previously revolved around chattel slavery in the South began to include discussions about New Mexico's peculiar institutions of Indian captivity and debt peonage, a conversation that expanded American understandings of involuntary servitude to include multiple variations of the practice (Kiser 2017, 15–56). Thus, as captive Indians living in a state of coercive bondage, Genízaros and other servile men and women in New Mexico began to play into the political debates that accompanied America's painstaking march toward emancipation in the mid-nineteenth century.

Because alternative modes of enslavement were so deeply ingrained in New Mexico culture and society, the region's landholders and political elites worked diligently to prevent manumission in much the same way that Southern slaveholders resisted abolition below the Mason-Dixon Line. Acting under the premise of popular sovereignty, the territorial legislature passed a "master-servant" statute in 1851 that protected the right to hold peons, and then its members approved two separate Slave Codes in 1857 and 1859 that upheld chattel slavery as a legal practice ("Law regulating contracts between masters and servants," NA, RG46, Roll 14; *Laws of the Territory of New Mexico 1857*, 48–50; *Laws of the Territory of New Mexico 1859*, 64–80). Although Indian captivity did not come under the purview of any new laws during this time, the forced servitude of Native peoples continued mostly unabated as armed slave raiders took the field against surrounding tribes and abducted as many women and children as possible during hostile encounters.[15] By the dawn of the Civil War, New Mexico had become a veritable slave territory, with multiple laws supplementing cultural tradition in order to protect the right of masters to detain the thousands of involuntary servants—Genízaros, captives, peons, and even a handful of chattels—living throughout the territory.[16]

Just as New Mexico's slaves came up as a discussion point during the political debates leading up to the Civil War, so too did they have an important role in the sweeping emancipations that Congress enacted at the conclusion of that conflict. Ratified in December 1865, the Thirteenth Amendment banned slavery and involuntary servitude, except by punishment for crime, in all US states and territories. The language of this constitutional addendum, however, left plenty of latitude for New Mexican slaveholders to circumvent the law, because they simply redefined debt peonage as a voluntary institution and similarly claimed that Indian captives willingly remained under the rule of their masters and adoptive families (NMSRCA, TANM, Reel 3, entry for January 26, 1866; Memorial to Congress 1863, NA, RG46, Roll 14). Through these sly means, New Mexico's cultural systems of slavery remained intact even after the South's chattel system crumbled in the wake of the Civil War. The cunning maneuvers to retain regional institutions of servitude quickly caught the attention of radical Republicans and abolitionists and, contrary to the wishes of local masters and *patrones*, had the unforeseen impact of expanding the constitutional abolition of slavery to specifically include debt peons and Indian captives.

In direct response to the refusal of Nuevomexicanos to liberate their Indian slaves, President Andrew Johnson issued an executive order on June 9, 1865, requiring Interior Department and Bureau of Indian Affairs officials to emancipate indigenous captives (Johnson Executive Order 1865, NA, RG75, OIA, T21, Roll 6). Three years later, when General William T. Sherman met with Navajo leaders at the Bosque Redondo Reservation in eastern New Mexico, he reaffirmed this commitment to freedom by assuring the chiefs that the government would assist them in reclaiming abducted family members from the territory's settlements (Correll 1979, 137–38). Congressional abolitionists strode a step further in 1867, targeting debt peonage in a new law that banned that institution along the same lines as chattel slavery (US Statutes 1867, 546). The following year, a federal investigator visited towns throughout New Mexico's northern counties to enforce these laws and search out captives and peons who remained in bondage. Subsequent legal proceedings charged 224 Hispanos with illegally holding slaves and prosecuted 363 separate cases in court, resulting in the liberation of all but 11 of the servants (Brooks 2002, 385–402).

By the 1870s, the majority of New Mexico's slaves had attained freedom through the ideological transformations that swept the nation during the age of emancipation. Also important to this evolution of American democracy, however, was the role that peons, captives, and Genízaros played in promulgating the legal and political revolutions that helped to end most forms of coercive labor in the United States. To be sure, New Mexico's Genízaros occupied an important place in the fabric of their local society and culture, as evidenced by the perseverance of group consciousness, community identity, and collective historical memory demonstrated at recurring festivals and ceremonies (Córdova 1973, 63; Córdova 1999, 2–3; Lamadrid 2015, 229–56).[17] But an equally significant aspect of Genízaro history involves its contribution to the emergence of free labor ideology and the concomitant abolition of slavery and involuntary servitude in nineteenth-century America, a movement that had far-reaching implications for the future of the democratic nation.

Notes

1. The percentage of enslaved depends on the scope of inclusivity. The 33 percent estimation seems high for Genízaros alone, but if all types of servants—debt peons, *partideros*, unbaptized Indian captives, Genízaros, and the offspring and dependents of these groups—are all taken into consideration, then the estimate becomes quite tangible.

2. For scholarship on Genízaros, see Swadesh 1974; Chávez 1979; Córdova 1979; Horvath 1979; Magnaghi 1994; Poling-Kempes 1997; Brooks 2001; Lamadrid 2003; Ebright and Hendricks 2006; Avery 2008; Brooks 2009; Gutiérrez 2010; Ebright 2014; and Gonzales 2014.

3. On Indian captivity and debt peonage, see Kiser 2017. For a comparative analysis, see Martin and Brooks 2015.

4. For the origins and etymology of the term, see Weber 2005, 240; Swadesh 1974, 39–48; Poling-Kempes 1997, 38–42; and Ebright and Hendricks 2006, 30–32.

5. On the role of Abiquiú in the Indian slave trade, see Blackhawk 2005, 70–81.

6. For Indian slavery in colonial North America, see Usner 1992; Gallay 2002; Snyder 2010; Rushforth 2012; and Reséndez 2016.

7. Evidence of Genízaros being granted citizenship dates at least as far back as 1765, when a census report on New Mexico enumerated 36 "Genízaros with the status of citizens" out of a total Genízaro population of 677 people (Cutter 1975, 351–52).

8. See also Horvath 1979, 157–59; Archibald 1978, 213; and Blackhawk 2005, 81, 100.

9. On Genízaro land grants, see Ebright 1996, 315–17.

10. For cases involving Genízaros, see NMSRCA, SANM II, Reel 9, Frames 524, 949; and NMSRCA, MANM, Roll 13, Frames 738–83. On the legal empowerment of Genízaros, see Brooks 2001, 150–80.

11. The same source identified these Genízaros as follows: Jumano, 14; Apache, 13; Kiowa, 12; Aa, 10; Panana, 7; Pawnee, 6; Tano, 6; Ute, 1; Unidentified, 8.

12. See also Nieto-Phillips 2004, 34–38; and Mora 2011, 19, 33–46.

13. On the impact of the Santa Fe trade in New Mexico, see Moorhead 1958, 55–75; Weber 1982, 122–46, 207–41; Boyle 1997; and Hyslop 2002.

14. For Mexican warfare with the Navajos after 1821, see Brugge 1964, 223–44; and McNitt 1972, 52–91.

15. The Navajos became the primary targets of these raids. See McNitt 1972, 363–429; and Trafzer 1982, 81–83.

16. Estimates of the total number of slaves in New Mexico vary. The seventh US census lists just twenty-four black slaves in the territory in 1850, and the eighth census sixty-four of them in 1860. Historian Andrés Reséndez has found that between 2.5 and 5 million Indians were enslaved during the long period from 1492 to 1900, of whom at least 147,000 were in North America (2016, 4–6, 324). The figures for New Mexico are spotty at best. When interrogated on the matter in 1865, Governor Henry Connelly estimated that between 1,500 and 3,000 Navajos were held as slaves, and Judge Kirby Benedict placed that number closer to 3,000 and perhaps more ("Condition of the Indian Tribes" 1867, 326, 332). A visitor to Santa Fe in 1866 guessed that about 2,000 to 4,000 Indians lived as slaves in the territory (Meline 1966, 120). All of these figures neglected to include Genízaros, for whom no clear estimates exist from that time period. Nor is there any concrete evidence on the number of debt peons

living in New Mexico, who would have added at least several thousand to the total number of bound people in the territory.

17. In 2007, the New Mexico legislature passed resolutions recognizing Genízaros as a distinct tribe (House Memorial 40, State of New Mexico, 48th Legislature, First Session, 2007; Senate Memorial 59, State of New Mexico, 48th Legislature, First Session, 2007).

References

Adams, Eleanor B., ed. 1953. "Bishop Tamarón's Visitation of New Mexico, 1760." *New Mexico Historical Review* 28: 192–221.

Ahlborn, Richard Eighme. 1990. "The Will of a New Mexico Woman in 1762." *New Mexico Historical Review* 65: 319–55.

Anderson, Gary Clayton. 1999. *The Indian Southwest, 1580–1830*. Norman: University of Oklahoma Press.

Anderson, H. Allen. 1985. "The Encomienda in New Mexico, 1598–1680." *New Mexico Historical Review* 60: 353–73.

Archibald, Robert. 1978. "Acculturation and Assimilation in Colonial New Mexico." *New Mexico Historical Review* 53: 205–17.

Avery, Doris S. 2008. "Into the Den of Evils: The Genízaros of Colonial New Mexico." Master's thesis, University of Montana.

Babcock, Matthew. 2016. *Apache Adaptation to Hispanic Rule*. Cambridge: Cambridge University Press.

Blackhawk, Ned. 2005. *Violence over the Land: Indians and Empires in the Early American West*. Cambridge, MA: Harvard University Press.

Boyle, Susan Calafate. 1997. *Los Capitalistas: Hispano Merchants and the Santa Fe Trade*. Albuquerque: University of New Mexico Press.

Brooks, James F. 2001. "'Lest We Go in Search of Relief to Our Lands and Our Nation': Customary Justice and Colonial Law in the New Mexico Borderlands, 1680–1821." In *The Many Legalities of Early America*, edited by Christopher L. Tomlins and Bruce H. Mann, 150–80. Chapel Hill: University of North Carolina Press.

———. 2002. *Captives and Cousins: Slavery, Kinship, and Community in the Southwest Borderlands*. Chapel Hill: University of North Carolina Press.

———. 2009. "We Betray Our Nation: Indian Slavery and Multi-Ethnic Communities in the Southwest Borderlands." In *Indian Slavery in Colonial America*, edited by Alan Gallay, 319–51. Lincoln: University of Nebraska Press.

Brugge, David M., ed. 1964. "Vizcarra's Navajo Campaign of 1823." *Journal of the Southwest* 6: 223–44.

———. 1985. *Navajos in the Catholic Church Records of New Mexico, 1694–1875*. Tsaile, AZ: Navajo Community College Press.

Bustamante, Adrián. 1991. "'The Matter Was Never Resolved': The 'Casta' System in Colonial New Mexico, 1693–1823." *New Mexico Historical Review* 66: 143–63.

Calloway, Colin G. 2003. *One Vast Winter Count: The Native American West before Lewis and Clark.* Lincoln: University of Nebraska Press.

Chávez, Fray Angélico. 1957. *Archives of the Archdiocese of Santa Fe, 1678–1900.* Washington, DC: Academy of American Franciscan History.

———. 1979. "Genízaros." In *Handbook of North American Indians*, vol. 9, *Southwest*, edited by Alfonso Ortiz and William C. Sturtevant, 198–200. Washington, DC: Smithsonian Institution.

"Condition of the Indian Tribes." 1867. 39th Cong., 2nd Sess. Senate Report No. 156.

Conrad, Paul Timothy. 2011. "Captive Fates: Displaced American Indians in the Southwest Borderlands, Mexico, and Cuba, 1500–1800." PhD diss., University of Texas.

Córdova, Gilberto Benito. 1973. *Abiquiú and Don Cacahuate: A Folk History of a New Mexican Village.* Los Cerrillos, NM: San Marcos Press.

———. 1979. "Missionization and Hispanicization of Santo Tomás Apóstol de Abiquiú, 1750–1770." PhD diss., University of New Mexico.

———. 1999. "The Genízaro." Paper presented at a conference in Taos, New Mexico.

Correll, J. Lee. 1979. *Through White Men's Eyes: A Contribution to Navajo History.* Vol. 6. Window Rock, AZ: Navajo Heritage Center.

Cutter, Donald C., trans. 1975. "An Anonymous Statistical Report on New Mexico in 1765." *New Mexico Historical Review* 50: 347–52.

DeLay, Brian. 2008. *War of a Thousand Deserts: Indian Raids and the U.S.-Mexican War.* New Haven, CT: Yale University Press.

Domínguez, Fray Francisco Atanasio. 1956. *The Missions of New Mexico, 1776: A Description by Fray Francisco Atanasio Domínguez, with Other Contemporary Documents.* Edited and translated by Fray Angélico Chávez and Eleanor B. Adams. Albuquerque: University of New Mexico Press.

Ebright, Malcolm. 1996. "Advocates for the Oppressed: Indians, Genízaros, and Their Spanish Advocates in New Mexico, 1700–1786." *New Mexico Historical Review* 71: 305–39.

———. 2014. *Advocates for the Oppressed: Hispanos, Indians, Genízaros, and Their Land in New Mexico.* Albuquerque: University of New Mexico Press.

Ebright, Malcolm, and Rick Hendricks. 2006. *The Witches of Abiquiu: The Governor, the Priest, the Genízaro Indians, and the Devil.* Albuquerque: University of New Mexico Press.

Elliott, J. H. 2006. *Empires of the Atlantic World: Britain and Spain in America, 1492–1830.* New Haven, CT: Yale University Press.

Ferguson, R. Brian, and Neil L. Whitehead. 1992. "The Violent Edge of Empire." In *War in the Tribal Zone: Expanding States and Indigenous Warfare*, edited by R. Brian

Ferguson and Neil L. Whitehead, 1–30. Santa Fe: School of American Research Press.

Gallay, Alan. 2002. *The Indian Slave Trade: The Rise of the English Empire in the American South, 1670–1717*. New Haven, CT: Yale University Press.

Gallegos, Bernardo P. 2010. "'Dancing the Comanches': The Santo Niño, La Virgen (of Guadalupe), and the Genizaro Indians of New Mexico." In *Indigenous Symbols and Practices in the Catholic Church: Visual Culture, Missionization and Appropriation*, edited by Kathleen J. Martin, 205–23. Farnham, Surrey, England: Ashgate.

Gammel, H. P. N., comp. 1898. *The Laws of Texas, 1822–1897*. Vol. 1. Austin: Gammel Book Company.

Gómez, Laura E. 2007. *Manifest Destinies: The Making of the Mexican American Race*. New York: New York University Press.

Gonzales, Moises. 2014. "The Genízaro Land Grant Settlements of New Mexico." *Journal of the Southwest* 56: 583–602.

Gutiérrez, Ramón A. 1991. *When Jesus Came, the Corn Mothers Went Away: Marriage, Sexuality, and Power in New Mexico, 1500–1846*. Stanford, CA: Stanford University Press.

———. 2010. "Indian Slavery and the Birth of Genízaros." In *White Water Shell Place: An Anthology of Native Reflections on the Founding of Santa Fe, New Mexico*, edited by F. Richard Sánchez, 39–56. Santa Fe: Sunstone Press.

Hackett, Charles W., ed. 1937. *Historical Documents Relating to New Mexico, Nueva Vizcaya, and Approaches Thereto*. Vol. 3. Washington, DC: Government Printing Office.

Horvath, Steven M., Jr. 1979. "The Social and Political Organization of the Genízaro of Plaza de Nuestra Señora de los Dolores de Belén, New Mexico, 1740–1812." PhD diss., Brown University.

Hyslop, Stephen G. 2002. *Bound for Santa Fe: The Road to New Mexico and the American Conquest, 1806–1848*. Norman: University of Oklahoma Press.

John, Elizabeth A. H. 1975. *Storms Brewed in Other Men's Worlds: The Confrontation of Indians, Spanish, and French in the Southwest, 1540–1795*. College Station: Texas A&M University Press.

Kinniard, Lawrence, ed. 1958. *The Frontiers of New Spain: Nicolás de Lafora's Description, 1766–1768*. Berkeley, CA: Quivira Society.

Kiser, William S. 2014. "'A Charming Name for a Species of Slavery': Political Debates on Debt Peonage in the Southwest, 1840s–1860s." *Western Historical Quarterly* 45: 169–89.

———. 2017. *Borderlands of Slavery: The Struggle over Captivity and Peonage in the American Southwest*. Philadelphia: University of Pennsylvania Press.

Lamadrid, Enrique R. 2003. *Hermanitos Comanchitos: Indo-Hispano Rituals of Captivity and Redemption*. Albuquerque: University of New Mexico Press.

———. 2015. "Cautivos y Criados: Cultural Memories of Slavery in New Mexico." In *Linking the Histories of Slavery: North America and Its Borderlands*, edited by Bonnie Martin and James F. Brooks, 229–56. Santa Fe: School for Advanced Research Press.

Lawrence, Deborah, and Jon Lawrence. 2016. *Contesting the Borderlands: Interviews on the Early Southwest*. Norman: University of Oklahoma Press.

Laws of the Territory of New Mexico, Sixth Legislative Assembly, 1856–1857. 1857. Santa Fe: Office of the Democrat.

Laws of the Territory of New Mexico, Eighth Legislative Assembly, 1858–1859. 1859. Santa Fe: A. DeMarle.

Magnaghi, Russell M. 1994. "The Genízaro Experiment in Spanish New Mexico." In *Spain and the Plains: Myths and Realities of Spanish Exploration and Settlement on the Great Plains*, edited by Ralph H. Vigil, Frances W. Kaye, and John R. Wunder, 114–30. Niwot: University Press of Colorado.

Martin, Bonnie, and James F. Brooks, eds. 2015. *Linking the Histories of Slavery: North America and Its Borderlands*. Santa Fe: School for Advanced Research Press.

McNitt, Frank. 1972. *Navajo Wars: Military Campaigns, Slave Raids, and Reprisals*. Albuquerque: University of New Mexico Press.

Meline, James F. 1966. *Two Thousand Miles on Horseback: Santa Fe and Back*. Albuquerque: Horn and Wallace.

Moorhead, Max L. 1958. *New Mexico's Royal Road: Trade and Travel on the Chihuahua Trail*. Norman: University of Oklahoma Press.

Mora, Anthony. 2011. *Border Dilemmas: Racial and National Uncertainties in New Mexico, 1848–1912*. Durham, NC: Duke University Press.

National Archives (NA). Record Group 46 (RG46). Territorial Papers of the US Senate. Roll 14 (New Mexico, 1840–1854).

———. Record Group 75 (RG75). Office of Indian Affairs (OIA). Microfilm T21. Letters Received (LR). New Mexico Superintendency (NMS).

New Mexico State Records Center and Archives (NMSRCA). Mexican Archives of New Mexico (MANM).

———. Spanish Archives of New Mexico I (SANM I) and Spanish Archives of New Mexico II (SANM II). Microfilm Translations.

———. Territorial Archives of New Mexico (TANM).

Nieto-Phillips, John M. 2004. *The Language of Blood: The Making of Spanish-American Identity in New Mexico, 1880s–1930s*. Albuquerque: University of New Mexico Press.

Nostrand, Richard L. 1992. *The Hispano Homeland*. Norman: University of Oklahoma Press.

———. 2003. *El Cerrito, New Mexico: Eight Generations in a Spanish Village*. Norman: University of Oklahoma Press.

Poling-Kempes, Lesley. 1997. *Valley of Shining Stone: The Story of Abiquiu*. Tucson: University of Arizona Press.

Reséndez, Andrés. 2016. *The Other Slavery: The Uncovered Story of Indian Enslavement in America*. New York: Houghton Mifflin Harcourt.

Rushforth, Brett. 2012. *Bonds of Alliance: Indigenous and Atlantic Slaveries in New France*. Chapel Hill: University of North Carolina Press.

Simmons, Marc, ed. and trans. 1977. *Father Juan Agustín de Morfi's Account of Disorders in New Mexico, 1778*. Isleta Pueblo: Historical Society of New Mexico.

Snow, David H. 1983. "A Note on Encomienda Economics in Seventeenth-Century New Mexico." In *Hispanic Arts and Ethnohistory in the Southwest*, edited by Marta Weigle, 347–57. Santa Fe: Ancient City Press.

Snyder, Christina. 2010. *Slavery in Indian Country: The Changing Face of Captivity in Early America*. Cambridge, MA: Harvard University Press.

Swadesh, Frances Leon. 1974. *Los Primeros Pobladores: Hispanic Americans of the Ute Frontier*. Notre Dame, IN: University of Notre Dame Press.

Torget, Andrew J. 2015. *Seeds of Empire: Cotton, Slavery, and the Transformation of the Texas Borderlands, 1800–1850*. Chapel Hill: University of North Carolina Press.

Trafzer, Clifford E. 1982. *The Kit Carson Campaign: The Last Great Navajo War*. Norman: University of Oklahoma Press.

Usner, Daniel H., Jr. 1992. *Indians, Settlers, and Slaves in a Frontier Exchange Economy: The Lower Mississippi Valley Before 1783*. Chapel Hill: University of North Carolina Press.

US Statutes at Large. 1867. 39th Cong., 2nd Sess. Ch. 187.

Weber, David J. 1982. *The Mexican Frontier, 1821–1846: The American Southwest under Mexico*. Albuquerque: University of New Mexico Press.

———. 2005. *Bárbaros: Spaniards and Their Savages in the Age of Enlightenment*. New Haven, CT: Yale University Press.

Worcester, Donald E., ed. and trans. 1949. "Notes and Documents: Advice on Governing New Mexico, 1794." *New Mexico Historical Review* 24: 236–54.

CHAPTER FOUR

Genízara Self-Advocacy in Eighteenth-Century New Mexico

CRISTINA DURÁN

The title of a newspaper article from the January 31, 1992, edition of the *Albuquerque Journal* reads, "Historians Debate Genízaro Question"—the Genízaro, the "Hispanicized, detribalized" Indian. I begin with a pivotal point in the emerging interest in *mestizaje* in New Mexico, the year of the Columbus Quincentennial. The Smithsonian National Museum of American History inaugurated an exhibit titled *American Encounters* (1992–2004) that featured New Mexico, as did the Smithsonian Folklife Festival that same summer. A central consultant for the exhibit was anthropologist Gilberto Benito Córdova, whose 1979 dissertation argued for the persistence of Genízaro identity. A year prior, Fray Angélico Chávez summarized the assumption of New Mexico historians that Genízaros culturally disappeared after the 1821 independence from Spain, when the term was abolished in census reports. The implications of mixing the Indian and the European, for contemporary notions of identity and for Indo-Hispano relations, had scarcely been discussed in the case of New Mexico.

This interest leads us to look at colonial New Mexico and the interrelationships between Indians and Spanish, since our "relationship" was in its early formative stages and was relatively uncomplicated. It is also during this time when something unique in New Mexico developed as a result of the coexistence of Indian and European peoples—Indians who, by force rather than by choice, became "detribalized" and to a large extent adopted the ways of life of the Español/mestizo. As the scholarship in the present volume attests, it is impossible to erase the cultural legacy of Genízaros, a group of people who constituted up to one-third of the population of New Mexico by the latter part of the eighteenth century, but who had been absorbed into the larger mestizo population by the nineteenth century (Archibald 1978; Magnaghi 1990).

Until Benito Córdova, relatively few studies had been written on the Genízaro, and the Genízaro voice had not been part of the conversation. For the most part, we are left to read the accounts of the interpretations of others regarding not only how Genízaros are defined but also who they were as people, as men and women whose lives seemed to be dictated by others; who, based on most characterizations of them, apparently had little if any control over the shape and direction of their lives. Many of these characterizations are included in reports and descriptions written by the Franciscans, who had substantial contact with Genízaros and Indians in the region. But as I continued to peruse archival literature, I began to see accounts here and there where the Genízaro voice clearly emerges. Among these stories, I was struck by a different set of possibilities for the Genízaro, reflecting a sense of agency and a broadening of the lens through which they have traditionally been viewed.

One of the ways the Genízaro voice can be heard is through instances, and there were many, when Genízaros accessed the Spanish-controlled courts to protect their rights. Steven Horvath, in his study of the Genízaros of Belén (1979), states: "The most valuable documents proved to be records of confrontations between Genízaros and Español hosts. Criminal trials, hearings, and land grant disputes produced some very important insights into the life of the Genízaros of Belén" (185). Based on portrayals of Genízaros found in Spanish colonial documents, which characterize them as unwanted, dependent, lost, and criminal, but good fighters, the fact that Genízaros took action to assert their rights is significant. During the conflicts in the Belén area, Genízaro leaders traveled as far as Mexico City to argue their case in the court of the viceroy (Sisneros 2017). It is even more significant that women, Genízaras on their own, took such action. The system of protection of the rights of Indians and Genízaros established in colonial New Mexico, and the survival of written legal documents and court records that chronicle these cases, provide us with an opportunity to foreground the lives of Genízaros in a way that allows us to begin to view them as complex figures in the shaping of Indian-Hispanic relations in colonial New Mexico. Before bringing some of these cases to light, it is necessary to provide some background on how we are defining that group of people known as Genízaros, and also to outline the system of protection of the rights of Indians and Genízaros in colonial New Mexico.

Emergence of the Genízaro

Most sources agree that Genízaros were Indians from various tribes, primarily Plains, who were ransomed from Indian captors by Spanish/mestizo settlers in the eighteenth century and who then became Hispanicized (and therefore detribalized) through years of servitude in Spanish households. According to Eleanor Adams and Fray Angélico Chávez,

> Church and civil records reveal such varied derivations as Apache, Comanche, Navajo, Ute, Kiowa, Wichita, and Pawnee. Many had Spanish blood, clandestinely and otherwise. They all bore Christian names from baptism and Spanish surnames from their former masters; belonging no longer to any particular Indian tribe they spoke . . . Spanish. (1956, 42n71)

Once in servitude, the law required that Spanish masters provide Indian servants with instruction in religion and language/culture as part of the assimilation process (Horvath 1979, 2). After serving a certain number of years in the home of a Spanish master, the Indian servant would gain his or her freedom, "when debts were paid, when manumitted by their masters, or when removed by officials for mistreatment or failure to be instructed in the tenets of faith and Spanish civilization" (Archibald 1978, 210–11). Then, either through advocacy of Spanish officials or on their own through petitioning the courts, Genízaros were awarded land grants and formed settlements. They were often assigned to frontier posts, where their talents as warriors were exploited to help protect the frontier from Indian raids (Archibald 1978). Towns mentioned as those that began as Genízaro settlements are: Belén, Valencia, Cerro de Tomé, San Miguel del Vado, Ojo Caliente, Abiquiú, San Miguel de Carnué, Socorro (near El Paso), and Analco (in Santa Fe) (Magnaghi 1990, 89).

Points of divergence regarding how narrowly or broadly the term "Genízaro" is defined and described is of interest. Horvath, in an article discussing Genízaros as both an ethnic category and an ethnic identity (1977), critiques some of the major definers of Genízaros from the eighteenth century, noting in particular how one might emphasize the deficits of Genízaros (Fray Francisco Atanasio Domínguez) while another might emphasize their virtues (Fray Miguel de Menchero). Horvath is unique among writers on Genízaros in that he attends carefully to pointing out exactly how the biases (such as class and duty) of these chroniclers might affect their interpretations.

Another area of some disagreement among scholars regards the actual process by which people became Genízaros and the extent of Pueblo representation. While many sources suggest that the ransoming of Plains Indians was the primary way that Genízaros were brought into Spanish households, initially as servants (Magnaghi 1990; Archibald 1978; Dozier 1970), others suggest that there were, in fact, other methods for how Indians, whether Plains or Pueblo, and even an occasional Español, could become a Genízaro. Pueblo Indians did become Genízaros, though for different reasons. Both Frances Swadesh (1974) and Ramón Gutiérrez (1991) agree that Pueblo Indians joined the ranks of Genízaros because they had been expelled from their pueblos, or had become overly assimilated with the Spanish settlers. Gutiérrez, whose work on colonial New Mexico centers in part on Pueblo life, states that Pueblo women who worked in Spanish households during the *repartimiento* (labor distribution) system would often return to their pueblo impregnated by a Spanish master. In such cases, the woman's pueblo would reject not only her but later her mixed-blood offspring. These outcasts would often have no other option but to return to Spanish households and become part of the Indian servant (and later presumably Genízaro) population (Gutiérrez 1991, 156).

Edward Dozier, on the other hand, states that "disaffected" Pueblos entered Spanish villages, but he does not indicate that Pueblos became Genízaros. He instead focuses on how Pueblos and Genízaros (after servitude) were partners, working side by side particularly in their assignments as auxiliary soldiers to protect the frontier (1970, 85). Horvath makes a similar statement, pointing to how Pueblos and Genízaros were allied through a shared sense of being stigmatized: "Pueblo Indians exiled from their pueblos were never indebted servants in Spanish houses, yet they shared the stigma with those Indians who were or had been indebted servants" (1979, 15). Horvath believes, however, that Pueblos became Genízaros as a necessary step to entering Spanish society, stating: "In order to begin assimilation into the Español population, a Christianized Pueblo Indian would have to move to a Spanish town and accept the stigma of Genízaro" (1979, 19). Horvath views the category of Genízaro as having permeable boundaries, and could include anyone who might share characteristics of Genízaros. He states:

People with visible Indian traits (complexion, accent) and people with a known history as Indian servants or descendants of Indian servants were all stigmatized with the label Genízaro (indebted Indian servant) and assigned to the lowest status in the society. Even Españoles could be temporarily labeled as Genízaros if they lived in a barrio or locality that was a known center of Genízaro residence. Españoles could also be stigmatized as Genízaros as a form of negative sanction or chastisement. (1979, 16)

Finally, one cannot provide an overview of Genízaros without also taking into account their subjugated status within Spanish society. Gutiérrez attends to this subject in some depth, comparing the status of Pueblos with that of the Genízaros, stating:

> As a vanquished class they paid tribute and labor to the nobility, but because the crown protected their legal rights and the integrity of their villages and of their lands, they fared far better under colonial rule than did the Genízaros, who were deemed sociocultural outsiders forced to live in Spanish towns. (1991, 149)

Although, as we will soon learn, Gutiérrez may have been mistaken to infer that Genízaros' legal rights were not also protected along with the Pueblos', his point regarding the liminal status of Genízaros is well taken. But Horvath articulates most clearly the stigma facing Genízaros, speaking directly to how power relationships based on race and class were involved:

> When the original reason for the existence of the Genízaro groups was examined it became clear that there was one general theme that shaped the observable behavior pattern of the Genízaros. The Spanish created the Genízaros as a category, and this category carried with it the stigma of Indianness. This stigma and its positive aspect, prowess as warriors, shaped or influenced all the behavior patterns observed for the Genízaros. In New Mexico, land and trade were in the hands of the Spanish-Mestizo settlers. Indianness had many negative connotations for these people, so consequently the Genízaros (who were stigmatized by their Indianness) had little access to power or mobility. (1979, 7)

This statement is also supported by Gutiérrez, who claims that the system of honor-status among those who had something to protect could be defined more clearly with the existence of Indian slaves, stating: "Much of what was considered Spanish culture on this northern frontier of new Spain gained its meaning in opposition to and as an exaggeration of what it meant to be an Indian or a Genízaro" (1991, 180).

When talking about Genízaros, most writers seem to use the term "Indian servant" or "slave" when referring to the period of servitude in a Spanish household, and the term "Genízaro" itself when referring to the period once the servant had been freed. It is not clear when one stops being a servant and becomes a Genízaro. For purposes of this chapter, I will use the term "Genízaro" to include the periods during and after servitude, unless otherwise indicated.

With a clearer picture of what has been said about Genízaros, let us now move on to describe the legal system of protection that in part allows the Genízaro voice to emerge and provides us with an opportunity to learn a little about what life was like for Genízaros before and after servitude.

Protecting the Rights of Genízaros

In *When Jesus Came, the Corn Mothers Went Away* (1991), Ramón Gutiérrez infers that Indian slaves, in their quest to seek redress against their Spanish masters, would not meet with success, stating, "Contemporaries seemed to regard slave and servant deaths as matters of minor importance, which deserved little comment" (185), and later, "New Mexico's authorities listened to slave complaints, albeit with feigned concern, because they feared apostasy" (186). However, instances did occur when the Spanish legal system of protection often worked to the advantage of Indians and Genízaros alike, softening the image of the cruel and barbarous Spanish leaders.

It makes sense that a lawyer-historian might help shed some light on this debate. Malcolm Ebright, in his article titled "Advocates for the Oppressed: Indians, Genízaros, and Their Spanish Advocates in New Mexico, 1700–1786" (1996), foregrounds the many legal cases initiated by Indians and Genízaros, with special attention to the role of the Spanish advocate, the Protector de Indios. It is in the legal arena where Genízaros were able to express their resistance to the history of their enforced subjugation, most often as individuals rather than organized as a group, as Horvath indicates:

> Group or category-wide responses to stigmatization are more likely to be recorded in the documentary record as "incidents" or confrontations. It is per-

haps rare for all the members of a stigmatized category to respond as a unit on an issue. (1979, 27)

Ebright provides us with a brief history of efforts to preserve Indian (and Genízaro) rights in the New World during the eighteenth century, well worth summarizing here.

A philosophical debate regarding the moral inferiority/superiority of the Indians and Spanish was necessarily part of the discussion regarding the ethics of conquest. While, as we know, the notions of Indians as inferior prevailed, Ebright states that "the moral force of Las Casas' argument found its way into the numerous laws and practices adopted by Spain to protect and preserve Indian rights" (306). He, of course, is referring to Fray Bartolomé de las Casas, "the most famous advocate for the oppressed" (305), who argued that Indians were "rational beings equal to and in some respects superior to Spaniards" (305). Ebright proceeds to show how Las Casas's assumptions about Indians were reflected in court cases whose outcomes favored the Indians.

The Recopilación, instituted by the Spanish after the Pueblo Revolt, is what we sometimes first think of as what some consider an act of "benevolence" on the part of the Spaniards, which included the "Christian obligation to ransom captive Indians enslaved by other Indian tribes" (Magnaghi 1990, 87). But Ebright notes that in the valley of Mexico, the office of Protector de Indios, the "sole attorney for indigenous claimants" (306), predated the Recopilación and was established by the Spanish government in 1591 as part of the establishment of the Juzgado General de Indios, a special court designed to hear only Indian claims. This had come about, according to Ebright, to help stop the abuses of interpreters and intermediaries who, among others, were assigned to defend the claims of Aztecs against the Spanish Crown. Ebright then goes on to highlight successful instances in Latin America when this legal system was used (primarily related to land rights) to the advantage of Indians, such as the Incas, Aztecs, and Maya. Ebright is careful to point out that one cannot conclude that challenges to Spanish authorities by indigenous groups, through accessing the courts, might be or become a form of resistance on a large scale, stating:

> By setting up a bureaucracy dedicated to the protection of Indian rights, the Spanish government allowed the Indians to limit Spanish dominance to some extent, but the capacity of the Indians to challenge colonial rule at its root was weakened when they became part of the system. (306)

Nevertheless, as much as it might have been part of the larger system that dominated and subjugated powerless members of society, it was the only formal means by which the Indians could seek redress, and they learned to access it and make it work for them.

Beginning his discussion with the Pueblos, Ebright states that finding a "case in which a Pueblo Indian is treated fairly in litigation against the Spanish" (307) before the Pueblo Revolt is difficult. After the revolt, the Spaniards were more reluctant to exploit the Indians, and complaints and cases were filed against the Spanish in New Mexico as they had been in other parts of Latin America. Ebright summarizes:

> If they were not always equals in this process, Indians and other oppressed groups like Genízaros and poor Spanish settlers on community grants achieved major victories in court, often as a result of the assistance of advocates for their cause and sympathetic government officials. (307)

James F. Brooks likewise corroborates the measure of protection available to Genízaros and others who carried a similar status:

> These and other servile peoples fell under the Spanish laws governing the slavery that had originated in las Siete Partidas in A.D. 1265, doctrines noteworthy for their "liberal" position, "that all laws of the world should lead towards freedom." Under these regulations, slaves were conferred rights in marriage and against cruel treatment. They were allowed to hold property and testify as plaintiffs or defendants and to pursue manumission. (2002, 124)

Frances Leon Quintana contributes to the discussion by adding that the Spanish had a "milder side" than other conquering powers:

> What is less apparent is the fact that Spanish colonial law from early times was more observant of common humanity than some other colonial codes and that, to the extent that this body of law was observed, Spanish colonies had more capacity for intercultural give and take than, for instance, nations under British or United States sway. (1991, 7)

Finally, regarding the Protector de Indios in New Mexico, Ebright states that the official operated from the mid-1600s until 1717 and "reappears as a Spanish official in 1810" (307). In the interim, according to Ebright, "self-appointed protectors like Felipe Tafoya and Carlos Fernández appeared in litigation as representatives of various pueblos" (307). A very well-known

Protector de Indios was Alfonso Rael de Aguilar, who helped to successfully represent cases involving primarily Pueblos.

To demonstrate the confidence Genízaros must have had in how the legal system might respond to their petitions, complaints, or requests, and/or how the system might work to their benefit, consider the following:

- In 1733, one hundred Genízaros filed a petition for their own land grant at Belén (Ebright 1996).
- Antonio Casados, a Genízaro from Belén, filed a lawsuit in 1746 against Governor Joaquín Codallos y Rabal himself, claiming that the rights of the Genízaro pueblo had been violated (Ebright 1996).
- Ventura Bustamante, a Genízaro lieutenant of a Genízaro auxiliary troop, traveled to Arizpe in 1780 to protest the threatened destruction of Analco, a Genízaro barrio in Santa Fe (Magnaghi 1990).
- In 1812, José Cristobal Guerro, a Genízaro from San Miguel del Vado, led a drive for a resident priest, submitting a very "persuasive" petition to the bishop of Durango (Magnaghi 1990).
- In 1745, Lieutenant Alcalde Francisco Gutiérrez was "deprived of his office and fined" after having been found guilty of killing Pedro García's Indian servant (Archibald 1978).
- Manuel Martín and Salvador Torres were found guilty, imprisoned, and ordered to pay a fine for attempting to kill an Indian servant in 1741 (Archibald 1978).

What is perhaps even more significant is that Genízaras, women, also somehow knew about and initiated moves to protect their rights as well, sometimes on their own, sometimes with the help of others. Let us turn now to a discussion of Genízaras to appreciate how the injustices committed against them stood out from some of the abovementioned cases, due to their gender.

Genízaras: A Sense of Agency

Because one rarely even sees the word "Genízara" appear in the literature that exists on Genízaros, one might conclude that perhaps the majority of Indian slaves (who would later become Genízaros) ransomed by the Spanish were males. The question "were there Genízaras?" becomes an appropriate one. The answer, of course, is yes. In fact, there may have been more Genízaras than Genízaros (Archibald 1978; Chávez 1978). When one considers this possibility, then the lives of Genízaras suddenly take on more importance. Before considering what we do know about the Indian women who were first taken as servants/slaves by Spanish/mestizo households and who would later become Genízaras, the story of Sarita from the Mora Valley puts flesh and emotive experience into the drama of uprooted and replanted lives that result from ransom redeemed even under the most difficult of human experiences.

SARITA, LA GENÍZARA

In *The Book of Archives and Other Stories from the Mora Valley* (2017), A. Gabriel Meléndez retells the story of Sarita, la Genízara, from his collection of narratives of the cultural history and memory of the Mora Valley, one of many corridors through which Genízaros entered New Mexican villages in the eighteenth and nineteenth centuries. All of the Genízara narratives in this chapter are drawn directly from archival sources, except Sarita's story. It imaginatively evokes oral tradition but is not intended by the author to be read as history, but rather as a way to register the emotional impact of the Genízara experience. The story illustrates Brooks's concern to understand "the quality of the day-to-day relationships between Genízaros and lower order New Mexico vecinos, and historical transformations in the nature of their servile status as the borderlands economies and societies transformed" (2002, 127). Meléndez puts flesh and emotive experience into the drama of uprooted and replanted lives that result from ransom, redeemed even under the most difficult of human experiences.

In Meléndez's story "Comanchero," slavers drive Sarita and her three-year-old daughter like human livestock across the open plains until they arrive in the first Spanish/Mexican settlements on the eastern edge of New Mexico. There, they barter over Sarita and their other captives with the local residents. Sarita's story is told from the point of view of a woman named doña Romancita Maés, who in turn tells the story as she came to learn it from her great-grandmother:

> Nanita told me that it so happened that one day at the plaza in Mora, some Comancheros had just returned from the llanos and had some captives with them, most of them women and children. Among them was the mother of the Sánchez boys, a woman who would later be called Sarita. Sarita already had a

three-year-old daughter, and both were full of sores and cuts from traveling for days over open country. (2017, 36)

Doña Romancita's retelling of Sarita's plight focuses on how she was inhumanly victimized by her captors, who not only sell her to the highest bidder but separate her from her child:

> Don José Antonio is said to have asked for both mother and daughter, but the Comancheros refused and would not sell him the little girl, claiming she had been bought and paid for in Taos. My nana Romancita was there when this happened, and she remembered how distraught Sarita became, pulling out her hair for want of her daughter. But this was to no avail, since these were very cruel men who took the child with them to Taos. (37)

Distraught and disoriented, Sarita is taken into the Sánchez family household. Romancita's story, a compressed and compact version of many ensuing years of forced assimilation, tells of Sarita having two sons, Benito and Hilario, while living in the Sánchez household. One of her sons, Benito, will favor his mother in appearance; the other, Hilario, grows up with disdain for his mother and her background and seeks to assert a more Spanish identity. Romancita's great-grandmother comes to befriend Sarita, becoming her *comadre* and passing on the story of their friendship in stories she passes on to the community. Years later, when Sarita is an old woman, she continues to ask her husband to take her to Taos to find her daughter, but he turns a deaf ear to her suffering (Meléndez 2017).

Regarding female Indian servants, such as someone like Sarita, some writers mention, almost parenthetically, that the price paid for these women on the Indian slave trade market was twice that of men (Adams and Chávez 1956). Robert Archibald goes a little further, stating, "Prices for female servants, as opposed to male servants, and the preponderance of females in available census records suggests many purchasers were in the market for concubines" (1978, 210). But Ramón Gutiérrez articulates most clearly the plight of Indian slave women in colonial New Mexico:

> The preference for female slaves is easy to understand. In a province where only one out of every three children born was likely to reach the age of twenty, female slaves were essential for social and biological reproduction. The pretensions of aristocratic households were hollow without slaves. Who would perform the menial household chores? Corn had to be shucked and wheat

threshed, ground into flour, and baked into bread. Chili peppers had to be tied into *ristras* and hung out to dry. Any meat that was not immediately consumed after a slaughter had to be salted and dried into jerky. There were buildings to construct and to plaster—all women's work. When not otherwise caring for household needs female slaves undertook production for the market. Animal pelts had to be tanned and sewn into shoes and saddles. Cotton and wool were spun and knit into socks, gloves, and caps, or woven into blankets and rugs, all of which would be sold in Chihuahua for manufactured goods and luxury items. And the illegitimate children slave women bore often remained in the household as additional working hands. (1991, 186–87)

Thus, Gutiérrez provides us also with the additional motive of the Spanish elite to bring in female slaves to help "keep up appearances," as it were, and protect their class status. But while Gutiérrez helps us to understand that bringing in female slaves was a matter of labor economics, he also ventures into the realm of relationships as he points to the inevitable, once female slaves were in Spanish households, in close physical proximity with Spanish families. He states: "Masters enjoyed enough access and time with their female slaves for sexual intimacies, whether won through seductive ploys or taken through force" (184). It is not difficult here for one to reflect on the legacy of the early stages of the conquest, which included misogyny and sexual exploitation of Indian women. Again, quoting Gutiérrez: "But the Spaniards as a group would interpret their subjugation of the Pueblos as a supreme assertion of masculine virility, and as such, would see 1598 as a sexual conquest of women" (51). Although in a different region and cultural context of North America, Angela Davis foregrounded the experience of black slave women, exposing how their status as slaves was impacted because of their gender. She states: "Again, it is important to remember that the punishment inflicted on women exceeded in intensity the punishment suffered by their men, for women were not only whipped and mutilated, they were also raped" (1981, 23).

So while Genízaras were targets of sexual exploitation due to their gender, we also have cases that show how Genízaras asserted themselves to protect their rights in other arenas. Let us look at some of the cases regarding Genízaras who took steps to safeguard the privileges and rights they felt they did have.

GERTRUDE CUÉLLAR

Benito Córdova states in his dissertation on Abiquiú that if a Genízaro felt unjustly treated or exploited by his overseer, "he could and frequently petitioned civil authorities for retribution." (1979, 82). We need to add "she" to this quotation, for this is exactly what Gertrude Cuéllar, "along with her husband, Joseph María Montaño," did in 1766, bringing action against their master, Juan Bautista Montaño. This case is interesting in that it resulted in the defendants receiving much more than what had been requested. Gertrude and her husband charged that their master refused to allow them to leave his household until they paid him one hundred pesos, which he claimed they owed due to his having provided for them over the course of their servitude, a total of nine years. Working from primary sources, Córdova states that Governor Tomás Vélez Cachupín decided, after having the matter investigated, that not only would the couple be allowed to leave the master's household, but they themselves should receive retroactive payments for the nine-year "tutelage." Governor Vélez Cachupín also appears to have been so moved by the plight of this Genízaro couple that he proposed that Santo Tomás de Abiquiú be established for Genízaros, and assigned the couple to go there, where they were allotted farmland and a house (Córdova 1979, 83).

MANUELA, THE SERVANT

Another case illustrates an instance when a Genízara, on her own, sought redress and retribution after having been "mistreated" by her mistress. Again relying on Benito Córdova's archival work: "During the administration of Governor Tomás Vélez Cachupín, Manuela alleged that she had been treated harshly by Isabel Chavéz. She charged that her master had failed to teach her to pray and perpetually had her out herding sheep, where Domingo Chávez had gotten her pregnant" (1979, 57). Regarding the identity of Domingo Chávez, it is worth mentioning here that Córdova is so thorough in his research that, indicated in a footnote, he looked at documents that might indicate who Chávez was, making some speculations but not being able to prove his identity for sure. In explaining that this was another case in which the governor decided in favor of the servant, in this instance Manuela, and against the Spanish mistress, Isabel Chávez, Córdova states that we must not let knowledge of such cases lead us to generalize and "view with contempt" the behavior of all Spanish settlers, since "the fact remains that the Spanish government did attempt to safeguard the rights of the Genízaro" (1979, 57).

In situations where Genízaras, specifically, were protected, Archibald states that the courts, citing the case of one Mr. Ortega, took the rape of Genízaras seriously: "In 1740 Antonio de Ortega was charged with raping his Indian servants and was accordingly found guilty. Such occurrences were commonplace" (1978, 210).

JUANA, THE SERVANT

The case of Juana, the servant/slave of Alejandro Mora of Bernalillo, illustrates how the wife of a master, another woman, albeit part of the Spanish elite, was instrumental in advocating on behalf of the household servant. It also shows the degree of physical violence and torture Genízaras suffered at the hands of their masters. The story of Juana is as follows:

> In 1751 Mora's wife complained to the authorities that Juana, a slave she had brought to the marriage, was being treated inhumanely. Bernalillo's constable investigated and found Juana's body totally covered with bruises. Her neck and body had burns from the application of live coals. Her ankles were scabbed from restraining manacles. Her knees had festering ulcers. Mora had initially broken Juana's knees to keep her from fleeing. The knee wounds never healed because Mora periodically reopened them, mincing the flesh with a sharp flint stone. (Gutiérrez 1991, 185)

Gutiérrez goes on to recount how Mora, in his own defense, tried to persuade the court that his treatment of Juana had more to do with his attempts at preventing her from becoming like other women in Bernalillo, who were "too sexually lax" (1991, 185). Mora's actions certainly indicate something other than protecting her virginity. At any rate, the result of the complaint was that Juana was removed from Mora's household, albeit probably nine years too late. In this case, Gutiérrez also points out that Mora himself did not receive "even a reprimand" (1991, 185).

TWO GENÍZARAS

Together, two anonymous Genízaras in 1763 decided to take their case to the authorities, which involved "excessive beatings and denial of life's necessities" (Archibald 1978, 209). Although the decision of the court was not in their favor (they were refused freedom), Archibald notes that the case is significant because it forced the Genízaras' masters, Tomás and Isabel Chávez (yes, probably Manuela's Isabel Chávez), to go on trial and defend themselves against the charges, "indicating substantial legal rights of Indian servants" (1978, 209).

Conclusion

Based on the few cases presented above, I would like to suggest some possibilities regarding how these situations might come about: that while in servitude, a Genízara (or Genízaro) would know when she had been legally wronged, that she would communicate this to someone in authority, and that the case would be investigated and those responsible held accountable.

First, Genízaras would have had to possess enough self-worth to come to the conclusion that they had been wronged, that they deserved better, and that their attackers or abusers deserved to be punished. Second, Genízaras must have had the knowledge that a formal system of redress existed and the wherewithal to access it for their own purposes. Lastly, and importantly, Genízaras, by accessing the court in their defense, must have also known that there existed the possibility that they would be successful in their attempt to seek redress. Otherwise, why bother? Related to this final point is that Genízaras' sense of confidence in the system must have outweighed the possible retaliation they could anticipate had the cases not been decided in their favor, which sometimes happened. In other words, they were taking quite a risk to publicly accuse their masters of wrongdoing. All of this indicates that there must have been, perhaps through word of mouth, a communication network operating that allowed Genízaras and Genízaros to obtain this valuable information, as well as develop a belief that it could actually work to their benefit. These speculations speak directly to the sense of agency these women and men were expressing by initiating the processes to protect themselves from harm and exploitation, to the extent that was possible, given their status as servants/slaves. These possibilities and others point to a need to continue to consider the social and cultural significance of Genízaros, and add to their complexity as subjugated peoples who somehow managed to see themselves as worthy of protection.

Genízaros have become part of the ongoing debate on whether Nuevomexicanos are more Spanish, or more Indian. In 2007, the New Mexico legislature passed "A Memorial Recognizing the Role of Genízaros in New

Mexico History and Their Legacy" (Rael-Gálvez 2007). Bronze statues and plaques honor colonial governors, the controversial first governor don Juan de Oñate (Trujillo 2008), and Juan Bautista de Anza (Christmas 2009), who negotiated peace with the Comanches in 1786. A new mural in Santa Fe honors Tomás Vélez Cachupín, who developed a defensive plan for New Mexico that resulted in a series of Genízaro land grants (Stelnicki 2017). A future monument may even honor José Gonzales, the first Genízaro governor of New Mexico (Chávez 1955).

References

Adams, Eleanor B., and Fray Angélico Chávez, eds. and trans. 1956. *The Missions of New Mexico, 1776: A Description by Fray Atanasio Domínguez*. Albuquerque: University of New Mexico Press.

Archibald, Robert. 1978. "Acculturation and Assimilation in Colonial New Mexico." *New Mexico Historical Review* 53, no. 3: 205–17.

Atencio, Tomás. 1985. "Social Change and Community Conflict in Old Albuquerque, New Mexico." PhD diss., University of New Mexico.

Brooks, James F. 2002. *Captives and Cousins: Slavery, Kinship, and Community in the Southwest Borderlands*. Chapel Hill: University of North Carolina Press.

Bustamante, Adrián Herminio. 1982. "Los Hispanos: Ethnicity and Social Change in New Mexico." PhD diss., University of New Mexico.

Chávez, Fray Angélico. 1955. "José Gonzales, Genízaro Governor." *New Mexico Historical Review* 30, no. 3 (July): 190–94.

———. 1979. "Genízaros." In *Handbook of North American Indians*, vol. 9, *Southwest*, edited by Alfonso Ortiz and William C. Sturtevant, 198–200. Washington, DC: Smithsonian Institution.

Christmas, Henrietta M. 2009. "Early Colonial Military and the Camino Real." *Chronicles of the Trail* (Camino Real de Tierra Adentro Trail Association, Santa Fe) 5, no. 3 (Fall): 14–19.

Córdova, Gilberto Benito. 1979. "Missionization and Hispanicization of Santo Tomás Apóstol de Abiquiú, 1750–1770." PhD diss., University of New Mexico.

Davis, Angela Y. 1981. *Women, Race, and Class*. New York: Vintage.

Dozier, Edward P. 1970. "Genízaros." In *The Pueblo Indians of North America*, 84–86. New York: Holt, Rinehart and Winston.

Ebright, Malcolm. 1996. "Advocates for the Oppressed: Indians, Genízaros, and Their Spanish Advocates in New Mexico, 1700–1786." *New Mexico Historical Review* 71, no. 4 (October): 305–39.

Gutiérrez, Ramón. 1991. *When Jesus Came, the Corn Mothers Went Away: Marriage,*

Sexuality, and Power in New Mexico, 1500–1846. Stanford, CA: Stanford University Press.

Horvath, Steven M. 1977. "The Genízaro of Eighteenth-Century New Mexico: A Reexamination." *Discovery* (School of American Research, Santa Fe): 25–40.

———. 1979. "The Social and Political Organization of the Genízaros of Plaza de Nuestra Señora de los Dolores de Belén, New Mexico." PhD diss., Brown University.

Magnaghi, Russell M. 1990. "Plains Indians in New Mexico: The Genízaro Experience." *Great Plains Quarterly* 10, no. 2 (Spring): 86–95.

Meléndez, A. Gabriel. 2017. *The Book of Archives and Other Stories from the Mora Valley, New Mexico*. Norman: University of Oklahoma Press.

Quintana, Frances Leon. 1991. *Pobladores: Hispanic Americans of the Ute Frontier*. Notre Dame, IN: University of Notre Dame Press.

Rael-Gálvez, Estevan. 2007. "A Memorial Recognizing the Role of Genízaros in New Mexico History and Their Legacy." Forty-Eighth Legislature, House Memorial 40, Senate Memorial 59. Santa Fe: New Mexico State Legislature.

Reno, Philip. 1965. "Rebellion in New Mexico, 1837." *New Mexico Historical Review* 40, no. 3 (July): 197–213.

Saltzstein, Katherine. 1992. "Historians Debate Genízaro Question." *Albuquerque Journal*, January 31.

Sisneros, Samuel E. 2017. "Los Genízaros and the Colonial Mission Pueblo of Belén, New Mexico." *New Mexico Historical Review* 92, no. 4 (Fall): 453–94.

Stelnicki, Tripp. 2017. "Redone Mural on County Guilding Paints More Pleasant Picture." *Santa Fe New Mexican*, July 19.

Swadesh, Frances Leon. 1974. *Los Primeros Pobladores: Hispanic Americans of the Ute Frontier*. Notre Dame, IN: University of Notre Dame Press.

Trujillo, Michael L. 2008. "Oñate's Foot: Remembering and Dismembering in Northern New Mexico." *Aztlán: A Journal of Chicano Studies* 33, no. 2 (Fall): 91–119.

White, Robert R. 1994. *New Mexican Genízaros and Turkish Janissaries*. Albuquerque: Las Lomas Press.

CHAPTER FIVE

The Genízaro Origins of the Hermanos Penitentes

RAMÓN A. GUTIÉRREZ

This chapter is a work of the historical imagination.[1] It is speculative, generative, and particularly hopeful that it will spark deeper research among others. Writing history is the process of piecing together shards from the past, fashioning them into plausible narratives about how events may have unfolded with a certain amount of verisimilitude. For several decades now we have learned a great deal about the historical emergence of Genízaro identity in New Mexico and southern Colorado. A much older published literature on the Hermanos Penitentes, officially the Cofradía de Nuestro Padre Jesús Nazareno (Confraternity of Our Father Jesus Nazarene), hereafter cited simply Hermanos Penitentes, has existed since the US annexation of New Mexico, trailed by Protestant missionaries and cultural promoters of the Southwest, who arrived during the last quarter of the nineteenth century. Is there a connection between the emergence of Genízaro identity and the rise of the Penitente Brotherhood? Since 1954, scholars have so suggested, but the answer to this question remains just that, a suggestion. My argument here is that the rise of Genízaro identity, which included the development of a distinct oppositional consciousness, occurred in tandem with the florescence of the Cofradía de Nuestro Padre Jesús Nazareno, indeed was a manifestation of the emergence of a distinct ethnic identity with religious and political dimensions. I hope that this historical connecting of dots serves as a provocation to conversation, and ideally more research.

New Scholarship

Scholarship on the history of New Mexico under Spanish, Mexican, and American rule has undergone considerable revision since the 1960s. Why is easy to explain. Every generation produces individuals animated to understand the preoccupations of their age and turn to history to explore what used to be, to understand what is. Fifty years ago, there were few histories of women in New Mexico. Now there are many. Revisionary works on the Native American past have appeared, written by indigenous scholars offering knowledge and viewpoints that previously were esoteric or secret, committed exclusively to memory and oral tradition. Histories of what became the American Southwest used to be narrated as the victorious Spanish, French, British, and, later, US Americans wanted it remembered. It was a triumphalist tale, a story of civilization taming savagery, of victors righteously vanquishing enemies, and of Christianity prevailing over the darkness of heathenism. This older view has been profoundly challenged in tomes chronicling the rise and fall of the Comanche and Apache not as simple, wayward, and irksome nomads but as denizens of powerful empires that for close to two centuries rivaled, bedeviled, and ultimately rendered helpless the military force that Spain, France, England, and the United States could muster against them. The Comanche empire, for example, could mobilize thousands of equestrian warriors in a flash to take whatever strategic goal or goods they wanted, which none of the European powers could do. Truth be told, more than four European imperial powers vied for control over Mexico's far north, what eventually became the American Southwest; counting the Apache and Comanche, that made six competing powers (Webb 2017; Ortelli 2007; Hämäläinen 2008; DeLay 2008; Velasco Ávila 2012).

In light of these findings, it is now easy to speculate that Mexico might not have lost Texas in 1836 or the large swath of territory the United States seized in 1848 had the Apache and Comanche not weakened Mexico's northern defenses as profoundly as they did. The larger story that starts circa 1730 was that France, Great Britain, and later the United States began constricting Apache and Comanche hunting grounds, forcing them southwestward into northern New Spain, hoping thus to weaken Spain's hold over the northern buffer colonies it had created to protect approaches to its silver mines. Their strategy embroiled colonists in New Mexico and Texas in endless Indian wars with the Apache and Comanche, who soon were deplored as *indios bárbaros* (barbaric Indians) (Weber 2005).

While the Spanish were responsible for transforming both indigenous groups into mounted warriors, leaving behind horses after the Pueblo Revolt that rapidly reproduced and were quickly tamed, the French, British, and Americans armed and liquored them, a combination lethally felt in northern New Spain. The Spanish initially responded by gifting and hosting the Apache and Comanche, signing treaties and smoking peace pipes, promising goodwill. But peace proved temporary and always too transitory. In 1764, the Crown dispatched José de Gálvez to New Spain as inspector general to assess the situation and offer defensive solutions. Gálvez proposed reforms—administrative, military, and economic—to safeguard the area from further incursions by indigenous and European imperial rivals. He reorganized New Spain's north into the Provincias Internas (Interior Provinces), which would report more directly than before to the king, militarily constructing a cordon of presidios across the North manned by light cavalry, *compañías volantes* (flying dragoons), who were prepared to give chase when Apache and Comanche depredations occurred. Finally, Gálvez had commercial advisers in tow assessing resources in the North that might stimulate investment and attract population, thereby fortifying defenses.

Comanche and Apache warfare was variously motivated, but the capture of enemies and their transformation into slaves was essential in meeting the need for labor, particularly hunting, processing animal hides, and, for women, reproduction, to generate additional laborers. Captives were held until their work potential was spent, until their indigenous owners tired of them, or until someone offered something even more coveted in return. These slaves sometimes included European captives. They were all routinely sold to the Spaniards as *indios de rescate* (bartered, ransomed, or rescued Indians) (Rister 1955).

Slave raids on Spanish settlements invariably produced immediate consequences, prompting retaliatory war against the Apache and Comanche and the abduction of their kin, who were in turn pressed into slavery. These indigenous captives started entering the Kingdom of New Mexico in significant numbers from the 1740s on. It was from these two forms of nomadic Indian enslavement that the category "Genízaro" emerged, eventually becoming a distinct oppositional identity. By 1848, Genízaros represented about a third of New Mexico's total population. The Spanish residents of colonial New Mexico deemed Genízaros enemy outsiders, the disposables of the indios bárbaros whom they feared and despised for wreaking so much death and destruction. Genízaro oppositional consciousness emerged as a reactive identity of self-affirmation, a frequent sociological response found when ethnicity becomes the source of stratification and the marked boundaries between social groups. When newcomers see themselves economically exploited, segregated, and racially discriminated against, they fashion oppositional cultures that coalesce as an identity that establishes their distinctiveness and their own self-worth, particularly in opposition to those they define as their oppressors (Gutiérrez 2016b).

Penitente Historiography

In the years following the 1848 territorial annexation of New Mexico into the United States, an extensive and highly polemical literature emerged on the Penitentes initially animated by proselytizing Protestant missionaries seeking Native American and Hispano converts. These publications reviled New Mexican Catholicism for its barbarity, using Penitente rituals as their prime example, amplifying putative "eyewitness" accounts of the savagery and bloodiness of human crucifixions into everyday occurrences. Catholic writers responded with their own anti-Protestant diatribes, elbowing aside Anglo cultural entrepreneurs promoting the strange peoples of the Southwest. Durango's bishops and later Santa Fe's archbishops contributed plenty to this war of words against the Cofradía de Nuestro Padre Jesús Nazareno, demanding restraint in their penitential rituals, the acceptance of Catholic Church supervision, and depoliticization. Of course, this print culture addressed a host of topics related to the area's religious practices, but the emergence and modes of existence of the Hermanos Penitentes was one of its central focuses (Weigle 1976b).

For many years, Penitente history has been obscured by what many still consider the hegemonic origin story Angélico Chávez articulated. In 1954, when he was still a Franciscan friar, a prolific writer on topics New Mexican, and the prickly organizer and custodian of the Archives of the Archdiocese of Santa Fe, jealously protecting the kingdom's Catholic history and the white supremacist lineage he articulated for its original Spanish settlers, Chávez published "The Penitentes of New Mexico" (1954). In this essay, Chávez argued that the Penitente brotherhood was a new organizational form that emerged sometime after 1776 and before 1833. He claimed that when Fray Francisco

Atanasio Domínguez undertook his ecclesiastical visitation of the kingdom in 1776, he did not mention any organization or religious practice so denominated. The cofradía only became known in 1833, or so said Chávez, when Durango's bishop, José Antonio Laureano de Zubiría y Escalante, railed against it as he unsuccessfully tried to impose the rule of the Third Order of Saint Francis on their *moradas* (chapels and meeting houses). Durango's bishop was intent on reining in what he read as Franciscan penitential brotherhoods intent on maintaining their increasing autonomy as he, the bishop, replaced the remaining resident Franciscans with secular parish priests, a transformation that had been approved and in the works since the 1760 New Mexican visitation by Durango's bishop, Dr. Pedro Tamarón y Romeral (Tamarón y Romeral 1954). Increasingly influenced by the emergent culture of science, the Catholic Church no longer deemed bloody public penitence appropriate. Interestingly enough, almost as if dropping a trail of crumbs, Chávez noted that in this fifty-seven-year period (1776–1833), the hermanos often referred to themselves as "the slaves of Jesus," numerically and spatially spreading their hermandad "into every hamlet and town," particularly to those New Mexican and southern Colorado villages that were "greatly populated by Genízaros" (1954, 119–20).

Chávez's own hypotheses about the post-1776 origin of the Cofradía de Nuestro Padre Jesús Nazareno were slippery at best, lacking much of an empirical foundation, often testing common sense. He maintained that the hermandad might have been a late transplant from Spain to central Mexico that simply had not reached the Kingdom of New Mexico before 1776. Alternatively, "some book, which described the old Spanish penitential societies and their rules had found its way to New Mexico at this time, in the quarter-century after 1776, to inspire the first Hermandad" (1954, 119–20).

Since religious brotherhoods with strikingly similar Lenten rituals existed then and now in many of the villages and towns that dot the old Camino Real de Tierra Adentro (Royal Road to the Interior) linking Mexico City to Zacatecas and then north to Durango, Parral, Chihuahua, El Paso, Santa Fe, and Taos, is it possible that the Cofradía de Nuestro Padre Jesús Nazareno totally bypassed New Mexico until after 1776, given the traffic on this route? Maybe. The Kingdom of New Mexico was founded in 1598 and remained under Spanish control despite the catastrophic 1680 Pueblo Revolt, primarily as a supply colony for the silver mines of north-central Mexico, provisioning them with indigenous slaves, livestock, hides, cotton and woolen products, salt, pine nuts, and pottery. Don Juan de Oñate, a wealthy silver miner who hailed from Zacatecas, was the principal investor in the kingdom's colonization, receiving his *capitulación* (royal charter) from King Philip II in 1595. Although many writers of the New Mexican past love to wax lyrically but ignorantly about New Mexico's utter isolation—a land unlike any other—it was developed as a supply colony for the mines that soon produced two-thirds of the world's silver. Far from isolated, New Mexico was intimately tied through regular trade to the forces of global capitalism that the mining, smelting, and circulation of bullion produced through human sweat.

Chávez's second hypothesis is that a Spanish penitential book may have ended up in New Mexico, been read, and its rituals mimicked. We know that there were very few books in church convents and even fewer in the kingdom's homes. If New Mexico in 1776 had had a literate population, the proposal might seem more plausible, but only about 15 percent of northern New Mexicans then could read. The few who could were largely of elite Spanish ancestry living in Albuquerque and Santa Fe, who were mostly Crown administrators, soldiers, and priests. Is it possible that a totally new confraternity emerged in New Mexico bearing a strikingly similar name and performing familiar Franciscan penitential rituals because of a book's arrival? Books such as the Bible were very important even to illiterates, but the appearance of such a work was never mentioned (Gallegos 1992, 52).

Some twenty years after Chávez's article, two books appeared: Elizabeth Boyd's *Popular Arts of Spanish New Mexico* (1974) and Marta Weigle's *Brothers of Light, Brothers of Blood: The Penitentes of the Southwest* (1976a). Boyd's capacious survey of Spanish colonial arts in New Mexico includes a lengthy chapter titled "The Third Order of St. Francis and the Penitentes of New Mexico." She begins the chapter gently questioning Chávez's hypotheses, arguing instead that the Penitentes were an outgrowth of Third Order Franciscanism (about which we will have much more to say below), and the departure of Franciscans from New Mexico as their parishes were secularized and transferred to secular priests known as *curas*. Genízaros were left with few priests to guide their spiritual needs. They fended for themselves first under Mexico in 1821, and then under the United States, which in 1848 took over jurisdiction of their towns and villages. They began conducting their own penitential rituals, increasingly surrounded by a profoundly different American socioeconomic and political culture. Although Boyd does not articulate an oppositional consciousness among the Genízaros, she does note their communal solidarity and self-help, their sense of otherness, and their rising political autonomy.

In rapid fire, Weigle summarized the hypotheses about the pre-1833 period, focusing her own ethnohistorical research instead on the post-1833 period, for which the documentary records are richer. She explored various hypotheses but gingerly sidestepped the origins debate. Were the Penitentes influenced by the ritual forms medieval European flagellants employed (unlikely), by early Mexican passion plays (no explicit link found), by Iberian penitential confraternities (many similarities existed), or by New World confraternities and penitential practices (absolutely)? Weigle's important contributions to the post-1833 history of the Cofradía de Nuestro Padre Jesús Nazareno are many, including a splendid appendix, which reproduces much of the correspondence between the leaders of Penitente moradas and Durango and Santa Fe Episcopal sees.

Below, let me focus on several topics: slavery, Franciscanism, and Genízaro identity.

Genízaro Slave Origins

From the Kingdom of New Mexico's establishment in 1598 to the 1680 Pueblo Revolt, the goal of its Spanish colonists was to extract as much wealth as possible from the sedentary Pueblo farmers they had conquered. The Spaniards divided indigenous towns and villages into forty-one *encomiendas* (assignments of land with labor), which Oñate awarded to the notables of the conquest, called *encomenderos* (grantees), who regularly demanded tribute from their encomienda Indians as labor, food, and locally produced goods for export (Snow 1983; Bloom 1939). The infamous squabbles between New Mexico's Spanish governors and Franciscan friars that marked the history of the seventeenth century leading to the 1680 Pueblo Revolt were precisely about who would commandeer Pueblo tribute. As early as 1598, the right to extract it was viciously demonstrated when don Juan de Oñate punished Ácoma Pueblo. As the Spaniards tell it, the conflict began on December 4, 1598, when Captain don Juan de Zaldívar and thirty-one of his soldiers en route to Zuñi Pueblo stopped at Ácoma demanding corn. Bushels were offered, but Zaldívar wanted it ground into flour, an additional effort that, in his mind, then proceeded way too slowly. The version Ácoma's residents tell is that, while the corn was being ground, a Spanish soldier stole two turkeys and assaulted an

Indian maiden, provoking a skirmish that ended with Zaldívar and twelve of his men dead. When Governor Oñate learned of this, he retaliated immediately, taking eighty men and five hundred women and children as prisoners on January 21, 1599, leaving behind some eight hundred dead. The Ácomans were found guilty of murder and failing to pay the demanded tribute. For this insubordination, all men and women over the age of twelve were condemned to slavery in Spanish households for twenty years. All children under the age of twelve were distributed to monasteries and households as servants. And all men over the age of twenty-five had one foot cut off, leading to sure death, but one that was agonizingly painful and slow. Several years later, Oñate razed the Tompiro pueblos of southern New Mexico for similar resistance, condemning all of the inhabitants to slavery. By 1630, Santa Fe counted 250 Spanish residents of various ages who were served by more than 700 Indian servants and slaves (Hammond and Rey 1953, 427–66, 247, 252).

The encomendero soldier-settlers of seventeenth-century New Mexico were "enemies of all kinds of work," noted Fray Jerónimo de Zárate Salmerón in the 1620s. In this, they were not unlike their Spanish compatriots elsewhere. For as New Spain's viceroy, don Luis Velasco, complained in 1608, "no one comes to the Indies to plow and to sow, but only to eat and loaf" (Zárate Salmerón 1966, 56). If they were to live idly but still gorge, they needed slaves. Don Francisco de Sosa Peñalosa, who entered New Mexico with Oñate's colonizing party, had in his service "three female negro slaves, one mulatto slave and other men and women servants" (Hammond and Rey 1953, 247, 252). Doña Teresa de Aguilera y Roche, the wife of Governor Bernardo López de Mendizábal, said in 1661 that when she set up her Santa Fe household, she owned two African slaves, four Apache slave girls, and an indigenous slave woman from central Mexico. Her husband had his own bevy of thralls (AGN Historia 25-3, 50–61; Hackett 1942, 142, 146, 153; Gutiérrez 2016a, 12).

When we think of slavery in the United States today, about its painful history and toxic racial legacies, we usually conjure up images of Africans being marched in chains to Africa's coasts for sale to Portuguese and Spanish merchants for shipment to ports in the Americas. The dimensions and nature of this history are well known. What is rarely mentioned in American history books is that slavery was a widespread institution among Native Americans, too, both before and after 1492. Settler colonialism intensified Indian slavery as an institution of labor appropriation and as a means of social and sexual reproduction. Indian slavery was well known to every indigenous group who claimed farming or foraging ground in what became New Mexico (Brooks 2002; Rael-Gálvez 2002; Gallay 2002; Olexer 2005; Ekberg 2007; Brooks and Martin 2015).

Indigenous slavery originated in war. Whenever contests over land, well-watered spots, or particular hunting grounds provoked conflict, captives were among the spoils. Throughout human history and across the globe, death on the battlefield is the standard way one vanquishes enemies, in times past parading their heads and scalps, their ears and genitals, as trophies that attested to one's own virility and military superiority. If death came in battle, one suffered no humiliation. But by being spared, captured alive, and condemned to slavery, there was. Such thralls were defeated enemy outsiders, the humiliated living who could have been honorably killed but instead now served the men who captured them as living dead (Patterson 1982).

Slavery, a well-known institution in medieval Europe, was transported via Spain to Hispaniola and Cuba in the years following 1492. It was fully lawful to enslave Natives who resisted Christianity and Spanish rule. Indian slavery in the Caribbean took a horrendous toll. Encomienda demands quickly wiped out Natives, forcing colonists to repopulate Hispaniola and Cuba with African slaves. Clerical critics of Spain's settler colonialism voiced opposition to slavery as early as 1610. Fray Bartolomé de las Casas, an encomendero turned priest, was among the most vociferous, articulating an ethics of empire that eventually stirred the monarch's conscience to temper this genocide. The 1542 New Laws of the Indies explicitly outlawed Indian slavery. The 1680 Recompilation of the Laws of the Indies reiterated the prohibition with a caveat. The enslavement of Indians remained legal on the empire's margins, in places like Chile, the Amazon, Paraguay, and New Mexico, as an enticement to attract the capital investment necessary for colonization. Indigenous peoples who refused to submit to Spanish rule, who resisted the word of God, were routinely enslaved and held in bondage for ten to twenty years, as was legal. In practice, most remained thralls their entire lives, and it was only their children ultimately who were deemed free, but nevertheless carrying slavery's stigma for generations (Zavala 1967, 107–14, 179–92, 223).

New Mexico's Spanish colonists waged endless Indian war in the seventeenth century. It was premeditated, intentionally provoked, and only later rationalized as retaliatory and "just." Their goal was singular. To seize slaves to work, breed, pimp, and sell. This was a basic fact of life. At first, the Spanish enslaved Pueblo dissidents as proximal targets. But by 1630 the colony's indigenous landscape had become more complex, as Apache nomads began surrounding the kingdom's settlements and farms, covetous of the livestock gathered there. They too soon became objects of Spanish hatred and desire. The enslavement and hyperexploitation of the Puebloans was one of the major grievances that provoked their 1680 revolt. A new set of indigenous enemies emerged within a decade of the kingdom's reconquest in 1692, who were more troublesome, militarily more adept, and increasingly mounted and armed. The Spaniards denigrated them as indios bárbaros, who eventually became ethnically legible as Navajo, Comanche, Ute, Pawnee, and Apache. Hesitant to do anything that might spark another Pueblo revolt, the Spanish shifted the focus of slave raids onto these "barbaric" nomads, deeming themselves and their Pueblo charges "civilized" farmers, cloaked and living in houses, monogamously married, and worshiping the one true god. In times of peace, these "barbarians" entered Pecos, Taos, and Picurís to trade their hunt products and indios de rescate for wool blankets, pottery, corn, turquoise, and Spanish manufactured goods. Governor Tomás Vélez Cachupín encouraged the trade in 1752, fearing that if it were curtailed, endless bloodshed would follow. What was better, the governor asked vicaregal officials, to allow the Indians to kill their prisoners during war or to permit the Spanish colonists to "ransom" them? Through such rescues, the governor continued, they would "be instructed in Our Holy Catholic Faith and made cognizant of the Divine Precepts, so that they may win their own salvation in honor and glory of God, our Lord" (SANM 8, 1070–105). The 1680 Recompilation of the Laws of the Indies stated that such ransomed Indians should be treated well and not "marketed as slaves," but as Fray Pedro Serrano testified in 1761, no one in New Mexico paid such decrees much heed. "The greed for slaves displayed by the citizens reaches such extremes, that, heedless of God, or the king, or the law, or the kingdom, or even of themselves, these men with their wrongs and injustices conspire so that they can be warred against" (Hackett 1937, 3:487).

New Mexico's Spanish residents swore that these wars were "just." Colonial ledgers expose their brutal intentions and grander dimensions. In mineral-poor New Mexico, Indian slaves were "the kingdom's gold and silver and the richest treasure" that one could find, claimed Father Serrano in 1761. They were the realm's coin, infinitely mutable. "I owe Felipe Saíz, a resident of Parral, a few pesos, which I agreed to pay with a little Indian girl," stated a 1718 will. Don Joseph Reaño paid for his purchases in Chihuahua in 1761 with a few *inditos* (Indian children), as did many others New Mexican merchants between 1598 and 1870 (Hackett 1937, 3:487; SANM 9, 410–44; SANM 9, 262–67).

The extent of warfare and its cultural impact on Spanish New Mexicans can be gleaned by comparing Spanish burial records listing men killed during nomadic Indian raids and the number of nomadic Indian baptisms that followed. Since Indians captured in war had to be baptized before incorporation into Christian homes, the number christened is a reasonable index of enslavement. Admittedly, baptisms underestimate slavery's dimensions, because captives destined for sale elsewhere did not have to be baptized. Because indios de rescate were already slaves, they did not have to be baptized and were thus not listed in these registers. Instead, they appear on silver mine musters, on the work rolls of henequen plantations in the Yucatán, and on slave manifests bound for Cuba's sugarcane fields (Sartorius 2013).

Between 1700 and 1820, 584 New Mexican Spaniards were killed in skirmishes with nomadic Indians; during the same period, 2,708 indios bárbaros were baptized. Approximately one Spaniard was killed for every five Indians captured (Gutiérrez 1991, 153–54). Baptismal records further reveal that between 1700 and 1849, 3,294 nomadic Indians entered New Mexican households. Two out of every five were identified explicitly as slaves, with notations that they were "in the power of," "in the dominion of," or "a captive of" a particular person. Ethnically, the Navajo represented the largest group of captives, totaling 37.5 percent. In the seventeenth century, Spanish colonists referred to the Navajo as *apaches de navaju* (Navajo Apaches). In the eighteenth century, the Spanish ethnic lexicon began differentiating Apaches by location. Those identified simply as Apache represented 24 percent; when aggregated with the Navajo, they totaled 61.5 percent. The Ute represented 16 percent of the total, and the Comanche 5 percent (Brugge 1968).

A total of 33 percent were listed as "adopted," again obfuscating the nature of their captivity. One out of every five slaves was listed as a *criado* or servant (from the Spanish verb *criar*, "to rear"). Criados were boys and girls usually captured in infancy and reared servicing a household's needs. To skirt the laws against Indian slavery, New Mexicans avoided the term *esclavo* (slave), preferring the more nurturing euphemism "criado" (Simmons 1973, 34). Fray Juan Agustín Morfi made this explicit when he wrote in 1776 that these slaves were "called Genízaros; they are Comanche and Apache captives obtained as children and reared [criados] among us" (AGN Historia 25-8, 147). Over time, "Genízaro" and "criado" were words used interchangeably to refer to all persons living or originating in a servile status. Indeed, the emancipated residents of Abiquiú, resettled in this segregated buffer town in 1754 to thwart Apache, Navajo, Ute, and Comanche raids, referred to themselves in 1820 as "Genízaros criados" (SANM 20, 419).

The number of Native Americans residing in New Mexico's nominally Spanish towns grew during the eighteenth century from a third population source: expulsions from Indian pueblos. This Pueblo Indian category was complex. Some expulsions resulted from Spanish labor demands. Although the encomienda was slowly curtailed in New Mexico with the Spanish reconquest in 1692, it was replaced by the *repartimiento*, a rotational labor levy. The entry of Pueblo women into Spanish towns to perform this required work sometimes led to sexual assaults. The governors of fourteen pueblos complained bitterly about this to New Spain's viceroy in 1707 (AGN Historia 25-4, 62–63). "When Indian women enter Santa Fe to mill wheat and spin wool, they return to their pueblos deflowered and crying over their dishonor or pregnant," explained Father Serrano in 1761 (AGN Provincias Internas 36-3, 128–29). When Pueblo men discovered such defilement, said Fray Carlos Delgado in 1750, these women were banished (AGN Historia 25-2, 31). If somehow a woman managed to conceal her shame but gave birth to a child of apparent mixed ancestry, the baby was abandoned at the doorstep of the local church. Baptismal registers list these infants as *hijos de la iglesia, padres no conocidos* (children of the church, parents unknown). Hijos de la iglesia were baptized and reared in Christian homes; they were likewise known as criados and subsequently considered Genízaros, among whom they lived once they became adults. Approximately one out of every ten persons living in Spanish households during the eighteenth century was a child of the church.

How many Genízaros were living in eighteenth-century New Mexico? If one counts only persons explicitly identified as Genízaros on census forms, the number is modest. The first census to report Genízaros as a distinct ethnic group appeared in 1765, listing 677 in a total population of 15,354—15 percent, or roughly one out of every seven residents (Cutter 1975). If one aggregates slaves, criados, Pueblo outcasts, and abandoned infants, the number of Genízaros reaches one-third, or one out of every three persons. This is extremely important culturally, because in a supply colony that had been ravaged by the Pueblo Revolt, and then endlessly decimated by indios bárbaros, a deep and visceral hatred developed against Genízaros, largely the offspring of these enemy Indians.

The Treatment of Genízaros

Bondage in colonial New Mexico was a household institution, and its meanings for Genízaros are to be found at the interpersonal level. Before slaves entered a Spanish household, they were stripped of their former name, baptized, and given a Christian name. Manuel A. Chávez in the early 1800s said that "on arriving home [after a slaving expedition,] the first thing to do was to take the children to the priest to baptize them and give them a name. They would naturally take your name" (Simmons 1973, 35). Kinship was the dominant mode of affiliation in colonial New Mexico; everyone was enmeshed in its web. Lacking genealogical ties to the community, slaves and criados entered households as part of its symbolic capital. The enmeshment of Indian servitude in the language of kinship has led some historians to conclude erroneously that the treatment of Indian slaves was "benevolent." This claim is based primarily on litigation before judicial courts in which slaves spoke of their masters and mistresses as "father" and "mother," and in turn were referred to as "son" and "daughter" (Chávez 1979, 198–200).

The use of filial terms to refer to detribalized Indians in legal documents tells us little about whether slavery was benevolent or brutal. Rather, they were statements concerning authority relationships within the household, particularly of a father's right to rule over his wife, children, slaves, and strays. The Crown tolerated slavery in New Mexico as a way of "civilizing" Indians. When slave owners came before the courts to contest charges of slave mistreatment, it was in their interest to portray slave relations as governed by the same rules that regulated families. Fathers ideally were loving and guiding, but equally stern and demanding. To have presented any other picture would have exposed masters to the risk of losing their servants and slaves.

Within New Mexican households, the treatment of Genízaros ran the gamut from kind, to neglectful, to utterly sadistic, or some combination thereof. To be a slave or a criado in a Spanish household was to be a marginal and stigmatized person. This was evident in the type of duties Genízaros were reported performing. They emptied chamber pots, clipped the master's toenails, hauled water, and chopped wood in the dead of winter; they were exposed to all sorts of dangers blood kin were not. Inside the household and outside of it as well, Genízaros were addressed as minors, in the second-person informal *tú*, but had to address their masters and the local citizenry with the formal *usted*. In the natal societies from which Genízaros hailed, advancing age brought increasing respect, but not for Genízaros in Spanish households. Many of them were infantilized permanently, even by their owners' own children. Take the case of Bárbara, an Indian slave described in 1762 as old, sickly, and no longer capable of much productive work. She expected that when her master died, his son, Joseph Gallego, whom she had suckled as an infant with her own breast milk, would free her. Bárbara requested her freedom, which he refused, beating her every time she asked. Bárbara's children, who were not allowed to visit their mother, sought the governor's intercession. Joseph Gallego arrogantly explained to Governor Vélez Cachupín that he had taken Bárbara to his house "not because of her service but because my deceased father bought her." His behavior could not be considered cruel, because he was simply preserving his father's property. The governor agreed. Bárbara had "no basis" for demanding emancipation (SANM 9, 172–78).

The sheer proximity between masters and slaves, and the slaves' status as dishonored outsiders lacking genealogical ties to the community, regularly made them scapegoats for all sorts of frustrations. A poor harvest, the low price one's livestock brought at market, a wife's infidelities, or an affront to one's honor could, and often did, get vented on slaves. Trivial insubordination or impertinences, whether real or imagined, produced beatings that sometimes resulted in death. When slaves were murdered, usually through severe beatings, local authorities rarely identified or punished the culprit.

Becoming Genízaros

The presence of significant numbers of Genízaro slaves and criados who had no genealogical ties to the Spanish community, who were dishonored by their status in households governed by men legally recognized as "honorable," and who were the very embodiment of the war between barbaric nomads and civilized farmers, generated negative stereotypes of what it meant to be a Genízaro, which in time crystallized, provoking a defensive ethnic identity. Indeed, much of what was considered Spanish culture on New Mexico's frontier gained its meaning in opposition to, and as an exaggeration of, what it meant to be an indio bárbaro, a detribalized slave, and ultimately a Genízaro. It was by contrasting themselves with Genízaros that Spanish aristocrats and peasants alike defined themselves, their honor, their standing, and their superior social worth.

Fray Francisco Atanasio Domínguez in 1776 vividly described the condition of Genízaro life. They were "ransomed from the pagans by our people, [they] are then emancipated to work out their account." Because Spaniards "only as a last resort . . . serve themselves," he continued, "Genízaros are servants among our people" (1956, 42). Two years later, in 1778, Father Morfi further elaborated. Genízaros were:

> Captive Comanches, Apaches, etc., who were taken as youngsters and raised among us. . . . Since they are the offspring of enemy tribes, the natives of this province, who bear long grudges, never admit them to their pueblos. Thus [Genízaros] are forced to live among Spaniards, without lands, or other means to subsist. . . . [T]hey desire sites for villages but fail to obtain any, either because no one wants to provide them or because most of the lands have been occupied. . . . On account of their poverty, which leaves them afoot and without arms . . . they bewail their neglect and they live like animals. (AGN Historia 25-8, 147–48)

Domínguez, ever observant of the smallest details, noted the variants of Castilian spoken in New Mexico. The kingdom's Spaniards spoke "with courtly polish," while peasants talked "simply and naturally among themselves." But the Genízaros did "not wholly understand it [Spanish] or speak it without twisting it somewhat." As for Genízaro character, Domínguez summarized the learned opinion of his compatriots: they were "weak, gamblers, liars, cheats, and petty thieves" serving as "examples of what happens when idleness becomes the den of evils." What exactly defined their idleness? Domínguez never said. This comment is hard to interpret because of the servitude in which many Genízaros lived. While describing the Genízaros resettled in the village of Belén in 1740, Domínguez added that they had no way of supporting themselves and lived by their luck: "Only they and God know whether they have managed to get their hands on what belongs to their neighbors" (1956, 42, 259, 126, 208). The dominant modes of subsistence in eighteenth-century New Mexico were farming and hunting. Reading these two Domínguez statements together seems to indicate that even after Genízaros were congregated in their own villages, they lived at the margins of existence without sufficient land or livestock to sustain themselves, hunting with bows and arrows and gathering what edibles they could.

The collective portrait of Genízaros that emerges is one of individuals of mostly nomadic indigenous origin, initially captured or purchased as slaves, not speaking Spanish well, owning inadequate land, livestock, and firearms to sustain themselves, despised, and deemed to be living much as their depraved *bárbaro* kindred. Salvador Martínez, a Spaniard from Albuquerque, offered a very similar depiction when he complained in the early 1800s that the Genízaros living in the vicinity of Belén "were fugitives from their masters, odious people, vagabonds, gamblers, and thieves without the political or economic organization of a Republic" (Horvath 1979, 78).

These depictions of Genízaros soon became constantly repeated stereotypes that entered the popular consciousness and remained deeply enmeshed as an evaluation of human worth, particularly among New Mexico's white *españoles*, who bore long grudges against their indigenous enemies. To this day, mischievous and unruly New Mexican children are taunted: "*¡Genízaro! ¡Genízaro! Puro indio de rescate!*" (Genízaro! Genízaro! Pure bartered Indian!). When New Mexicans today say, "*No seas Genízaro*" (Don't be a Genízaro), they mean: "Don't be a liar." Anthropologist Frances Swadesh wrote that in northern New Mexico in the early 1970s, when someone was referred to as a Genízaro, it meant crude, low-class, or *indiado* (Indian-like) (1974, 45). In the 1950s, anthropologist Florence Hawley Ellis was told similar things about Belén's Genízaros by the descendants of Spaniards who resided just across the Río Grande in Tomé, which itself originated as a large Spanish land grant. Belén's Genízaros, said Ellis's informants, were "semi-slave, low class and without ability" (1955, 45).

If "barbaric" Indian origins, dishonored slave ancestry, distorted language, crude character, and bad habits defined the Genízaros, a list of antonyms characterized what it meant to be Spaniards. Differences between aristocrats and peasants were of degree, not kind. Spaniards, whatever their estate, were men of honor in comparison to Indian slaves. Even the lowliest Spaniard felt a grand sense of honor among women and men reared in servility. Landed peasants shared fully in this timocratic culture because, unlike Genízaros, they were Old Christians, longtime members of the kingdom, putatively white, and as such had been given land by Spain's kings to farm and ranch. Landowners were *vecinos* (citizen neighbors) with full voting rights in the governance of town affairs. As men of honor, they owned horses and firearms and spoke Castilian well. When such men said that Genízaros "lived like animals," they deprecated the "wild" Indian nomads who ate what they hunted or stole, were scantily clad, and showed little modesty or restraint in their social and sexual comportment, capturing women and keeping them as their sex slaves. Because slave women bore illegitimate mixed-race children, rarely married (instead living in informal unions), and were reputed to be frisky and licentious, they were frequently the victims of sexual assault. To be a Spanish woman, on the other hand, regardless of status, meant that one was concerned for one's sexual purity and reputation, guarded one's virginity, and valued marital monogamy. Finally, men of honor were men of their word; their words carried force and were as binding as modern contracts. Genízaros were described as liars and cheats, hardly men who could be trusted to keep their word.

By the 1770s, stigmatization, segregation, and demographic growth had transformed Genízaros into a distinct and dangerous ethnic group. Spanish society so avoided them as marriage partners, explained Father Delgado, that the only option they had was to marry within their own group, taking "women of their own status and nature." More importantly, at least according to Delgado, was that Genízaros had begun to live in great unity, "*como si fueran una nación*" (as if they were a nation) (AGN Historia 25-25, 229). Here at last is the evidence of the emergence of a Genízaro ethnic identity, at least as recognized by an astute outsider who had worked his entire life among a range of indigenous groups in New Spain. In Spain and New Spain, when distinct peoples were referred to as a *nación*, it implied that they shared a common origin, spoke a similar language, and had developed a common culture and sense of collective identity tied to territory.

New Mexico's Franciscan Imprint

The origins of the Cofradía de Nuestro Padre Jesús Nazareno are to be found in the evangelization strategies, rituals, and organizational forms the Franciscans brought to New Mexico in 1598 and over which they presided for nearly two hundred years.

The evangelization model the Franciscans utilized to lead New Mexico's Indians to God was created by the order's founder, Saint Francis of Assisi. In the hagiographic tomes written by Tommaso da Celano (*Vita Beati Francisci*) and Saint Bonaventure (*Life of Saint Francis*), both early devotees, we learn that Francis was the first person ever to receive the stigmata, the physical wounds inflicted on Christ's hands, feet, and breast during his crucifixion. Francis received these because his internal love for the crucified Christ was so intense that eventually that love was displayed externally on his body for everyone to behold. To reach spiritual perfection, then, as Saint Francis had done when he carried the crucified Christ internally, one began by demonstrating it externally, purging the body of all physicality by fasting, deadening the palate, engaging in extensive flagellation, and silencing the libido and sources of pleasure through painful acts, even by self-mutilation. Once purged of bodily sensation, the soul was free of its body and ready for illumination through God's words. If these words were followed perfectly, they would lead to a mystical marriage with Christ. Purgation, illumination, and union were the steps necessary for the spiritual re-formation of any person who wanted to become a Franciscan. This was the evangelization model the Franciscans brought to New Mexico. If the Pueblo Indians were someday to carry the crucified Christ in their souls and enter heaven, they had to begin by carrying the crucified Christ on their bodies.

The Franciscans imported into New Mexico two other innovations that Saint Francis bequeathed to Catholicism. In the thirteenth century, he created three categories of Franciscan membership. The first was the Order of Friars Minor, for men ready to vow chastity, poverty, and obedience as Franciscans. The second was the Order of Saint Clare, for women seeking conventual life. And the Third Order of Saint Francis, originally known as the Brothers and Sisters of Penance, was for the laity ready to follow the Franciscan rule, wearing the habit and waist cord, but without living its vows. The Franciscans who ventured into New Mexico in 1598 were the First Order of Friars Minor. There is no mention of the Second Order or Third Order between 1598 and 1692.

Franciscanism was also profoundly felt in New Mexico through the introduction of the Stations of the Cross, a processional rite invented by Saint Francis in Jerusalem in 1217 to allow Christians to meditate on Christ's final day. The devotion was organized around fourteen pictures showing the ordeal Christ endured on his way to Golgotha, as a sort of meditative pilgrimage, which became widespread in Christendom and now adorns the naves of most Catholic churches. The stations begin with Christ's condemnation and scourging at the pillar; proceed through three falls; then to meetings with his mother, with Veronica, and with three women from Jerusalem; to Simon's assistance; and culminating in the stripping, crucifixion, death, and entombment. Throughout the year, individuals could traverse a church's nave or the perimeters of the church cemetery, where similar stations were displayed, meditatively walking side by side with Christ along his *via crucis*.

During Lent and Good Friday, processions started at the altar, where statues of Jesús Nazareno and the Mater Dolorosa were housed; these were placed on platforms and paraded through the town's streets and back, accompanied by flagellants, cross bearers, and others performing various acts of penitence. For the rest of the year, these statues remained at their designated altars, allowing devotees of Jesús Nazareno to nurture acts of personal piety spontaneously. The Stations of the Cross and its grander Lenten rituals are well recorded in New Mexico from the 1710s on.

The Catholic ritual geography established in the kingdom at its start was much larger than the devotions the Franciscans imported and authorized. Sodalities formed an older sacral topography consisting of religious associations created to advance personal piety, enhance the love of God, and provide charity through *obras pías* (pious works), cofradías, *archicofradías* (archconfraternities), and *hermandades*. The obras pías reported in eighteenth-century New Mexico include a visit by the Holy Office of the Crusade collecting donations to fund the reconquest of Jerusalem, as well as the construction of several private chapels underwritten by individuals to honor familial devotions. Archicofradías, which were aggregates of confraternities of the same name, such as the Confraternity of the Blessed Sacrament, were widespread in New Spain but not in New Mexico until the twentieth century. While there are a few passing references to cofradías and hermandades before the 1680 Pueblo Revolt, their existence after the kingdom's 1692 reconquest is abundantly documented. The former required episcopal license for their creation; the latter emerged more spontaneously from local devotion, had little ecclesiastical oversight, and operated without the formal license or infrastructure bishops demanded of confraternities. The distance between New Mexico and its episcopal seat, coupled with infrequent inspections, meant that a great deal of variance developed in the functioning of confraternities and brotherhoods. If a confraternity's founding documents still existed, members tried to honor those obligations. If not, members pretty much poured out their religious sentiments, as they deemed appropriate, eyeing what other confraternities did. If and when bishops discovered that rituals significantly deviated from those sanctioned, they would dispatch sternly worded letters, retire to the comfort of their lairs, and in time perhaps send inspectors to report on the state of affairs. With no effective local sanctions, ritual practice continued largely uninterrupted (Taylor 1996).

The Franciscans only had jurisdictional power over those confraternities they had founded before the 1729 transfer of episcopal power over the missions of New Mexico to the bishop of Durango, who retained this control until 1850. But the Franciscans nevertheless actively participated as parish priests in confraternity activities, saying Masses, preaching sermons, offering blessings, and leading processions, for which they were paid by the confraternities.

The word "cofradía" comes from the Latin *confrater*, which means "cobrother." A confraternity was a group of persons who gathered as members of a larger mystical family. They originated in Europe during Christianity's early years, before state-sponsored social services existed, emerging as voluntary associations of the Christian faithful committed to acts of charity. Cofradías attended to victims of catastrophe, disease, and poverty. By performing such acts, cobrothers earned grace and indulgences, deemed sure routes to sanctity and salvation (Gutiérrez 1993, 672–82; Bermejo y Carballo 1882, 2–5).

The familial language confraternities employed made them vibrant forms for the expression of identities. Joined together in religious brotherhood for purposes of larger social good, Catholics momentarily could put aside the enmities and distrust that typically marked the daily interactions of families, households, and clans. Through the creation of cofradías, Catholic prelates and theologians intentionally attacked secular understandings of family as exclusively rooted in blood, hoping thus to whittle away at the power of biological kinship networks (Gudeman 1971; Foster 1969; Mintz and Wolf 1950).

Confraternities dedicated themselves to different personifications and life-course transformations of Christ and the Virgin Mary, and to a range of local patron saints. To gain license for their creation, first the prelates of the religious orders and later bishops elaborated a constitution, a set of rules, requisite rituals, works of mercy, and festival days, along with a fee schedule and an income ledger to track membership dues. Despite the variance in confraternities and brotherhoods, the common thread that bound them was an obligation to lead model lives of virtue, care for the welfare of the needy, bury the dead, and pray for the redemption of departed souls (Foster 1953).

Two types of cofradías, vertical and horizontal, often existed side by side in larger towns, often with their own private oratories, chapels, and devotional paraphernalia. Vertical confraternities integrated a locality's social groups, momentarily obliterating status distinctions by joining the rich and the poor, Spaniards and Indians, slave and free, through acts of mutual aid. The most common vertical cofradía in New Spain was dedicated to the Blessed Sacrament, promoted mostly by the clergy to sponsor regular community Masses

(Moreno Navarro 1974, 12–35). If vertical brotherhoods integrated a town's social groups, horizontal cofradías were segregated by social status, by honor, race, ethnicity, and wealth. Relationships of domination and subordination between groups were often articulated through confraternity rivalries and the symbolic oppositions frequently evident in their names. The Cofradía de Nuestro Padre Jesús Nazareno was just that, a self-governing horizontal cofradía composed mainly of Genízaros, its influence growing significantly after the secularization of Franciscan missions, the arrival of US Americans, and the transfer of the Catholic Church to American control. Though not well documented, there can be little doubt that in many of the small villages and plazas of northern New Mexico and southern Colorado, there were other small community devotions to Christ, Mary, and particular saints. The Cofradía de Nuestro Padre Jesús Nazareno was not the only one that existed.

Below is a history of Catholic ritual practices in New Mexico divided into three periods, admittedly with somewhat fuzzy transitional dates, that provides a chronology for the emergence of the Hermanos Penitentes.

Period One: 1598–1691

The clerics who accompanied don Juan de Oñate's colonizing party to the Kingdom of New Mexico in 1598 were twelve First Order Franciscans, denominated the "Twelve Franciscan Apostles," to honor the original "Twelve Franciscan Apostles" who arrived in 1524 to begin the Christianization of New Spain. These twelve were a radical lot. Many had seen their millenarian evangelical fantasies dashed in central Mexico and now sought a new missionary field for the realization of their apocalyptic dreams. They believed that the conversion of New Mexico's Pueblo Indians would usher in the thousand years of Christian rule preceding Christ's return and the destruction of the world.

The first use of the word "penitente" in New Mexico appears in 1610, not 1833, in the epic poem *Historia de la Nueva México*, recounting the feats of Oñate's conquest, penned by a participant, Captain Gaspar Pérez de Villagrá. As Oñate's convoy advanced northward, it stopped on March 20, 1598, not far from what is today El Paso, Texas, to observe Holy Thursday and Good Friday. Oñate ordered a chapel constructed, well canopied with trees. There, the Franciscans kept vigil all Holy Thursday night "on their knees.... There were many contrite penitents and bloody and great discipline asking God with tears and prayers" to reveal the way to New Mexico. The following day, on Good Friday, barefoot women and children asked for God's mercy, as did the soldiers "using whips to flagellate their backs with both hands, until they bled." The "humble sons of Francis clad in haircloth . . . with clamor and prayers . . . sought God's aid." Don Juan de Oñate did not participate in these public rites, as had his two nephews. Instead, he went off alone, and, according to Villagrá, on his knees "shed two fountains from his eyes and then, lashing his shoulders, he poured out a sea of crimson blood while imploring His Divine Majesty that he have mercy on us all" (Pérez de Villagrá 1992, 102–3, my translation).

Once the kingdom was under Spanish rule, Franciscan Holy Thursday and Good Friday rituals were celebrated in similar canonical fashion, but perhaps now with grander processions and more exemplary public penitence, hoping to show the Pueblo Indians how to carry the crucified Christ on their bodies to eventually carry him in their hearts. Fray Alonso de Benavides recounted an argument with a Chililí medicine man in 1630. The medicine man was shocked by a Good Friday via crucis, or Stations of the Cross, and began shouting: "You Christians are crazy; you desire and pretend that this pueblo shall also be crazy. . . . You go through the streets in groups, flagellating yourselves and it is not well that the people of this pueblo should commit such madness as spilling their own blood by scourging themselves." Benavides tried to explain the ritual, but the medicine man refused to listen, muttering as he departed that he had no intention of being afflicted by such Christian madness (Benavides 1945, 66).

The Good Friday processions at Curac and Tajique in 1655 were reported to have included some six hundred persons carrying "large and small crosses on their shoulders." That same year, the Hopi dressed themselves "like penitent hermits walking about praying in penitence, carrying crosses, large beads, and wearing haircloth shirts." The winter of 1666 was so cold that, to keep warm, the friars at the Tompiro pueblos burned six hundred of the large crosses they normally used for Good Friday processions (AGN Inquisición 512, 99–101).

When a number of Isleta Pueblo men were discovered in a *kiva* (ceremonial chamber) invoking their ancestral gods in 1661, the Franciscans had the men rounded up and publicly flogged (AGN Inquisición 593, 17). Later that year too, Fray Salvador de Guerra emerged from his convent only to find his charges performing the idolatrous *katinsa* dance and viciously beating a lifeless infant, whom everyone suspected Guerra had fathered. Guerra begged them to stop. When his exhortations were ignored, he stripped naked, began violently beating himself with a whip, placed a rope around his neck and a crown of thorns on his head, and crisscrossed the pueblo under the weight of a large cross. On seeing this, the residents of Isleta are said to have immediately stopped dancing. Some begged the friar's forgiveness; others scurried to the safety of their homes, fearing that soldiers might soon arrive with more severe punishments (AGN Inquisición 573, 100).

The whips or *disciplinas* so evident in Lenten penitential rituals were ever present. Whips used for European self-discipline quickly served another function, the punishment of Puebloans. Most missions had a coterie of indigenous assistants who helped keep neophytes focused. If one did not appear to be carrying the crucified Christ internally, a round of disciplinas certified that they now clearly carried him externally. Sherburne F. Cook, in his monumental study of relations between the Franciscans and California's Indians, documents how disciplinas became the master symbol of Franciscan authority, used mercilessly to curb disobedience, sexual liberties, and particularly apostasy (1976, 112–40).

I have found only one small shard documenting the existence of confraternities in New Mexico before the 1680 Pueblo Revolt. The Franciscans denounced New Mexico's Governor Juan de Eulate in 1626, claiming that during the colony's early years both the Confraternity of the Blessed Sacrament and the Confraternity of the Immaculate Conception (Madre de Dios de la Concepción) existed. Because of the governor's bad influence and disrespect for the church, or so claimed the friars, the settlers deserted the confraternities and now spent their time playing cards in the governor's house (AGN Historia, 356, f278v). There is also evidence of Good Friday Franciscan penitential processions but without enough description to tell us more than that they occurred. In 1662, the Franciscans accused Governor Bernardo López de Mendizábal of having intentionally missed the procession that "commemorates the Passion of Christ Our Lord and the death He suffered at the hands of the perfidious Jews" on Good Friday of the previous year out of his disdain for the friars (Gutiérrez 2016a, 16).

Except for these fragments, little more remains in the archival records about how Christian rituals were actually conducted before the revolt. Perhaps the most poignant testament that was left by the Pueblo rebels was discovered by the fleeing colonists in the rubble of Sandía's church. There, all the paint and plaster on the church's crucifix had been completely stripped off with whips. The arms of the statue of Saint Francis had been hacked to bits with an ax. The Holy Communion table had been covered with human excrement (Hackett 1942, 177–78).

Period Two: 1692–1830

A group of Franciscans returned to New Mexico in 1692 chastened by the revolt, now less radical, sometimes wayward, certainly more lax, and lacking much of the power and authority they wielded before 1680. Lenten penitential processions with large crosses, statues of Jesús Nazareno and the Mater Dolorosa, and flagellants wearing haircloth shirts, some in the habit of Saint Francis, regularly occurred, as did the Stations of the Cross. The First Order Franciscan friars were back. No Second Order nuns were ever mentioned. And by 1776 the Third Order of Saint Francis existed in Santa Fe, Santa Cruz de la Cañada, and Albuquerque. Writing to New Mexico's governor in 1794, Fray Cayetano José Bernal, the kingdom's Franciscan custodian, explained that the Third Order of Saint Francis had arrived in New Mexico following the 1692 reconquest, though "the exact date is unknown. . . . The Third Order . . . is distinct from the cofradías, with which it has no relation [por no pertenecer en nada]" (Weigle 1976a, 197, my translation). There could have been a thousand reasons for Bernal to draw this distinction precisely at the moment the Franciscan missions were being secularized and their personnel departing. Whatever else may have been happening among episcopally authorized confraternities, the Lenten rituals were still largely celebrated according to Franciscan Third Order molds.

What we know about the organization of Catholic rituals and practices in New Mexico in the eighteenth century largely comes from the encyclopedic ecclesiastical inspection Fray Francisco Atanasio Domínguez conducted in 1776. Fifteen years earlier, in 1760, Dr. Pedro Tamarón y Romeral, Durango's bishop, conducted a similar but more superficial review in which he recommended that the Franciscans missions be secularized; this was soon approved, with the further recommendation that the transition proceed slowly. The objective of Domínguez's inspection was to provide the Franciscan Province of the Holy Gospel with an accurate inventory of the Order's material possessions and interests in New Mexico in anticipation of the transfer.

Domínguez reported that, in 1776, Third Order Franciscan chapters existed in Albuquerque, Santa Fe, and Santa Cruz, but only at this last parish was it functioning well. There were 127 dues-paying men and women here, with a transept altar on which they kept a "very large image in the round of Jesús Nazareno clothed . . . [in a] purple tunic . . . crown, cross, and rope and a rather large Dolorosa" of the sort used during Good Friday processions. Here too was a "Holy Sepulcher [and] casket." Domínguez urged this Third Order to draw up better rules and keep more accurate accounts (1956, 75–76). Santa Fe's Third Order was in disarray, but it did have a nave altar on which stood "a clothed image" of Saint Francis. These Tertiaries were poor ("all its juice consists chiefly of misfortunes") and had no account books or sacra, borrowing what they needed from local confraternities (Domínguez 1956, 17, 18–19). In Albuquerque, the state of the Third Order Franciscans was even worse. Its members were broadly dispersed, gathering only once yearly on Holy Thursday and Good Friday. It had no altar of its own and no account or rule books, although the church did have a Holy Sepulcher containing a reposed Christ in loincloth, a statue of Our Lady of Sorrows, and a small image of Saint Francis. Domínguez urged Albuquerque's Tertiaries to "abandon the lethargy and laziness in which they have lived up to now" (1956, 147–48).

As for the confraternities under the jurisdiction of Durango's bishop, there were several in Santa Fe, Santa Cruz, and Albuquerque. Two of them were prospering; the rest were not. Santa Fe had a Confraternity of the Blessed Sacrament, for which there were no founding documents. Old-timers vaguely remembered that it merged with the Confraternity of Our Lady of the Light, but no one could recall a date. Santa Fe's residents, even "persons of the upper classes," believed that a Confraternity of the Poor Souls existed. It was a "devotion and not a confraternity," Domínguez explained, "evident from the fact that there are no brothers or other characteristics of a confraternity." Attached to one end of Santa Fe's church's transept, but very self-contained, was the chapel of the Confraternity of Our Lady of the Rosary, which locals called La Conquistadora, Our Lady of the Conquest. Her bejeweled statue stood about a *vara* (yard) high and was richly cloaked and adorned. Her chapel contained many beautiful things that had been donated by the town's elites. In the same chapel's nave was a small altar to the Blood of Christ "with a very nice large crucifix," and at its feet, a Mater Dolorosa also about a yard high. The confraternity was under the jurisdiction of Durango's bishop despite its lack of foundation and governance papers (Domínguez 1956, 19, 20, 24–27).

Santa Fe had two privately owned freestanding chapels in 1776. New Mexico's governor, don Francisco Marín del Valle, had the Chapel of the Confraternity of Our Lady of the Light constructed in 1760. He developed this ardent devotion, gained episcopal license for it, and largely funded most of its ritual activities. When Domínguez visited the chapel, he described it as well adorned, with many generous members, prospering, even loaning its sacra to the town's Third Order. The origin of the Chapel of San Miguel, Santa Fe's second freestanding oratory, was murky. Allegedly, it was first constructed in the 1640s, razed during the Pueblo Revolt, and restored in 1710 as a hospital. It, too, had no foundational documents, was very modestly furnished, mainly serving Santa Fe's Genízaros, and was jurisdictionally under episcopal control (Domínguez 1956, 32–39).

Santa Cruz had two cofradías in 1776. The first, devoted to the Blessed Sacrament, had obscure origins, lacked documents, and was bankrupt. Its devotees sometimes sponsored the celebration of a Mass. The second cofradía was devoted to Our Lady of Carmel. It was authorized in 1710 by the Provincial of the Carmelite Order in New Spain and licensed anew in 1760 by Durango's bishop to ensure that no one questioned it episcopal sanction or right to distribute indulgences. It owned a freestanding chapel that was well equipped, containing the many gifts its seven hundred members had donated. With so many dues-paying members, it was undoubtedly the biggest and richest confraternity in the kingdom (Domínguez 1956, 76–82, 249).

The only confraternity in Albuquerque was dedicated to the Poor Souls. Captain Antonio Montoya, a citizen of Bernalillo, started it in 1718 under Franciscan sanction. Its few possessions were kept in a small room attached to the church, which included dresses for the statue of its unnamed Virgin. Though largely moribund, the confraternity occasionally collected alms to pay for burials (Domínguez 1956, 148–49).

Finally, José Martín began what he thought was a Confraternity to the Poor Souls in Abiquiú sometime after 1754. Domínguez again explained that it was an unauthorized devotion. He ordered the devotion abolished, its assets liquidated, and its proceeds dispatched to the Franciscan provincial to pay for the Masses the friars had prayed but remained unpaid. Martín was insolvent. He lacked the 588 ewes owed for the Masses. Domínguez quickly stated that he had abolished the devotion but could not collect the debt (1956, 148).

Eighteen years later, in 1794, Governor Fernando Chacón was queried on the number and names of the kingdom's confraternities. His list was identical to Domínguez's. Nothing had changed. Not even the dogged insistence of Santa Fe's residents that they had a Confraternity of the Poor Souls (AGN Historia, 313, 348–50).

This exhaustive survey of New Mexican Third Order chapters, confraternities, oratories, and devotions establishes several facts. Only the Third Order Franciscans owned or easily could procure the objects necessary for Lenten rituals that later became associated with the Hermanos Penitentes: cross bearing, the processing of statues of Jesús Nazareno, the Mater Dolorosa, Tinieblas (Tenebrae) services around a Santo Entierro (Holy Sepulcher), and penitents undertaking acts of piety of various sorts including flagellation. Neither Franciscan, episcopal, nor local records easily established the origins of most religious organizations in New Mexico in the eighteenth century. Only Santa Fe's Confraternity of Our Lady of the Light, founded in 1760, and Santa Cruz's Confraternity of Our Lady of Carmel, relicensed that same year, had a clear, documentary provenance. The founding documents of most were lost. Few account books, inventories, and rules existed, and those that did were crumbling, missing pages, water stained, or vermin infested. Even the Third Order Franciscans at Santa Cruz, whom Domínguez found to be the most vibrant in the kingdom in 1776, were urged "to draw up new ones [i.e., foundational documents, rules, inventories, and accounts] and with the clarity specified" (1956, 75). It is hard to imagine that this prosperous Third Order with many members in a comparatively large Spanish town did not continue holding its Lenten rituals after secularization in 1797. There is no later mention of its implosion or declension. Aware that the friars would soon be replaced at Santa Cruz, Domínguez urged these Third Order Franciscans to draft documentation to avoid confusion whenever the next episcopal inspector arrived.

Equally important to this survey was the autonomous emergence of locally inspired devotions by groups committed to burying the poor at Abiquiú and Albuquerque. Above, we noted how many of New Mexico's Spanish residents were killed during Apache and Comanche raids in the second half of the eighteenth century, which helps explain why devotions emerged to bury the dead. They denominated themselves as confraternities despite clerical warnings that they were only technically local devotions.

The Franciscan Province of the Holy Gospel created the Custody of the Conversion of Saint Paul in 1616 to oversee the missions of New Mexico. Episcopal jurisdiction over them was transferred to Durango's bishop in 1729. Missions were originally imagined as transitional institutions chartered ideally for ten to fifteen years. In that time, they were to Christianize and Hispanicize their charges. Soon after 1760, the Crown concluded that it was time for their secularization. Indeed, it was way past due. New Mexico's missions, funded almost exclusively by royal subsidies, had been under Franciscan rule for 162 years. It was time for the kingdom's residents to support their own priests through obventions, those "offerings" or fees the faithful paid for Masses, special prayers, candles, baptisms, marriages, and burials. In 1797, secular priests were appointed at El Paso, Albuquerque, Santa Fe, and Santa Cruz, and in 1826 at Belén, El Vado, Abiquiú (these three were Genízaro villages), Taos, and San Juan.

New Mexico's Franciscans had numbered twelve in 1598, sixty-six in 1630, seventy in 1657, twenty-two in 1776, twenty-two in 1812, and nine in 1826. The last Franciscan, Fray Mariano de Jesús López, who died in 1848, was undoubtedly spread very thin, ministering to Zuñi, Ácoma, Laguna, and Isleta. In 1812, there were only four secular priests in New Mexico, the same number in 1817, five by 1826 (several of their parishes were *visitas*, visitation parishes without a resident priest), and ten by 1851. In 1812, New Mexico had twenty-six Indian pueblos and more than a hundred Spanish and Genízaro settlements. Had Durango's bishops ordained more secular priests to meet its needs, perhaps New Mexicans might not have created their own devotions. These staffing shortages arose because neither the seminaries of the religious orders nor episcopal sees admitted men of African, indigenous, or mixed racial ancestry to the priesthood until the middle of the nineteenth century. The dire straits New Mexico's Catholic faithful found themselves in for lack of priests was described by don Antonio Barreiro in his 1831 pamphlet, *A Quick Look at New Mexico*. Cadavers often went unburied for days, infants got baptized only at great cost, many died without confession or last rites, and most went a whole year without having a priest celebrate Mass (Carroll and Haggard 1942, 53).

The transition from Franciscan to secular control was also evident in a transformation of the sacral topography marked by altars and oratories. In 1776, Domínguez reported separate altars to Jesús Nazareno in Santa Fe, Santa Cruz, Abiquiú, Albuquerque, and Tomé (1956, passim). By 1814, Santa Fe's altar had been moved to a freestanding chapel in the church's courtyard, presumably funded by Antonio José Ortiz and his wife Rosa Bustamante, well-to-do Third Order Franciscans. By 1821, this chapel, too, was moved onto private property (SANM 21, 686; Boyd 1974, 445; Weigle 1976a, 44).

The constructions of privately owned chapels and oratories proliferated. They occurred in the instances noted above and quickened during secularization. Construction of the now famous Santuario de Chimayó was begun in 1813 by Bernardo Abeyta, a wealthy local merchant, to venerate the Santo Cristo de Esquipulas, a Franciscan devotion to the crucified Christ first promoted officially in 1594 in Esquipulas, Guatemala. Abeyta apparently visited the shrine in Guatemala and imported the cult to Chimayó, although the shrine's origin stories are much more bizarre, attributed to the apparition of crosses Abeyta putatively rescued. As his oratory grew in popularity and became a popular pilgrimage site, construction on an adjacent chapel dedicated to the Santo Niño de Atocha was begun in 1856. Both remained under family control until the middle of the twentieth century (Gutiérrez 1995, 71–86). Thomas Steele and Rowena Rivera conjecture that Bernardo Abeyta was intimately connected with the emergence of the Cofradía de Nuestro Padre Jesús Nazareno, his oratory serving as a meeting place beyond ecclesiastical control. Steele and Rivera further propose that the Hermanos Penitentes emerged in 1797, presumably with the secularization of the parishes at El Paso, Albuquerque, Santa Fe, and Santa Cruz, but without offering evidence or explanation (1985, 16–19).

Period Three: 1831–1886

By 1833, the emergence of devotions in northern New Mexico and southern Colorado calling themselves Cofradías de Nuestro Padre Jesús Nazareno, their members referring to each other as "hermanos," came to the attention of Durango's bishop, don José Antonio Laureano de Zubiría y Escalante. Recall Domínguez's 1776 insistence that for a confraternity to exist, members had to refer to each other as brothers. They now were. With only nine remaining Franciscan friars left in New Mexico in 1826, all stretched thin, ministering mostly to the Pueblo Indians, whom they vastly preferred, the Catholic faithful began conducting their own rituals independently based on collective memory, probably tutored by the many Third Order Franciscans still in their midst, fashioning their own crosses and statues or using the sacra previously stored in churches, which were now largely abandoned without resident custodians. The hermanos called the oratories where they congregated "moradas," which began proliferating in the 1820s (Ahlborn 1968). Weigle identified more than 120 moradas in New Mexico and southern Colorado's Río Arriba, and only twenty along Río Abajo (Weigle 1976a, fig. 3). These numbers loosely correspond to don Pedro Pino's 1812 count of 26 Indian Pueblos and 102 Spanish and Genízaro settlements in New Mexico.

Bishop Zubiría y Escalante took charge of Durango's see in 1831 and two years later visited New Mexico to assess the state of the church and the faith of its residents. In a letter of July 31, dispatched from Santa Cruz to the area's priests, he condemned the "Hermandad de Penitentes that had existed there for some years [*ya de bastantes años atrás*] without any authorization or even being known to the bishops." Their rituals were contrary to spirit of religion and the rules of the Holy Church because of the "excessive, indiscreet corporal penitence they publicly perform." He decried their large crosses, what he deemed their ritual "butchery [*más bien de carnicería*]," which could not be considered acts of legitimate penitence. He ordered priests not to allow such rituals, and to abolish this penitential brotherhood anywhere it was found (Chávez 1954, 110–11; Weigle 1976a, 195–96, my translation). In 1833, in 1845, and again in 1850, Bishop Zubiría y Escalante ordered his curas to prohibit any manifestation of the Hermanos Penitentes.

The bishop seemed unaware that the biggest and best-organized Third Order chapter was at Santa Cruz, with 127 dues-paying members. Likewise, since 1776, the village of Abiquiú, which began as a *congregación* (a consolidation or gathering) of "Christian Genízaro Indians," had been conducting the via crucis on Lenten Fridays. At day's end, "after dark, discipline [was] attended by those who come voluntarily." The pastor, Fray Sebastián Fernández, a Spaniard from Asturias, simply announced that the penitential ritual would occur but did not order anyone to attend (Domínguez 1956, 124).

New Mexico was occupied by US troops in August 1846 and with the signing the Treaty of Guadalupe Hidalgo in 1848, which ended the Mexican-American War, was annexed by the United States. Soon after, in 1850, New Mexico's Catholic Church was placed under the jurisdiction of St. Louis's bishop as an apostolic vicariate, became an independent diocese in 1853, and an archdiocese in 1875. The first American bishop, the French-born Jean-Baptiste Lamy, like his predecessor, attempted to curb the devotional zeal of the Cofradía de Nuestro Padre Jesús Nazareno, imposing two sets of rules on the "Brotherhood of Penance" in 1856 and 1857. Although Lamy did not refer to them as Third Order Franciscans, he did address them as the "Brotherhood of Penance" or "Brothers of the Catholic Confraternity of Penance." The Third Order of Saint Francis was originally known as the Brothers and Sisters of Penance. In New Mexico, this hermandad in the 1800s included women and men. Lamy never referred to the brotherhood by its proper name, Cofradía de Nuestro Padre Jesús Nazareno. Internalist accounts of the organization and rituals of this emergent cofradía are beyond my scope or interest here. I pause only to note that to join the hermandad, one began with instruction from the *maestro de novicios* (novice master), as was required when one wanted to join any of the three Franciscan Orders (Steele and Rivera 1985, 12–34).

Finally, this story comes full circle in 1886 when Santa Fe's archbishop, John Baptist Salpointe, concluded that the Hermanos Penitentes were a local variant of the Third Order Franciscans. He dispatched a circular to all known moradas in the archdiocese with the rule of the Third Order of Saint Francis that Pope Leo XIII had approved in 1883. Salpointe urged the wide distribution of the circular so that all the brothers would understand "that the devotion of the Penitentes absolutely comes from the Third Order Franciscans and should return to [the Order's rule] if they wish to gain its enriching indulgences" (*La Revista Católica*, March 21, 1886, 138–39). The Hermanos Penitentes, particularly those with moradas close to Santa Cruz, might have first known and later sensed this genealogy, but they were unwilling to do as the archbishop ordered.

Between the 1790s and 1890s, the Hermanos Penitentes morphed beyond the simple penitential confraternities of their birth and became the religious and political organization of the towns and villages in which they existed, eschewing the clear separation of church and state that American conquerors were imposing on subalterns. Perhaps because Bishop Salpointe had already retired from active duty and left Santa Fe for Banning, California, he must have felt freer to opine without moderating filters. In his 1898 ecclesiastical history of New Mexico, Arizona, and Colorado, entitled *Soldiers of the Cross*, he described the Cofradía de Nuestro Padre Jesús Nazareno in much harsher and less redemptive words. Salpointe stated categorically that the origin of the Penitentes was the Third Order of Saint Francis, which had "so degenerated that it is nothing to-day but an anomalous body of simple credulous men, under the guidance of some unscrupulous politicians. Their leaders encourage them . . . in the practice of their unbecoming so-called devotions, in order to secure their votes for the times of political elections." To further underscore his point, the ex-archbishop immediately quoted "N . . . de la Peña," who claimed: "The Penitentes, it is true, have framed a constitution somewhat resembling that of the Third Order, but entirely suited to their own political views. In fact, they have but self-constituted superiors; they do what they please and accomplish nothing good" (Salpointe 1898, 162). Peña here echoed the most pernicious caricatures Spanish New Mexicans had of Genízaros as criminals and good-for-nothings.

Angélico Chávez believed that the Penitentes were initially of Genízaro origin and that their organizational influence spread beyond their own communities into adjacent ones that were increasingly being settled by poor españoles and mestizos. They all wanted land and got it from the Mexican government after 1821 mainly as a way of thwarting Apache and Comanche depredations in northern New Mexico and southern Colorado. The Cofradía de Nuestro Padre Jesús Nazareno took on social and political roles, as they became the autonomous governance structure of the towns and villages they formed. This developmental pattern is not unique. It forms part of the larger history of how religious brotherhoods became labor unions and mutual aid societies, sodalities morphed into political parties. Even the Italian Mafia took the brotherhood mold as its own.

The Emergence of Genízaro Identity

As the number of Genízaros residing in Spanish towns increased, many were resettled and segregated into independent villages located at the margins of the kingdom. Belén was created as a Genízaro settlement in 1740, as were Abiquiú and Ojo Caliente in 1754, and San José del Vado and San Miguel del Vado in 1794. By strategically locating these independent, self-governing villages along known nomadic Indian raiding routes, the residents of Santa Fe, Albuquerque, and Santa Cruz purged their towns of persons they deemed dangerous. If Apache and Comanche raiders first attacked Genízaro villages, their force would be blunted before they reached wealthier Spanish towns. This is precisely what the word "Genízaro" means (etymologically from the Turkish *yeni*, "new," and *çeri*, "troops"). Like the Janissaries, the captured slaves of the Ottoman Empire pressed into battle as a forward line of shock troops, Genízaros were relocated to hold such defensive positions against the indios bárbaros.

Gradually, adult Genízaros were pressed into military service against their former kin. Father Delgado reported in 1744, just four years after Belén was established, that its Genízaros were obliged to "go out and explore the country in pursuit of the enemy, which they do with great bravery and zeal" (AGN Historia 25-25, 229). By 1782, Father Morfi described the kingdom's Genízaros as "great soldiers, very warlike and the ones most feared by our enemies" (AGN Historia 25-8, 147). Governor Pedro Fermín de Mendinueta must have been of similar opinion, for when he ordered that a band of Apache be given chase by flying dragoons in 1771, he dispatched fifty-five Genízaros in their pursuit (SANM 10, 925). For their services as soldiers, scouts, and interpreters during the second half of the eighteenth century, Genízaros solicited and sometimes received military posts, such as Manuel Antonio in 1768 at Santa Fe's presidio (AGN Provincias Internas 102-7, 256).

New Mexico's most comprehensive colonial census was carried out in 1790. It listed a few Genízaros as artisans, blacksmiths, silversmiths, masons, carders, spinners, and weavers—far from the stereotypes Spaniards had of them. One out of every five Genízaros reported owning land with "farmer" as their occupation. But the majority of Genízaros were recorded as day laborers, field hands, and servants. As the development of export-oriented agriculture and livestock production progressed during the first half of the nineteenth century, those Genízaros who had been emancipated quickly became debt peons of their former masters. Father Morfi summarized this Genízaro predicament when he wrote in 1776 that "without land, without livestock, without any other manner of subsisting than with their bows and arrows . . . they [Genízaros] have surrendered themselves into wage labor and suffer all sorts of tyrannies" (AGN Historia 25-8, 147). By Mexican independence in 1821, they remained marginal to the kingdom's affairs, but as their autonomous villages grew in size and number, they began developing a distinct and prideful Indo-Hispano reactive identity (Langham Olmsted 1975). Marcos Sánchez demonstrates this. A resident of the Genízaro village of Belén, he was forcefully apprehended by the authorities of Tomé, the Spanish village just across the Río Grande, for maltreating his concubine in 1793. He was reported to have vociferously protested, saying, "I am a Genízaro unworthy of such base treatment (SANM 13, 346).

When Father Domínguez described the kingdom's social stratification in 1776, he said that it was broadly divided into three groups: "superiors, middlemen, and the infamous" (1956, 241). This chapter has described and documented the origins of those made infamous by virtue of their intrusion, initially as the captive enemy indios bárbaros and as extruded Puebloans, primarily exiled women and infants of unknown parentage. Throughout the eighteenth century, Genízaros gradually demonstrated their personhood, shattering some of the caricatures by which they had been persistently reviled.

The most important of these were their slave and ex-slave status, their lack of kinship ties, their lack of community membership, and their location at bottom of social hierarchies. Men who should have been killed in battle lived as slaves, as shunned living dead. Boys and girls who had been torn from their natal fathers and mothers were pressed into domestic servitude. As such, they fundamentally lacked fathers, the principal defenders of one's personhood, membership, and social standing in Spanish society.

How might a confraternity provide social connection? Why might have Genízaros found the rituals of the Cofradía de Nuestro Padre Jesús Nazareno compelling for their own identity formation and emergence as adults in a society that had infantilized, marginalized, and deprecated them? Were these men and women, who had grown up as orphans, seeking an omnipotent father? Were oedipal dramas and displaced rage being enacted when the hermanos crucified their father on Good Friday? Initiates into the confraternity, known as Hermanos de Sangre (Brothers of Blood), in time became Hermanos de Luz (Brothers of Light), and town leaders only after they had demonstrated their penitential piety zealously throughout the course of the year, and especially after they had ushered their Padre Jesús to his crucifixion, death, and burial as bloody flagellants. In the theology of the crucifixion, Genízaros found a particularly powerful metaphor for a death of human bondage, for in it one finds ideas of both death and renewal. Christ died because of humanity's slavery to sin. His resurrection assured Christians access to eternal life anew through redemption. The word "redemption" means to ransom one from the bondage of slavery through the martyrdom of a sacrificial victim. Christ was that victim. Through his death, Christians atoned for their sins and were reconciled. Those who had been separated by sin were integrated anew.

Christ's crucifixion and resurrection offer a series of status elevations—from slavery to freedom, from death to life, from separation to integration—that parallel the status changes that characterized the psychic condition of Genízaros as they moved into their own villages, forged independent identities, and asserted their stature as independent landholders. For as Marcos Sánchez so proudly proclaimed in 1793, "I am a Genízaro unworthy of...base treatment" (SANM 13, 346).

Note

1. Very special thanks to William B. Taylor for his careful reading of an earlier draft of this chapter and for offering his incisive comments. I have also drawn on a much older critique of some of the material herein by Ross Frank; thanks to him, too.

References

Ahlborn, Richard E. 1968. *The Penitente Moradas of Abiquiú*. Washington, DC: Smithsonian Institution Press.

Archivo General de la Nación (AGN). Documents are cited by the archive's category, followed by the volume and number, finally with the folio page numbers.

Benavides, Alonso de. 1945. *Fray Alonso de Benavides' Revised Memorial of 1634*. Edited and translated by Frederick W. Hodge, George P. Hammond, and Agapito Rey. Albuquerque: University of New Mexico Press.

Bermejo y Carballo, José. 1882. *Glorias religiosas de Sevilla*. Seville: Imprenta y Librería del Salvador.

Bloom, Lansing B. 1939. "The Vargas Encomienda." *New Mexico Historical Review* 14, no. 4 (October): 367–71.

Boyd, Elizabeth. 1974. *Popular Arts of Spanish New Mexico*. Santa Fe: Museum of New Mexico Press.

Brooks, James F. 2002. *Captives and Cousins: Slavery, Kinship, and Community in the Southwest Borderlands*. Chapel Hill: University of North Carolina Press.

Brooks, James F., and Bonnie Martin, eds. 2015. *Linking the Histories of Slavery in North America and Its Borderlands*. Santa Fe: School for Advanced Research Press.

Brugge, David M. 1968. *Navajos in the Catholic Church Records of New Mexico, 1694–1875*. Window Rock, AZ: Navajo Tribe.

Carroll, H. Bailey, and J. Villasana Haggard, trans. 1942. *Three New Mexico Chronicles: The* Exposición *of Don Pedro Bautista Pino, 1812; The* Ojeada *of Lic. Antonio Barreiro, 1832; and the Additions by Don José Agustín de Escudero, 1849*. Albuquerque: Quivira Society.

Chávez, Angélico. 1954. "The Penitentes of New Mexico." *New Mexico Historical Review* 29, no. 2 (April): 97–123.

———. 1979. "Genízaros." In *Handbook of North American Indians*, vol. 9, *Southwest*, edited by Alfonso Ortiz and William C. Sturtevant, 198–200. Washington, DC: Smithsonian Institution.

Cook, Sherburne F. 1976. *The Conflict between the California Indian and White Civilization*. Berkeley: University of California Press.

Cutter, Donald C., trans. 1975. "An Anonymous Statistical Report of New Mexico in 1765." *New Mexico Historical Review* 50, no. 3 (October): 347–52.

DeLay, Brian. 2008. *War of a Thousand Deserts*. New Haven, CT: Yale University Press.

Domínguez, Fray Francisco Atanasio. 1956. *The Missions of New Mexico, 1776: A Description by Fray Francisco Atanasio Domínguez, with Other Contemporary Documents*. Edited and translated by Fray Angélico Chávez and Eleanor B. Adams. Albuquerque: University of New Mexico Press.

Ekberg, Carl J. 2007. *Stealing Indian Women: Native Slavery in the Illinois Country*. Urbana: University of Illinois Press.

Ellis, Florence Hawley. 1955. "Tomé and Father J.B.R." *New Mexico Historical Review* 30 (July): 89–144.

Foster, George M. 1953. "Cofradía and Compadrazgo in Spain and Spanish America." *Southwestern Journal of Anthropology* 9, no. 1 (Spring): 1–28.

———. 1969. "Godparents and Social Networks in Tzintzuntzan." *Southwestern Journal of Anthropology* 25, no. 3 (Autumn): 261–78.

Gallay, Alan. 2002. *The Indian Slave Trade: The Rise of the English Empire in the American South, 1670–1717*. New Haven, CT: Yale University Press.

Gallegos, Bernardo. 1992. *Literacy, Education, and Society in New Mexico, 1693–1821*. Albuquerque: University of New Mexico Press.

Gudeman, Stephen. 1971. "The Compadrazgo as a Reflection of the Natural and Spiritual Person." *Proceedings of the Royal Anthropological Institute of Great Britain and Ireland*, no. 1971: 43–49.

Gutiérrez, Ramón A. 1991. *When Jesus Came, the Corn Mothers Went Away: Marriage, Sexuality, and Power in New Mexico, 1500–1846*. Stanford, CA: Stanford University Press.

———. 1993. "Family Structures." In *The Encyclopedia of the North American Colonies*, vol. 3, edited by Jacob Ernest Cooke, 672–82. New York: Charles Scribner's Sons.

———. 1995. "El Santuario de Chimayo: A Syncretic Shrine in New Mexico." In *Festivals and Celebrations in American Ethnic Communities*, edited by Ramón Gutiérrez and Geneviève Fabre, 71–86. Albuquerque: University of New Mexico Press.

———. 2016a. "Doña Teresa de Aguilera y Roche before the Inquisition: The Travails of a Seventeenth-Century Aristocratic Woman in New Mexico." In *Women in Early America*, edited by Thomas A. Foster, 7–42. New York: New York University Press.

———. 2016b. "What's in a Name? The History and Politics of Hispanic and Latino Panethnicities." In *The New Latino Studies Reader: A Twenty-First-Century Perspective*, edited by Ramón A. Gutiérrez and Tomás Almaguer, 19–53. Berkeley: University of California Press.

Hackett, Charles W., ed. 1937. *Historical Documents Relating to New Mexico, Nueva Vizcaya, and Approaches Thereto, 1773*. 3 vols. Washington, DC: Carnegie Institution.

———. 1942. *Revolt of the Pueblo Indians of New Mexico and Otermín's Attempted Reconquest, 1680–1682*. Albuquerque: University of New Mexico Press.

Hämäläinen, Pekka. 2008. *The Comanche Empire*. New Haven, CT: Yale University Press.

Hammond, George P., and Agapito Rey. 1953. *Don Juan de Oñate: Colonizer of New Mexico, 1595–1628*. Albuquerque: University of New Mexico Press.

Horvath, Steven M. 1979. "The Social and Political Organization of the Genízaros of Plaza de Nuestra Señora de los Dolores de Belén, New Mexico, 1740–1812." PhD diss., Brown University.

Langham Olmsted, Virginia, trans. and comp. 1975. *New Mexico Spanish and Mexican Colonial Censuses, 1790, 1823, 1847*. Albuquerque: New Mexico Genealogical Society.

Magnaghi, Russell M. 1998. *Indian Slavery, Labor, Evangelization, and Captivity in the Americas: An Annotated Bibliography*. Lanham, MD: Scarecrow Press.

Mintz, Sidney W., and Eric R. Wolf. 1950. "An Analysis of Ritual Co-parenthood (Compadrazgo)." *Southwestern Journal of Anthropology* 6, no. 4 (Winter): 341–68.

Moreno Navarro, Isidro. 1974. *Las Hermandades Andaluzas: Una aproximación desde la antropología*. Seville: Secretariado de Publicaciones de la Universidad de Sevilla.

Olexer, Barbara J. 2005. *The Enslavement of the American Indian in Colonial Times*. Columbia, MD: Joyous Publishing.

Ortelli, Sara. 2007. *Trama de una guerra conveniente: Nueva Vizcaya y la sombra de los apaches (1748–1790)*. México: Centro de Estudios Históricos, El Colegio de México.

Patterson, Orlando. 1982. *Slavery and Social Death: A Comparative Study*. Cambridge, MA: Harvard University Press.

Pérez de Villagrá, Gaspar. 1992. *Historia de la Nueva México, 1610*. Albuquerque: University of New Mexico Press.

Rael-Gálvez, Estevan. 2002. "Identifying Captivity and Capturing Identity: Narratives of American Indian Slavery in Colorado and New Mexico, 1776–1934." PhD diss., University of Michigan.

Rister, Carl Coke. 1955. *Comanche Bondage: Dr. John Charles Beales's Settlement of La Villa de Dolores on Las Moras Creek in Southern Texas of the 1830's, with an Annotated Reprint of Sarah Ann Horn's Narrative of Her Captivity among the Comanches, Her Ransom by Traders in New Mexico, and Return via the Santa Fé Trail*. Glendale, CA: A. H. Clark.

Salpointe, John Baptist. 1898. *Soldiers of the Cross: Notes on the Ecclesiastical History of New Mexico, Arizona and Colorado*. Banning, CA: Saint Boniface's Industrial School.

Sartorius, David. 2013. *Ever Faithful: Race, Loyalty, and the Ends of Empire in Spanish Cuba*. Durham, NC: Duke University Press.

Simmons, Marc. 1973. *Little Lion of the Southwest: A Life of Manuel Antonio Chaves*. Chicago: Sage Books.

Snow, David H. 1983. "A Note on Encomienda Economics in Seventeenth-Century

New Mexico." In *Hispanic Arts and Ethnohistory in the Southwest*, edited by Marta Weigle, 350–59. Santa Fe: Ancient City Press.

Spanish Archives of New Mexico (SANM). Microfilm edition, listed by reel and frame number.

Steele, Thomas J., and Rowena A. Rivera. 1985. *Penitente Self-Government: Brotherhoods and Councils, 1797–1947*. Santa Fe: Ancient City Press.

Swadesh, Frances Leon. 1974. *Los Primeros Pobladores: Hispanic Americans of the Ute Frontier*. Notre Dame, IN: Notre Dame University Press.

Tamarón y Romeral, Pedro. 1954. *Bishop Tamarón's Visitation of New Mexico, 1760*. Albuquerque: University of New Mexico Publications in History.

Taylor, William B. 1996. *Magistrates of the Sacred: Priests and Parishioners in Eighteenth-Century Mexico*. Stanford, CA: Stanford University Press.

Velasco Ávila, Cuauhtémoc. 2012. *La frontera étnica en el noreste mexicano: Los comanches entre 1800–1841*. México: Centro de Investigaciones y Estudios Superiores en Antropología Social.

Webb, Daniel. 2017. "Mapping the Apachería: American Indian Sovereignty and State Power in the U.S.-Mexico Borderlands, 18th–19th Century." PhD diss., University of Chicago.

Weber, David J. 2005. *Bárbaros: Spaniards and Their Savages in the Age of Enlightenment*. New Haven, CT: Yale University Press.

Weigle, Marta. 1976a. *Brothers of Light, Brothers of Blood: The Penitentes of the Southwest*. Albuquerque: University of New Mexico Press.

———. 1976b. *A Penitente Bibliography*. Albuquerque: University of New Mexico Press.

Zárate Salmerón, Jerónimo de. 1966. *Relaciones: An Account of Things Seen and Learned by Father Jerónimo de Zárate Salmerón from the Year 1538 to Year 1626*. Albuquerque: Horn and Wallace.

Zavala, Silvio Arturo. 1967. *Los esclavos indios en Nueva España*. México: El Colegio Nacional.

CHAPTER SIX

The Colonial Genízaro Mission Pueblo of Belén

SAMUEL E. SISNEROS

The cruel practices of Native American tribes and Spanish settlers of obtaining indigenous captives, selling them, and placing them in servitude deprived these unfortunate victims of every personal and cultural component they had known. Battles, raids, trade fairs, and the exchange of hostages, as well as Spanish colonial institutions all contributed to the sad fate of captured Indians. These tribal people became classified as Genízaros, assuming an identity and low social caste not of their choosing. Despite their status, some astute and valiant members of this group used newly established Spanish institutions for their gain, becoming well informed about the indoctrination process of the Catholic Church, Spanish law, and land ownership to seek justice and improve their lives and those of their descendants. The little-known mission pueblo of Nuestra Señora de Belén is a testament to this astonishing legacy in eighteenth- and early nineteenth-century New Mexico.

The following chronology of historical documents, oral histories, genealogies, and local folk traditions validates Belén as one of New Mexico's earliest and key Genízaro settler communities. The Genízaros' Native American identity and new Spanish Christian social status were used initially by both the Genízaros and the Spanish authorities to construct Belén as a Pueblo Indian enclave. Essential to Belén's foundation was a strong connection to the Pueblo Indian world, particularly that of the Tiwa Isleta Pueblo, and to the mission communities of El Paso del Norte. The following accounts of periodic self-governance, political unity, and mobility will help to provide a compelling story of this elusive group, whose presence has escaped the annals of colonial history. This work will also demonstrate that Belén's original segregated communities of Genízaro and Spanish citizens grew tremendously and through cultural transition and miscegenation became a mestizo or mixed-race, mixed-culture village. Consequently, the small village lost its Genízaro Indian identity by the mid-1800s. Nevertheless, Belén's indigenous legacy survives through various manifestations, as will be discussed below.

Belén is located thirty-five miles south of Albuquerque along the Río Grande agricultural corridor in the Río Abajo (south-central New Mexico). It was settled alongside the ancient Camino Real, the trading route that connected New Mexico to Mexico City. As a modern railway and commercial crossroads, Belén lays claim to being a "Hub City." Various civic plaques and signage as well as web pages extol Belén's Spanish colonial beginnings, such as the following statement: "Two Spaniards, Captain Don Diego Torres and Antonio Salazar, Torres' brother-in-law, founded Belén in 1740" (City of Belén, n.d.).[1] From this one-line introduction, the narrative jumps to nostalgic railroad history of the 1900s and to anecdotes about Belén's "pioneer," John Becker.[2] There is only minimal note of Belén's Genízaro origins and pioneering history. Also, little attention is given to Belén's historic parish church, Franciscan convent, and *plaza* site, known as La Plaza Vieja, whose adobe ruins were abandoned to the point of disappearance by the 1940s.[3] Aside from the current limited narratives of local history, the complete history of Belén is far more complex and requires further illumination.

The Belén area was initially populated much earlier than the 1740 "official settlement date." There were settlements between Isleta and Socorro by Tiwa and Piro indigenous groups as early as AD 1200. A pre–Spanish contact Pueblo pit house is located on the archaeological site on the east side of the Río Grande from Belén. During the 1500s, there were various Franciscan missions to the Tiwa, Piro, and Tompiro Indians in the Manzano Mountains and nearby Salinas areas located east of the Río Grande. These remarkable missions were abandoned by the 1670s because of Apache attacks and droughts, causing mission members to abandon the area and join the Isleta Pueblo and Piro settlements near the Río Grande (Wiseman 1995; Marshall and Walt 1984; Bletzer 2013). As the Piro settlements grew in the Río Grande Valley, the descendants of colonists who arrived in don Juan de Oñate's settlement in 1598 began to migrate from northern New Mexico to the Río Abajo area and to cluster around the Isleta mission district. These Spanish families had experienced one hundred years of Spanish colonization and settlement. They established *estancias* (large landholdings) near the present towns of Los

FIGURE 6.1 Los Genízaros signature, with rubric from "Petition by Los Genízaros to populate the Old Pueblo of Sandía," 1733 (SANM, Series I: 1208). Courtesy of New Mexico State Records Center and Archives, Santa Fe, New Mexico.

Padillas, Los Lunas, Valencia, and Tomé. In 1680, Spanish citizens along with Isletans and Piros fled New Mexico to the Guadalupe del Paso area (modern Ciudad Juárez) in order to escape the Pueblo Revolt. Over a decade later, don Diego de Vargas, in a move to recolonize the region, brought back many El Paso del Norte refugees; a few families chose to resettle in the Río Abajo area.[4] Their contemporaries, the Genízaros, also began to migrate to the area as early as the 1720s. They played an important role in the settlement process for several decades thereafter.

An organized group of Río Abajo Genízaros advocated for participation in the Spanish system of community land ownership in 1733. The group petitioned Gervasio Cruzat y Góngora, the governor of New Mexico, to grant them permission to establish their own settlement and assign them a pueblo at the site of the abandoned Sandía Pueblo.[5] The petition, although not granted, sheds important information about Genízaros in general and in particular those who were dispersed throughout the Río Abajo. The term *indios dispersos* (dispersed Indians), as this Río Abajo Genízaro group described themselves, was used at the time for Indians who were not "wild" but rather pacified, little or poorly evangelized, and living on the margins of Spanish society (Rieu-Millan 1990, 140–41).

This unique request was written in a formal tone, embellished with many religious metaphors and patronizing epithets. It appears by its plural first-person sentence construction, along with its ease and familiarity with the issues at hand, to have been written by one of the Genízaros who had acquired literary skills and the facility of diplomacy.[6] Amazingly, the petition for reassignment was signed "Los Genízaros," with an attached rubric. This distinguishes the document as the only known example of Genízaro group self-representation and evidence of a wide, regional Genízaro unity.

Throughout the appeal, the Genízaros stressed contentment at being new Christians by stating that they were grateful to be in the fold of both the Catholic Church and the Spanish Crown. Yet they expressed they were disadvantaged and desperate, with no land or work to care for their families. They also asserted their position as Christianized Indians to differentiate themselves from the "enemy pagan" Plains Indians, a status they emphasized they had been freed from, and from the Pueblo Indians, who they claimed were involved in idolatry and witchcraft. Although they had once lived in servitude, their petition did not include Indians still living as *criados*, noting that they were obligated to pay their own ransom through service. According to the social meaning of the verb *criar*, after being ransomed or bought, criados were raised as Christians and given the surnames of their families, who benefited from their labor as servants and ranch hands, and their talents with crafts such as weaving.[7] Yet perhaps as a persuasive tactic, they connected themselves to these "other" indigenous groups by stating the possibility of returning to the heathen life if they did not get assistance. Not only did "Los Genízaros" invoke their religiosity and indigeneity, they proposed a tactical defensive network to protect frontier communities against enemy raids, including building defensive structures such as a fortress wall around Sandía Pueblo.

The petition also included the revelation that "Los Genízaros" comprised more than one hundred families scattered throughout New Mexico. This demonstrates that Genízaros were unified and, although from many nations (tribes), were aware of the demographics of their separate communities. The governor's first response was to request a list of the "Indian" petitioners' names and their distinct nations. The resulting list was produced, written in the same penmanship as the petition. The title as translated into English reads: "List of the Native Genízaro Sons found dispersed in this Kingdom of New Mexico. First in this Río Abajo Jurisdiction are the following married families." Perhaps another list was forthcoming with names from the northern region (Río Arriba), since this first list enumerated only seventeen of the said one hundred families. It included their Spanish first and last names, the Indian ethnic group of the male heads of each family and of the eight single adult males, the wives' first names, and the number of children in each family unit. The list totaled seventy-six persons and represented Genízaros from the Pánana (Pawnee), Jumano, Ndé (Apache), Caigua (Kiowa), Yuta (Ute), Aa (Jicarilla Apache?), and Tano Pueblo Nations.[8] The governor responded that he would not allow this type of settlement in an unpopulated village, and the petition was not granted. "Los Genízaros" remained "dispersed" in the Río Abajo (see the petition and petitioner list in Appendix A to this chapter). This group may have been freed servants and exiled Tiwas living in the town of Bernalillo, but many of Los Genízaros began to appear in the Isleta mission jurisdiction even before petition was submitted. They and other Genízaros are recorded in Isleta mission church sacramental records in the late 1720s and 1730s. These records provide insight not only into the assimilation of Genízaros living in the Río Abajo but also of their origins, identity, social status, and familial relationships.

Starting in the late 1720s, some of the first non-Pueblo Indians were annotated in the Isleta church registers, mostly Apache children and adults of unknown parentage, indicating that they had been uprooted and taken during military excursions or purchased from Nuhmuhnuh (tribal Comanches) at trade fairs, becoming household servants at Isleta or nearby Hispanic villages and later absorbed into Tiwa Isleta society or the Genízaro class. The earliest non-Pueblo marriages were performed in 1727. The first was the marriage of Antonio Curuna, a Tiwa Indian, to Isabel, from the Apache Nation. Later, two indigenous couples were wed, these being Sebastian married to Rosa and Miguel paired with Gertrudes—all Apaches with no surnames. The first person specifically identified as a Genízaro was noted in the 1728 marriage entry of Andrés Trujillo, a Pánana Indian, and Pascuala Felisiana, who is listed with no surname and as a Genízara. A person listed with no surname was an indication of the early process of assimilation.

Another early non-Pueblo Indian family was documented in the mission church of Isleta on July 9, 1730, at the baptism of Antonio Grolé, child of Antonio Grolé and Teresa Gallego.[9] This couple was the first family listed in the 1733 petitioner list of Los Genízaros. Antonio Grolé or Gurulé once resided in the Bernalillo district near old Sandía Pueblo, where he was one of the many Indian servants of Jacques Grolet's large family estate in the neighboring town of Bernalillo. Jacques "Santiago" Grolet was a Frenchman who was one of the three survivors of the failed La Salle Expedition on the Texas Gulf Coast in 1684. Living among various Indian groups in the area, Grolet and the others surrendered to a Spanish military detachment and were taken to the interior of Mexico and then to Spain, where they served two years in prison for leaving the shipwreck. They got permission to return to New Spain, where they made their way to Zacatecas and joined a group of colonizers headed to New Mexico in 1692. Grolet's children and his Indian servants would take the Hispanicized version of "Gurulé" as a surname (Lewis 2019). Apparently, the Antonio Gurulé family moved from the Sandía/Bernalillo area to the Isleta/Belén area according to the record of their child's baptism and other documents.

In addition to the Gurulé family, Isleta church parish registers give insight into the lives of other early Belén area families such as Reymundo Jójola and Francisca (no surname). Jójola is a Tiwa Isleta surname. This family was apparently important in Isleta Pueblo society during the first half of the 1700s. In 1730, they were listed as residents of Isleta at the baptism of their first child, Juan Pedro Jójola. In the 1750 Isleta Pueblo census, Reymundo Jójola and Francisca's household is listed first, indicating that they were the head family and prominent in the community's social hierarchy (Langham Olmsted 1981). In addition, Reymundo and Francisca often acted as godparents at many Pueblo baptisms and marriages as early as 1726. In one marriage record, Reymundo is given the honorific titles of *Don* and in another *Fiscal Mayor*, or local juridical official. He also appeared consistently as the lead official witness in many church records from 1755 to 1757. By August 1757, Isleta tribal officials, Governor Joseph Costal, War Captain Eucebio, and Domingo the *casique* accused Reymundo of extortion. Witnesses identified Reymundo (his surname is not provided in the document) as *el fiscal* and a native Isleta Indian during testimony. They said that Reymundo went from house to house instigating dissention and requesting paybacks. They also accused him of severely injuring Andrés Lente to the degree that he was not able to testify against him. Reymundo was consequently charged and imprisoned. It is not known what his final punishment was; perhaps he was banished from Isleta.[10] This episode appears to be lost in the historical memory of Isletans today, although oral tradition recounts "Te'é Reymundo" (Grandfather Reymundo), remembered for uniting Isleta after the return from the Pueblo Revolt.[11]

Nevertheless, shortly after Reymundo's troubles in Isleta, he and his family appeared as residents of Belén. On October 30, 1760, Reymundo Jójola and Francisca were noted as Indians from Belén instead of Indians from Isleta in the marriage investigation of their son Tomás Jójola. Reymundo and Francisca's other sons, Juan Pedro, Juan José, and Santiago, all appear as residents of Belén after 1760. Their daughter, Juana María, was married at San Agustín de Isleta Church in 1756 to Juan Ramos (also Martín), also an Isleta Tiwa. This couple was living in Sabinal (a Belén satellite plaza discussed later) by the 1780s, and they were either listed as general Indians or as Genízaros. Reymundo and Francisca's son Juan José moved to El Paso del Norte, where on July 7, 1781, at the mission church of Nuestra Señora de Guadalupe, he married Manuela (no surname), a Native Indian woman. The marriage record listed him as Juan JoJana, Genízaro Indian, widow of Josefa Rivera, and the legitimate son of Reymundo JoJana and María Francisca, natives of Belén, New Mexico. A later record has Juan with the regular "Jojola" spelling—listed as an Indian from the mission pueblo of El Paso del Norte.

Reymundo and Francisca's children established the Tiwa family line of the Belén "Genízaro" and then "Hispanic" branches of the families surnamed Jójola, Ramos, and Martín (Buxton 1998, 27), and apparently a branch in the El Paso area. The cultural transition of this Jójola family demonstrates how a Pueblo Indian person or family could move into the Genízaro category even without having experienced captivity or servitude. Families such as this might have functioned as cultural brokers between the Pueblo, Genízaro, and Spanish cultures, and between the El Paso area and northern New Mexico.[12]

The family of Ventura Jójola and Jacinta Baca was a different Jójola family but had similar beginnings in Belén. In the San Agustín de Isleta Church marriage register in 1737, they appear without surnames, but in subsequent records they are identified as Ventura Jójola (or Cruz) and Jacinta Baca. He was most likely a Tiwa Indian, and she was often listed as a Coyote. In New Mexico and in particular Belén, the "Coyote" label was usually synonymous with Genízaro and suggested that a person was born into an Indian servant family.[13] In 1750, Ventura Jójola and Jacinta Baca resided in Los Chávez (a village near Belén) but eventually moved to Belén, where they and subsequent generations were listed as Genízaros or Indians of Belén. The mostly females in this family went by the surnames Jójola, Cruz, or Baca and married into various local Belén families, resulting in the eventual loss of the Jójola surname in this family. The 1762 prenuptial investigation of Ventura Jójola and Jacinta Baca's daughter Josefa noted that she, along with her fiancé, José Manuel Gurulé, were Belén Indians. José Manuel Gurulé was the son of Antonio Gurulé and Teresa, mentioned previously. Another daughter married the son of the Spanish "founder of Belén," Diego Torres, at San Agustín de Isleta Church on January 1, 1759.[14] Ventura and Jacinta's daughters became the matrons of key families of Belén's Plaza de los Genízaros, Plaza de Jarales, and Sabinal. These families and communities will be discussed later on.

Another Ventura (surname unknown) whose life and travels were noted in the historical record was of particular interest to colonial officials because he offered them a better strategic understanding of Navajo affairs.[15] Ventura's testimony reveals that he was from the Kiowa Nation and was captured by Comanches in the early 1700s and sold at age eight to Ventura Mestas, who in turn sold him to Antonio, a rich Indian from Senecú in the El Paso del Norte region. Ventura returned to northern New Mexico in the service of don Carlos Fernández for one year, and then became the household servant of Diego Torres in Belén, where he married Rosa in 1745. She was an Indian criada who had been brought up from childhood by Diego Torres. Ventura and Diego Torres had an altercation resulting in Ventura's exile to the Navajo province. After a year and a half with the Navajos, Ventura went to San Géronimo de Taos Pueblo, where he joined a military campaign against the Utes; upon completing his service, he returned to Belén to his wife Rosalía or Rosa, where he started a family in his own house as a free Genízaro.[16]

The preceding stories of the origins of early Belén Genízaro families and their social, cultural, and political interactions show that Genízaros were established in the Belén area prior to and during the Spanish land grant settlement of 1740. They also relate that Genízaros became participants in Spanish religious, civil, and legal systems, were multitribal, had kinship and political ties to Isleta, and were unified under a unique cultural identity. In 1744, Fray Juan Miguel Menchero made a very telling and keen observation about a group of fifty Río Abajo Genízaro families who were congregated at Tomé. He might have confused the Tomé area for the location of the Genízaros at Belén, for there is evidence of only a couple of Genízaro families ever residing at Tomé. Nevertheless, he said that this large Genízaro group comprised of Indians from "distinct and distant nations" who had been captured by the Apaches and Comanches and eventually joined together, numbered fifty families living "in great union as if they were their own nation."[17]

After the initial Genízaro migrations to the Río Abajo areas of Isleta and Belén, Spanish families began to arrive in the 1740s. They came from Santa Cruz de la Cañada (near Española and Chimayó) and from other areas in northern New Mexico. These migrants petitioned Governor Gaspar Domínguez de Mendoza for a royal land grant, and on December 9, 1740, they received and took possession of the Nuestra Señora de Belén Grant, which included 121,633 acres. The lead petitioner was Captain Diego de Torres, along with thirty recipients.[18] The other lead petitioner was Antonio de Salazar, who was the husband of Diego de Torres's sister María Torres. Antonio de Salazar was also of Pueblo Indian ancestry, even though he was categorized as a Spanish colonizer. Antonio's father, Agustín Salazar, was noted as being an interpreter of the Zuni language, which was his mother's native Indian language (Sisneros 1996).

Shortly after the grantees arrived in Belén, a group of Genízaros claimed that Spanish settlers were trespassing on their land and committing many injustices toward them. The leader of the Belén Genízaros was Antonio Casados, a captive from the Apache Kiowa Nation and previous servant of Captain Diego de Torres. In 1745, Casados traveled 2,500 miles to Mexico City to petition the viceroy to protect the rights of his "pueblo" and to evict the Spanish settlers from Belén. Historians suggest that Casados went by himself to Mexico City, but a closer look at the viceroy's report and the court records reveals that Casados joined others on his trip and became involved in a much larger unified Pueblo and Genízaro effort to challenge Governor Joaquín Codallos y Rabal and the Spanish citizens of New Mexico.

Upon arriving at El Paso del Norte, Casados was confronted by the cohort of Francisco Padilla and Manuel de la Cruz, who were also on the road from New Mexico to Mexico City to take their demands to the viceroy.[19] Padilla had already been in confrontation with Spanish officials at Laguna Pueblo in 1737, where he was accused of sedition for inciting Laguna Indians to revolt and for trying to insert himself as mayor of the pueblo. Padilla's accomplice in the Laguna affair was a Belén Genízaro named Cristóbal Caraquis, a Pánana (Pawnee) Indian;[20] Padilla also proved to be an instigator in Casados's case. When the New Mexico group arrived at El Paso, Padilla began to pressure Casados to speak against New Mexico's governor, but Casados would not concede and planned on denouncing only the Spanish of Belén. However, Padilla convinced Casados to continue on to Mexico City along with him and Manuel de la Cruz to jointly take their grudges to the viceroy. Cruz, an Indian, was identified by the viceroy's report as the chief war captain and representative of the twenty casiques and another twenty *capitanes de guerra* (war captains) of the "twenty Pueblo Indian villages" of New Mexico consisting of "twelve to thirteen thousand" persons.[21]

Arriving at Mexico City, the group assembled at a house located on Puente Blanco Street. It was there that Padilla continued to insist that Casados decry Governor Codallos y Rabal, but Casados was still reluctant. The group soon encountered Luis Quintana, an Apache, who had apparently arrived in Mexico City around the same time and was staying in the same house. Quintana, reportedly, had just escaped from the town of Encinillas in the Chihuahua region and made his way to Mexico City in order to seek permission to return to New Mexico. He had been imprisoned in Encinillas for a sentence that he'd received in 1741 at Santa Cruz de la Cañada for apostasy and flight; he was an escaped servant of Juan de Tafoya. His punishment was two hundred public lashes, banishment from New Mexico, and four years of labor in the mines at San Felipe el Real de Chihuahua. Apparently, the prisoner Quintana had been sent to the hacienda of don Manuel de San Juan at Encinillas instead of the mines.[22] Whether or not Luis Quintana or the other New Mexico cohorts influenced them, Casados and Manuel de la Cruz separately presented their complaints to the viceroy.

Regarding the Casados case, the viceroy ordered court in Santa Fe, and in 1746 Casados and Quintana (now noted as a Belén Genízaro) brought legal suit against Diego de Torres, Antonio Salazar, and the other Belén Spanish land grant settlers. On the day of the trial, Casados appeared with an escort of seventy Pueblo Indians. The governor was angered by this rebellious display, along with the fact that Casados had left the province without license. After nine exhausting days of testimony, the issue was apparently laid to rest, and both groups remained in Belén.[23]

Manuel de la Cruz's grievances, on the other hand, although heard by the viceroy, did not make it to the courts in New Mexico, or at least no record of such a proceeding exists. Therefore, nothing has been recorded about Manuel de Cruz's bold leadership and advocacy for the Pueblo people. Cruz, unlike Casados, did complain to the viceroy about Governor Codallos y Rabal. The Pueblo leader claimed that since the governor had taken possession of New Mexico, his people had suffered continuous hardship. Cruz told the viceroy that the governor did not punish or break off commercial ties with an enemy Indian group that had attacked and killed forty-one Pueblo individuals. Cruz also mentioned that the governor imposed excessive demands and unjust tariffs on them. He complained that during their trade with peaceful tribes, the governor seized the merchandise, including Indian captives who were exchanged. Another complaint was that not only would the governor not furnish the Pueblo Indians with arms during their campaigns against enemy tribes, he would also confiscate the spoils of war that the Pueblo warriors obtained. Cruz also interjected that don Francisco Padilla exposed the injustices toward the Pueblos and the recently converted Indians (Genízaros), who, he asserted, were returning to their pagan ways as a result of the current governor's wrongdoings.[24] The Pueblo leader's intentions, along with his involvement with Casados and the other New Mexican protesters in Mexico City (previously unknown by New Mexico historians), demonstrates the formation of Genízaro and Pueblo collaboration and unity and explains the presence of seventy Pueblo individuals attending Casado's and Quintana's trial in Santa Fe. The Indian personages involved in this early Belén and New Mexico–wide conflict and resulting legal maneuvers were remarkable because of their political finesse and their commitment to acquiring justice for their indigenous communities.

While doing research for this chapter, I have made an intriguing discovery related to Cristóbal Caraquis, the Belén Pawnee Genízaro sidekick of Francisco Padilla mentioned above, and a connection to a previously unknown Río Arriba Genízaro identity. The unusual surname "Caraquis" or "Caraques" appears in a source that is often used by researchers—the 1750 New Mexico censuses extracted by Virginia Langham Olmsted. In the heading for the census of the Taos jurisdiction, Olmsted listed the parishioners (*feligresía*) as "Española, Coyote, and Genízara." A closer look at the original handwritten census shows that she left out another caste category, or rather a subcategory of Genízara. The original has "feligresía Española, Coyota, y Genízara o Caraques." The *y* indicates the last category in the heading list, and the *o* refers back to Genízara. In English, this would be "Spanish, Coyote, and Genízara or Caraques," designating "Caraques" or "Caraquis" perhaps a subcategory of Genízara. The word "Kawarakis," which bears resemblance to "Caraquis," is associated with an early southern group of Pawnees (Parks 2001, 517). The connection between Cristóbal Caraquis, the Pawnee Genízaro, and the discovery of the Taos Caraques identity strand could indicate that the Taos Genízaros were primarily Pawnees (Langham Olmsted 1981).

The new, amalgamated community of Belén persisted and was, along with the rest of New Mexico, enumerated in the 1750 census just a few years after the aforementioned initial confrontation. The Belén census recorded two settlements of segregated groups within the jurisdiction of Belén. These included thirteen households with seventy Spanish land grantees and twenty-three Indian house servants. A separate section included twenty Genízaro family units with a total of sixty-nine persons (Langham Olmsted 1981). This first census reveals that Belén's Spanish and Genízaro population ratio was half-

and-half. The Spanish population amounted to 43 percent, and the Genízaro group was also 43 percent. The total Indian population (Genízaros and Indian servants) was 57 percent.

As the Belén settlers were in the early stages of community formation, there is evidence of further cultural and social tension. In 1746, two Genízaros from Belén were accused of stealing items from the San Clemente home of don Juan Miguel Álvarez del Castillo and were arrested. The accused were identified as "Genízaros de Nación," which translates as either "Nation Genízaros" or "from the Genízaro Nation." The former indicates that they had recently arrived from Plains nations and were not local generational Genízaros. The latter implies they belonged to the Genízaro ethnic, tribal, and cultural group or nation. Regardless, the two suspects found themselves, perhaps, in a rebellious and desperate place in this new society. They were most likely newcomers, given the fact that they had not yet acquired a Spanish surname and by the rash treatment that officials meted out, such as giving them derogatory nicknames. The head suspect was "El Cuajo" (the Mucus, snot-nose, crybaby, or Slimy One), and his accomplice was Antonio "El Pelón" (Poor Scoundrel or Baldy). This criminal case reveals insightful anecdotes about the colonial period's social conditions and cultural relationships. While jailed in prison at Isleta, El Cuajo used an interpreter and requested that the padre of Isleta, Fray Juan José Padilla, and the military captain, Bernabé Baca, be present during his interrogation. Apparently, he believed that these officials would advocate for him. When questioned about the whereabouts of the stolen goods, El Cuajo confessed where he had buried his loot, but Antonio el Pelón testified that he had sold his ill-gotten treasure to individuals from Belén and Isleta. The outcome and punishment of the accused are unknown.[25]

As some Genízaros of Belén became intertwined in local conflicts, others were in exile, venturing to El Paso del Norte as fugitives. In 1759, a group of Genízaro fugitives of Belén were attacked and murdered by Apaches. This notable episode in colonial frontier life was brought to light by a prenuptial investigation that was begun on June 15, 1778. Lucas Baca petitioned to marry María Josefa Rael—both Genízaros from Belén. The focus was to verify the death of María Josefa's first husband, Miguel Padilla, in order to determine if she was free to marry Lucas.[26] Witnesses testified during the investigation that nineteen years previously, Josefa Rael's missing husband, Miguel Padilla, along with three other Genízaros left Belén for El Paso de Norte as fugitives and never returned. Pascual Vigil, also a Genízaro from Belén, testified that at the time of these events, he, too, left New Mexico as a fugitive. While on the road near El Paso, he encountered the footprints of four persons, and he tracked them to a place called El Alemán. There, they found many additional footprints and scattered arrows indicating that a skirmish had taken place. The footprints went off in different directions, so he went on to El Paso, where he was questioned by María Josefa Rael, who apparently was there in search of her missing husband. The governor of New Mexico also arrived at the scene to aid in the search. A second witness, José Atanasio ("Apache Genízaro") from Belén, said that he was living in El Paso at the time of the incident when he came across an Apache acquaintance who told him that his parents had recently participated in dancing for the scalps of the Belén Genízaro fugitives. Despite the testimony, church officials denied the marriage request due to insufficient evidence.

Other Genízaros also traveled to the El Paso area not as fugitives but as warriors in sanctioned Spanish military excursions. In 1777, fifty-five Genízaros from New Mexico completed a successful campaign against the Apaches at Sierra Blanca just east of El Paso.[27] There were many such accounts of clashes between Apaches, Navajos, and Comanches with the Spanish, Puebloans, and Genízaros. Fray Francisco Atanasio Domínguez's letter dated November 4, 1775, to Fray Isidro Murillo mentions that in September of the same year, Comanches attacked and "devastated" the "missions of Sandía and Belén" (Domínguez 1956, 271). Belén obviously recuperated from this tragic attack.

A year later, in 1776, Domínguez reported that Belén's occupants included ninety-six Spanish family units with 593 persons (most likely including castes and Indian servants), and a Genízaro community that totaled forty-nine family units with 209 persons. He also gave the population count for Belén's extended community of Sabinal (discussed later), which consisted of fifty-one family units and 214 persons. Fray Domínguez's report referred to Belén as a settlement of "widely separated ranchos" that contained rich and productive irrigated land. In his discussion of Genízaros in Belén, the friar said that they were similar to those in Santa Fe. He also stated negatively that they were impoverished and maintained themselves on small plots of land with whatever they could "get their hands on" from their neighbors (Domínguez 1956, 208).

Two years after Domínguez's report, a subsequent account, "Disorders in New Mexico," was given by Fray Juan Agustín de Morfi in 1778, which provided a rare critical view of provincial affairs. Morfi wrote that the Spanish

FIGURE 6.2 Detail of "Plano geográfico de la tierra descubierta nuevamente a los rumbos" (Geographical map of the land newly discovered in the directions), don Bernardo Miera y Pacheco, San Felipe el Real de Chihuahua, 1778. Map detail courtesy of the Center for Southwest Research, University of New Mexico. The church steeple symbol marking Belén designates it, according to the legend, as a village of Christian Indians ("Pueblo de Indios Cristianos").

lacked discipline and were cruel and oppressive profiteers, as opposed to the orderly Pueblo Indians. The Genízaros, on the other hand, he described as the poorest of the groups, rejected by the Pueblo Indians and forced to live with the Spaniards, among whom they were neglected and left with little land or work but yet were good soldiers and "very warlike." He stated that the Genízaros comprised some sixty families and lived in Belén and Tomé—he did not mention any other New Mexico locations. The friar reported that the Genízaros had a chief spokesman (whose name was not given) at the time, who had recently taken his petition for community rights to Durango. This account provides further evidence of Genízaro mobility and self-governance. Morfi also discussed that the Genízaros requested permission to establish El Sabinal, but the Spanish citizens from Belén attempted to move in on the attempted Genízaro settlement. He suggested that the Spanish stay in Belén and the Genízaros remain in Sabinal, where they were to "live in the manner of the Pueblo Indians" with privileges and exemptions. He reasoned that the Genízaros were deserving of this because of their loyalty and military service.[28] Morfi's report, and evidence taken from other documents about Sabinal, offer unique insight into the settlement process of Belén's plazas.

The plaza of Sabinal was farthest from Belén's main plaza. It was a contested space between the two founding groups, Spanish and Genízaro, as was the original Belén settlement. In 1765, the two groups filed joint but separate requests to the governor asking for permission to settle Sabinal. They were referred to as the Nueve Blancos and the Nueve Indios Genízaros (Nine Whites and Nine Genízaro Indians), and they claimed to have already been working the land in the area and even constructed acequia systems. Both groups provided a list of persons wishing to settle there. Permission was granted to both groups under the condition that they be given equal opportunity and land to build their homes, fashioned around a public square. The Genízaros were separately instructed to build their houses at the entrance of the village along with the construction of a protective fort for the whole community.[29] This formative episode in Sabinal's settlement reveals that the Genízaros and the Spanish were still segregated but becoming dependent on one another.

Just two years into the settlement, in 1767, the Spanish and Genízaro residents of Sabinal complained about obstacles and abuse by the son and grandsons of the deceased Captain Diego de Torres. Josef Torres and his sons were attempting to control Sabinal by halting the construction of ranchos and not allowing the complainants to pasture their horses there. The Genízaros said that the Torres family abused them to the point of threatening their lives and that of their *governadorsillo* (local community governor).[30] Antonio Gurulé was one of nine Genízaros involved in both the request to establish the Sabinal settlement and the complaint against the Torres sons; in both documents, he was listed as "El Casique" (War Lord or spiritual leader). This Genízaro leader was most likely the same Antonio Gurulé who was lead petitioner of the "Los Genízaros" petition previously discussed. Reymundo Jójola was also on the list of Sabinal Genízaro settlers, along with his sons Juan Pedro and Tomás. Interestingly enough, Ventura Jójola (alias de la Cruz), the Isleta Genízaro who was discussed earlier, was listed with the group of Nueve Blancos. Among the nine Genízaro Indians was Matías Frésquez, who was of Piro Indian derivation from Los Lentes, an early Isleta village. In 1775, Matías married María Magdalena Jójola, the daughter of Reymundo Jójola. It can be observed from these intertwined families that the settlers of Sabinal moved back and forth between their original plazas in Belén and Sabinal.

The settlement of Sabinal sheds light on how the other Belén plazas

FIGURE 6.3 Detail of a map made in 1779 by don Bernardo Miera y Pacheco. Notice that Belén is represented by a cluster of dispersed ranchos, while Sabinal is represented as a square defensive fort. Map detail courtesy of the Center for Southwest Research, University of New Mexico.

might have also been settled, but the most comprehensive population report on Belén's plazas was provided in the second census enumerated in 1790 by Fray Cayetano Bernal, the resident priest of Isleta. (Langham Olmsted 1975). The 1790 census listed seven plazas in Belén including Sabinal, farthest from the central plaza. The first two plazas were primarily home to Spanish privileged-class families along with their Indian servants. Don Diego Antonio Sánchez was the head rancher of Plaza no. 1. The largest of the Belén plazas was Plaza no. 2, which was later called Los Bacas.[31] It was headed by the family of Miguel Antonio Baca, followed by seven ranching families (core elite landowners), a few subsistence-farming families (laboring working class), and seventeen Indian household servants.

The third plaza of Nuestra Señora de los Dolores de los Genízaros was home to some of the original Belén Genízaro families but was also populated with newly arrived Genízaro and mestizo migrants. The head family was that of Comandante Marcos Velásquez and his wife, María Rosa Baca. Although Marcos is listed as mestizo, his parents were noted as Genízaros living in

Belén in the 1770s, who were originally from Alburquerque.[32] Marcos's wife, María Rosa, was the daughter of Genízaros, Ventura Jójola and Jacinta Baca. Four heads of families originated from the El Paso area, three of whom were from Socorro del Paso. The only Genízaro in the Belén census listed with tribal affiliation is also in this plaza. His name was Matías Montaño, a Navajo criado of Bernabé Montaño. Several modern-day Belén families can trace their ancestry to Matías and his Genízara wife, Juana María Silva, who were married in 1775. The demographic breakdown for this Genízaro-designated plaza in 1790 was 40 percent Genízaro, 14 percent Spanish, 32 percent mestizo, 2 percent Coyote, and 12 percent Indian servants. Combining the Genízaro, Coyote, and Indian servants would make the total Indian population for Plaza de los Genízaros 54 percent.

Los Trujillos (Plaza no. 4) had a large percentage of people categorized as Spanish (89 percent), with a few mestizos, Coyotes, and Indian servants but no Genízaros. The heads of households were Lieutenant don Santiago Trujillo, a rancher, and Nicolás Torres, grandson of Diego de Torres. Nuestra Señora del Pilar de los Garcías (Plaza no. 5) was headed by the family of rancher Joaquín Torres and his wife, Isabel Chávez, along with their three Indian and Coyote servants. Nombre de Dios de los Jarales (Plaza no. 6) is separated from the previous core plazas by a distance of two miles, located downriver. It comprised a small cluster of ranchos housing only five families. The head family belonged to Comandante José García and María Bárbara de la Cruz, who was listed as a mestiza. Although José García's birthplace is listed as Socorro, in the El Paso region, he was actually of the Spanish class from Sonora—his full surname was García Sandarte Lechuga.[33] María Bárbara, on the other hand, although listed as a mestiza, was in fact the daughter of Ventura Jójola (Cruz) and Jacinta Baca. The plaza of Jarales had the least number of Indian residents and the largest number of mestizos. Also, as at Plaza de los Genízaros, Jarales had no ranching families or servants.

San Antonio de Sabinal was the last plaza enumerated in the 1790 census of Belén. It was located even farther downriver, was the second largest in population, and had mostly farming families, like Plaza de los Genízaros and Jarales. The head family of Sabinal was that of farmer, Comandante Francisco Suazo, a native of El Paso, and wife Ana Gregorio Torres, both of whom were categorized as Spanish. Sabinal's two ranching families do not appear to have been leading families in the community, as were the rancher families in the central plazas, for they did not have Indian servants—although one had a Spanish servant. Sabinal had the highest number of Coyotes and was second in population of total Indian residents, after the Plaza de los Genízaros. This provides evidence that Genízaro families were in the Sabinal settlement from 1765.

The plazas of Sabinal, Los Genízaros, and Jarales were socially and politically connected to the original Genízaro and Tiwa Belén founders and were also structured as Pueblo villages with a governadorsillo, comandante, and cacique (social and spiritual leader), as evidenced by the documents and the census of the Sabinal settlement. This kind of organization also existed in the Genízaro community of Abiquiú. The Genízaro communities of Abiquiú and neighboring Ojo Caliente were organized in the same manner as the other Indian pueblos including the designation of a governor, a *teniente* (lieutenant governor), a comandante, and two assistants (Ebright 2014, 67n36).

The Pueblo of Belén and its plazas were becoming mixed-ethnic communities, according to the 1790 census. Over the course of two generations from 1750 to 1790, the ethnic component of Belén reversed its population ratio of Indians to Spanish. In the 1750 census, Belén was populated by 57 percent Indians and 43 percent Spanish. Belén's population in 1790 was composed of 57 percent Spanish citizens, 24 percent Indians (Coyotes, Indians servants, and Genízaros), and 19 percent mestizos.

The decline in persons identified as Indian and the increase in those listed as mestizos informs us that there was an increase in Spanish and Indian mixed marriages or unions. This also indicates that some of the Indian residents shifted into the category of the mestizo class. There is also evidence that a few males from all of the ethnic categories migrated to Belén. Some arrived from the Guadalupe del Paso area, introducing additional Isleta/Piro Indian components. Interrelationships between Genízaro, Piro, and Tiwa Indians had also existed in the Guadalupe del Paso missions. According to an account in 1773 by Fray Joaquín de Jesús Ruiz, the Piro community in Socorro del Sur (near present-day El Paso, Texas) was dwindling due to the fact that the mission was primarily composed of Genízaros who were originally brought in from New Mexico. Fray Ruiz further stated that these Genízaros were Apaches, captured by the Comanches and having no particular inclination toward the Apache Nation, nor did they know their own Apache language. Therefore, they lived peacefully in El Paso, first marrying their own and later marrying Spanish and mestizos, all benefiting from the rich, fertile land.[34]

Regardless of their ethnicity, class status, or place of origin, Belén residents witnessed more than forty years of change from the town's precarious origin

TABLE 6.1 Population Data of Belén, from the Spanish Census of 1790. Courtesy of Samuel Sisneros.

SETTLEMENT / PLAZA	FAMILY UNITS	PERSONS	SPANISH	GENÍZARO	MESTIZO	COYOTE	INDIAN	INDIAN / COYOTE / GENÍZARO /
No. 1	4	18	12 (67%)	0	2 (11%)	0	4 (22%)	4 (22%)
No. 2	47	251	143 (57%)	9 (4%)	56 (22%)	21 (8%)	22 (9%)	52 (21%)
No. 3, Nuestra Señora de los Dolores de los Genízaros	34	145	22 (14%)	56 (40%)	46 (32%)	3 (2%)	18 (12%)	77 (54%)
No. 4, San Antonio de los Trujillos	8	54	48 (89%)	0	2 (4%)	1 (2%)	3 (5%)	4 (7%)
No. 5, Nuestra Señora del Pilar de los Garcias	30	157	115 (73%)	0	19 (13%)	10 (6%)	13 (8%)	23 (14%)
No. 6, Nombre de Dios de los Jarales	5	36	15 (42%)	0	20 (55%)	1 (3%)	0	1 (3%)
San Antonio de Sabinal	52	227	149 (65%)	6 (3%)	24 (11%)	35 (15%)	13 (6%)	54 (24%)
Combined Belén Plazas	180	888	504 (57%)	71 (8%)	169 (19%)	71 (8%)	73 (8%)	215 (24%)

in two ethnically separated sections of the community. In 1790, Belén was in the early stages of blurring ethnic and class designations and becoming an interdependent colonial village. Soon after the 1790 census was enumerated in Belén, the village saw the birth of its parish and the construction of the mission church. The Nuestra Señora de Belén mission church and convent was constructed from 1791 to 1793 with the labor of Genízaros and *vecinos* (meaning "neighbor" but here referring to Spanish and mestizo residents), under the supervision of Fray Cayetano Bernal. In 1794, Bernal reported on the formation of Belén parish and the construction of the mission church while stressing that the Genízaros were the focus of the community. This suggests that Bernal was using their identity as Indians and new status as baptized Christians to achieve the goal of claiming Belén as a mission and Genízaros as mission Indians.

The Franciscan friar administered Belén as a single Indian mission village with nearby rancho communities. In his report, he further emphasized the Indian mission aspect of Belén, naming the settlement "La Misión de Nuestra Señora de Belén de Indios Genízaros de Diversas Naciones" (The Mission of Our Lady of Belén of Genízaro Indians from Diverse Nations) and highlighting that in the mission there were 36 Genízaro families with 87 persons, followed by fifteen *puestos* (outpost plazas) of Spanish and castes with 416 families and 1,316 persons. Regardless of the fact that the overall Genízaro population was minimal, Fray Bernal continued to emphasize Genízaros as the primary inhabitants of the central plaza of the mission or pueblo, and the Spanish and mixed castes as the populace of outlying ranches. Fray Bernal also gave the same designation of "indios genízaros de diversas naciones" to the Pueblo of Santo Tomás de Abiquiú.[35] In his continued efforts to obtain funding, Bernal corresponded with officials in 1795 noting the increase of forty Belén families of the "Genízaro race." This gives further credence to the perception or function of the Genízaros as a tribe, nation, or distinct group.[36]

The Genízaro community of Abiquiú was Belén's northern New Mexican counterpart, and it also functioned as a quasi-Pueblo and Genízaro nation. Both communities shared similar origins and social constructs, as discussed earlier. In addition, the Genízaros of Belén and Abiquiú shared common family ties as a result of migrations between the two pueblos from the mid-1700s to the early 1800s in spite of the 140-mile distance. The first emigrant from Belén to Abiquiú was Bartolomé Gutiérrez, who was listed as a Genízaro in the 1750 census of Belén. He was in Abiquiú by 1759, when he wed Bárbara

Martín, a Coyota from the area. Bartolomé was back in Belén as a widower by 1785, when he married María Josefa Baca, a Genízara from Belén. Several of Bartolomé's children remained in Abiquiú. Other Genízaros from Belén, namely Luis Silva, José Antonio Sierra, and Juan Andrés Ramos, married local Abiquiú Genízara, Indian, or Coyota women at the mission church of Santo Tomás in Abiquiú. Another example is Salvador Matías Lente, a Genízaro widower from Isleta of Tiwa and Genízaro origin.³⁷ He married Juana María Roybal at Abiquiú in 1784. In the record of his first marriage in 1780 to an Isleta Tiwa woman, Salvador Matías is designated as Apache. In Abiquiú, he was noted as a Genízaro and sometimes with the surname Coruna or Coruña. The Coruña surname might indicate that other early Lente Isleta families were children or grandchildren of the first Pueblo/non-Pueblo Indian union in the Isleta church marriage registers, as noted earlier of Antonio Coruña (or Curuna), a Tiwa, and Isabel, an Apache.³⁸

Another Genízaro migrant from Belén to Abiquiú was Juan Cristóbal Manchego, son of Juan Manchego and María Rosa Miranda, both Genízaros of Belén. Also in the early 1790s, María Antonia García, a Jarales expatriate, was in Abiquiú with her husband, Vicente Trujillo. Two Genízaro families that relocated from Abiquiú to Belén were those of Mariano Trujillo and his wife, Rosalía Apodaca; and José Uvaldo Martín, who arrived in Belén as a widower and later married María Teresa Chávez of Sabinal in 1790.

Migrations and steady population increase at the end of eighteenth century saw tremendous growth throughout New Mexico, and particularly in Belén, which was due in part to Fray Cayetano José Bernal's work to establish a productive mission community. From 1799 to 1801, Fray Bernal issued a series of demographic reports on Belén's population. He stated that in 1799 there were 1,283 Spaniards and castas living in Belén along with 124 Genízaros. This tallied a total of 1,407 residents. On a tabular chart, he included the Isleta and Belén missions under the jurisdiction of the village of Alburquerque. He described Belén as a mission of Genízaro Indians from *distintas naciones* (different nations), with ten plazas *agregados* (attached). Again, this was an indication that the Nuestra Señora de Belén mission church *was* the Genízaro mission. For 1800, Fray Bernal gave an account of Belén's continued expansion, which now encompassed up to fifteen settlements including Nuestra Señora de los Dolores de la Joya de Sevilleta. In 1801, he gave the total population of Belén as 1,794 souls. Of these citizens, Genízaros numbered 105, and the rest Bernal described as having a "nature that cannot be defined, because they all want to call themselves Spaniards, even though there are people of every caste."[39]

The last colonial tabulation of Belén residents was a list of contributions of the members of the Confraternity of the Blessed Souls of Purgatory inscribed in 1802. Although it was not a true census, it noted the adult members and their dues to the confraternity, which were paid in kind primarily with sheep, serapes, goats, stockings, and some silver currency. The members of the Belén area specified as their first and principal plaza the "Mission de Nuestra Señora de Belén, Plaza de Los Bacas." The following plazas were then listed in order: the Plaza de Francisco Chávez (probably plaza no. 1 in the 1790 census), the Plaza de los Genízaros de Belén, the Plaza de los Trujillos, the Plaza de los Garcías, and the Plaza de los Jarales.[40] The added description of "de Belén" after "Plaza de los Genízaros" indicates that this plaza was directly connected to the mission plaza (Los Bacas) either in proximity or administratively.

While New Mexico's clerics were reporting on their parish populations and conditions and scrambling for funding from the bishop and the king, Spain was weakened by the invasion of France (1808–1813), igniting Mexico's independence movement (1810–1821). Ironically, the province of New Mexico, although on the outer periphery of Spanish control, was finally advancing in the eyes of the Spanish Crown, and don Pedro Bautista Pino was granted the opportunity to travel to the Spanish royal court as a representative of the province. In 1811, Pino presented a detailed report of New Mexico's frontier communities, including a notation that designated Belén and Abiquiú as Indian pueblos. Many of Pino's suggested reforms never took place, with the independence of New Spain from Spain and the formation of the Republic of Mexico (Carroll and Haggard 1942, 27).

The caste system began to collapse during the Mexican governance of New Mexico (1821–1848), and Belén's Genízaro identity along with its unique Genízaro plaza place name began to fall out of use by local officials. Beginning in the early 1800s, Belén's Genízaros were intermittently and broadly labeled as Indians, or often with no specific identity. Despite this identity marker decline, a core group of families maintained Indian identity (imposed or self-proclaimed) and linkage to the Plaza de los Genízaros or the Plaza de los Bacas through generational residency, endogamous unions, and affinity with a *compadrazgo* (ritual kinship) system. Between 1810 and 1846, these old Belén Genízaro families were noted in eighty-seven baptisms, nineteen burials, and two marriages as residents of Los Janchis (Janches,

TABLE 6.2 Members of the Confraternity of the Blessed Souls of Purgatory, Plaza de los Genízaros de Belén, 1802. Courtesy of Samuel Sisneros.

1	Hurtado	Francisco	
1a	Atencio	Pascuala	wife
2	Saavedra	Francisco	
2a	Hurtado	Antonia Lucía	wife
3	Romero	Feliciano	
3a	Romero	Rosalía	daughter
3b	Romero	María Antonia	daughter
4	Montoya	Manuel Antonio	
4a	García	María de los Santos	wife
5	García	Joaquín	
6	Montoya	Pedro (Antonio)	
6a	Gurulé	Juana María	wife
7	Gurulé	Paulín	
7a	Cachiya	Juana María	
8	Góngora	Marcos	
8a	Manzanares	Victoria	wife
9	Baca	Antonio	
9a	Padilla	Dominga	wife
10	Gonzales	Antonio	
11	García	Marcelino	
11a	Peña	Quiteria	wife
12	Cachiya	José	
12a	Baca	Gertrudes	wife
13	Velásquez	Martín	
13a	Tenorio	María Cristina	wife

Xanchis) including two individuals who were listed as Janchi Indians. The core surnames were Gurulé, Gonzales, Moreno, Cachiya, Castillo, Galindro, and Tiburcio. The most numerous was the Gurulé family, the children and grandchildren of Antonio Gurulé and Rita Quiteria Baca discussed earlier. Their son, Rafael Gurulé, and his wife, María de la Luz Otero, incidentally were the last persons listed as Genízaros in Belén, in 1817. The last mention of Plaza de los Genízaros was in 1819.[41]

The transition from Los Genízaros to Los Janchis is first noted in the 1810

Nuestra Señora de Belén Church burial record of Felipa Romero, in which she was noted as an adult resident of Los Janchis; the word "Jancha" is written on the entry margin. Felipa was listed in the 1790 census as a Genízara of the Plaza de los Genízaros. Her son, Pedro Antonio Montoya, was married to Juana María Gurulé, daughter of José Manuel Gurulé and Josefa Baca. In the 1802 census, Pedro and Juana María are listed as residents of Plaza de los Genízaros. The first baptismal entry to note Los Janchis residency was in the 1811 baptism of María Josefa de Jesús, natural daughter of José Antonio Castillo and Getrudis Sanches.[42] The *padrinos* (godparents) were Agustín Gonzales and María de la Luz Baca, who were also padrinos for many other Los Janchis residents including their own grandchildren. This Gonzales/Baca couple was an old Belén Genízaro family, recorded as residents of Plaza de los Genízaros in the 1750 and 1790 censuses.

The two persons annotated as Janchi Indians are found in 1813 and 1816 burial records. The first was that of the deceased Juan Felipe Moreno, who was noted as the son of Santiago Moreno, "Indio Janchi." Santiago Moreno and wife Isabel Tiburcio are listed in other records as residents of Los Janchis.[43] The other person identified as a Janchi Indian was Rafael Castillo. His 1816 burial record gives his wife's name as María Gertrudes Gurulé. This couple had just married a few months before Rafael's death, and their marriage record lists Rafael (born in 1789) as an Indian servant (Indio criado) of don Joaquín Castillo.[44] Castillo had many Indian criados and was a resident of Los Bacas plaza.

The last Los Janchis references appeared in 1840s. The prenuptial investigation of José Antonio Castillo and María Cruz Cervantes on October 17, 1842, listed the groom as a resident of the "Plaza de los Janchis." This is the only record designating Los Janchis as a plaza, which strengthens its connection to the Plaza de los Genízaros or the Plaza de los Bacas. The last mention of a Los Janchis resident was made in the year that Texas and US military forces entered and occupied the city of Santa Fe. Juana María Gurulé was baptized as an infant on May 18, 1846; she was described as a resident of Los Janchis and daughter of José Gurulé and Concepción Gonzales, both descendants of Belén Genízaros.

The expressions "Janchi," Janchi Indian identity, and Los Janchis residency were in use for nearly fifty years. There are a few possible explanations as to how and why the word "Janchi" developed, particularly in association with Comanche history, culture, ancestry, and language. The regional New Mexican

Spanish word for Comanche was "Cumanchi," and "Janchi" could have been a derivative of that word. The earliest Janchi mention is found in the 1750 Isleta burial record of Rosa, Genízara Indian of Belén. The burial noted that she was married to Pedro Xanchi (the use of *X* for *J* is common in colonial Spanish documents, similar to "Xavier" instead of "Javier"). Perhaps Pedro was Comanche, and the "Xanchi" tribal affiliation or moniker was used as a surname or attribution. No more is known about this couple, and they are not listed in the 1750 Belén census. There were Comanche persons residing in the Belén area throughout this period. Soledad Vigil was a Comanche criada, as noted in the record of her Belén baptism in 1795. In 1812, Soledad was listed as a resident of Los Janchis in the burial records for José Vigil, her natural son.

Another possible Comanche association with the word "Janchi" may stem from Comanche raids on Belén, Tomé, and other villages in New Mexico in the late 1770s, still remembered in narrative legends and reenacted in the Christmas Eve folk dramas of "Los Comanches."[45] Comanche attacks throughout the Río Arriba were led by a Comanche war chief named Cuerno Verde (Green Horn), whose defeat in August 1786 by Governor Juan Bautista de Anza is celebrated in a heroic equestrian play titled *Los Comanches*. In the play, Cuerno Verde's warriors face off with their antagonists from a previous campaign, led by Capitán don Carlos Fernández. Shuttling between the Spanish and Comanches with his tobacco-and-white flag is a (presumably Comanche) character enigmatically named Tabaco Chupa Janchi (Tobacco-Smoking Janchi). His petitions for peace fail, and he flees just as the battle begins.[46] As the script traveled from village to village, his name was shortened to Tabaco, but the word "Janchi" is included in one of his lines, spoken in an unknown language: "Chupa janchi nimaca" (Espinosa 1907; Campa 1942). Aurelio M. Espinosa Sr., a pioneer Spanish New Mexican folklorist, speculated that this verse could have been from the Comanche language, but its meaning was unknown. In his famous *arenga* (battle harangue), Cuerno Verde boldly summons the "valiant Genízaros" to join the Comanches in a call to war against the Spanish citizens. Ironically, Genízaros historically defended their own, neighboring Pueblo, and Spanish communities against the Comanches. They were also first in line to trade with them in times of peace. Although the Janchi word associations might appear to be circumstantial, the Indo-Hispano folk drama *Los Comanches* was, surprisingly, historically accurate, and it demonstrates that the word "Janchi," along with the Pedro Xanchi reference, had historical usage in New Mexico relating to the Comanche tribe, Genízaros, and settlers in the Río Abajo as well as the Río Arriba.

According to the late Rubén Cobos, who was a preeminent New Mexico Spanish-language linguist, the regional Spanish word *janche* or *janchi* traditionally means "to grab" or "grabby" (Cobos 1983, 128). The ascription of the word "Janchi" to a particular group of people could come from early derogatory attitudes toward Genízaros as thieves. Recall the observation made by Fray Domínguez that Genízaros "would take whatever they could get their hands on," and also the investigation of the thievery of Antonio el Pelón and El Cuajo.

Another possible Janchi derivation could be connected to a group of Indian soldiers in the colonial period who were allied to the Spanish and who operated in central and northern Chihuahua and were referred to as Janches or Indios Jancha. In 1771, the commanding military officer of the Sonora/Chihuahua region, Hugo O'Conor, described this band as part of a large, generic group of Indians in Chihuahua and Sonora called Indios Norteños.[47] Also, an Ácoma word that would sound similar to the Spanish *janche* means a kind of Mexican dance or round dance (Miller 1960, 44).

Further complicating the Janchis identity and locality are references to both Los Janchis and Plaza de los Genízaros residents as residents of "the Pueblo" (del Pueblo).[48] This offers a deeper correlation to Belén's Pueblo mission status and indicates that the Plaza de los Genízaros and Los Janchis (most likely the same place) could have been physically located on the outskirts of Belén's historic main plaza and the colonial mission church of Nuestra Señora de Belén.[49] The Genízaro plaza could have also been located at the entrance of the Belén mission pueblo, like the settlement formation in the village of Sabinal. Regardless of their former associations, the Genízaro and Los Janchis place names and identities no longer remain in the current historical memory of Belén's Hispanic natives.[50]

The decline of Genízaro identity during the Mexican period coincided with the transition of Janchis identity and its eventual demise at the time of the Texas/US invasion and subsequent occupation during 1846–1848. Although Indian captivity and displacement continued throughout US territorial administration, there was no more mention of Belén's Indian legacy until 1867. In that year, federal official John Ward, special agent for Pueblos, mentioned Belén in a letter to the New Mexico superintendent of Indian affairs.

Ward stated that a census enumeration of the "Village Indians" of Abiquiú, Pecos, and Belén had not been done since 1809. Ward obtained information from colonial records, which gave the "Belén Indian Pueblo" population for 1790 as having "no data"; in 1808 it had 135 citizens, and in 1809 it had 133. Abiquiú's population in 1790 was 216, dropping to 122 in 1808 and 126 in 1809. Pecos Pueblo was eventually disbanded, and a small group from there joined Jémez Pueblo in 1845. Superintendent Ward stated further that Abiquiú and Belén had ceased to exist as Indian communities, although he said Indian heritage could be easily traced among the Mexicans residing in and around those places. Ward brought up these demographics to offer evidence of the supposed disappearance of New Mexico Indian tribes and general Pueblo Indian depopulation in order to support the view, or expectation at the time, that Indians would become extinct.[51]

Needless to say, the extinction never took place, and the decline or disappearance of segments of New Mexican Native Americans can be attributed to identity transformation, acculturation, intermarriage, and emigration—which are all components of the process of mestizaje.[52] This process continued during the Mexican and US territorial periods throughout New Mexico, including Belén. Captives from various Indian tribes were constantly brought in, particularly from the Navajo Nation. Although these later captives were introduced into the Mexican population through Catholic baptism and compulsory servitude in the same manner as during the Spanish colonial period, these unfortunates were never labeled, grouped, or united under the Genízaro category, and thus they were able to blend much more quickly into Mexican or Pueblo cultures.[53]

Belén's Genízaro and Native American identity and ties to the location of the original Plaza de los Genízaros were superficially lost despite continuous reinvigoration of Native American blood. But perhaps subliminal linkages have been surfacing through Belén's local "Indian Princess" legend of La Indita and by way of traditional *indita* ballads, some of which were composed and sung by Belén area residents like Abeytas/Sabinal natives Norberto Abeyta and his son Amador, principal forces behind the twentieth-century continuation of inditas cultural production.[54] Inditas are a genre of Spanish devotional and popular song and dance, essentially ritual performances of poetic petitions (for protection in war or against illness, requests for rain, etc.), and were dedicated to a variety of saints' devotions, including Guadalupe, San Antonio, Santo Niño de Atocha, and San Luis Gonzaga, who became the patron saint of dancing and protector of soldiers in New Mexico. The prayers are blended with Native American tradition, which provides the language, rhythm, sacred dance, choruses, and chants. The word "inditas" means "little Indian girl" and implies songs about little Indian girls or about Indians in general (Lamadrid 2002). Arthur Campa, Spanish folklorist, wrote this about inditas: "To see it written one would take it for a ballad (Spanish), and to hear it sung one would think it was an Indian chant" (1930, 9). Espinosa said: "I am inclined to think that the origin of the indita is as natural as the mixture of Spanish and Indian blood by intermarriage." Along the same lines, Enrique Lamadrid, in his exceptional work on Indo-Hispano folk traditions, wrote of the genre: "There is no better musical demonstration of the unique New Mexican style of pluralistic mestizaje or cultural blending" (2002, 181).

In addition to the Indo-Hispano folk tradition of indita songs, the other possible manifestation of the Belén Genízaro–Native American legacy or "blood memory" can be found in the local Belén legend of La Indita.[55] The story is told that a mysterious Native American women called La Indita or Aztec Princess came from the interior of Mexico to Belén, where she lived in a room behind the church on the Plaza Vieja. It is said that she was "regal and noble in appearance," with piercing dark eyes and long hair, and wore fine jewelry and clothing. She was the splendor of the pueblo. One version recounts that she suddenly disappeared, either returning to Mexico or moving away with a Spanish military officer. Another version reveals that her Spanish officer deserted her and that she died broken-hearted. The story concludes that the princess was buried in the Plaza Vieja Church, where many would hear her spirit's mournful cries begging to return to Mexico or longing for her lover (Baca 2008).[56] Recounting La Indita through oral tradition expresses a local foundational narrative that complicates the identity negotiation of a particular Plaza Vieja family, linking them and the larger Belén community to the factual Genízaro Native American history of Belén.

The story of La Indita has been told by four generations of Manuel García-O'Neal and Antonia Rael's extended family, who still reside at the family property located on the site of Belén's Plaza Vieja and the colonial church. Manuel García (he later appended the "O'Neal" surname) was the natural son of Delfinia "Virginia" García (born 1869), who was the daughter of José Isidoro García and María Petra Montaño. José Isidoro (born ca. 1840) and his mother, María Antonia García (born ca. 1820), were listed as Indian servants in the 1860 US census of Belén.

FIGURE 6.4 José Isidoro García seated outside his home in Belén, undated. Courtesy of Alberta O'Neal.

FIGURE 6.5 Delfinia "Virginia" García with Charles O'Neal, undated. Courtesy of Alberta O'Neal.

María Petra Montaño was the daughter of José Victorio Montaño, the son of Bartolo Montaño, himself the son of Matías Montaño (a Navajo) and Juana Silva (a Genízara). These were eighteenth-century residents of Plaza de los Genízaros, as mentioned earlier. Manuel García-O'Neal's wife, Antonia Rael, was the daughter of Lázaro Rael and Josefa Tafoya, who were the original owners of the family property site at the Plaza Vieja, near the church ruins that were still visible in the 1940s.

The Manuel García (O'Neal) family history enlightens this Belén Genízaro legacy story, as many other families' stories also would. Manuel was baptized on March 5, 1885, as recorded in the Nuestra Señora de Belén Catholic Church register, where it was noted that he was the natural child of Delfinia García.[57] Manuel was not Delfinia García's only child born out of wedlock. A couple of years earlier, in 1883, Delfinia gave birth to her first child, María Adela, and, as in Manuel's baptismal entry, no father was mentioned.[58] Just two years after María Adela's birth and during the same year as Manuel's birth, the 1885 census for Belén lists Delfinia ("Virginia" in this and other records—a phonetic corruption) García as a nineteen-year-old unwed mother living with her parents, José Isidoro García and Petra.[59]

Close to ten months after Manuel's birth, Delfinia "Virginia" García married an Irish American newcomer to Belén, Charles "Carlos" O'Neal, on January 20, 1886.[60] Before the end of the year, Virginia and her husband gave birth to a legitimate son, Luis Carlos O'Neal.[61] It appears that this child did not live long, passing away sometime prior to 1900, when Delfinia left her children Manuel and Adela in the care of her parents while moving away from Belén with her husband. Adela married in 1900 at the age of seventeen to Melquiades García. In the marriage registry, Adela's mother was noted as Virginia García, with no notation of a father.[62] At Manuel García's April 8, 1907, marriage to Antonia Rael, the register did not mention a father either but simply noted that Manuel was the son of Delfinia García and had been brought up (*criado por*) by Isidoro García (his grandfather).[63] As demonstrated by their respective marriage records, both Manuel and Adela had been raised by their grandparents and continued to reside in Belén. But what became of their mother, Delfinia, and her husband?

The Belén family oral tradition holds that Charles O'Neal and Delfinia went to California on several occasions, where they eventually got a divorce. Family lore also maintains that Charles O'Neal (the spellings "O'Neal" and "O'Niel" are used interchangeably in the records) ended up in Globe, Arizona, where he died and was buried. He was believed to have been a lawman and was somehow related to roughrider Bucky O'Niel.[64] Interestingly, the historical record shows that the family did move to Arizona and eventually to California. In Globe, Charles and Delfinia had five children of their own but divorced prior to 1900. In the 1900 census for Globe, Delfinia is listed as Delphine O'Neil, birthdate October 1868, divorced, head of household, from New Mexico, and with occupation of laundress. The 1900 Globe census notes that she gave birth to eight children, with five living. This is very telling, given that she indeed did give birth to eight children—three in Belén and five in Arizona. Perhaps claiming that three had died was an attempt to avoid the stigma of leaving her first-born children in Belén. The 1900 Globe census lists three daughters and two sons ranging from one to twelve years of age, all listed as born in Arizona and all listed with the surname O'Neil. On October 20, 1906, Delfinia married again, to Charles Quinn, a well-known Arizona miner.[65] The couple remained in Globe and had three daughters and one son of their own, as indicated in the 1910 census. By 1916, the family is listed as still living in Globe.[66] Charles Quinn died on January 1, 1919.[67] A year later, in 1920, Delfinia is listed as a fifty-two-year-old widow living in Globe with her Quinn children. By 1930, she and part of her family were in Redondo Beach, California, where, interestingly, her race was listed in the census as "Mexican" while the rest of her family was listed as "White." Delfinia Quinn remained in Los Angeles until her death on March 8, 1940. It is unknown what became of Charles O'Neil.

There is much mystique in this story of how a stunning, young, petite woman standing next to an older, gun-toting outsider in a family photo, at fourteen or fifteen years old was initiated into motherhood, setting her life in a new direction, exiling to Arizona and later California, and mothering at least twelve children. Fading family memories and lore along with the historical record shine some light on this story, enlightening us with more information about the Belén Genízaro legacy as it expanded to Arizona and California. This is one example of the many stories of life, love, family, community, migration, identity, and legend that could be told by the extended descendent community of the early Belén Genízaro people.

Although the García-O'Neal family was grounded in a sense of place through family memory and through continued land ownership, the family's Genízaro ancestry was unknown by current family members prior to this study. Their identity is generally Hispanic. Therefore, this family might

FIGURE 6.6 Manuel García O'Neal and Antonia Rael and family, undated. Courtesy of Alberta O'Neal.

have been unconsciously attempting, through their rendition of the Indian princess story, to legitimize their own and Belén's Native American heritage, a people who became delegitimized and erased.

Besides the local manifestations of the Indita story, inditas, and the sense of place and identity established by the Genízaro, Coyote, Indio, and Janchis associations as agencies of continuity, memory, and recovery, the most tangible link to Belén's unique Native American experience are the many Genízaro descendants still living in the town or "dispersed" throughout New Mexico and beyond. Besides the García/O'Neal family discussed in this chapter, another case in point of this innate recovery process involves this author, as I am also a descendant of Belén Coyotes.[68] It is my hope that this illumination of a complex regional history begins not only to recover but also to recognize Belén's Genízaro legacy, thereby extending the scope of Native American identity and scholarship.

A further understanding of the broader theoretical aspects of Native American identity could come from reviewing the definition of the word "Genízaro" as found in eighteenth-century Spanish dictionaries—"the child of parents from diverse nations and the mixed object [*lo mesclado*] from two diverse things."[69] The word "Genízaro" as transferred to the Americas, designating various Indian nations, corresponds with Fray Cayetano Bernal's description of Belén's Indian residents as "Indios Genízaros de diversas naciones." The unique Native American Genízaro community should be celebrated as one of the earliest and most widespread models of pan-tribalism that has occurred within current US boundaries. The second definition of the word Genízaro as "lo mesclado" can also be applied to the transformative experience of the New Mexican Genízaro. The Genízaros, starting out as an intertribal assemblage, went through another admixture with the Spanish, thus circumstantially becoming mestizo, as demonstrated in this chapter. Belén exemplifies this unique unity and cultural transformation, irrespective of the tragic circumstances that brought these indigenous and Spanish Mexican people together.

APPENDIX A Petition by Los Genízaros to Populate the Old Pueblo of Sandía, 1733

Señor Gobernador y Cappitan General

Los hijos Genizaros de este Reino, los quales por la missericordia de Dios N[uest]ro Senor fuimos traidos al Gremio, y Abrigo de N[uest]ra Santa Madre Iglesia, rrecibiendo por Nra gran dicha el Agua de el Bautismo, y con el la fe de los misterios santos de el mui alto señor, favor tan excelente, y singular, a que nos hallamos obligados y rreconocidos; pues siendo tantas las Almas que sosobran en el mar immenso de la Gentilidad, a nossotros, por particular [de] decreto, y Providiencia se digno de sacarnos al Puerto Seguro de su Yglesia, en ella pues, gososos de tan crecida dicha, esperamos, mediante su divina gracia, darle colmados frutos de virtudes, y buenas obras, con las quales, llegado el Termino de la Temporal Vida, pasaremos alegres a dar la buena quenta de la distribución, que hizo en nossotros de sus Talentos; y esta supuesta, gosaremos el Prometido premio a los que fieles obserbaron su Ley, y mui Santos preceptos. mas porque para conseguir tanta Dicha, es prescisso, y Anexo, al servicio, y agrado de el Señor, dar el nessesario sustento al Cuerpo, como assi lo Dispusso, ordeno, y prebino, su infinita sabiduria y soberana Probidencia; para el qual, aunque en el Principio de n[uest]ra Creacion, esto es, en Adan, y Eva, nos probeio de todo aquello que conducia, a n[ues]tro Natural manteni[mi]ento, sin que para ello nessecitassemos de poner de nra parte algun trabajo, o medio; quisso Nra Desgracia que olvidados Nros primeros P[adr]es de tanto bien, y Beneficio, y soltando las Riendas a su desordenado deseo, quebrantando de Dios aquel tan santo, y saludable precepto, perdiendose ellos, y tanbien a Nosotros; en penitencia, de tan Atros Delitos salimos sentenciados, a la pena, y tormento, de cultivar la tierra, a fuerza de la fatiga, y propio trabajo de cada uno, Regandola con Prolijo sudor de N[uest]ro Rostro, como hasta aora, esperimentamos, y sabemos; y aunque en aquel entonces de N[uest]ra Pen[st]encia, era toda la Tierra Campo libre e immenzo para nra labranza, por ser Pocos los hombres e habitadores de ella, oi, por la probidencia, y disposicion de el señor esta tan llena, y Poblada de Gentes, que es nessessario, el avenirse todos a no pasar de aquellos limites, que por los superiores o Reies de la Tierra les son asignados en possecion a cada Uno, segun el fundamento, o motibo que se viere combenir para ello. por lo qual, y lo arriba supuesto, Paressemos ante la Grandeza de V[uestr] S[enoriya] los Referidos hijos en la mejor via, y forma, que en Derecho Conbenga y decidimos que hallandonos Dispersos en las Villas, y Poblazones de este Reino, sin Abrigo, y forma de poder mantener N[uest]ras Personas y familias, pues no tenemos tierras proprias para ello, por lo qual pasamos la inconbeniencia y nessecidad q[ue] Dios sabe, y la Gracia de V[uestr]s[enori]a puede considerar, assi en el vestido, como la comida, y otros nessessarios de el cuerpo, sujetos a la Toleranzia de las estorciones, que la condicion humana de cada sujeto puede hacernos; y Arriesgados q[uan]do no todos, algunos de Nosotros que compelidos de sus grandes trabajos, y miserias, o otras estorciones que acaeser puedan en nuestro del abrigo, los incinte el Demonio, como nuestro enemigo, a que abrazando la abominable Apostacia Vaian a la Gentilidad, a buscar a sus trabajos el rremedio; esto prebenimos, en atención a que siendo, como son las inclinaciones, y Juicios de los hombres tan muchos y diversos, si Unos conociendo el maior bien que gosan en la Yglecia de Dios N[uest]ro Senor, sufren con humildad, y amor qualesquiera trabajos, e incombeniencias que en la Compania, y aiuntamiento de los demás se ofrecen, a trueque de no perder sus Almas, otros puede ser desatiendan todo esto, y olvidando lo principal, y puesto su cuidado en lo menos, como es lo Corporal, sugeridos de el Enemigo, (que embidiosso no sessa de Rodearnos) y instigados de sus nessecidades, executen lo dicho. y aunque pudiéramos pedir a la piedad, y grandeza de Vsa como a Nro. Sr y P[adr]e. y que goso la Regia Authoridad para el Gobierno militar, y Politico de este Reino, el que nos agregase a los Pueblos de Yndios Christianos, que componen este distrito, no queremos pedirlo, considerando la Renuencia, y mala inclinación de dichos Yndios, pues despues de tantos anos de Doctrina, y predicacion Evangelica, en lugar de ir a mas, cada dia ban a menos, hallandose como se hallan, entre ello cada dia, mucho idolatras y hechizeros; y asi por no contaminarnos, con tan Pestilencia al [Docma], y costrumbres Perversas assi Nossotros, con Nuestros hijos, pedimos a la Grandeza de Vsa sea mui servido, de Asignarnos por Pueblo, para Nuestra manutención, y bien estar el Pueblo, que llamando Sandia, puesto que al Pressente se halla, como se ve despoblado, y yermo; lo qual demas de ser conbeniencia para nossotros, lo es tanbien para el Reino pues siendo una frontera, y Puerta de los Enemigos Apaches, conseguirse ha con esto, el que se les estorbe la entrada, y assi mesmo que con las continuas Recorridurias de Tierra que nosotros haremos, esplorando sus huellas, no tan facil, y libre les sera el venir a sus hurtos, Asaltos, y homicidios; pues aiudados nossotros, de los Espanoles sercanos de Alburquerque, nos hacemos un muro fuerte, para Resistirse su deprabado intento. Y por que para la determinación de Vsa discurramos ser necesario, el que sepa el Numero de que dichos Genizaros nos componemos, decimos ser mas de siento las familias, que están dispersas por todo el reino. Assi en los Pueblos de Yndios, como en lugares de españoles. Y no es Nra intención que en esto se intrometan los criados de Españoles, que por derecho de haverlo rescatado y tener como los hijos en sus casas deben servirles sino solos nossotros, los que como hemos dicho nos hallamos desacomodados, y dispersos.

Por todo lo qual a Vsa volvemos a suplicar con todo rrendimiento se ha mui servido de concedernos lo arriba dicho, pues allí conviene al servicio, y agrado de ambas majestades y de ser assi como esperamos de su fiel, y catholico pecho, agradeceremos, se nos de el despacho, o orden en esta ocacion, para que siendo, como es tan oportuno el tiempo de sembrar, y hacer casa, pasemos luego a hacerlo; y Juramos en debida forma este nuestro escrito no ser de malicia, si por el motivo tan justo arriba dicho, y en lo nessesario ett[ceter]a

Los Genizaros (rubric)

En la Villa de Santa Fe en viente y un dia del mes de Abril de mil sette sientos trenta y tres anos vista por mi el Coronel Dn. Gervacio Cruzat y Gongora Governador y Capitan General de este Reyno de la Nueva Mexico y sus Provincias por su Mag. la huve por presentada en lo que ha lugar en derecho y devía mandar y mande que los suplicantes presenten una nomina de los Yndios que pretenden poblarse con la distincion de sus Nombres y Naciones. Asi lo provey mande y firme con los testigos de mi asistensia a falta de escribano Publico y Real que no lo ay en este Reyno

    Don Gervasio Cruzat y Gongora
    Witnesses: Gaspar Bitton Juan Antonio de Unanue

Nomina de los hijos Genízaros, que se hallan dispersos en este Reino de la Nuevo Mexico: Primeramente en esta jurrisdiccion de el Río Abajo los casados son los sigientes / List of the Native Sons (Genízaros) who are found scattered in this Kingdom of New Mexico: First, in this Río Abajo Jurisdiction are the following married families:

1. Antonio Gurule, casado, su mujer Theresa, sus hijos dos hombres, y una muger.
2. Sebastian Gallegos, Juman, casado con Quiteria, sus hijos tres hombres. Joseph Fernandes.
3. Juman, su muger Angelina, sus hijos tres: un hombre y dos mugeres.
4. Antonio Padilla, Panana, casado con Maria, su hijo un hombre.
5. Antonio Padilla, Panana, casado con Isabel, una hija.
6. Francisco Baca, Apache, casado con Maria, sus hijos: dos hombres y una muger.
7. Rafael Montoia (Montoya), Caigua, casado con Rosa, una hija.
8. Juan Antonio, Apache, casado con Maria, un hijo.
9. Pablo de Chaves, Caigua, casado con Rosa, dos hijos: un hijo y una muger.
10. Francisco de Chaves, Tano, casado con Mariana, sus hijos: dos hombres y dos mugeres.
11. Domingo Martines, de la Nacion A, casado con Antonia, sus hijos tres hombres y una muger.
12. Antonio Jaramillo, Caigua, casado con Pascuala, sus hijos: dos hombres y una muger.
13. Agustin Garcia, de la Nacion A, casado con Maria, sus hijos un hombre y una muger.
14. Joan Antonio Gurule, Panana, casado con Maria, sus hijos tres: dos hombres y una muger.

15. Joan Ulibarri, Apache, casado con Rosa, un hijo.
16. Cristobal Lujan, Panana, casado con Maria, sin hijos.
17. Cristobal Romero, Apache, casado con Antonia, sin hijos.

SOLTEROS / BACHELORS
1. Francisco Sedillo, Panana.
2. Francisco Baca, Panana.
3. Andres Martin, Yuta,
4. Agustin Fernandes, Juman, viudo
5. Antonio Tagle, Juman
6. Francisco García, Juman
7. Bernardo, soltero
8. Joseph, juman, soltero

En la Villa de Santa Fee en viente y tres de Abril de mil sette sientos trenta y tres anos vista por mi el Coronel Dn. Gervasio Cruzat y Gongora Governador y Capitan General de este Reyno de la Nueva Mexico y sus provincias por su Mag. la nomina de los Indios que en ella se expresa como asi mismo lo que pretenden en su escripto, devía declarar y declaro no tener lugar la poblasión que pretenden y solo se les permitira el ponerse en los Pueblos ya formados, para cuio efecto podía acudir el que quisiere a este superior Gobierno para que se les segnale el Pueblo a donde debe ponerse. Asi lo provey y mande y firme con los testigos de mi asistencia a falta de escribano Publico y Real q[ue] no lo ay en este Reyno
Don Gervasio Cruzat y Gongora
Witnesses: Gaspar Bitton Juan Antonio de Unanue (Original petition transcribed by María Feliza Monta Collaguazo)

English Translation of Petition to Populate the Old Pueblo of Sandía, 1733

Sir Governor and Captain General,

We, the Genízaro native sons in this Kingdom, whom by the mercy of God our Lord were brought to the fold and protection of Our Holy Mother Church, receiving, for our great joy, the water of baptism and with it the faith of the holy Mysteries of the Most High Lord, it being an excellent and singular favor of which we recognize and find ourselves thankful. Therefore, being many the souls that suffer in the immense sea of paganism, but by decree and providence found it worthy to bring us into the safe harbor of the Church, where we are joyful of such a progressive act and we hope through His Divine Grace to return to Him abundant fruits of virtue and good works and at the end of our temporal life, we would wish to perish happily voicing the good account of the blessings of His talents bequeathed us. Therefore, it is apparent that we enjoy the promised reward anticipated for those who faithfully observe His law and very holy precepts. In order to acquire such fortune, it is necessary that we give service to Him and depend on the satisfaction of the Lord to provide us the necessary sustenance for the body that in His infinite wisdom and sovereign providence, [He] has mandated, ordered, and prepared. For it is that in the beginning of our creation—that is, of Adam and Eve—He gave us all that provides for our natural maintenance, for which we needed not employ any type of labor or means. Due to the disgrace of our first parents, the dismissal of all things good and beneficial and releasing the reins of its disordered actions, breaking God's holy and sound precepts which were lost by them and also by us. We are now sentenced by such cruel offenses and penanced with the punishment and torment to cultivate the land, and each person working to the point of fatigue and watering the land with the sweat dripping down from our faces, which we are still experiencing. And even though, during the time of our penance, the lands were free and immense for our tillage with just a few men and inhabitants on the land. But today, by the provenance and disposition of the Lord, it is now full, and populated by people; that it is known by all to accommodate and not cross those boundaries which the kings and owners of the land assigned to each person's possession according to the legal foundations or intentions that they were in agreement with.

For this reason and the abovementioned suppositions, we, the referred native sons, present ourselves to your grandeur in the best manner, that asserting our rights, we declare that we now find ourselves dispersed in the villages and populaces of this kingdom, without protection or without means to maintain our persons and families. In addition, because we do not have our own land, we experience the discomfort and hardship that only God knows, and Your Magnificence can consider, that in our clothing and food and other necessities of the body are subject to tolerating the pressures that this condition can impart upon each one of us; and not all but some of us are at risk of getting trapped into such a plight, compelled by our hard work, misery, and pressures which might incite the Devil our enemy and then embrace the repugnant apostasy of the pagan world to find remedy and employment. This calls attention to the inclinations and judgments of the diverse populace, some knowing the better good and enjoying the Church of our God and Lord, but who suffer with humility and love for whatever chore and inconvenience but receive the company and council offered from others in exchange of not losing their souls; others might lose sight of this and put their care in the carnal world by the suggestions of the Enemy (that its jealousy doesn't cease to surround us) and, instigated by their own needs, execute the aforementioned. And even though we can ask for pity from Your Splendor as our master and father with your royal authority over the political and military government of this kingdom who would include us with the Christian Indian pueblos that are in this district, but we will not do so because considering that the said Indians renounce you and have bad inclinations despite years of doctrine and evangelical teaching do each day find themselves going backward and involved with idolatry and witchcraft; and not to contaminate ourselves with such pestilence toward dogma and perverse customs so it is that we with our children ask that in your well served greatness assign us as a pueblo for our care and well-being at the pueblo called Sandía, which presently appears to be unpopulated and gloomy; and also regardless of its convenience for us it would also be good for the kingdom since that it is at the border region and at the gateway to the enemy Apaches who disturb the entrance and in this way with our continued traversing of the land and exploring all its features we will be free and prepared for their future robberies, attacks, and murders; but also with the help of the Spanish people from nearby Alburquerque, we will make a walled fortress to resist their vicious intentions. Thus for your determination we believe it necessary that you know the number of said Genízaros that we comprise of which we believe to be more than one hundred families dispersed throughout the kingdom in Indian pueblos as well as in the territories of the Spanish [citizens]. And it is not our intention to include the house servants of the Spanish because it is their right, for they rescued them and brought them into their homes as their children to serve them, but rather this applies to only us whom, as we have explained, find ourselves discomfited and scattered.

For all the abovementioned reasons we again request with our humility that it would be of great service and to the liking of Both Majesties and as we would expect from your faithful and Catholic bosom, we would appreciate if you would give us the discharge or order in this case since it is such an opportune time to plant and build our homes which we would immediately proceed to do; and we swear that our writ is in due form and not of malice but rather motivated by a just and imperative cause.

Los Genízaros (rubric)
(English translation by Samuel E. Sisneros and Carlos Vélez-Ibáñez)

Notes

1. These renditions of Belén's history were corroborated during the City of Belén and Belén Chamber of Commerce's 2007 renovation of the civic plaza located on Becker Avenue in downtown Belén. In the English lexicon, a plaza is a town square. In colonial New Mexico, *plaza* is synonymous with settlement, which, according to the Laws of the Indies, should be constructed around a central civic space. Then, as now, plaza refers to a Hispano town, whereas pueblo means an Indian town (Sisneros 2016).

2. John Becker came to Belén in the 1870s and became a successful banker and merchant.

3. The locations of the old ruins of the mission church and convent and some of the secondary plazas are known by locals. Since 2018 there is ongoing archaeological excavation to positively identify the Plaza Vieja site. The last documented reference to the ruins of the colonial church was in 1943, with a photographic image of Brother Andrew Hayes pointing to the then remaining structural ruins (Sisneros 2018; Hayes 1943).

4. Río Abajo pre-revolt and reconquest families are discussed in Chávez 1992.

5. Los Genízaros Petition to Governor Gervasio Cruzat y Góngora, April 21, 1733, Spanish Archives of New Mexico (SANM), Series I: 1208.

6. Historians Malcolm Ebright and Rick Hendricks (2006) assume that the petition was not written by one of the Genízaro petitioners but rather by "an advocate." Borderlands scholar Carlos Vélez-Ibáñez, while assisting me by analyzing and translating the petition, concluded that the document was drawn by Genízaro authorship. He commented: "I would speculate that it may not have been anonymous but rather a literate Genízaro who assumed the collective identity of the rest of the petitioners as 'Genízaros,' providing group identity rather than that of an individual and topping it off with their own rubric" (personal communication, March 2019).

7. Servitude in New Mexico was different from the chattel and plantation black slavery of the southern United States, because the former involved a complex regional system of economic codependency, caste and ethnic identity, social positioning, and kinship ties that led to a totally separate outcome from that of the African American slave experience (Brooks 2004; Rael-Gálvez 2002).

8. The heading in Spanish reads "Nomina de los hijos Genízaros que se hallan dispersos en este Reino de la Nueva México. Primeramente en esta jurisdicción de Río Abajo los casados son los sigientes." *Hijos* or sons are often used in conjunction with *principales* (principles) and would be equivalent to the English term "native sons," analogous to the concept of the neophyte-infant category used during the colonial period.

9. The baptisms, marriages, prenuptial investigations, and burials discussed throughout this chapter can be found in the sacramental church registries of San Agustín de Isleta and Nuestra Señora de Belén, and in the prenuptial records and loose documents in the Archives of the Archdiocese of Santa Fe. Microfilm editions and extraction publications are widely available.

10. Peticion de los principales indios del pueblo de San Agustín de la Isleta contra el indio Reymundo del mismo pueblo, August 7, 1757, A. L. Pinard Collection, Bancroft Library, University of California, P-E 50: 3, CSWR microfilm 110: 5, roll 6. The Reymundo mentioned is this case could only be Reymundo Jójola. There were no other persons by the name of Reymundo in the records for this time period, and the fact that witnesses called him "El Fiscal" also verifies the identification. This Reymundo Jójola appears to be the Indio baptized on June 6, 1703, in Bernalillo. He was a son of Juan Jójola and María de los Reyes.

11. Personal conversation with an Isleta tribal member whose name is withheld by request, Albuquerque, 2015.

12. "Cultural broker" is a term used for a person retaining cultural identity while proactively living in another cultural setting, acting as a mediator between the two. Other notable Indian-to-Spanish cultural brokers were Bartolomé de Ojeda and don Juan de Ye of the colonial period and twentieth-century Pablo Abeita of Isleta Pueblo (Guggino 1955).

13. There are many examples in the church records of the Coyote category and, in the Belén/Isleta area, my research shows that the term in synonymous with "Indian" or "Genízaro." Sometimes, two identity markers were combined; for example, María Salome is identified as an "India Coyota" of Belén, daughter of José Baca and Marta Vásquez, as found in the Belén baptismal record of October 25, 1815. Ross Frank defines "Coyote" as a term that "often referred to offspring of Plains Indians born as captives or servants in Spanish households" (2000, 281).

14. Manuel Torres, son of Captain don Diego de Torres and María Martín, was married to María Tomasa Cruz, Coyota, daughter of Buenaventura de la Cruz and Jasinta Baca. Witnesses were Captain don Joseph Baca and Juana Torres.

15. Cadallos y Rabal to Viceroy, Santa Fe, copy of statement of Genízaro Indian Ventura regarding conditions in the Navajo country, July 2, 1748, SANM II: 827.

16. Steven Horvath postulates that this Ventura is the same Ventura who was married to Jacinta, not noticing that in the actual biography there is mention that Ventura was married to Diego Torres's servant Rosa (1979, 84–85).

17. Declaracion, "Nueva Poblacion de Indios Genízaros," Fr. Juan Miguel Menchero, May 10, 1744, Legajo 9, doc. 11, Biblioteca Nacional de México, México, DF; photocopy, Center for Southwest Research, University of New Mexico, MSS 867, Vol. 126A, 2887–88. I corroborate with Horvath's conclusion that this Tomé location was a mistake on the part of Menchero. Horvath goes further to state that it is "Menchero's fabrication that has led many historians astray" to include Tomé as a Genízaro forefront (1979, 81).

18. SANM I, Land Records, SG 13.

19. Antonio Casados and Luis Quintana, Genízaros, proceeding against "Fulano" Barrera, Diego de Torres, and Antonio Salazar over lands at the Puesto de Belén, February 12, 1746, SANM I: 183.

20. Proceedings against Francisco Padilla for inciting trouble within the Pueblo of Laguna, Santa Fe, March 8–June 4, 1737, SANM II, 415b, CSWR Roll 7, fr. 561. Nothing more is known of Caraquis, although, his widow, Gregoria (no surname), apparently moved to Abiquiú, where she married a Genízaro in 1759. Padilla appears to be of the Spanish category.

21. Don Pedro Cebrián, Conde de Fuenclara, and Viceroy of New Spain don Félix de Sandoval, concerning complaints by Indians, October 22, 1745, Bancroft Library, P-E 228, doc. 32-33, CSWR microfilm, 868: 7 reel 12. Manuel could have been of Piro or Isleta del Sur origin, because it is noted that the group stayed at Manuel's mother's house in El Paso del Norte.

22. Proceedings against Luis Quintana, Apache servant of Juan de Tafoya, and others, Santa Fe, July 8–31, 1742, SANM II: 441.

23. SANM I: 183. See also Bancroft Library, P-E 228, doc. 32-33, .

24. Bancroft Library, 0040, October 20, 1745, Mexico City.

25. Proceedings in the complaint of Juan Pino against two Genízaros of Belén for the theft of goods, June 19–August 5, 1747, SANM II: 480.

26. Prenuptial investigation of Lucas Baca and María Josefa Rael, June 15, 1778, Belén, Loose Documents, no. 24, AASF.

27. Caballero de Croix, México, regarding Genízaro attack on Apaches, July 2, 1777, SANM II: 701.

28. Fray Juan Agustín de Morfi, "Account of Disorders," 1778, Archivo General de la Nación (AGN), Historia, vol. 25. A translation can be found in Simmons 1991, 127–61.

29. Proceedings by settlers of Sabinal, 1765–1767, SANM I: 869.

30. The nine Indios Genízaros were Joseph Manuel Gurulé, Matías Frésquez, Juan de Luna, Antonio Gurulé, Antonio Rubí, Gerónimo Silva, Juan Ramos, Reymundo Jójola, and Juan Pedro Jójola de la Cruz. Many other names of Genízaros appear in the 1767 complaint. The name of the governadorcillo was not noted.

31. The August 7, 1803, Belén church baptism of the child of Jóaquin Álvarez del Castillo notes the family's residency at the second plaza, Belén de los Bacas.

32. Marcos Velásquez and María married at San Felipe de Neri Church in Alburquerque on February 14, 1765.

33. For a discussion of this family, see Chávez 1992, 185.

34. AGN, photocopy no. 25, pt. 3, 338–40, Center for Southwest Research, University of New Mexico.

35. Fray Cayetano José Bernal, "Certificaciones de las misiones de Nuevo Mexico," Belén, September 1, 1794, Biblioteca Nacional de México, legajo 10, num. 70; photocopy at CSWR, MSS 867, vol. 127D; transcription at CSWR, MSS 22.

36. Fray Cayetano José Bernal to Francisco Paula Soto, Secretario de Gobierno, May 16, 1795, "Expediente sobre licencia de decir misa en la capilla de la Mision de Belén feligresia de Alburquerque en el Nuevo Mexico, solicitandose haga parroguia," AHAD, roll 195, frame 0484.

37. A few generations earlier, Matías Lente and wife Juana (surname unknown) were the head of the large Lente family of the southern Isleta village of Los Lentes, which was early on populated by Isletans, Piros, and Genízaros.

38. It was brought to my attention in a personal communication with art historian Felipe Mirabal (2016) that the word *coruña* was used for an embroidered overshirt that Pueblo men traditionally wore to show their status in the community.

39. Fray Cayetano José Bernal, Informe, Belén, June 27, 1801, Archivo Histórico del Archobispado de Durango (microfilm edition: reel 205, frames 561–65, 619–20). An English translation can be found in Hendricks 2008, 123–30.

40. Cofradía de las Benditas Almas del Purgatorio, 1802, loose documents, AASF, University of New Mexico, microfilm, roll 53, frame 395.

41. This last mention was the 1819 baptism of María Bartolomé, daughter of Manuel Galindo and María Ysabel Chávez.

42. This couple apparently never married, and both appear to have later married Los Janchis persons.

43. Santiago was most likely the brother of José María Moreno, a Los Janchis resident. Santiago therefore would have been the son of José Moreno and Verónica Fresquis, Genízaros from Los Lentes who later moved to Plaza de los Genízaros.

44. María Gertrudes Gurulé is noted as the widow of Juan Pedro Paseño. This couple appears to be the Juan Pedro Baca and María Gertrudes Gurulé who married in Belén in 1810. Both are listed as Indians; Juan Pedro's parents were Juan de Dios Baca and María Juana Tiburcio. María Gertrudes was listed as the natural daughter of María Antonia Gurulé.

45. For a pioneering and excellent examination of Los Comanches and Indo-Hispano folk celebrations, see Lamadrid 2003.

46. Arthur L. Campa provided this translation of the Comanche emissary's name (Kanellos 2002; Campa 1942).

47. *Boletín del Archivo General de la Nación*, vol. 30, no. 3 (1959).

48. Isletans were also referred to as "Indios del Pueblo" or simply "del Pueblo." In this case, it means of the Pueblo mission of Belén.

49. One of the last families listed as being from the Plaza de los Genízaros, in 1819, is that of Manuel Galindo and María Isabel (Ysabel) Chávez.

50. Steven Horvath purports to have located the Plaza de los Genízaros near the railroad roundabout near the Harvey House Museum in present-day Belén, but a closer look at his source reveals that the informant only mentions playing at ruins of an old building in that area. It could have just as easily been the ruins of the Plaza de los Trujillos.

51. John Ward, Special Agent for Pueblos, Santa Fe, July 10, 1867, *Report of the Secretary of Interior*, nos. 55–56, Records of the Bureau of Indian Affairs, Secretary of the Interior, 210-13.

52. Mestizaje is the process of racial mixing between Spanish and Indian individuals, thus creating mestizos. This process was prevalent in the Americas during the colonial period.

53. For an exceptional examination of nineteenth-century Indian captivity, see Brugge 2010.

54. Rubén Cobos Collection of Southwestern Folklore and Folk Music, Center for Southwest Research, University of New Mexico, Box 2, CD 227; Box 3, CD 239, 243, 264. Amador Abeyta, born in 1883 in Sabinal, sang and recorded his inditas around 1946.

55. Blood memory is a concept in Native American literature that counters blood quantum by instead looking at ancestry, heritage, beliefs, storytelling, and communal memory in order to blend an ethnic and cultural identity with history and to reimagine and retell the past so as to claim a self-identity (Harkin 2014).

56. Corroborating versions of this story were told to me by Alberta O'Neal, Patsy Tórrez, and Rosendo Lovato, grandchildren of Manuel García-O'Neal, in 2014; they were also the informants for Matt Baca's article.

57. Extraction in "Bautismos: Nuestra Señora de Belen Church, January 1, 1866, through March 13, 1895," Santa Fe, New Mexico: Archdiocese of Santa Fe, 1998. I also checked with microfilm copy of original record (AASF, r., 313) and determined that the extraction is accurate.

58. Extraction in "Bautismos: Nuestra Señora de Belén Church."

59. The given name "Delfinia" is expressed in various documents as Delfina, Delphine, and Derfinia, the latter probably being the form that prompted the phonetic alteration to Virginia.

60. Extraction in "Bautismos: Nuestra Señora de Belén Church," 78. The entry reads: "On the 20th of January of 1886, in the Church of Belén, I married and veiled Carlos O'Neil, legitimate son of Carlos O'Neil and of Susan Bechtal, deceased, from

Waukan (Iowa) with Virginia García, legitimate daughter of Isidoro García and of Petra Montaño, from Belén. Witnesses, Juan Poniente and Francisca Montoya."

61. Extraction in "Bautismos: Nuestra Señora de Belén Church," 342. The entry reads: "O'Neil, Luis Carlos, of Belen, born on 1 Dec. 1886. Bap. on 19 Dec. 1886. Hijo de Charles O'Neil y Virginia Garcia. Godparents: Luis Boul y Manuela Garcia." Luis Carlos may have died as an infant, since he doesn't show up in further documents.

62. The entry reads: "In this Church of Belén, today the 10th of September of 1900, I married Melchiades García, single, legitimate son of Theodoro García and of Juana [blocked out by black line], with Adela García, daughter of Virginia García, from Belén. Padrino, Martín Ortega. Madrina, Manuela García."

63. AASF, POS reel 111A, 214.

64. Conversation with Alberta O'Neal, June 2015.

65. Ancestry.com.

66. Globe city directory.

67. *Bisbee Daily Review*, January 2, 1919, 7.

68. Samuel E. Sisneros ancestry: Samuel Sisneros > Rosalía Padilla > Josefina Moraga > Crespín Moraga > Antonio Aban Moraga > Juana Trujillo > Manuel Trujillo > and Rosa María Lucero, daughter of Bernardo Lucero and Brianda Chávez. Bernardo and Brianda were married on September 25, 1740, and listed in the marriage register of San Agustín de Isleta Pueblo mission church as Coyotes and without surnames. The 1750 census of Los Chávez (most likely servants of Nicolás Chávez) and other historical documents state that they were Coyotes, and the 1790 Belén census has the family enumerated as Coyote residents of Plaza no. 2.

69. Real Academia Española, "Nuevo tesoro lexigráfico de la lengua española," available at http://ntlle.rae.es/ntlle/SrvltGUILoginNtlle.

References

Baca, Matt. 2008. "Who Was the Indian Princess?" La Historia del Rio Abajo, *Belén News-Bulletin*, September 20.

Bletzer, Michael. 2013. "'The First Province of That Kingdom': Notes on the Colonial History of the Piro Area." *New Mexico Historical Review* 88, no. 4 (October): 437–59.

Brooks, James F. 2004. *Captives and Cousins: Slavery, Kinship, and Community in the Southwest Borderlands*. Chapel Hill: University of North Carolina Press.

Brugge, David M. 2010. *Navajos in the Catholic Church Records of New Mexico, 1694–1875*. 3rd ed. Santa Fe: School for Advanced Research Press.

Buxton, Margaret L. 1998. "Jójola: An Indian Ancestry." *Herencia* (Hispanic Genealogical Research Center) 6, no. 4 (October).

Campa, Arthur L. 1930. "A Bibliography of Spanish Folk-lore in New Mexico." *University of New Mexico Bulletin* 3, no. 3 (September): 9.

———. 1942. "Los Comanches: A New Mexican Folk Drama." *University of New Mexico Bulletin* 7, no. 1 (April).

Carroll, H. Bailey, and J. Villasana Haggard, trans. 1942. *Three New Mexico Chronicles: The Exposición of Don Pedro Bautista Pino, 1812; The Ojeada of Lic. Antonio Barreiro, 1832; and the Additions by Don José Agustín de Escudero, 1849*. Albuquerque: Quivira Society.

Chávez, Fray Angélico. 1992. *Origins of New Mexico Families: A Genealogy of the Spanish Colonial Period*. Santa Fe: Museum of New Mexico Press.

City of Belén. N.d. "Belén: The Hub City." History. Available at http://www.belen-nm.gov/history.aspx.

Cobos, Rubén. 1983. *A Dictionary of New Mexico and Southern Colorado Spanish*. Santa Fe: Museum of New Mexico Press.

Domínguez, Fray Francisco Atanasio. 1956. *The Missions of New Mexico, 1776: A Description by Fray Francisco Atanasio Domínguez, with Other Contemporary Documents*. Edited and translated by Fray Angélico Chávez and Eleanor B. Adams. Albuquerque: University of New Mexico Press.

Ebright, Malcolm. 2014. *Advocates for the Oppressed: Hispanos, Indians, Genízaros, and Their Land in New Mexico*. Albuquerque: University of New Mexico Press.

Ebright, Malcolm, and Rick Hendricks. 2006. *The Witches of Abiquiú: The Governor, the Priest, the Genízaro Indians, and the Devil*. Albuquerque: University of New Mexico Press.

Espinosa, Aurelio M. 1907. "Los Comanches: A Spanish Heroic Play of the Year Seventeen Hundred and Eighty." *Bulletin University of New Mexico* 1, no. 1 (December).

Frank, Ross. 2000. *From Settler to Citizen: New Mexican Economic Development and the Creation of Vecino Society, 1750–1820*. Berkeley: University of California Press.

Guggino, Patricia Burke. 1955. "Pablo Abeita (1871–1940): Cultural Broker between Isleta Pueblo in New Mexico and the United States Government." PhD diss., University of New Mexico.

Harkin, Natalie. 2014. "The Poetics of (Re)Mapping Archives: Memory in the Blood." *Journal of the Association for the Study of Australian Literature* 14, no. 3.

Hayes, Andrew, O. S. M., ed. 1943. *150th Anniversary of the Founding of the Parish of Our Lady of Belen, 1793–1943*. Belén, NM: Our Lady of Belén Church.

Hendricks, Rick. 2008. *New Mexico in 1801: The Priests Report*. Albuquerque: Río Grande Books.

Horvath, Steven M. 1979. "The Social and Political Organization of the Genízaros of Plaza de Nuestra Señora de los Dolores de Belén, New Mexico, 1740–1812." PhD diss., Brown University.

Kanellos, Nicolás, ed. 2002. *Herencia: The Anthology of Hispanic Literature of the United States.* Oxford: Oxford University Press.

Lamadrid, Enrique R. 2002. "History, Faith, and Intercultural Relations in Two New Mexican *Inditas*: *Plácida Romero* and *San Luis Gonzaga.*" In *Nuevomexicano Cultural Legacy: Forms, Agencies, and Discourse,* edited by Francisco A. Lomelí, Victor A. Sorell, and Genaro M. Padilla, 164–84. Albuquerque: University of New Mexico Press.

———. 2003. *Hermanitos Comanchitos: Indo-Hispano Rituals of Captivity and Redemption.* Albuquerque: University of New Mexico Press.

Langham Olmsted, Virginia. 1975. *New Mexico Spanish and Mexican Colonial Censuses: 1790, 1823, 1845.* Albuquerque: New Mexico Genealogical Society.

———. 1981. *Spanish and Mexican Censuses of New Mexico, 1750–1830.* Albuquerque: New Mexico Genealogical Society.

Lewis, Angela. 2019. "Grolet-Gurulé: Los Franceses de Nuevo Mexico." Available at http://www.gurulefamily.org.

Marshall, Michael P., and Henry J. Walt. 1984. *Rio Abajo: Prehistory and History of a Rio Grande Province.* Santa Fe: New Mexico Historic Preservation Program.

Miller, Wick R. 1960. "Spanish Loanwords in Acoma: II." *International Journal of American Linguistics* 26, no. 1 (January): 41–49.

Parks, Douglas R. 2001. "Pawnee." In *Handbook of North American Indians,* vol. 13, *Plains,* edited by Raymond J. DeMallie and William C. Sturtevant, 515–47. Washington, DC: Smithsonian Institution.

Rael-Gálvez, Estevan. 2002. "Identifying Captivity and Capturing Identity: Narratives of American Indian Slavery in Colorado and New Mexico, 1776–1934." PhD diss., University of Michigan.

Rieu-Millan, Marie Laure. 1990. *Los Diputados Americanos en Las Cortes de Cádiz.* Madrid: Consejo Superior de Investigaciones Científicas.

Simmons, Marc. 1991. *Coronado's Land: Essay on Daily Life in Colonial New Mexico.* Albuquerque: University of New Mexico Press.

Sisneros, Samuel. 1996. "Salazar and Hinojos Family Ties." *Herencia* (Hispanic Genealogical Research Center) 4, no. 1 (January).

———. 2016. *Belen's Plaza Vieja and Colonial Church Site: Memory, Continuity and Recovery.* Capstone Project, UNM School of Architecture & Planning.

———. 2018. *The Plaza Vieja and Colonial Church of Nuestra Señora de Belén, New Mexico.* San Bernadino, CA: CreateSpace Publishing.

Wiseman, Regge N. 1995. *The Belén Bridge Site and the Late Elmendorf Phase of Central New Mexico.* Archaeology Notes 137. Santa Fe: Office of Archaeological Studies, Museum of New Mexico.

CHAPTER SEVEN

Genízaro Ethnogenesis and the Archaeological Record

CHARLES M. CARRILLO

An emergent interest in the Genízaros of New Mexico, and archaeological inquiry about these peoples, have caused me to rethink my own conceptual treatment of archaeological evidence from locations identified as Genízaro sites. I argue that the historicity of material practices and material culture should be reconceptualized as an active, constitutive element of social practice.

Ethnogenesis is defined as a process by which a social group comes to regard itself or be regarded as a distinct people; in other words, when a group of people acquires an ethnicity—either through a process of self-identification or an imposed-outside identification (Anderson 1999). On the other hand, the concept of transculturation implies that "native" culture is abandoned, swept aside, or left behind (Ortiz [1940] 1995). Genízaro consciousness suggests otherwise. Did the Genízaros of New Mexico purposely scheme their own ethnogenesis? Marshall Sahlins points out that cultural change through the process of ethnogenesis is "externally introduced, yet indigenously orchestrated" (1985). So what about the Genízaros of Abiquiú, Belén, Jarales, and other villages in New Mexico? I can speak clearly about the Abiquiú Genízaro experience—the first Genízaros in Abiquiú were Hopi-Tewa, they were identified as Genízaros by colonial authorities, they were externally named as Genízaros, yet they indigenously orchestrated themselves with a Genízaro identity. At least a dozen different Native groups came to populate the eighteenth- and early nineteenth-century Pueblo de Abiquiú. The externally induced mechanism that influenced Abiquiú's ethnogenesis were the local Franciscans assigned to the pueblo, and the Spanish Crown's involvement as agents for the placement of Genízaros in the pueblo. The question then is, did the Abiquiú Genízaros operate as power brokers between mainstream New Mexican Hispano society and other Native American groups? In other cases from colonial New Mexico, certain families and even groups of people self-identified as Genízaro. Many scholars have suggested that Genízaros were the product of interracial unions. Baptismal records from Abiquiú tell a different story. Recently discovered baptismal records from Abiquiú indicate that infant children of the nomadic Ute, Apache, Paiute, Kiowa, and Navajo Nations, as well as infant children from many pueblos including Cochití and Isleta, were baptized on a regular basis. By 1800, the Franciscan missionary at Abiquiú, Teodoro Alcina, only notes in the baptismal records the Native group from which the captives are derived, such as Ute, Apache, Navajo, and so on. Alcina does not assign social status to the baptized captives. It is impossible to know if these children were the products of interracial relations. Frances Leon Swadesh writes:

> The word "Genízaro" supposedly refers to detribalized, nomadic Indians, often of mixed ancestry, who came from both east and west of New Mexico and who had been ransomed from captivity among the nomadic tribes. In Abiquiú the church records tell a somewhat different story. In addition to the record of Hopis settled at the Montoya homestead in 1750, records of later years show that people from Hopi Villages, Zunis, Isletas, Santa Claras and other Pueblo Indians continued to come to Abiquiú throughout the eighteenth century, apparently forming the majority of the local Genízaro population. Those Genízaros identified as nomadic or of non–New Mexican origin were in the minority. (1974, 40)

Gilberto Benito Córdova argues in his work "Missionization and Hispanicization of Santo Tomás Apóstol de Abiquiú, 1750–1770" that the Genízaros of that community simply transculturated from Genízaros to Hispanos, by first being detribalized, then baptized, and finally acculturated into the customs of eighteenth-century Hispanos (1979).

Fray Angélico Chávez pointed out that long before Genízaros were described by eighteenth-century Franciscans or colonial authorities for their military role, they were simply called Genízaros as an ethnic designation applied to detribalized Indians (1979). Their role as soldiers came later. Fray Juan Agustín Morfi describes them as "fine soldiers, very warlike, and most formidable against our enemies" (Horvath 1979, 99–100). Additionally, Teodoro

Croix commented on the Genízaros' "prosperous" clashes with Apaches (Horvath 1979, 99–100). Croix does not define his use of "prosperous"; however, it is likely that he was suggesting that the outcome of these clashes benefited the settler communities, perhaps even with war booty! Another question surfaces: did Genízaros use their perceived "military/soldier" role to advance their social position in New Mexican society?

More recently scholars such as Ramón Gutiérrez and James Brooks have equated Genízaros with military auxiliaries (Gutiérrez 1991, 151; Brooks 2002, 374). As part of the New World caste system employed by the Spanish, the term "Genízaro" applied to perceived genetic qualities and/or racial admixtures. This caste system did not rank castes according to occupation; therefore, its use as a designator suggesting military service or "shock troops" becomes questionable, suggesting the possibility that Genízaros themselves applied an occupational category to their social status. Hence, they carved out for themselves a status of note that demonstrates my assertion that they were involved in their own ethnogenesis. They differentiated themselves from other Native Americans and Hispanos with a distinct Genízaro identity. The question presented to us is—did Genízaros reinvent themselves through the process of ethnogenesis, and was this social cultural transformation a strategy for survival?

Today, Abiquiuseños celebrate their Genízaro heritage through spoken narratives and by preserving elements of their cultural identity, as is the case in their performance narratives, which include song and dance. These narratives reaffirm and help maintain a collective memory of "Genízaroness" (Lamadrid 2003).

Let us now turn to ethnicity, understood as shared cultural practices, perspectives, and distinctions that set apart one group of people from another; that is, shared cultural heritage. The most common characteristics distinguishing ethnic groups are ancestry, a sense of common history, language, religion, and, often, forms of dress. Ethnic differences are learned and not inherited. Typically, members of an ethnic group share a common history but not necessarily a common language. In Abiquiú, the first groups of settled Genízaros did not share a common group history or a common language. Included in the Genízaro population were Hopis, Hopi-Tewas, Kiowas, Pawnees, Paiutes, Utes, Navajos, Apaches, and peoples from many pueblos. This varied conglomeration of people with different histories and different languages formed the Pueblo de Abiquiú, with a common language, Spanish, a common religion, Catholicism, and a shared "new" history as they struggled to establish themselves in an ongoing social and political process.

I would argue that the Abiquiú Genízaros minimized most indigenous cultural practices and selectively preserved others. The performance narratives still celebrated for the Feast Day of Santo Tomás in Abiquiú are an example of a preserved cultural practice. These dances likely survived the scrutiny of church and civil authorities because they were nonthreatening. Córdova argues that the eighteenth-century missionization and Hispanicization efforts were so effective that the descendants of the Genízaros are now considered in legal terms as members of a Hispanic/Chicano/Mexican American/Spanish American/Latino community and not a part of a defined "Native American" population (1979). I would argue that the "shared" cultural history of Abiquiú is its incomplete Hispanicization. Governor Tomás Vélez Cachupín's 1754 placement of the Genízaros in Abiquiú is understood as his attempt to totally acculturate the Native population as Hispanos. The very fact that some residents of Abiquiú still self-identify as Genízaro, and still maintain their Genízaro dances and vocalizations, is a testament to the fact that the colonial process of acculturation was incomplete.

With all that I have said, I now get to play devil's advocate and ask this question to my fellow archaeologists: Can we find Genízaros in the archaeological record? Archaeologists investigate architecture, food practices/foodways, pottery, lithics, and other material culture. I suggest that this material culture should be studied in the context of eighteenth- and nineteenth-century regional processes, group fission, and group fusion. Archaeological research is an important alternative to archival-based research for understanding Genízaro villages; however, my concern is that material culture does not elicit Genízaros. So let us examine two different types of material from the archaeological record, faunal remains and pottery.

As a case in point, recently excavated faunal remains from a Hispanic settlement were used as evidence to elicit Indianness/Genízaros via differences in the butchering practices from different loci at the site (Sherman 2002, 57). Butchered horsemeat was linked to lower-status families and by default to Genízaros with the simplified argument that "vecino tastes" would evoke disgust at the thought of equine consumption. *Vecino*, literally "neighbor," is a term used in colonial documents to designate relatively acculturated, high-status groups (Frank 2000). In other words, the more "Spanish" families were, the less likely they would be to eat horsemeat. The assumption in examining social status is that pork was served to upper-class families while venison was served to "Indians."

Simply stated, the "colonizer" is different from the "Indian" because they have different "tastes" and food practices. Concerning Europeans, David Sherman writes: "'waste not, want not,' and when horses reached the end of their productive lives as work animals, they found their way to the livestock markets and onto the dinner plates" (2002, 57). Concerning the archaeology of eighteenth-century Cape Cod, Anne Yentsch writes: "[W]hile horsemeat was culturally taboo among English settlers in the New World, when the animals died, they were used as food" (1988, 150). In our case, the butchering practices among different families in the same village do not determine lower status, whether indigenous or "Genízaro." Horsemeat consumption at Hispanic sites informs us that meat was meat—a food commodity, used by anyone who had access to it, not necessarily Genízaros.

Until recently, pottery produced in Hispanic villages (Abiquiú qualifies as one) was assumed to be the manufacture of nearby Pueblo potters or Athabascan potters. My own research has provided the theoretical basis for understanding pottery produced in Hispanic villages (Carrillo 1996).

An operational definition may prove helpful: a traditional New Mexican Hispanic was a person who chose to live or was forced to live in a Hispanic manner by residing in a Hispanic village or settlement. They included residents of Genízaro villages that are now Hispanic villages. Other locations are home sites occupied by Hispanic settlers that were not attached to larger planned plazas, such as scattered ranch sites and extended family *placitas*. These individuals chose to or were forced to live in New Mexico rather than New Spain; and they chose to or were forced to speak Spanish rather than an Indian language as their primary language, and to believe in and practice Catholicism rather than a Native American religion. Biologically, many of the people in this situation were totally or predominantly Native American.

That being said, I do not believe that archaeologists can elicit "Genízaro" pottery from the archaeological record. Pottery manufacture is a learned behavior—it is not an inherited behavior. Recall that ethnicity is learned, not inherited. As archaeologists, we need to be more aware of the unexamined presuppositions that we bring to our research and our theorizing—colonizer/Hispano versus indigenous. We need to be aware of the limits of archaeological knowledge about social groups like Genízaros. Margaret Conkey questions:

What if we question the assumption that groups are continuous integrated bounded entities that can be stopped in their time-space tracks as traditional ethnography has led us to believe? What if we question the assumption that social groups in the past changed transformationally and gradually, as the pervasive kind of evolutionary theory has led us to believe: that there was tribalization or complexification of a "progressive" sort. At minimum, we should recognize the weight of our own particular historically contingent world view that has emphasized social and cultural boundaries. Even those stylistic studies that work with inferences about social interaction, as a process, are dependent upon the demonstration or hypothesized existence of social boundaries. At a very fundamental level, questioning these taken-for-granted notions about the inherent boundedness of groups or the inevitable transformations of social units through time should lead to a radical change not just in the way we conceptualize culture but in how we practice cultural description or representation. (1990, 12)

What I am asking archaeologists working in seventeenth-, eighteenth-, and even nineteenth-century New Mexican Genízaro villages is to consider a reconceptualization of culture. James Clifford postulates that culture is not even a unified corpus of symbols that can be definitively interpreted; rather, he informs us that culture is "contested," "temporal," and "emergent" (1986, 19).

Can this be said of the Genízaros of New Mexico? The implications are these: our view of culture is produced historically, and because of this, we need to reexamine Genízaro culture. In short, these peoples were in production, produced historically, contested, and emergent. So what does this mean for archaeologists, and for the material culture produced by Genízaros? Our reexamination should challenge the notion of material culture as a product or output that reflects social entities. Genízaro material culture is itself an active essential element of social practice. The question arises then—can we separate this material culture from what we term "Hispanic"? In the context of village archaeology, objects understood to be clearly of Hispanic/European and even Asian origin—such as imported ceramics and metal—were not rejected by Genízaros; rather, they made these "outsider" objects their own. These objects were used in the context of Genízaro village life—so as archaeologists, how do we perceive them?

As a student of "New Archaeology," I was taught to view culture as an adaptive system with material outputs and specific archaeological correlates.

Material culture was thought of as a code to be read by archaeologists, as coded information about variability in the operation of past cultural systems. I propose to view Genízaro material culture as an active, fundamental element of social practice. Therefore, we should challenge ourselves as ethnographers, historians, and archaeologists to understand the contexts in which social/cultural experiences are activated as practice. Rather than focus on the identification of Genízaro material culture or the characterization of Genízaro material culture, it is the dynamics of Genízaro culture or the mutability of this material culture as embedded in contexts of social life and social relations that we should examine.

In short, if archaeologists are looking for Pueblos—Hopis, Tewas, Towas, Tiwas, Keres—or Athabascans, Comanches, Pawnees, Kiowas, Utes, or other tribal groups in the archaeological record of Genízaro communities, then, as Benito Córdova might say in one of his picaresque moods, they may be joining Mano Fashico, the Brother Francis character of Indo-Hispano joke cycles, a numskull (Lamadrid and Steele 1998), "pidiendo peras al olmo" (looking for pears in the elm tree) in La Tierra de Jauja, the Neverland of wishful thinkers.

References

Anderson, Gary Clayton. 1999. *The Indian Southwest, 1580–1830: Ethnogenesis and Reinvention*. Norman: University of Oklahoma Press.

Brooks, James F. 2002. *Captives and Cousins: Slavery, Kinship, and Community in the Southwest Borderlands*. Chapel Hill: University of North Carolina Press.

Carrillo, Charles M. 1996. "Hispanic New Mexican Pottery: Evidence of Craft Specialization, 1790–1890." PhD diss., University of New Mexico.

Chávez, Fray Angélico. 1979. "Genízaros." In *Handbook of North American Indians*, vol. 9, *Southwest*, edited by Alfonso Ortiz and William C. Sturtevant, 198–200. Washington, DC: Smithsonian Institution.

Clifford, James. 1986. "Introduction: Partial Truths." In *Writing Culture: The Poetics and Politics of Ethnography*, edited by James Clifford and George E. Marcus, 1–26. Berkeley: University of California Press.

Conkey, Margaret W. 1990. "Experimenting with Style in Archaeology: Some Historical and Theoretical Issues." In *The Uses of Style in Archaeology*, edited by Margaret W. Conkey and Christine A. Hastorf. Cambridge: Cambridge University Press.

Córdova, Gilberto Benito. 1979. "Missionization and Hispanicization of Santo Tomás Apóstol de Abiquiú, 1750–1770." PhD diss., University of New Mexico.

Frank, Ross. 2000. *From Settler to Citizen: New Mexican Economic Development and the Creation of Vecino Society, 1750–1820.* Berkeley: University of California Press.

Gutiérrez, Ramón A. 1991. *When Jesus Came, the Corn Mothers Went Away: Marriage, Sexuality, and Power in New Mexico, 1500–1846.* Stanford, CA: Stanford University Press.

Horvath, Steven M. 1979. "The Social and Political Organization of the Genízaros of Plaza de Nuestra Señora de los Dolores de Belén, New Mexico, 1740–1812." PhD diss., Brown University.

Lamadrid, Enrique. 2003. *Hermanitos Comanchitos: Indo-Hispano Rituals of Captivity and Redemption.* Albuquerque: University of New Mexico Press.

Lamadrid, Enrique, and Thomas J. Steele, S. J. 1998. "Indigenous Voice in Nuevomexicano Anti-Clerical Satire: Humor, Rumor, and Marginalia, from the 'Mano Fashico Numskulls' to the 'Anti-Cristo of Taos.'" *Catholic Southwest* 9, 53–74.

Ortiz, Fernando. (1940) 1995. *Cuban Counterpoint: Tobacco and Sugar.* Durham, NC: Duke University Press.

Sahlins, Marshall. 1985. *Islands of History.* Chicago: University of Chicago Press.

Sherman, David M. 2002. *Tending Animals in the Global Village: A Guide to International Veterinary Medicine.* Baltimore: Lippincott Williams and Wilkins.

Swadesh, Frances Leon. 1974. *Los Primeros Pobladores: Hispanic Americans of the Ute Frontier.* Notre Dame, IN: University of Notre Dame Press.

Yentsch, Anne E. 1988. "Farming, Fishing, Whaling, Trading: Land and Sea as Resource on Eighteenth-Century Cape Cod." In *Documentary Archaeology in the New World*, edited by Mary C. Beaudry, 138–60. Cambridge: Cambridge University Press.

CHAPTER EIGHT

Survival of Captivity
Hybrid Identities, Gender, and Culture in Territorial Colorado

VIRGINIA SÁNCHEZ

The history of the enslavement of indigenous women and children in Colorado Territory is well documented in US military and civil records between 1861 and 1874. These narratives begin with trade and settlement, then continue with historical information about some descendants of indigenous enslaved persons, their ancestors' lives, the owners under whose rule they served, and how they had become acculturated into Hispano, Anglo, and Indio society, culture, and religion. However, this important information is a forgotten and untold part of Colorado history.

Life on the far northern frontier was complicated by the cycle of warfare, raids, and retaliation to redeem property and family members, and to secure laborers. Before 1861, the Hispano settlements along the Conejos, Costilla, and Culebra Rivers were part the northern frontier of New Mexico Territory. When the US Congress created Colorado Territory on February 28, 1861, it annexed land from the territories of New Mexico, Kansas, Nebraska, and Utah to create the new, almost square-shaped territory. The nearly seven thousand Nuevomexicanos impacted by this action continued to live under the customs and traditions practiced in New Mexico during the Spanish, Mexican, and territorial periods.

Documented episodes of trade with, raids on, and enslavement of indigenous peoples by Hispanos in early Colorado reveal ongoing interethnic and intercultural relations. The kinds of trades and purchases made underscore

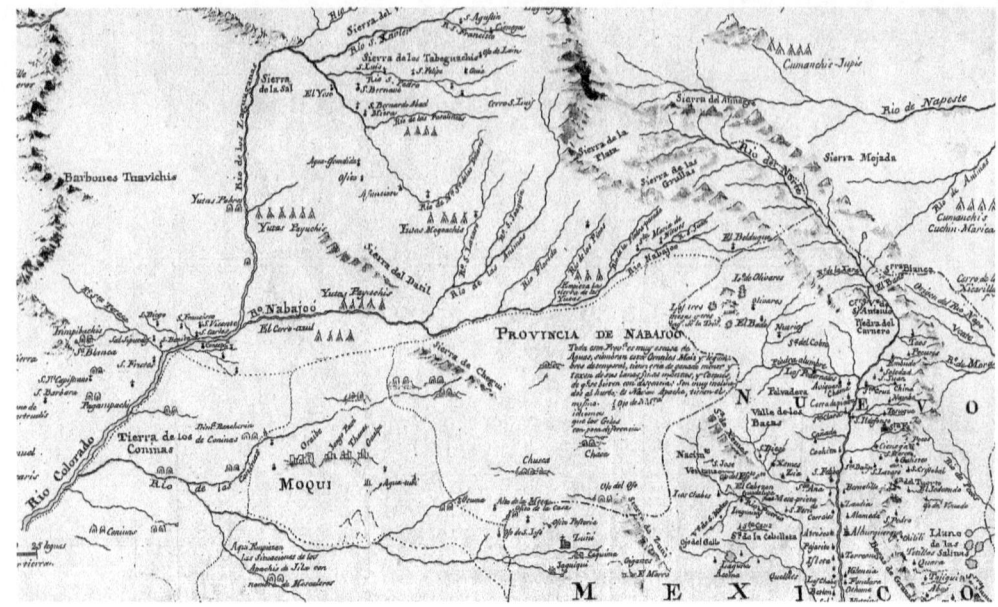

FIGURE 8.1 Drawn nearly a century before the boundary of Colorado was drawn in 1861, the vast landscape shows the Río Napeste (Arkansas River) in the east, the Río del Norte (upper Río Grande), the entire Río Nabajoó (San Juan River), the Sierra de Chegui (Canyon of Chelly), and the villages of Moqui (Hopi) in the south. "Plano geográfico de la tierra descubierta nuevamente a los rumbos" (Geographical map of the land newly discovered in the directions), Bernardo Miera y Pacheco, San Felipe el Real de Chihuahua, 1778. Map detail courtesy of the Center for Southwest Research, University of New Mexico.

the need for goods and laborers on the far northern frontier. Newly found historical documents help identify, acknowledge, and give voice to the untold history of trade, raids, and enslavement in southern Colorado.

Indigenous people in southern Colorado were being incorporated into Nuevomexicano families throughout Colorado's territorial period. A number of Hispano militiamen and settlers maintained close relations with the Utes, and languages and culture were shared. Many Utes had served as auxiliaries during various Spanish, Mexican, and US campaigns against the Navajos, and they spoke Spanish. Likewise, many hunters and comancheros or unlicensed traders who visited Ute lands became fluent speakers of Ute.

The information in this chapter diverges from the Genízaro theme to include an indigenous identity in southern Colorado. By the time the region was permanently settled by Nuevomexicanos during the 1850s, the term "Genízaro" was no longer in use. In 1821, after independence from Spain, the

Plan de Iguala abolished the system of *castas*. Genízaro was not a caste term, but it was abolished as well. Settlers who migrated far north of the Chama River Valley never lived in isolated groups, nor did any identify themselves as Genízaro. In addition, no civil or ecclesiastical records identified any individuals living in this far northern frontier as Genízaro. This chapter examines the frontier heritage and cultural mingling of some intercultural households living in southern Colorado and examines the linkage and historical trauma associated with enslavement and assimilation.

Legal and Illegal Trade as a System of Survival

Information about southern Colorado's traders, licensing, routes, and locations is a record of the interethnic and intercultural interaction that occurred on the frontier. Legal and illegal trade expeditions created economic opportunities for both cultures. To discourage illicit trading, the US government relied on Indian agents to issue trade licenses to reputable applicants. Such regulations were intended to keep contraband away from hostile nations. From his agency at Abiquiú, in New Mexico, agent Christopher "Kit" Carson issued licenses to several men who had ties to southern Colorado. To obtain a license, applicants had to be US citizens, produce testimonies of their good character, provide one or more sureties, and post a bond of $500. By making his mark or signing the license, each man agreed to conform to and observe all government trade and communications laws and regulations with indigenous nations. Traders were forbidden to sell any liquor, guns, or ammunition. Any violation of the terms revoked the licenses.

For years, the Apache, Navajo, Comanche, Ute, Arapahoe, and Kiowa Nations kept Hispano and Anglo settlers from encroaching on their lands in present-day Colorado. The increasing number of Anglo trappers and miners in Colorado resulted in a devastating loss of buffalo and other wild game and available natural resources. This loss, combined with the onslaught of disease and the government's failure to provide fresh, sufficient, and timely rations, forced many nations to trade or abandon family members as a means of survival. James F. Brooks refers to this action as "self-exchange" (2002, 193–94). An 1865 report shows that at least fourteen indigenous women and children were traded or sold by slavers of their same nation or band (table 8.1). For example, in about 1867, José Francisco Vigil traded three cows for a three-year-old indigenous lad whom Vigil named Vicente (Colorado Humanities

1979b; US Census 1870). This trade provided the toddler's indigenous parents and band with much-needed food to survive the coming winter.

Atanacio Trujillo was one Nuevomexicano who regularly ventured north from El Rito to Los Conejos to trap beaver and trade with the Ute. During a visit in spring of 1848, he planted corn and wheat, then returned to El Rito (Trujillo 1990, 55–58). On about May 3, Trujillo returned to the area he had previously planted to *presionar* (determine the value/growth of) his crops. According to oral history, at some point a band of Utes arrived, and one spoke Spanish. The band, pleased with what they saw of Trujillo's crop, traded dressed deer hides and buffalo robes for a shared portion of the harvest. Trujillo and his men spent four days with the Utes in their camp. When they were ready to return to El Rito, about a dozen Utes provided them with safe escort to the San Antonio Mountains to protect them from the raiding Navajo. Using the "great, classic west side trail" from the San Antonio Mountains, Trujillo traveled south to Tres Piedras, past the Arroyo de la Aguaje de Petaca, a spring on La Petaca Creek to El Rito (Colville 1984; Colville 1996, 229, 270).

On March 8 of the following year, Trujillo returned to Los Conejos and found several Utes camped near Los Cerritos Largos. Through dialogue and trade, the two cultures formed friendly relations. In the practice of "respectful behavior," Trujillo requested the band's permission to settle the area the following spring (Quintana 1991, 190). Two months later, on May 1, Trujillo returned and settled near Los Rincones. Sometime later, the band announced their arrival by "firing a salvo of greeting," and in the spirit of friendship they brought gifts of meat and tanned deerskins, and trade items of silver, beads, horses, and saddles (Colville 1996, 229). This amicable inaugural dialogue and exchange resulted in the permanent settlement in Ute country by Hispanos (Trujillo 1990, 55–58).

The following stories introduce several traders who traveled to the northern frontier and detail their licenses and the likely trade locations located in southern Colorado. On June 1, 1856, Antonio José Vallejos obtained a short-term, one-month license to trade with the "Muache Utahs" within their boundaries, including the "Sanguachi [Saguáche] and the bounds" of agent Kit Carson's agency.[1] Huérfano County historian Louis B. Sporleder described him as a man of valor who "could command a company of volunteer fighters, or trail a band of fugitives through mountains and desert for hundreds of miles" (1932, 103).

Before leaving on trade expeditions, *criadas* or enslaved indigenous domestics baked a variety of hard breads to be used as trade items. Such breads included *pan de comanche*, *panocha*, and *pan de cemita*. The Natives regarded pan de comanche a delicacy and traded as much as "a good pony for a sack of the nutritious loaves" (Kenner 1969, 84). Women baked it until it was dark, dry, crisp, and "almost imperishable" (Louis B. Sporleder Collection, 86). Panocha was a slightly sweet wheat bread made from sprouted wheat flour that "the Indians liked like the devil." It was baked into "little pones" (cakes). They also traded pan de cemita, another variety of coarse wheat bread. Comanches, Kiowas, and Mescalero Apaches often traded buffalo robes, deerskins, and horses for this bread (Cobos 1983, 30, 125; Haley 1935, 163).

The name Charles "Carlos" Beaubien, heir to the Sangre de Cristo Land Grant, appeared on six known trade licenses between 1855 and 1858. These licenses authorized trade with the "Muache Utahs" and other indigenous nations within the boundaries of New Mexico.[2] Because he was not listed as a mayordomo (leader of an expedition), presumably Beaubien posted money for the bonds and likely obtained a share in the profits. These trading expeditions enabled Beaubien, or his men, to monitor the progress of the settlers living on his land grant. Trade in captives likely supplied his settlers with much-needed laborers.

On February 21, 1858, forty-four-year-old José Celedonio Valdez paid a $500 bond for a three-month license to trade with the "Utahs within the limits of New Mexico."[3] Valdez lived at La Isla de don Celedonio, a "long point" of fertile land that lay between the San Antonio and Conejos Rivers (Gibson ca. 1930, 68). That fall, with the help of his enslaved indigenous laborers, Valdez sold $1,383 worth of sheep, cattle, wool blankets, and wheat to the US government as provisions for the Utes of the Conejos Agency, led by US agent Lafayette Head (NARA 1860; see also table 8.3).

Routes, Trades, and Raids

Although no trade licenses issued by Conejos agent Lafayette Head or Colorado territorial governor William Gilpin have survived, additional historical records document trades that occurred near the river valleys south of and including the Río Napeste (Arkansas River). Traders met at the Sierra de la Plata, Río San Miguel, Río de los Pinos, Río de las Ánimas Perdidas (Purgatoire), Río Navajo, and along the Uncompahgre, Gunnison, and Colorado

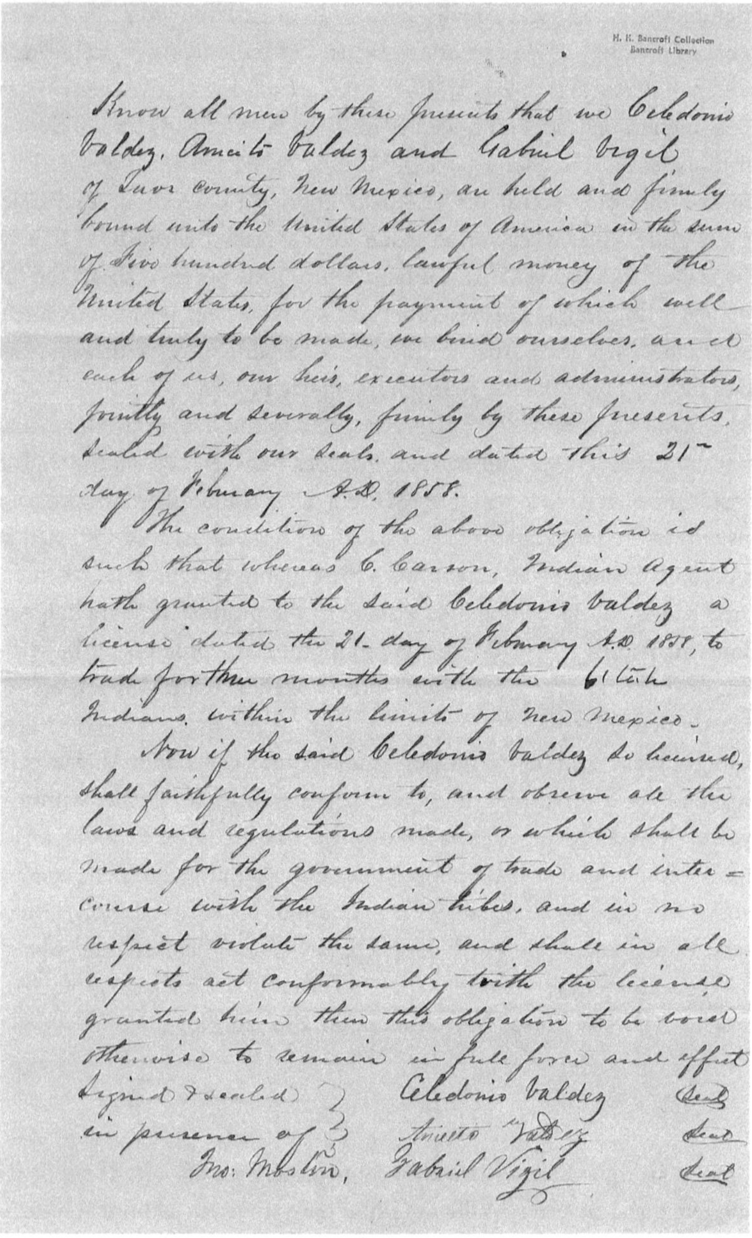

> Know all men by these Presents that we Celedonio Valdez, Aniceto Valdez and Gabriel Vigil of Taos County, New Mexico, are held and firmly bound unto the United States of America in the sum of Five hundred dollars, lawful money of the United States, for the payment of which well and truly to be made, we bind ourselves, and each of us, our heirs, executors and administrators, jointly and severally, firmly by these presents, sealed with our seals, and dated this 21st day of February A.D. 1858.
>
> The condition of the above obligation is such that whereas C. Carson, Indian Agent hath granted to the said Celedonio Valdez a license dated the 21 day of February A.D. 1858, to trade for three months with the Utah Indians, within the limits of New Mexico.
>
> Now if the said Celedonio Valdez so licensed, shall faithfully conform to, and observe all the laws and regulations made, or which shall be made for the government of trade and intercourse with the Indian tribes, and in no respect violate the same, and shall in all respects act conformably with the license granted him then this obligation to be void otherwise to remain in full force and effect
>
> Signed & sealed   Celedonio Valdez   {seal}
> in presence of   Aniceto Valdez   {seal}
>   Jno. Mostin,   Gabriel Vigil   {seal}

FIGURE 8.2 Trade bond of Celedonio Valdez, February 21, 1858. Courtesy of the University of California at Berkeley, Bancroft Library, Kit Carson Papers, Bonds of Traders (1856–1860), BANC MSS P-E 64, box 3.

Rivers (J. Sánchez 2015, 129). Traders also congregated on the Río Conejos near San Juan de Nepomuceno (El Mogote) settlement (Gibson ca. 1930, 75), established in 1854 about six miles west of Guadalupe (López-Tushar 1997, 40). Near the eastern part of Utah Territory, which the US Congress attached to Colorado Territory in 1861, traders gathered at Sierra Lanterna, between the Grand and Green Rivers (Jones 2000, 123; Brigham Young Collection 1853, Box 47, FF 36).

On one trip to Navajo land from southern Colorado, the comancheros traveled south, then entered New Mexico's Cañada del Ojo de la Cueva onto Navajo land and into Arizona Territory (Gibson ca. 1930, 75, 78–79). Along the way, they may have recited or sung a *verso* to remind each other of the danger they could certainly encounter. The following four versos were sung in Hispano communities in Costilla and Huérfano Counties.

El Gallegón	The big Galician
sentado estaba en su lumbre,	was sitting by his fire,
llovizándole la nieve,	under the drizzling snow,
cuando llegó el navajó.	when a Navajo came.
Le trió la fleche breve.	He shot a quick arrow,
El Gallegón se la sacó,	the big Galician removed it,
pero ya triste, no alegre.	but now was sad, not happy.

(López-Tushar 1997, 141).

In *The People of El Valle*, Olibama López-Tushar (1997, 141), stated that the following verso was an extension of El Gallegón.

Si tú andas en combate	If you are in combat
y tu tropa no ganó,	and your troops do not win,
pide a Dios que te rescate,	ask God to rescue you,
si el enemigo es navajó.	if your enemy is Navajo.

This verso is part of the repertory of the Comanches de la Serna, a Hispano Comanche community from Ranchos de Taos, New Mexico (Lamadrid 2003, 149).

Lucas Martínez, of Huérfano County, recalled the following verso about remaining cautious in Navajo land (2005, 3). This verso is still sung by the Comanches de la Serna (Lamadrid 2003, 149, 139):

Si fueres a nabajó,	If you should go to Navajoland,
lleba contigo morta[ja].	take your burial shroud with you.
Porque la muerte de allá	Because dying over there
es firme y no se rrebaga [*sic*].	is certain and cannot be negotiated.

The final verso, sung as a round in Costilla County, made fun of raiding mayordomos who were incompetent in leadership and warfare, and in equitably dividing booty (López-Tushar 1997, 132). They invoke the diminutive of the ancestral Spanish war cry "Santiago," to send or dispatch their enemies:

Si son muchos a huir,	If they are many we flee,
si son pocos a agazapar,	if they are few we hide,
si es la huella nomás,	if it is only their trail,
Santiguillo con ellos,	to the Devil with them,
al cabo para morir nacimos.	in the end we are born to die.

Juan de Dios Ruybal and his brothers, from the Río Conejos settlement of San Juan de Pomuceno, traveled southwest over the *cumbres* (mountain passes) to Dulce, New Mexico. They then crossed the southernmost part of Coraque (Cañón de Carracas) and traveled through the southern end of Cañada de Cabresto (Trail of the Lasso), and past the eastern side of the Mesa de la Fragua (Mesa of the Forge), then through Cañada de la Jara (Trail of the Willow) past "the Martínez Ranch" to Cañada del Ojo de la Cueva (Trail of Cave Spring).[4] When they reached this location, they found no Navajos or livestock. Running low on food and supplies, the comancheros decided to conduct trade with the Hopi or Moqui settlement further west at Oraibi (see fig. 8.1).

Ruybal and his men traveled into the *cañada*[5] identified only as where the "cliff dwellers" lived. Ruybal described these Natives as having fair skin and light hair and eyes. Because these people were timid and had no weapons, Ruybal's men "rushed on them." A type of stampede ensued in which Ruybal's men "captured [those] not quick enough to escape." Continued raiding of this timid tribe likely led to its disappearance (Gibson ca. 1930, 75, 78–79). The captors bound women and older children with leather ties so they could not escape, and they often gagged their prisoners to silence their screams. Younger children and infants were tied to their captors. A few indigenous *chichiguas* (wet nurses or lactating women), who remained under guard at

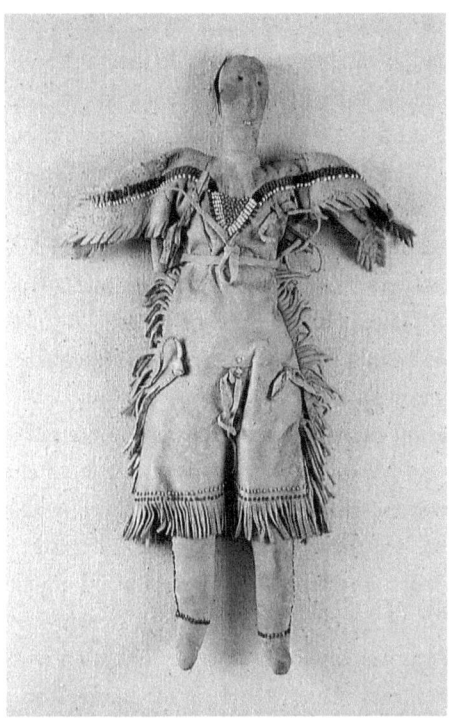

FIGURE 8.3 Doll, tanned hide, glass beads. Ute, Colorado or Utah, ca. 1875–1890. Courtesy of the Phoebe A. Hearst Museum of Anthropology and the Regents of the University of California, #2-15961.

designated locations, traveled with the comancheros to assist with newly orphaned infants and young toddlers. Small toys or woven dolls also helped calm a sobbing child. Because raiders had to be wary of noises that would attract unwanted attention, those captives who excessively cried, screamed, or resisted were often killed or abandoned on the trail.

Another raid campaign, comprising two comanchero expeditions from southern Colorado and northern New Mexico, likely met near Chama or Dulce. Juan Vigil of El Rito led the attack company, while men under the command of Manuel Gregorio Martín of Embudo were responsible for driving off the Moquis' sheep (NARA 1867a; NARA 1867b).[6] Information about this campaign coincides with the oral history of a Moqui elder, Lomawikvaya, regarding a similar campaign made during 1866–1867 by eighty Nuevomexicanos (Aitken 1931, 378–81; Kraemer 2013, 141–45). In December 1866, the raiders went into Oraibi, the land of the Moquis, under the pretense of "goodwill and trade"; they used a form of sign language to communicate their desire to trade. They remained in the village, trading and observing the Oraibi and their corralled livestock. After supper on the second day, they lay down for the night, but cautiously and repeatedly "raised their heads" to assess the situation. Suddenly, shots rang out. Some of the raiders used their guns to hold back the Moquis, while the others forced some women and children to drive the sheep away. A fatal stray shot from a rifle struck raider José Ignacio García in the head. The raiders killed three Moquis and wounded four. The captives they "violently" abducted were loaded onto carts; among these were one adult female, five girls, and six boys. The raiders escaped with 558 sheep and goats, and 2 burros. In their haste, they left García's body where he lay and "headed toward the east, [leaving] a yellow dust cloud [that] rose far . . . and floated on and on, then disappeared" (Kraemer 2013, 141–45).

The Moquis, unsuccessful in chasing their attackers, traveled to Santa Fe to report their grievances to the New Mexico governor and to A. Baldwin Norton, the New Mexico superintendent of Indian affairs. The Moquis had not realized or understood that as of 1863 they were now under the jurisdiction of the superintendency of Arizona Territory. However, Special Agent John Ward investigated the Moquis' allegation, which led him to Antonio Sierra, reportedly from Conejos. Sierra was one of the twenty-one men who had driven off the stock and captives, and received a share of the livestock. Sierra told Ward all about the campaign and named forty-two of the raiders involved. Nine of these were from southern Colorado—eight from Conejos County and one from Huérfano County (NARA 1867a).

Special Agent Ward located sixty of the raiders and learned they had "passed the captives off as Navajo." Ward located one captive in Conejos and the remaining eleven in northern New Mexico at Arroyo Seco, El Rito, Ojo Caliente, Taos, and Tierra Amarilla. In Río Arriba County, the raiders sold the captives after Mass on Sundays (Aitken 1931, 377). By March 1867, Ward successfully freed and returned twelve captives, fifty head of sheep and goats, and one burro to the Moquis. With sufficient evidence to indict the sixty raiders, Special Agent Ward and Superintendent Norton hoped to convince the grand jury of the New Mexico District Court of their guilt. However, because the actual crime had been committed in Arizona Territory, the court determined that the accused should be tried there.

Five months later, on August 1, 1867, Superintendent Norton wrote a letter to the commissioner of Indian affairs in Washington recommending indictment of these raiders by the Arizona Territorial District Court. Norton also recommended that the territorial governors of New Mexico and Colorado arrange transportation of the accused to Arizona for trial. To this letter, Norton attached a list of the names and residences of the raiders. Eight months later, Norton learned that the Arizona Territorial Court had decided not to indict any of the raiders (Kraemer 2013, 145).

Historic Memory and Trauma

As practiced in New Mexico during its Spanish, Mexican, and territorial periods, enslaved indigenous women and children in southern Colorado went through an assimilation process whereby each was baptized into the Catholic Church and received a Christian name, and was raised by an adoptive or foster family. Coincidentally, after President Abraham Lincoln decreed the Emancipation Proclamation in 1863, which changed the federal status of enslaved people in the US South from slave to free, priests began using various phrases for baptized indigenous slaves in southern Colorado: *padre no conocido* (father unknown), *indio huérfano* (orphaned Indian), or *adoptivo de* (adopted by). Prior to this time, priests at Arroyo Hondo, Taos, and Costilla used Spanish

TABLE 8.1 Raiders of the Moqui Pueblos at Oraibi, 1867

SETTLEMENT	# MEN	# PARTICIPATING IN RAID
Abiquiu	6	1
Arroyo Seco	3	3
Chama	2	1
Conejos, Colorado	8	4
El Rito	5	4
Embudo	2	0
Huerfano, Colorado	1	unknown
Mora	3	0
Ojo Caliente	3	3
Rincones	1	1
Rio Arriba	1	0
Taos	2	1
Tierra Amarilla	2	1
Vallecito	2	1

NARA 1867a.

FIGURE 8.4 Gabriel Woodson, ca. 1880s. Courtesy of Saguache County Museum.

terms and phrases denoting provenance, Indian purchased by, Indian of, adopted/foundling of, and in the family of. None of the priests identified any owners or any enslaved persons as Genízaros, nor did they identify any of those baptized as *esclavos* (slaves).

Older boys tended to resist any assimilation or performance of what they considered women's work. Many tried to escape and often suffered the consequences of those attempts (Brooks 2002, 143n56). In 1860, James Bernard Woodson, a business partner of John Lawrence, purchased a twelve-year-old Navajo boy from a band of Utes trading in southern Colorado. No information exists regarding the length of time he was with the Utes before being sold to Woodson. Woodson named the boy Gabriel. Woodson and John Lawrence later settled in Saguache with Gabriel and one other enslaved indigenous male named Andrés (tables 8.2, 8.3).

Gabriel suffered a difficult life, which author Janet Lecompte attributed to "a world that was foreign and sometimes hostile" toward him (1978, 139–40). Alcohol undoubtedly led to many of Gabriel's problems. Nor did it help that both James Woodson and John Lawrence enjoyed alcohol and had it readily available. Several times, Lawrence bailed Gabriel out of jail, settled his court costs, or paid his debts. During a Christmas Eve dance in 1872, Gabriel got into a fight. He fled after getting knocked down. "Some [Anglo] men . . . took [off] after him and beat him up some" (Martin 1990, 74–75). Lawrence attributed Gabriel's problems to his "damned mean Indian blood" (Lecompte 1978, 140).

Robert "Bob" A. Morrison, a paid laborer who also worked for Woodson and Lawrence, was addicted to alcohol and was often arrested for disturbing the peace (Lecompte 1978, 139–40). On the evening of July 4, 1873, Gabriel got in a fight with Morrison and threatened to kill him. Gabriel ran once Morrison pulled out a gun and fired two shots. The following morning, Lawrence and Woodson searched for and found Gabriel, dead as a result of the shooting. Morrison was arrested, and a judge sentenced him to three years in the territorial penitentiary at Cañon City. In a somewhat mordant twist, Woodson later obtained a pardon for Morrison. Lawrence wrote in his diary: "It was the greatest injustice to Bob that could possibly be done as he was justafiable [sic] in every way in killing the Indian" (Martin 1990, 78).

Treatment and Mistreatment

In 1866, Congress enacted the Civil Rights Act, and holding slaves became a violation of US law. Regarding the continued practice of enslavement of the indigenous in southern Colorado, Territorial Governor Alexander Cummings reported to Indian Commissioner Dennis N. Cooley that indigenous persons were "mostly taken in infancy" and resided with families, "where they [had] been for a long time . . . at their own will" (NARA 1866). Sporleder considered the "practice as a mild form of slavery" and believed that captives living in the Walsenburg area were "kindly treated and raised the same as the owner's children":

> When of age [they] often married into the ranch owner's own family, or were established in business. . . . A redeeming feature of this traffic was the kindness with which . . . child-prisoners . . . were treated. Invariably they . . .

became members of the family, with every right and privilege the legitimate children enjoyed. They were as carefully guarded as the sons and daughters of the family. Reverence and devotion to their foster parents usually lasted a lifetime. (Louis B. Sporleder Collection, F7, 84; F22, 198)

Occasionally, the enslaved received good treatment and developed a lasting relationship with their owners' family. The story of José Miguel Romero is an example of devotion that lasted a lifetime. About 1864, after a raid on Juan de Jesús Romero's livestock, Romero and his neighbors fired upon the indigenous raiders and followed them into the woods. Romero found a trail of blood leading him to a fatally injured Navajo mother still holding her baby boy. Although we do not know if the men buried the mother, Romero took the baby home and named him José Miguel. Learning a new language and culture was somewhat easier for young captives when they grew up among the owner's birth children. As Miguel grew into manhood, he became a respected member of the family and developed a lasting friendship with his owner's brother, José Gerónimo Romero (M. C. Martínez 2013). Although Miguel later married and moved to Vaughn, New Mexico, he returned to Cucharas when he learned that Gerónimo was gravely ill. Miguel continued to care for Gerónimo until his death in 1925 (Nellie Pacheco, personal communication, 2013). However, Governor Cummings and Sporleder failed to understand that, during capture, many indigenous persons witnessed the murder of family members; and during their enslavement, they were forced to live and work among strangers and subsequently lost their indigenous identities and heritage (Brooks 2002, 4, 253, 266; Rael-Gálvez 2002, 50). In 1863, on his return trip from Washington, Conejos agent Lafayette Head stopped in Illinois to visit his sister, Eliza Jane Head Downing. Reportedly, her eldest son had recently died fighting for the Union. Agent Head successfully convinced her to return to Conejos with him. Eliza and her two children traveled with Head as part of a military caravan. Soon after their arrival at Conejos, trouble ensued between Head's sister and his wife over the treatment of a newly acquired Navajo girl. Martina Martínez, the agent's wife, had recently purchased or traded for the young Navajo, who apparently needed assimilating, disciplining, and taming. Eliza abhorred the sound of the girl's screams when "tyrannical Mexican bosses" beat her with a rawhide whip "until bleeding and bruised." Martina became furious when she learned that Eliza helped the girl escape on horseback. Shortly after, Eliza and her children returned to Illinois (Downing 1945).

In another example of mistreatment, Higinio Córdova purchased four indigenous children, two girls and two boys, "from another of his race." Córdova was able to tame one boy, whom he named José de Gracia García, but he was "unable to tame" the other boy. Unfortunately, many boys were punished for running away or not assimilating as quickly as their owners wanted. Perhaps Higinio traded or sold him to recoup his purchase. In a worst-case scenario, the boy died as a result of the inhumane methods owners sometimes used to facilitate the assimilation. As for José de Gracia García, by 1870 he and his owner's family were living in Las Ánimas County (Richeson ca. 1930).

Examples of captivity narratives include ecclesiastical records, some of which show that many enslaved indigenous females bore the children of their owners or of their owners' sons. In most baptisms, the owner served as the illegitimate child's baptismal godparent. In 1864, forty-two-year-old Antonio José Vallejos purchased a fifteen-year-old Navajo female from comancheros trading in Colorado. US Marshal Edward R. Harris mistakenly reported her name as Colores (tables 8.2, 8.3). Upon baptism the following year, her name was changed to María Dolores Vallejos. By 1866, Dolores had migrated with the Vallejos family from Costilla County east to Huérfano County. The following year, Dolores bore the first of seven children fathered by Vallejos; the 1880 the census enumerator listed them as servants in the Vallejos household (US Census 1880). What is missing from these records is the number of births resulting from rape and the trauma associated with such violent actions. Incidentally, María Soledad Romero, the wife of Vallejos, who bore five of his children, died seventeen days after the birth of Dolores's last child fathered by her owner.

Ecclesiastical records also show that some owners married their enslaved indigenous females. As in the case previously mentioned, Antonio José Vallejos married Dolores in Walsenburg on August 29, 1885. Before the parish priest, Father Gabriel Ussel, Antonio declared that two daughters and a son were his by Dolores, and he "legitimized them through this marriage" (Nuestra Señora de los Siete Dolores 1885, 157). The following day, Father Ussel christened their infant and named her Soledad (Pino 1885, 184).

Dolores and another Navajo captive, José Hilario, continued to care for their aging owner, who remembered them in his will. Although considered free by age twenty-one, Hilario remained with Antonio José Vallejos for thirty-two years. When Antonio José died in 1892 at the age of eighty-five, his will divided his estate among his six living biological children, Dolores, and Hilario. As a beneficiary of her husband's estate, Dolores received "all household furniture, books, fuel, and provisions and stores" (Colorado State Archives 1892). By 1900, she took in boarders and lived with Hilario's growing family; the census enumerator incorrectly listed Dolores as Hilario's mother (Family History Center 1860; Nuestra Señora de los Siete Dolores 1885, 156–57; US Census 1900). Both Dolores and Hilario continued to raise their families in Huérfano County. As with their Navajo names, their original tribal culture, traditions, spirit, and language were expunged. Yet, their "fictive kinship" helped recover their missing connection or "blood links" to their Navajo heritage (Brooks 2002, 236; Huang 2006, 173–74). (Tables 8.2 and 8.3 list the other enslaved persons in the Antonio José Vallejos household.)

Ecclesiastical records, however, do not record the number of deaths that occurred as a result of suicide. Such records could not be recorded, as at that time, the Catholic Church did not allow ecclesiastical burials of victims who deliberately killed themselves. These baptized captives preferred death to enslavement; they hoped that death would heal their broken hearts.

Captivity Songs, Laments, and Lullabies

Some captivity songs evolved into children's lullabies or *arrullos*, and express cultural memory and trauma. After praying the rosary each night, Teresa and Victoria Velarde, of Huérfano County, remember that their father, José Desiderio Velarde, sang "one of his silly songs" before sending his "giggling" children off to bed. To ease children's fright that their misbehavior might cause their parents to sell or give them away, gentle animals, "el venau y la venanda" (el venado y la venada), replaced the song's original characters, "el Comanche y la Comancha" (Lamadrid 2003, 92–93, 243–44n8).

El venau y la venanda [*sic*]	The buck and the doe
se fueron pa santa fé,	went to Santa Fe,
a vender a sus hijitos	to sell their kids (fawns)
por asúcar y café [*sic*].	for sugar and coffee.
(Raleigh 2011, n.p.)	

Many Hispanos lost their homes and land due to back taxes and fines they had accrued. Little cash was available in the far northern frontier. To pay their taxes in hard cash, they faced three alternatives: sell some of their livestock or land, obtain a loan from a merchant or wealthy neighbor, or place a son or daughter in a labor or debt-peonage contract. By means of signed contracts, the patrón (contractor or boss) was responsible for the welfare of his laborers.

In 1851, Juan Antonio González of Taos County was in debt to attorney Theodore D. Wheaton in the amount of twenty-three dollars. Wheaton, who was born in Rhode Island, later served in the New Mexico Territorial Assembly and became the US attorney for New Mexico. He was also involved in a land title business (Lamar 2000, 68, 78, 124). According to the peonage contact Wheaton penned in English, González agreed to outsource his son, José María, for a minimum of two years, at the rate of one dollar per month. By this contract, if José María needed clothing, Wheaton would furnish it; however, José María would have to work to pay off the clothing cost at a rate of one dollar per month. González could not read or write in Spanish or English, so he signed Wheaton's contract by placing his mark. Furthermore, José María was to remain in the services of Wheaton until the said time of service expired; González could not reclaim his son by paying off the total debt owed.[7] The work that José María performed likely was not related to Wheaton's legal profession, nor did the type of work improve José María's education or social standing.

According to the 1860 Taos County census for the Northern District, which included Conejos, Costilla, and Culebra, forty-three men listed their occupations as peon (US Census 1860). The two youngest men were fifteen years old; the oldest was sixty. By reviewing the census for names of those persons who reported any real and personal property of substance, and those persons who lived close to wealthy neighbors, thirteen presumed contractors can be identified. These likely contractors, living in Conejos and Costilla Counties, include Harvey E. Easterday, James Bernard Woodson, Agent Lafayette Head, and Conejos farmer José Francisco Gallegos. Easterday and Ceran St. Vrain owned the St. Vrain and Easterday Mercantile in Costilla, which supplied and freighted US Army goods. In 1862, they reported company earnings at $4,700 (Steinel and Working 1926, 38; Colorado Tax Schedules 1863).

On March 2, 1867, Congress passed an antipeonage law aimed at the southwestern territories and the state of California. Because many military and civil officials did not enforce this law, peonage continued, at least in New Mexico and Colorado, for many more years. Additionally, many military reports erroneously reported captives as peons rather than slaves (Thompson 2015, 397). The following year, three Hispano owners arrived at the Costilla County courthouse, where five enslaved Navajos were giving testimony

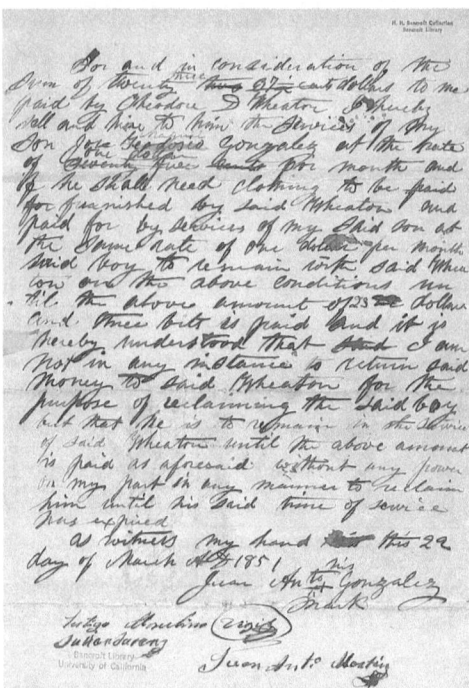

FIGURE 8.5 Peonage contract between Juan Antonio González and Theodore D. Wheaton, March 22, 1851. Courtesy of the University of California at Berkeley, Bancroft Library, Special Collections, Miscellaneous Accounts, 1851–1866.

under oath about their treatment. According to the testimonies recorded before County Clerk John L. Gaspar, Juana María Pacheco, María and Juan Miguel Martínez,[8] and Margarita[9] and María Antonia Trujillo testified that their owners allowed them "the Liberty of going wherever [they] wished to go, and of doing any and all things which [they] may have wished to do in the same manner and subject to the same laws as the people of the United States of America and the Territory of Colorado" (Rael-Gálvez 2002, 340–41; Costilla County Records 1868, 11–13). (For María Martínez, see tables 8.2 and 8.3; for all others, see table 8.3.)

Historical memories and trauma caused by these losses have been passed down. López-Tushar writes that her grandmother, María Regina Manzanares, sang an *indita* ballad about the tribulations of Marcelina, a captive adult who laments for the loss of her children, family, sheep, and home. Inditas, here referring to "little Indian songs," also translates as "little Indian girls." It is a lyrical narrative genre unique to New Mexico and southern Colorado. Unlike the heroic, male-inflected corrido ballad, inditas are sung from a female perspective. Many are voiced in the first person, capturing the experience of captivity and other travails of women. Unlike corridos, they often feature choruses, which give singer and listener the opportunity to reflect on the story being told. Some are used in religious rituals (Romero 2002, 56–80).

La cautiva Marcelina,	Marcelina the captive,
ya se va, ya se la llevan,	there she goes, there they take her,
y se va, ya se la llevan. ¡Ay!	and she goes, there they take her. Oh!
Coro: Por ese no quiero	Chorus: That is why I cannot love
en el mundo más amar,	in this world again,
que de mi patria querida	for from my beloved homeland
me van a desterrar.	they will take me into exile.
Cuando llega a los cerritos,	When she gets to the little hills,
voltea la cara y dice:	she turns back her face and says:
—Se quedaron mis hijitos. ¡Ay!	—My children stayed behind. Oh!
—¿Volveré a mi tierra? ¡No!	—Will I ever see my land again? No!

(López-Tushar 1997, 131–32)

Manuel de Jesús Salazar (personal communication, 2017), of Conejos County, remembers hearing the following two arrullos, which are still performed by the Comanches de la Serna (Lamadrid 2003, 148).

Los inditos de San Juan	The little Indians of San Juan
rique sí, rique son,	*rique* yes, *rique* they are,
los inditos de San Juan.	the Indian children of San Juan.
Piden pan y no les dan,	They beg for bread and do not get any,
piden queso y les dan un hueso,	they beg for cheese and get a bone,
se sientan a llorar	they sit down to cry
en el tronco de un corral.	on a rail of the corral.

The word *rique* is the kind of repetitive nonsense word that can appear in lullabies. As a pun, it ironically suggests the word *rico* or rich, which the Indian children are obviously not, as well as *requesón* or cottage cheese, which they are not getting any of, either. The little children of San Juan Pueblo beg for bread, but are given none. They ask for cheese and are given a bone. They weep while sitting on the railing of a corral.

The following verso refers to prowess in warfare and the historical dominance of the Comanches over the Apaches, many of whom took permanent refuge in New Mexico and became the Jicarillas.

El comanche y el apache	The Comanche and the Apache
el apache y el comanche	the Apache and the Comanche
se citaron a la guerra.	arranged a date for battle.
El apache gime y llora,	The Apache moans and cries,
y el comanche se le aferra,	and the Comanche bears down harder.
y el comanche se la aferra.	and the Comanche bears down harder.

(Lamadrid 2003, 148; López-Tushar 1997, 141).

Gambling and Gaming

The comancheros played games to pass the time and to relieve stress. Players gambled hoping to win money, slaves, or material goods. Along with card games and horse and foot races, two games played in Cucharas around 1870 were *el chueco* and *el cañute*. Chueco (crooked stick) was a team sport similar to field hockey. In Ute, the hockey stick was called a *beher* and the ball was the *pokunump*, about the size of a baseball wrapped in leather and tied with sinew (Jefferson, Delaney, and Thompson 1972, 66). The object was to move the pokunump across the field past the opposing team's goal line.

Cañute was played with a little stick, hidden in one of four cylindrical, hollow branches made from reeds or green cottonwood or pine. The object of the game was to correctly guess which branch contained the stick. The cañuteros (players) on the defending team often sang versos that gave clues as to the stick's location, or simply to taunt the players (Louis B. Sporleder Collection, F22, 207–8; V. Sánchez 2010, 37–39).

Allá viene el cañutero,	There comes the reed game player,
él no halla el palito.	he doesn't find the little stick.
Él perdió el juego.	He lost the game.
Há-lla-lo, há-llo-lo,	Find it, find it,
hálla-le, cañutero.	find it for him, reed game player.

(Colorado Humanities 1979a; V. Sánchez 2010, 37–39).

Conejos Agency Reports on Captivity

During most of Colorado's Territorial Period (1861–1875), the Utes, Hispanos, and US Army were at war with the Navajos. Those Navajos who gave in to US efforts at subjugation were militarily escorted on their "Long Walk" to Bosque

Redondo, a wretched prison camp the government established for them in east-central New Mexico. Some of the Navajos left their babies and children with Hispano families to spare them from the exposure of the dreaded march, some of which took place in freezing and bitter cold. Those making their way to army posts became easy prey for Hispano and Ute raiders, who captured and sold them to Hispanos and Anglos in New Mexico and southern Colorado for $100 per person, much higher if domesticated (Brugge 2010, 97). The evidence lies in two reports submitted by Indian agent Lafayette Head in 1865. Opportunistic Navajos also sold other Navajos along the way (Meketa 1986, 241).

In light of the Civil War during the early to mid-1860s, Congress discussed the issue of slavery and the Emancipation Proclamation. As instructed, on June 28, 1865, Colorado territorial governor and superintendent of Indian affairs John Evans asked his four agents to report instances of slavery of American Indians. In response, between July 10 and July 13, Agent Head interviewed eighty-eight male owners living in thirteen settlements in Conejos County. Two days later, US Marshal Edward R. Harris reported sixty owners who resided in settlements along the Culebra and Costilla Rivers of Costilla County; why Harris prepared that county's report is not known (NARA 1865a).

Information that Head and Harris collected resulted in two historical reports about the owners, slavers, and enslaved. Of the total 148 women and children enumerated, 116 were Navajo and 31 were Ute (Rael-Gálvez 2002, 243). Comancheros sold more Navajo captives to Hispanos and Anglos than did the Ute slavers. Some Ute, Apache, and Navajo slavers sold (or traded) women and children of their respective tribes. Head and Harris did not report married females (Brugge 2010, 97). The reports do not indicate how many times a captured indigenous person was traded before his or her final purchase; they also do not indicate from which nation the slave originated or was acculturated. (A compilation of the two reports appears in table 8.3). Incidentally, Agent Head recommended to Governor Evans that all reported Navajo captives be returned to their tribe, and then relocated to Bosque Redondo. The governor agreed to provide transportation to those who wished to be returned; however, no extant records suggest that any enslaved Navajos in Colorado were returned or militarily escorted to eastern New Mexico (NARA 1865b). Interestingly, Head participated in grubstaking (Lamar 2000, 226–27; Pfeiffer Papers 1868–1869); he was known to have provided expeditions with funds or provisions in return for a share of the profits. Such expeditions included indigenous slave raids and gold and land prospecting.

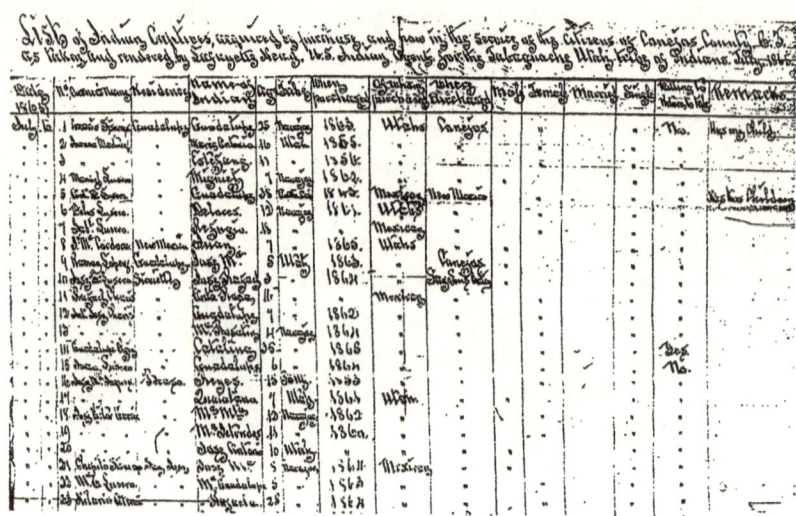

FIGURE 8.6 Conejos County captives enumerated by Indian agent Lafayette Head, 1865. Letters Received by the Office of Indian Affairs, 1824–1880. Courtesy of the National Archives and Records Administration, Washington, DC.

Although the two reports provide much information about a people, place, and time, several issues and additional questions come to mind. Who sponsored the Hispano and Ute slaving expeditions, since license bonds were expensive? How were the interviews conducted, and how accurate were the responses given? Who answered on behalf of the younger captives? For example, in 1864, comancheros trading in Colorado Territory sold a four-year-old Navajo boy to Juan de Jesús Gómez of Guadalupita. We can only imagine the extreme sadness and confusion this young boy experienced during his capture, enslavement, and acculturation. On August 14, the lad was baptized into the Catholic Church at his owner's bidding. In the sacramental register, the Conejos parish priest recorded his name as José Antonio Gómez; there are no family memories of his original Navajo name (D. Salazar 1864, 23–24). Head noted that José Antonio wished to remain with the Gómez family. He had been with the family for only one year. Did he understand the question about being returned to the Navajo, and did he realize that the Navajo were being forcibly relocated? Did owners use this information to induce their Navajo captives to remain? (Brugge 2010, 124–25). Unfortunately, there are no answers. By 1880, José Antonio was still living with the Gómez family, but now in Alamosa. As in his baptismal record, the census enumerator recorded him as an adopted member of the Gómez family. In 1887, José Antonio Gómez married Abrana Jacobs, the half-Ute daughter of the Reverend Albert G. T. Jacobs, a Methodist minister.

Outside of Conejos and Costilla Counties, no territorial official recorded information about the enslaved indigenous women and children held in Huérfano or Las Ánimas, two other Hispano-populated counties. By this time, the governor had other issues to attend to, such as the aftermath of the 1864 massacre of the Arapahoe and Cheyenne at Sand Creek, and depredations around Trinidad. During the 1870 census, some enumerators listed some enslaved as extended family members (e.g., nephews, nieces, stepchildren, adopted children). Researching civil and ecclesiastical records has shown that many of these were, in fact, enslaved indigenous persons. Reviewing Huérfano, Las Ánimas, and Saguache County records, and reexamining Conejos and Costilla County records, revealed 238 additional enslaved indigenous persons in southern Colorado. Territorial tax records prove that none of the owners itemized them as property. Although the enslaved were a valuable source of labor, their owners did not consider them chattel. Additionally, the records disclose that generational patterns of enslaving indigenous persons extended into Colorado Territory; owners, whose parents and grandparents had held captives, continued the practice (see table 8.3).

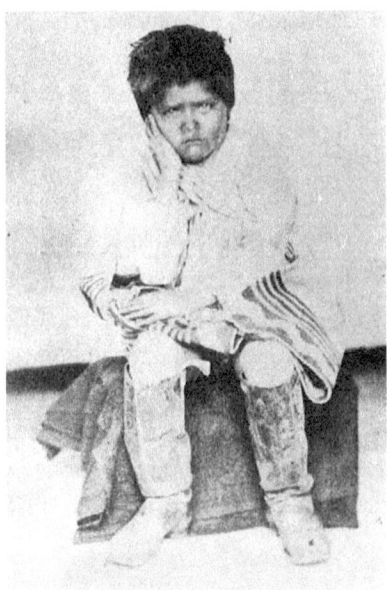

FIGURE 8.7 Navajo captive boy, undated. Courtesy of the Denver Public Library, Western History and Genealogy Department, X-33098.

Some Navajos, now released from Bosque Redondo, arrived in southern Colorado to search for their enslaved family members. Unfortunately, very few surviving historical documents record successful redemptions by any indigenous nations. Agent Alexander G. Irvine reported in 1877 that many owners in southern Colorado and New Mexico kept information from their enslaved Navajos about their tribe's desire for their return. Irvine thought that owners falsely reported about the "condition in which the Indians live. [They] work upon the fears of the captives [making them] afraid to return" (NARA 1877; Brugge 2010, 104).

Conclusion and Appendix

This chapter has examined the frontier heritage and cultural mingling that occurred in intercultural households in southern Colorado Territory due to trade, exchange, and sale. It has also examined the linkage among the various issues associated with enslavement. When José Antonio Gómez, a Navajo, married Abrana Jacobs, he assimilated into Anglo culture and became a Methodist. María Dolores Vallejos, also Navajo, assimilated into Hispano culture and became a Catholic. She was eighteen when she bore the first of her owner's seven children, and he was forty-two years her senior!

We can only imagine the experiences and historical trauma the captured and enslaved endured, their embedded memory of witnessing their family members murdered in raids, and the pain and suffering they endured when their owners imprisoned, beat, starved, raped, or maimed them into submission (Durán et al. 1998, 342). And, with each passing day, they lost more and more of their former identity, language, and heritage (Brooks 2002, 4, 253, 266; Rael-Gálvez 2002, 355).

Like many enslaved removed from the protection of family and community, Gómez and Vallejos dealt with their individual historical trauma while adapting to their new environment and culture. But, how were their bicultural children perceived and treated within Anglo and Hispano communities? Did their daughters fare better than their sons? What historical trauma did they pass on to their descendants? Although we do not know the answers to these questions, the histories of the survivors of captivity told here help identify, acknowledge, and give voice to the gender and culture of a forgotten and untold history of southern Colorado.

TABLE 8.2 Captives Reported by Indian Agent Lafayette Head, 1865

The following is a compiled alphabetical list (with verbatim spellings) of enslaved indigenous males and females residing in Costilla and Conejos Counties as reported in 1865 by Indian Agent Lafayette Head. The last column provides the line numbers and county report. National Archives and Records Administration microfilm of the "Records of the Colorado Superintendency of Indian Affairs," 1861–1864, RG 75, roll 198, Reports for Conejos and Costilla Counties. Agent Head's reports did not include married Indian women; female owners appeared under their maiden names. See also Combs 1973.

LAST NAME	OWNER'S FIRST NAME	RESIDENCE	NAME OF INDIAN	AGE	M	F	TRIBE	YEAR	PURCHASED FROM	PURCHASED IN	RETURN TO TRIBE	COUNTY/ LINE NO.
Aragon	F.E. (Franc Esteban)	Cenicero	Jose Antonio	6	x		Navajo	1862	Utahs	Colorado Territory	No	Conejos Line 49
Aragon	J. G.	San Rafael	Dolores	15		x	Navajo	1864	Mexicans	Colorado Territory	No	Conejos Line 69
Archuleta	Manuel (de Jesus)	Saritas	Guadalupe	15	x		Navajo	1864	Utahs	New Mexico Territory	No	Conejos Line 27
Archuleta	Manuel (de Jesus)	Saritas	Maria Dolores	10		x	Utah	1858	Utahs	Conejos	No	Conejos Line 26
Atencio	Hilario	San Jose	Jose Antonio	11	x		Navajo	1864	Mexicans	Conejos	No	Conejos Line 25
Atencio	Hilario	San Jose	Juan Quaro [sic]	15	x		Navajo	1860	Mexicans	"Navajo Country"	No	Conejos Line 24
Atencio	Hilario	San Jose	Rafaela	25		x	Navajo	1864	Mexicans	"San Luis Valley"	No	Conejos Line 23
Bernal	Juan B. (de Jesus)	Costilla	Margarita	25		x	Navajo	1863	Mexicans	Colorado Territory	Yes	Costilla Line 48
(B)orego	V (Buenaventura)	San Jose	M(a)delina	8		x	Navajo	1864	Utahs	Colorado Territory	No	Conejos Line 33

LAST NAME	OWNER'S FIRST NAME	RESIDENCE	NAME OF INDIAN	AGE	M	F	TRIBE	YEAR	PURCHASED FROM	PURCHASED IN	RETURN TO TRIBE	COUNTY/ LINE NO.
Bounay [sic]	J. (Joseph Bourcy)	Culebra	Resiona [sic]	20		x	Navajo	1864	Mexicans	Colorado Territory	Yes	Costilla Line 5
Casias	Ml.	Santa Cruz NM	Francisco Antonio	4	x		Navajo	1862	Mexicans	Colorado Territory	No	Conejos Line 50
Casias	Ml.	Santa Cruz NM	Juana	4		x	Navajo	1862		Colorado Territory	No	Conejos Line 51
Chacon	J. B. (Juan Bautista)	San Rafael	Juliana	15		x	Navajo	1864	Utahs	Colorado Territory	No	Conejos Line 70
Chacon	J. G. (Juan Gabriel)	San Rafael	Dolores	15		x	Navajo	1861	Utahs	Colorado Territory	No	Conejos Line 69
Chavis	Antonio Jose	Sirvietta	Guadalupe	4		x	Utah	1862	Mexicans	"San Luis Valley"	No	Conejos Line 12
Chavis	Antonio Jose	Sirvietta	Maria Rosalia	4		x	Navajo	1864	Mexicans	"San Luis Valley"	No	Conejos Line 13
Chavis	J.M. (Jesus Maria)	San Jose	Guadalupe	16		x	Pah-Ute	1852	Utahs	California	No	Conejos Line 73
Chavis	J.M. (Jesus Maria)	San Jose	Libr(a)da	4		x	Navajo	1864	Utahs	Colorado Territory	No	Conejos Line 74
Chavis	(Jose) Rafael	Sirvietta	Antonia Rosa	16		x	Utah	1864	Mexicans	"San Luis Valley"	No	Conejos Line 11
Chavis	V. (Vicente)	San Jose	Ma (Ignacia) Gracia	60		x	Navajo	1864	Mexicans	New Mexico Territory	No	Conejos Line 75
Chaves	Vicente	Culebra	Jose Rafael	11	x		Ute	1861	Mexicans	Colorado Territory	No	Costilla Line 37
Cordova	Jesus Maria	New Mexico	Juan	7	x		Navajo	1865	Utahs	New Mexico Territory	No	Conejos Line 8
Cordova	Juan (Bautista)	Culebra	Juan Jose	8	x		Navajo	1862	Mexicans	New Mexico Territory	No	Costilla Line 30
Cordova	Juan (Bautista)	Culebra	Valentina	7		x	Navajo	1864	Mexicans	Colorado Territory	No	Costilla Line 29
Cordova	Juan (Bautista)	Culebra	(Maria) Margarita	16		x	Navajo	1864	Mexicans	Colorado Territory	No	Costilla Line 28
Cruz	Domingo (Diego An)	San Antonio	Ramon	13	x		Navajo	1864	Navajos	Arizona Territory	No	Conejos Line 53

Surname	Given Name	Place	Captive Name	Age	X	Tribe	Year	Group	Territory	?	Reference
Duran	Pedro	Culebra	Juan Miguel	12	x	Ute	1864	Mexicans	Colorado Territory		Costilla Line 11
Duran	Pedro	Culebra	Maria Refugio	24	x	Navajo	1862	Mexicans	Colorado Territory	Yes	Costilla Line 10
Esquibel	Jose R(afael)	Culebra	Carmel	14	x	Navajo	1864	Mexicans	Colorado Territory	No	Costilla Line 36
Esquibel	Juan J. (de Jesus)	Culebra	Maria Luisa	35	x	Navajo	1860	Utes	Arizona Territory	No	Costilla Line 35
Gallegos	Francisco	Culebra	Maria Paula	14	x	Navajo	1862	Mexicans	Colorado Territory	Yes	Costilla Line 22
Garcia	Jose Victor	Braso	Jose Antonio	10	x	Utah	1860	Utahs	"San Luis Valley"	No	Conejos Line 20
Garcia	Jose Victor	Braso	Maria Gertrudes	11	x	Navajo	1860	Utahs	"San Luis Valley"	No	Conejos Line 19
Garcia	Jose Victor	Braso	Maria Miguela	12	x	Navajo	1862	Utahs	"San Luis Valley"	No	Conejos Line 18
Garcia	Pedro (Antonio)	San Jose	Guadalupe	8	x	Navajo	1862	Utahs	Colorado Territory	No	Conejos Line 32
Garcia	S. (Serafin) Garcia	Braso	D. M. Reta (Rita)	9	x	Navajo	1863	Utahs	Colorado Territory	No	Conejos Line 72
Gomez	Juan (de Jesus)	Guadalupita	Jose Antonio	4	x	Navajo	1864	Mexicans	Colorado Territory	No	Conejos Line 60
Gonzales	Albarieto (Evaristo)	Costilla	Maria	11	x	Navajo	1864	Mexicans	Arizona Territory		Costilla Line 61
Gonzales	Desiderio	Costilla	Juan Felipe	12	x	Navajo	1863	Mexicans	Colorado Territory	No	Costilla Line 43
Gonzales	Philipe (Felipe)	Costilla	Juan	6	x	Ute	1860	Mexicans	Colorado Territory	No	Costilla Line 59
Gonzales	Philipe (Felipe)	Costilla	Juliana	6	x	Navajo	1864	Mexicans	Colorado Territory	No	Costilla Line 60
Jacques	Jose U. (Eusequio)	Culebra	Pedro	7	x	Navajo	1862	Mexicans	New Mexico Territory	No	Costilla Line 23
Jaques	Jose Maria	Braso	Quaintaro [sic]	4	x	Utah	1861	Utahs	"San Luis Valley"	No	Conejos Line 17
Jaques	Jose Maria	Braso	Reyes	15	x	Pah-Ute	1853	Mexicans	"San Luis Valley"	No	Conejos Line 16
Jaramillo	(Juan) Francisco	Canon	Ramon	12	x	Navajo	1864	Apache	New Mexico Territory	No	Conejos Line 64
Jaraz [sic]	J. S.	Cenicero	Lue?a?	7	x	Navajo	1864	Navajo Country	Arizona Territory	No	Conejos Line 48

SURVIVAL OF CAPTIVITY *199*

LAST NAME	OWNER'S FIRST NAME	RESIDENCE	NAME OF INDIAN	AGE	M	F	TRIBE	YEAR	PURCHASED FROM	PURCHASED IN	RETURN TO TRIBE	COUNTY/ LINE NO.
Lobato	A. J. (Antonio Jose)	San Jose	Guadalupe	15		x	Navajo	1864	Mexicans	Colorado Territory	No	Conejos Line 42
Lobato	A. J. (Antonio Jose)	San Jose	Paulito	9	x		Utah	1861	Utahs	Colorado Territory	No	Conejos Line 43
Lobato	C. (Jo. Policarpio)	San Antonio	Catalina/Catarina	4		x	Navajo	1862	Utahs	Colorado Territory	No	Conejos Line 52
Lopez	Ramon	Guadalupe	Jose Manuel	5	x		Utah	1863	Utahs	Conejos	No	Conejos Line 9
Lucero	Antonio D(omingo)	Guadalupe	Guadalupe	38		x	Pah-Ute	1843	Mexicans	New Mexico Territory	No	Conejos Line 5
Lucero	Delos (?)	Guadalupe	Dolores	12		x	Navajo	1868	Utahs	New Mexico Territory	No	Conejos Line 6
Lucero	Gabriel	Guadalupe	Refugio	18		x	Navajo	1868	Mexicans	New Mexico Territory	No	Conejos Line 7
Lucero	J. M. (Jose Maria)	Cerritos	Maria Benina	15		x	Utah	1862	Mexicans	New Mexico Territory	No	Conejos Line 35
Lucero	J.Y.	Cerritos	Ana Maria	14		x	Utah	1858	Utahs	Utah Territory	No	Conejos Line 38
Lucero	J.Y.	Cerritos	Maria	16		x	Navajo	1864	Mexicans	Colorado Territory	No	Conejos Line 39
Lucero	Jose Francisco	Sirvietta	Jose Rafael	3	x		Utah	1864	Utahs	"San Luis Valley"	No	Conejos Line 10
Lucero	Juan	Sirvietta	Guadalupe	6		x	Navajo	1864	Mexicans	"San Luis Valley"	No	Conejos Line 15
Lucero	(Jose) Julian	Culebra	Macaria	6		x	Navajo	1859	Mexicans	New Mexico Territory	No	Costilla Line 34
Lucero	Manuel	Guadalupe	Miguel	7	x		Navajo	1862	Utahs	Conejos	No	Conejos Line 4
Lucero	Maria E.	San Jose	Maria Guadalupe	5		x	Navajo	1863	Mexicans	"San Luis Valley"	No	Conejos Line 22
Madrid	Juan R(afael)	Costilla	Miguel	3	x		Navajo	1864	Mexicans	Colorado Territory	No	Costilla Line 58
Mes (Maes)	(Jose) Benito	Culebra	Antonio	24	x		Navajo	1864	Mexicans	Colorado Territory	No	Costilla Line 7

Surname	Given Name	Location	Name	Age		Tribe	Year	Captors	Territory	?	Reference
Mes (Maes)	Juan Santos	Culebra	Lionor [sic]	10	x	Navajo	1861	Mexicans	Colorado Territory	No	Costilla Line 6
Mes (Maes)	Q[uerino]	Canon	Rafael	15	x	Navajo	1861	Utahs	Colorado Territory	No	Conejos Line 88
Mes (Maes)	Querino	Canon	(Jose) Gregorio	18	x	Navajo	1853	Mexicans	New Mexico Territory	No	Conejos Line 67
Mes (Maes)	Querino	Canon	Jose	15	x	Navajo	1861	Mexicans	New Mexico Territory	No	Conejos Line 68
Mes (Maes)	Querino	Canon	Seferina	28	x	Navajo	1853	Utahs	Colorado Territory	No	Conejos Line 66
Mes (Maes)	Teodoro	Canon	Juan Bautista	4	x	Navajo	1862	Mexicans	Colorado Territory	No	Costilla Line 3
Mes (Maes)	Teodoro	Canon	Juan Tomas	8	x	Navajo	1862	"Captured in"	Arizona Territory	No	Costilla Line 2
Mes (Maes)	Teodoro	Canon	Maria Rita	10	x	Navajo	1865	Utes	Colorado Territory	No	Costilla Line 1
Manzanares	Juan Andres	Culebra	Guadalupe	10	x	Navajo	1864	Mexicans	Colorado Territory	No	Costilla Line 4
Manzanares	Pedro	Costilla	Maria Tomasa	30	x	Ute	1864	"Captured in"	Arizona Territory	No	Costilla Line 57
Martin	Antonio J.	Culebra	Hilario	4	x	Navajo	1861	Utes	Colorado Territory	No	Costilla Line 42
Martin	Felipe (de Jesus)	Los Pinos	Juliana	12	x	Apache	1855	Apaches	New Mexico Territory	No	Conejos Line 58
Martin	J.M.	Pura y Limpia	Rita	45	x	Navajo	1864	Mexicans	Colorado Territory	No	Conejos Line 81
Martin	M[iguel] A[ntonio]	Mesitas	Dolores	10	x	Navajo	1864	Mexicans	Colorado Territory	No	Conejos Line 63
Martine [sic]	J[ose] G[abriel]	Canon	Margarita	18	x	Navajo	1864	Utahs	Colorado Territory	No	Conejos Line 65
Martine [sic]	Jose A[ntonio]	Culebra	Margarita	12	x	Navajo	1864	Mexicans	Colorado Territory	No	Costilla Line 38
Martinez	Antonio J.	Costilla	Guadalupe	18	x	Navajo	1864	Mexicans	Colorado Territory	Yes	Costilla Line 45
Martinez	Juan	Guadalupe	Estefana	11	x	Utah	1856	Utahs	Conejos	No	Conejos Line 3
Martinez	Juan	Guadalupe	Maria Antonia	16	x	Utah	1855	Utahs	Conejos	No	Conejos Line 2
Medina	(Buena) Ventura	Costilla	Guadalupe	50	x	Navajo	1863	Mexicans	Colorado Territory	Yes	Costilla Line 50
Medina	Faustin	Costilla	Margarita	16	x	Navajo	1863	Mexicans	Colorado Territory	No	Costilla Line 49

LAST NAME	OWNER'S FIRST NAME	RESIDENCE	NAME OF INDIAN	AGE	M	F	TRIBE	YEAR	PURCHASED FROM	PURCHASED IN	RETURN TO TRIBE	COUNTY/ LINE NO.
Montoya	Juan	Culebra	Miguel	4	x		Apache	1861	Apaches	New Mexico Territory		Costilla Line 31
Montoya	N.	Pinas	Guadalupe	11		x	Navajo	1864	Mexicans	Colorado Territory	No	Conejos Line 62
Ocayan (Ocaña)	P.	San Jose	Agapita	18		x	Navajo	1863	Mexicans	Colorado Territory	No	Conejos Line 79
Olzoriz [sic]	Guadalupe	Sirvietta	Catalina	35		x	Navajo	1865	Mexicans	"San Luis Valley"	Yes	Conejos Line 14
Pacheco	Mariano	Culebra	Juana Maria	17		x	Navajo	1864	Mexicans	Colorado Territory	No	Costilla Line 12
Padilla	Maria P.	Costilla	Catalina	17		x	Ute	1857	Mexicans	Colorado Territory	No	Costilla Line 56
Padilla	Maria P.	Costilla	Jose Antonio	12	x		Ute	1859	Utes	Colorado Territory	No	Costilla Line 54
Padilla	Maria P.	Costilla	Lupita	11		x	Ute	1856	Utes	Colorado Territory	No	Costilla Line 53
Padilla	Maria P.	Costilla	Maria	30		x	Navajo	1863	Utes	Colorado Territory	Yes	Costilla Line 52
Padilla	Maria P.	Costilla	Santana	7		x	Navajo	1862	Utes	Colorado Territory	No	Costilla Line 55
Quintana	Vicente	Costilla	Maria Antonia	20		x	Navajo	1860	Mexicans	Colorado Territory	No	Costilla Line 51
Rodriguez	M(artin)	San Rafael	Guadalupe	20		x	Navajo	1861	Utahs	Colorado Territory	No	Conejos Line 71
Romero	Ml.	San Jose	Maria Guadalupe	10		x	Utah	1864	Utahs	Colorado Territory	No	Conejos Line 40
Romero	Ml.	San Jose	Rosalia	19		x	Navajo	1863	Mexicans	Colorado Territory	No	Conejos Line 41
Ruiz	G.	San Antonio	Rosalia	6		x	Navajo	1864	Navajos	Arizona Territory	No	Conejos Line 54
Salazar	Francisco	Los Pinos	Guadalupe	17		x	Navajo	1864	Mexicans	New Mexico Territory	No	Conejos Line 55
Salazar	Francisco	Los Pinos	Juana	5		x	Navajo	1864	Mexicans	Colorado Territory	No	Conejos Line 56
Salazar	M A (Miguel Anto.)	Saritas	Trinidad	10		x	Navajo	1862	Utahs	Colorado Territory	No	Conejos Line 31
Salazar	Salvador	Saritas	Juan	7	x		Navajo	1862	Utahs	Colorado Territory	No	Conejos Line 30

Salazar	Salvador	Saritas	Carenya [sic]	9	x	Navajo	1862	Utahs	Colorado Territory	No	Conejos Line 29
Sanchez	(Jose) Amado(r)	Culebra	Maria Guadalupe	30	x	Navajo	1864	Mexicans	Colorado Territory	Yes	Costilla Line 13
Sanchez	(Jose) Amado(r)	Culebra	Maria Lucia	8	x	Ute	1864	Utes	Colorado Territory	No	Costilla Line 14
Sanchez	Damacio	Costilla	Antonio	7	x	Navajo	1864	Mexicans	Colorado Territory	No	Costilla Line 46
Sanchez	Francisco	Culebra	Dolores	10	x	Navajo	1862	Mexicans	New Mexico Territory	No	Costilla Line 19
Sanchez	Francisco	Culebra	Nicolas	7	x	Navajo	1860	Mexicans	New Mexico Territory	No	Costilla Line 18
Sisneros	A. R.	Los Pinos	Jose Sino [sic]	5	x	Pah-Ute	1864	Utahs	Colorado Territory	No	Conejos Line 57
Sisneros	Chepito	San Jose	Jose Maria	8	x	Navajo	1864	Mexicans	"San Luis Valley"	No	Conejos Line 21
Sisneros	Cresencio	Guadalupe	Guadalupe	25	x	Navajo	1863	Utahs	Conejos	No	Conejos Line 1
Sisneros	M. M.	Los Pinos	Encarnacion	16	x	Navajo	1864	Mexicans	Colorado Territory	No	Conejos Line 61
Tobin	Tomas Tate	Costilla	Dominga	25	x	Navajo	1863	Mexicans	Colorado Territory	No	Costilla Line 47
Trujillo	J. (Jose Ignacio)	Cerritos	Getrudes	8	x	Navajo	1863	Utahs	New Mexico Territory	No	Conejos Line 34
Trujillo	Juan Andres	Culebra	Margarita	15	x	Navajo	1861	Mexicans	New Mexico Territory	No	Costilla Line 8
Trujillo	Juan Andres	Culebra	Maria Antonia	14	x	Navajo	1863	Mexicans	Colorado Territory	No	Costilla Line 9
Trujillo	Manuel	Saritas	Juan	11	x	Navajo	1854	Utahs	New Mexico Territory	No	Conejos Line 28
Trujillo	S.	San Jose	Filomena	14	x	Navajo	1857	Utahs	New Mexico Territory	No	Conejos Line 77
Trujillo	S.	San Jose	Maria Guadalupe	52	x	California	1831	Utahs	California	No	Conejos Line 76
Trujillo	S.	San Jose	Nestor	12	x	Navajo	1864	Capote	New Mexico Territory	No	Conejos Line 78

LAST NAME	OWNER'S FIRST NAME	RESIDENCE	NAME OF INDIAN	AGE	M	F	TRIBE	YEAR	PURCHASED FROM	PURCHASED IN	RETURN TO TRIBE	COUNTY/ LINE NO.
Trujillo	Tofolo (Teofilo)	Culebra	Antonio (Maria)	7	x		Navajo	1865	Mexicans	Colorado Territory	No	Costilla Line 32
Trujillo	Topolo (Teofilo)	Culebra	Piedad	10		x	Navajo	1864	Mexicans	Colorado Territory	No	Costilla Line 33
Valdes	(Jose) S(eledonio)	San Jose	Getrudes	24		x	Pah-Ute	1848	Mexicans	New Mexico Territory	No	Conejos Line 44
Valdes	(Jose) S(eledonio)	San Jose	Luis	9	x		½ Indian				No	Conejos Line 46
Valdes	(Jose) S(eledonio)	San Jose	Paula	11		x	Pah-Ute	1858	Utahs	Colorado Territory	No	Conejos Line 45
Valdez	J.M.	Pura y Limpia	Rafaela	10		x	Navajo	1862	Utahs	Colorado Territory	No	Conejos Line 80
Valdez	Jesus	Pura y Limpia	Maria Antonia	12		x	Navajo	1864	Mexicans	Colorado Territory	No	Conejos Line 82
Vallejos	Antonio J(ose)	Culebra	Colores (Dolores)	15		x	Navajo	1864	Mexicans	Colorado Territory	No	Costilla Line 39
Vallejos	(Jose) Francisco	Culebra	Maria Paola (Paula)	14		x	Navajo	1862	Mexicans	Colorado Territory	Yes	Costilla Line 22
Vallejos	Joseph (Maria)	Costilla	Rosalia	18		x	Navajo	1864	Mexicans	Colorado Territory	Yes	Costilla Line 44
Vallejos	Maria D. (Dolores)	Culebra	Maria Vigil	40		x	Navajo	1859	Mexicans	Colorado Territory [sic]	No	Costilla Line 24
Vallejos	Maria D. (Dolores)	Culebra	Maria Rosario Vigil	7		x	Navajo	1859	Mexicans	New Mexico Territory	No	Costilla Line 25
Vallejos	Maria D. (Dolores)	Culebra	Jose Antonio Vigil	9	x		Navajo	1858	Mexicans	New Mexico Territory		Costilla Line 27
Vallejos	Maria G(uadalupe)	Culebra	Juan Antonio Vigil	6	x		Navajo	1860	Mexicans	New Mexico Territory	No	Costilla Line 21
Vallejos	Maria G(uadalupe)	Culebra	Ma. Alcaria Vigil	11		x	Navajo	1859	Mexicans	Colorado Territory [sic]	No	Costilla Line 20

Surname	Given Name	Place	Child	Age	X	Tribe	Year	Captors	Territory	?	Line
Vallejos	Miguel Antonio	Culebra	Felipe	8		Navajo	1863	Utes	Colorado Territory		Costilla Line 41
Vallejos	Miguel Antonio	Culebra	Josefa	8	x	Navajo	1860	Utes	Colorado Territory	No	Costilla Line 40
Velasquez	J M (Jesus Maria)	Guadalupita	Catalina	24	x	Navajo	1855	Mexicans	New Mexico Territory	No	Conejos Line 59
Vigil	F.	Guadalupe	Maria Rosalia	5	x	Navajo	1864	Mexicans	Colorado Territory	No	Conejos Line 47
Vigil	(Juan de Jesus)	Cerritos	Lucas	4	x	Utah	1864	Mexicans	New Mexico Territory	No	Conejos Line 37
Vigil	J. Maria	Canon	Juliana	22	x	Navajo	1862	Utahs	Colorado Territory	No	Conejos Line 86
Vigil	J. Maria	Canon	Lucas	18	x	Navajo	1863	Utahs	Colorado Territory	No	Conejos Line 87
Vigil	J.T.	Cerritos	Vicente	4	x	Utah	1864	Mexicans	New Mexico Territory	No	Conejos Line 36
Vigil	(Jose) Tomas	Culebra	Francisco Antonio	7	x	Navajo	1865	Mexicans	Colorado Territory		Costilla Line 26
Vigil	Juan M. (Miguel)	Culebra	Juan Antonio	8	x	Navajo	1864	Mexicans	New Mexico Territory	No	Costilla Line 16
Vigil	Juan M. (Miguel)	Culebra	Juliana	12		Navajo	1862	Mexicans	New Mexico Territory	No	Costilla Line 17
Vigil	Juan M. (Miguel)	Culebra	Pablo	7	x	Ute	1864	Mexicans	New Mexico Territory	No	Costilla Line 15
Woodson	(James Bernard)	Guadalupe	Andres	10	x	Navajo	1862	Utahs	Colorado Territory	No	Conejos Line 85
Woodson	(James Bernard)	Guadalupe	Gabriel	12	x	Navajo	1860	Utahs	Colorado Territory	No	Conejos Line 84
Woodson	(James Bernard)	Guadalupe	Maria Catalina	19	x	Utah	1860	Utahs	Colorado Territory	No	Conejos Line 83

TABLE 8.3 Captive Indians by Owner Surname, 1860–1880

This table includes known captives who lived in the counties of Conejos, Costilla, Huérfano, Las Animas, and Saguache. It does not include indigenous heads of households. A baptized individual was considered indigenous if his or her named adoptive parent(s) also served as the *padrino(s)* (godparents). Also, information provided on the 1880 census enumerations helped identify those indigenous persons who were traded or purchased before 1880. Spellings are verbatim.

LAST NAME	OWNER'S FIRST NAME	RESIDENCE	NAME OF INDIAN	M	F	TRIBE	ON HEAD'S REPORTS?
Abeyta	Lorenzo A.	Trinidad CO	Juana		x		
Abeyta	Pablo Antonio	Las Animas CO	Buenaventura	x			
		Las Animas CO	Francisco	x			
Aguilar	Jose Rafael	Costilla CO	Francisco Juarez	x			
Alires	Juan Ignacio	Las Animas CO	Juan Antonio	x			
Aragon (3)	Francisco Esteban	Conejos CO	Donaciano de Jesus	x			
	F. E. (Franco. Esteban)	Cenicero	Jose Antonio	x		Navajo	y
	Francisco Esteban	Conejos CO	Ma Francisca de Jesus		x		
Aragon	J. G.	San Rafael	Dolores		x	Navajo	y
Aragon	Pedro	Conejos CO	Agapita		x		
Archuleta	A. J. (Antonio Jose)	Las Animas CO	Jose Antonio	x			
Archuleta (5)	Jose Manuel de Jesus	Conejos CO	Juliana Gallegos		x		
	Jose Manuel de Jesus	Conejos CO	Juliana		x		
	Manuel (de Jesus)	Saritas	Maria Dolores		x	Utah	y
	Jose Manuel de Jesus	Conejos CO	Jacinta		x		
	Manuel (de Jesus)	Saritas	(Maria) Guadalupe		x	Navajo	y
Atencio (3)	Hilario	San Jose	Jose Antonio	x		Navajo	y
	Hilario	San Jose	Juan Quaro [sic]	x		Navajo	y
	Jose Hilario	San Jose	Rafaela		x	Navajo	y
Autobees	Charlie	Sand Creek CO	Mike	x		Cheyenne	

LAST NAME	OWNER'S FIRST NAME	RESIDENCE	NAME OF INDIAN	M	F	TRIBE	ON HEAD'S REPORTS?
Baca (3)	Felipe de Jesus	Guadalupita NM	Antonia		x	Navajo	
	Felipe de Jesus	Trinidad CO	Manuel	x			
	Ma Dolores Gonzales Baca	Trinidad CO	Rafael	x			
Baca (2)	Jose Trinidad	Huerfano	Librada		x		
	Jose Trinidad	Huerfano	Rita		x		
Baca (5)	Juan Antonio	Arroyo Seco NM	Encarnacion		x	Ute or Navajo	
	Juan Antonio	Arroyo Hondo	Jose Maria	x		Navajo	
	Juan Antonio	Costilla CO	Siriaco	x			
	Juan Antonio	Arroyo Seco NM	Juan Antonio	x			
	Juan Antonio	Arroyo Hondo	Maria Guadalupe		x	Ute	
Barela	Jesus Maria	Las Animas CO	Juan B.	x			
Bernal	Juan B. (de Jesus)	Costilla	Margarita		x	Navajo	y
Borrego	Felis de Jesus	Conejos CO	Maria Victoriana		x		
[B]orego (Borrego)	V (Buenaventura)	San Jose	M(ag)delina		x	Navajo	y
Bounay (Bourcy) (2)	J. (Joseph)	Culebra	Resiona [sic]		x	Navajo	y
	Joseph	Culebra	Guadalupe		x		
Bustos	Jose Ramon	Arroyo Hondo	Jose Antonio	x		Navajo	
Carson (3)	Christopher "Kit"	Taos NM and Boggsville CO	Juan	x		Navajo/Apache	
	Christopher "Kit"		Juan Bautista	x		Navajo	
	Christopher "Kit"		Maria Dolores		x	Navajo	
Casias (2)	Ml.	Santa Cruz NM	Francisco Antonio	x		Navajo	y
	Ml.	Santa Cruz NM	Juana		x	Navajo	y
Casias	Miguel	Del Norte CO	Santiago	x		Ute	
Casias	Miguel Antonio	Conejos CO	(Juan) Mateo	x			
Chacon	Jose Rafael Sotero, Capt.	Las Animas CO	Maria		x		
Chacon	J. B. (Juan Bautista)	San Rafael	Juliana		x	Navajo	y

LAST NAME	OWNER'S FIRST NAME	RESIDENCE	NAME OF INDIAN	M	F	TRIBE	ON HEAD'S REPORTS?
Chacon (2)	J. G. (Juan Gabriel) Fran.	San Rafael	(Maria) Dolores		x	Navajo	y
	Juan Gabriel (Francisco)	Conejos CO	Maria Rita		x		
Chavis (2)	Antonio Jose	Sirvietta	Guadalupe		x	Utah	y
	Antonio Jose	Sirvietta	Maria Rosalia		x	Navajo	y
Chavez/Chavis (5)	Jesus Maria de la Cruz	Conejos CO	(Francisca) Leonarda		x		
	Jesus Maria de la Cruz	Conejos	Guadalupe		x	Pah-Ute	y
	J. M. (Jesus Maria Cruz)	San Jose	Guadalupe		x		
	Jesus Maria de la Cruz	Conejo NM	Jose Antonio	x			
	J. M. (Jesus Maria Cruz)	San Jose	(Maria) Libr(a)da		x	Navajo	y
Chavez	Jose Guadalupe	Conejos CO	Maria Catarina		x		
Chavez/Chavis	(Jose) Rafael	Sirvietta	(Maria) Antonia Rosa		x	Utah	y
Chavez/Chavis	V. (Jose Vicente)	San Jose	Ma (Ignacia) Gracia		x	Navajo	y
Chavez/Chavis	Vicente	Culebra	(Juan) Jose Rafael	x		Ute	y
Cordoba	Juan Bautista	Trinidad CO	Maria Cayetana		x		
Cordoba (3)	Juan (Bautista)	Culebra	(Maria) Margarita		x	Navajo	y
	Juan (Bautista)	Culebra	Juan Jose	x		Navajo	y
	Juan (Bautista)	Culebra	Valentina		x	Navajo	y
Cordova (4)	Higinio	Las Animas CO	Jose de Gracia Garcia	x			
	Higinio	Las Animas CO	unknown	x			
	Higinio	Las Animas CO	unknown		x		
	Higinio	Las Animas CO	unknown		x		
Cordova	Jesus Maria	New Mexico	Juan	x		Navajo	y
Cordova (2)	Jose Rafael	Las Animas CO	Jose Antonio	x			
	Jose Rafael	Las Animas CO	Maria Antonia		x		

LAST NAME	OWNER'S FIRST NAME	RESIDENCE	NAME OF INDIAN	M	F	TRIBE	ON HEAD'S REPORTS?
Cordova	Manuel (A.)	Huerfano	Leonor Garcia		x	Navajo	
Cruz	Domingo (Diego Ant.)	San Antonio	Ramon	x		Navajo	y
Duran (2)	Pedro (Antonio)	Culebra	Juan Miguel	x		Ute	y
	Pedro (Antonio)	Culebra	Maria Refugio		x	Navajo	y
Espinosa (2)	Jose Julian, Capt.	Saguache	unknown		x	Ute	
	Jose Julian, Capt.	Saguache	Justo	x		Ute	
Esquibel (2)	Jose R(afael)	Culebra	Carmel		x	Navajo	y
	Jose Rafael	Costilla NM	Jose Antonio	x		Navajo	
Esquibel (3)	Juan de Jesus	Huerfano	(Jose) Manuel	x			
	Juan de Jesus	Arroyo Hondo	Maria Rita		x	Navajo	
	Juan J. (de Jesus)	Culebra	Maria Luisa		x	Navajo	y
Esquibel	Maria de la Cruz Mestas	Huerfano	Miguel	x			
Ford	James H., Capt.	Fort Garland CO	Lorenzo	x			
Fulton (Fullerton) (2)	James	Conejos/ Saguache	Margarita Trujillo		x		
	James	Conejos/ Saguache	Jose M. Trujillo	x			
Gallegos (5)	Dario	Costilla CO	Antonia		x		
	Dario	Arroyo Hondo	Guadalupe			Navajo	
	Dario	Costilla CO	Jose Antonio	x			
	Dario	Costilla CO	Maria (del) Refugio		x	Comanche	
	Dario	Arroyo Hondo	(Maria) Romula		x	Navajo	
Gallegos (3)	Diego Antonio	Costilla CO	Cayetano Gonzales	x			
	Diego Antonio	Arroyo Hondo	Maria Juana		x		
	Diego Antonio	Arroyo Hondo	Maria Trinidad		x		
Gallegos	Francisco	Culebra	Maria Paula		x	Navajo	y
Gallegos	Jose Benito	Conejos CO	Agapito	x			
Gallegos	Jose Eluterio	Arroyo Hondo	Juliana		x	Navajo	
Gallegos	Jose Eulogio	Conejos CO	Felipe	x			
Gallegos	Jose Narciso	Arroyo Hondo	Maria Antonia		x	Navajo	

LAST NAME	OWNER'S FIRST NAME	RESIDENCE	NAME OF INDIAN	M	F	TRIBE	ON HEAD'S REPORTS?
Gallegos	Jose Nazario	Costilla CO	Rita		x		
Gallegos	Juan de Jesus	Conejos CO	Francisco Antonio	x			
Gallegos (3)	Juan Gabriel	Costilla CO	Gabriela		x	Palluchi	
	Juan Gabriel	Arroyo Hondo	Martin	x		Navajo	
	Juan Gabriel	Arroyo Hondo	Maria Rita		x		
Gallegos	Manuel	Conejos CO	Catalina		x		
Gallegos	Manuel Antonio	Conejos CO	Maria Rita		x	Navajo	
Garcia	unknown	Conejos CO	Maria Teresa		x		
Garcia	Jose Simon	Conejos CO	Guadalupe Rafaela		x		
Garcia (7)	Jose Victor	Conejos	Antonio	x			
	Jose Victor	Braso	Jose Antonio	x		Utah	y
	Jose Victor	Conejos	Jose Inez	x			
	Jose Victor	Conejos	Maria Antonia		x	Utah	
	Jose Victor	Braso	Maria Gertrudes		x	Navajo	y
	Jose Victor	Braso	Maria Miguela		x	Navajo	y
	Jose Victor	Conejos	Sarifino	x			
Garcia	Pedro (Antonio)	San Jose	(Maria) Guadalupe		x	Navajo	y
Garcia (4)	S(erafin) Garcia	Braso	D. M. Reta (Rita)		x	Navajo	y
	Jose Serafin Garcia	San Juan, NM	Maria Antonia		x	Ute	
	Jose Serafin Garcia	San Juan, NM	Maria Guadalupe		x	Ute	
	Jose Serafin Garcia	San Juan, NM	Jose Feliciano	x		Ute	
Garcia (2)	Teodosio	Costilla CO	Maria Paula		x		
	Teodosio	Costilla CO	Rumalda		x		
Gomez (2)	Juan de Jesus	Conejos CO	Delfinia		x		
	Juan (de Jesus)	Guadalupita	Jose Antonio	x		Navajo	y
Gonzales	Desiderio	Costilla	Juan Felipe	x		Navajo	y
	Desiderio	Costilla	Maria Viviana		x	Navajo	
Gonzales (2)	Juan Evaristo	Huerfano	Dolores		x		
	Albarieto (Evaristo)	Costilla	Maria		x	Navajo	y

LAST NAME	OWNER'S FIRST NAME	RESIDENCE	NAME OF INDIAN	M	F	TRIBE	ON HEAD'S REPORTS?
Gonzales	Felipe	Costilla	Juan del Carmel	x			
Gonzales (6)	Manuel	Huerfano	Jose Francisco	x			
	Manuel	Huerfano	Maria Antonia		x		
	Manuel	Arroyo Hondo	Maria de los Dolores		x	Ute	
	Manuel	Arroyo Hondo	Maria Guadalupe		x		
	Manuel	Arroyo Hondo	Maria Guadalupe		x	Navajo	
	Manuel	Huerfano	Maria Rita		x	Navajo	
Gonzales (2)	Philipe (Felipe)	Costilla	Juan	x		Ute	y
	Philipe (Felipe)	Costilla	Juliana		x	Navajo	y
Gurule	Damaso	Trinidad	Maria Manuela		x		
Gutierrez	Cipriano	Trinidad	Pedro Antonio	x			
Head (6)	Lafayette	Conejos CO	Estefana		x		
	Lafayette	Arroyo Hondo	Felipe	x			
	Lafayette	Conejos CO	Juana		x		
	Lafayette	Arroyo Hondo	Maria Antonia		x	Ute	
	Lafayette	Conejos CO	Maria Guadalupe		x		
	Lafayette	Conejos CO	Miguel	x			
Herrera	Juan	Las Animas CO	Rita Herrera		x		
Hurtado (2)	Manuel	Huerfano	Guadalupe		x		
	Manuel	Huerfano	Rafaela		x		
Jacques (Jaquez)	Jose U. (Eusequio)	Culebra	Pedro	x		Navajo	y
Jaques (2)	Jose Maria	Braso	Quaintaro [sic]	x		Utah	y
	Jose Maria	Braso	Reyes		x	Pah-Ute	y
Jaramillo	(Juan) Francisco	Canon	Ramon	x		Navajo	y
Jaraz [sic]	J. S.	Cenicero	Lue? a?		x	Navajo	y
Jiron	Guadalupe	Conejos CO	Maria de la Ascencion		x		
Jiron	Secundo	Conejos CO	Maria Guadalupe		x		

LAST NAME	OWNER'S FIRST NAME	RESIDENCE	NAME OF INDIAN	M	F	TRIBE	ON HEAD'S REPORTS?
LeBlanc	Jose Antonio	Del Norte CO	Albino	x		Jicarilla Apache	
Lobato (3)	Antonio Jose	Conejos CO	Encarnacion		x		
	A. J. (Antonio Jose)	Conejos	Guadalupe		x	Navajo	y
	A. J. (Antonio Jose)	San Jose	Paulito	x		Ute	y
Lobato	(Jose) C(arpio) (Policarpio)	San Antonio	(Maria) Catalina/ Catarina		x	Navajo	y
Lobato (2)	Maria Dionisia	Conejos CO	Antonio	x			
	Maria Dionisia		Felipe	x			
Lobato	Teodoro Antonio	Conejos CO	Maria del Socorro		x	Navajo	
Lopez	Francisco Antonio	Conejos CO	Jesus Maria	x			
Lopez	Jose Bonifacio	Conejos CO	Jose Santiago	x			
Lopez	Ramon	Guadalupe	Jose Manuel	x		Utah	y
Lucero (3)	Antonio D(omingo)	Guadalupe	Guadalupe		x	Pah-Ute	y
	Antonio Domingo	Conejos CO	Maria Antonia		x		
	Maria Rufina Valdez Lucero	Conejos CO	Juan Nepomuceno Valdez	x			
Lucero	Delos (?)	Guadalupe	Dolores		x	Navajo	y
Lucero (2)	Gabriel Antonio	Conejos CO	Polonia		x		
	Gabriel Antonio	Guadalupe	Refugio		x	Navajo	y
Lucero	Jose Francisco	Sirvietta	Jose Rafael	x		Utah	y
Lucero (2)	(Jose) Julian	Culebra	Maria Macaria		x	Ute	
	(Jose) Julian		Macaria		x	Navajo	y
Lucero	J. M. (Jose Maria)	Cerritos	Maria Benina (Benigna)		x	Utah	y
Lucero	Jose Nemesio	Conejos CO	(Maria) Soledad		x		
Lucero	Juan	Sirvietta	Guadalupe		x	Navajo	y
Lucero (3)	J. Y. (Juan Ysidro)	Cerritos	Ana Maria		x	Utah	y
	J. Y. (Juan Ysidro)	Cerritos	Maria		x	Navajo	y
	Juan Isidro	Cerritos	Maria Escolastica		x		

LAST NAME	OWNER'S FIRST NAME	RESIDENCE	NAME OF INDIAN	M	F	TRIBE	ON HEAD'S REPORTS?
Lucero (2)	Luciano	Costilla CO	Francisco	x			
	Luciano	Costilla CO	Maria Cordoba		x		
Lucero	Manuel	Guadalupe	Miguel	x		Navajo	y
Lucero	Maria E.	San Jose	Maria Guadalupe		x	Navajo	y
Lujan	Juan de Jesus	Huerfano	Jose Antonio	x		Sioux	
Madrid	Juan R.	Costilla	Miguel	x		Navajo	y
Maes (2)	Bernardo Joaquin	Costilla CO	Jose Paz	x		Apache	
	Bernardo Joaquin	Costilla CO	Juan Claudio	x		½ Apache	
Mes (Maes) (2)	Jose Benito	Huerfano	Maria Antonia		x	Navajo	
	(Jose) Benito	Culebra	Antonio	x		Navajo	y
Maes	Jose de Jesus	Conejos CO	Maria Bernarda		x		
Mes (Maes)	Juan Santos	Culebra	Lionor (Leonor)		x	Navajo	y
Mes (Maes) (5)	Querino	Canon	Jose	x		Navajo	y
	Querino	Canon	(Jose) Gregorio	x		Navajo	y
	Quirino	Las Animas CO	Margarita		x		
	Q(uerino)	Canon	(Jose) Rafael	x		Navajo	y
	Querino	Las Animas	Seferina		x	Navajo	y
Mes (Maes) (4)	Teodoro	Canon	Juan Bautista	x		Navajo	y
	Teodoro	Canon	Juan Tomas	x		Navajo	y
	Teodoro	Huerfano	Juana Librada		x		
	Teodoro	Canon	Maria Rita		x	Navajo	y
Manzanares	Juan Andres	Culebra	Guadalupe	x		Navajo	y
Manzanares	Pedro	Costilla	Maria Tomasa		x	Ute	y
Martin	Antonio J.	Culebra	Hilario	x		Navajo	y
Martin	Felipe (de Jesus)	Los Pinos	(Maria) Juliana		x	Apache	y
Martin	J. M.	Pura y Limpia	Rita		x	Navajo	y
Martin	Luis Maria	Costilla CO	(Maria) Piedad		x		
Martin(ez) (2)	M[iguel] A[ntonio]	Mesitas	(Maria) Dolores		x	Navajo	y
	Miguel Antonio	Conejos CO	(Jose) Igancio	x			

LAST NAME	OWNER'S FIRST NAME	RESIDENCE	NAME OF INDIAN	M	F	TRIBE	ON HEAD'S REPORTS?
Martin	Pablo	Conejos CO	Victoria		x		
Martine [sic]	Jose A.	Culebra	Margarita		x	Navajo	y
Martine [sic]	J G (Jose Gabriel)	Canon	Margarita		x	Navajo	y
Martinez	Antonio J.	Costilla	Guadalupe		x	Navajo	y
Martinez (2)	Juan	Guadalupe	Estefana		x	Utah	y
	Juan		Maria Antonia		x	Utah	y
Martinez (2)	Juan Bautista	Huerfano	Lupe		x		
	Juan Bautista	Huerfano	Lupita		x		
Martinez	Juan Santos	Huerfano	Encarnacion Montoya		x	½ Navajo	
Martinez (2)	Ma. de la Luz Archuleta	Costilla CO	Juan Miguel	x			
	Ma. de la Luz Archuleta	Costilla CO	Maria		x	Navajo	
Mascarenas	Antonio Marcelo	Las Animas CO	Juan Lorenzo	x			
Mascarenas	Juan Jose	Conejos CO	Maria Guadalupe		x		
Medina	Antonio (Eusebio)	Costilla CO	Alvina		x		
Medina	Ventura	Costilla	Guadalupe		x	Navajo	y
Medina	(Jose) Faustin	Costilla	Margarita		x	Navajo	y
Montoya	Ana	Las Animas CO	Isabel		x		
Montoya	Juan	Culebra	Miguel	x		Apache	y
Montoya	N.	Pinas	Guadalupe		x	Navajo	y
Ocayan (Ocaña)	P.	San Jose	Agapita		x	Navajo	y
Olguin (2)	Jesus Maria	Conejos CO	Jose Antonio	x			
	Jesus Maria	Conejos CO	Jose Gregorio	x			
Olzoriz [sic]	Guadalupe	Sirvietta	Catalina		x	Navajo	y
Pacheco	Mariano	Culebra	Juana Maria		x	Navajo	y
Padilla (5)	Maria P.	Costilla	Catalina		x	Ute	y
	Maria P.	Costilla	Jose Antonio	x		Ute	y
	Maria P.	Costilla	Lupita		x	Ute	y
	Maria P.	Costilla	Maria		x	Navajo	y
	Maria P.	Costilla	Santana		x	Navajo	y
Pfeiffer (3)	Albert Hinrich	Costilla CO	Jose Lazaro	x		Navajo	
	Albert Hinrich	Costilla CO	Maria Antonia		x	Ute	
	Albert Hinrich	Costilla CO	Maria Juliana		x	Navajo	

LAST NAME	OWNER'S FIRST NAME	RESIDENCE	NAME OF INDIAN	M	F	TRIBE	ON HEAD'S REPORTS?
Quintana	Baltazar de los Reyes	Arroyo Hondo	Ignacio	x			
Quintana	Vicente	Costilla	Maria Antonia		x	Navajo	y
Rodriguez (2)	Juan Rafael	Conejos CO	Jose Julian	x			
	Juan Rafael		Miguela Noriega		x		
Rodriguez (2)	M(artin)	San Rafael	Guadalupe		x	Navajo	y
	Martin	Conejos CO	Julian	x			
Romero	Juan de Jesus	Huerfano	Jose Miguel	x		Navajo	
Romero (2)	Ml.	San Jose	Maria Guadalupe		x	Utah	y
	Ml.	San Jose	Rosalia		x	Navajo	y
Ruiz	G.	San Antonio	Rosalia		x	Navajo	y
Salazar (4)	(Jose Francisco) Eliseo	Conejos CO	Alejandro	x			
	(Jose Francisco) Eliseo	Abiquiu, NM	Maria Rita		x	Navajo	
	(Jose Francisco) Eliseo	Abiquiu, NM	Juliana		x	Pah-Ute	
	(Jose Francisco) Eliseo	Abiquiu, NM	Vicente	x		Navajo	
Salazar	Epifanio de Jesus	Conejos CO	Candelario	x			
Salazar (2)	(Jo Toribio) Francisco	Los Pinos	Guadalupe		x	Navajo	y
	(Jo Toribio) Francisco	Los Pinos	(Maria) Juana		x	Navajo	y
Salazar (2)	M A (Miguel Antonio)	Conejos CO	Maria Paula		x		
	M A (Miguel Antonio)	Saritas	Trinidad		x	Navajo	y
Salazar (4)	Manuel Sabino	Conejos CO	Antonia		x		
	Manuel Sabino	Conejos CO	Daniel	x			
	Manuel Sabino	Conejos CO	Marco	x			
	Manuel Sabino	Conejos CO	Maria Rita		x		
Salazar	Pedro Ignacio (Nabor)	Conejos CO	Juan Bautista	x			

LAST NAME	OWNER'S FIRST NAME	RESIDENCE	NAME OF INDIAN	M	F	TRIBE	ON HEAD'S REPORTS?
Salazar (6)	Salvador	Saritas	Carenya [*sic*]		x	Navajo	y
	Salvador	Conejos CO	Gertrudes		x		
	Salvador	Conejos CO	Jose Manuel	x			
	Salvador	Saritas	Juan	x		Navajo	y
	Salvador	Conejos CO	Juana		x		
	Salvador	Conejos CO	Maria Margarita		x		
Sanchez (2)	(Jose) Amado(r)	Culebra	Maria Guadalupe		x	Navajo	y
	(Jose) Amado(r)	Culebra	Maria Lucia		x	Ute	y
Sanchez	Damacio	Costilla	Antonio	x		Navajo	y
Sanchez (3)	Francisco	Culebra	(Maria) Dolores		x	Navajo	y
	Francisco	Culebra	Nicolas	x		Navajo	y
	Francisco	Conejos CO	Rafael	x			
Sanchez (3)	Jesus Maria	Costilla NM	unknown		x		
	Jesus Maria	Costilla NM	Maria Catarina		x	Ute	
	Jesus Maria	Costilla NM	Maria Guadalupe		x	Ute	
Sanchez	Joaquin	Costilla NM	Maria Antonia		x		
Sanchez	Vicente	Conejos CO	Maria Dolores		x	Navajo	
Silva (3)	Juan Bautista	Rio Grande CO	Alvino	x			
	Juan Bautista	Rio Grande CO	Carlota		x		
	Juan Bautista	Rio Grande CO	Juan	x		Ute	
Sisneros	A. R.	Los Pinos NM	Jose Sino [*sic*]	x		Pah-Ute	y
Sisneros	Chepito	San Jose	Jose Maria	x		Navajo	y
Sisneros	Cresencio	Guadalupe	Guadalupe		x	Navajo	y
Sisneros	M. M.	Los Pinos	Encarnacion		x	Navajo	y
Tafoya	Felipe de Jesus	Las Animas CO	Margarita		x	Navajo	
Tobin (2)	Tomas Tate	Costilla	Dominga		x	Navajo	y
	Tomas Tate	Conejos CO	Maria Helena		x	Navajo	
Trujillo	unknown	Conejos CO	Maria de la Luz		x		
Trujillo	J. (Jose Ignacio)	Cerritos	(Maria) Getrudes		x	Navajo	y
Trujillo	Jose Tiburcio	Conejos CO	Jose Antonio	x			

LAST NAME	OWNER'S FIRST NAME	RESIDENCE	NAME OF INDIAN	M	F	TRIBE	ON HEAD'S REPORTS?
Trujillo (5)	Juan Andres	Costilla County	Jose Irene	x			
	Juan Andres	Costilla County	Juan Bautis. Gallegos	x		Navajo	
	Juan Andres	Culebra	Margarita		x	Navajo	y
	Juan Andres	Culebra	Maria Antonia		x	Navajo	y
	Juan Andres	Costilla County	Mariana		x		
Trujillo	Manuel	Saritas	Juan	x		Navajo	y
Trujillo (3)	S.	San Jose	Filomena		x	Navajo	y
	S.	San Jose	Maria Guadalupe		x	California	y
	S.	San Jose	Nestor	x		Navajo	y
Trujillo (2)	Tofolo (Teofilo)	Culebra	Antonio (Maria)	x		Navajo	y
	Tofolo (Teofilo)	Culebra	Piedad		x	Navajo	y
Trujillo (3)	Vidal	Costilla County	Ferman	x			
	Vidal	Costilla County	Lupe		x		
	Vidal	Costilla County	Santana		x		
Valdez	J. M.	Pura y Limpia	Rafaela		x	Navajo	y
Valdez	Jesus	Pura y Limpia	Maria Antonia		x	Navajo	y
Valdez	Jose Leonides	Huerfano	Maria Dolores		x	Navajo	
Valdes/Valdez (6)	Jose Seledonio	Conejos CO	Cleofe	x			
	(Jose) S(eledonio)	San Jose	(Maria) Getrudes		x	Pah-Ute	y
	Jose Seledonio	Conejos CO	Gertrudes		x		
	(Jose) S(eledonio)	San Jose	Luis	x		½ Indian	y
	Jose Seledonio	Conejos CO	Pablo	x			
	(Jose) S(eledonio)	San Jose	Paula		x	Pah-Ute	y
Valdez (7)	Juan Benito	Taos	Cornelia		x		
	Juan Benito	Arroyo Hondo	(Maria) Guadalupe		x	Navajo	
	Juan Benito	Taos	Maria de la Cruz		x		
	Juan Benito	Arroyo Hondo	Maria Ramona		x	Navajo	
	Juan Benito	Taos	Maria Refugio		x		
	Juan Benito	Taos	Soledad		x		
	Juan Benito	Taos	Vicente	x			

LAST NAME	OWNER'S FIRST NAME	RESIDENCE	NAME OF INDIAN	M	F	TRIBE	ON HEAD'S REPORTS?
Vallejos (4)	Antonio Jose	Arroyo Hondo	Jose Hilario	x		Navajo	
	Antonio Jose	Huerfano	Jose Trinidad	x			
	Antonio Jose	Conejos	Maria Dolores		x	Navajo	y
	Antonio Jose	Conejos CO	Maria Isabel		x		
Vallejos (4)	Jose Francisco	Conejos CO	Maria Guadalupe		x		
	Jose Francisco	Conejos CO	Maria Guadalupe		x		
	Jose Francisco	Arroyo Hondo	Maria Josefa		x		
	(Jose) Francisco	Culebra	Maria Paola (Paula)		x	Navajo	y
Vallejos	Joseph (Maria)	Costilla	Rosalia		x	Navajo	y
Vallejos (6)	Miguel Antonio	Huerfano	Dolores		x		
	Miguel Antonio	Culebra	Felipe	x		Navajo	y
	Miguel Antonio	Culebra	Josefa		x	Navajo	y
	Miguel Antonio	Huerfano	Maria Rosalia		x		
	Miguel Antonio	Huerfano	Nestor	x			
	Miguel Antonio	Huerfano	Soledad		x		
Velasquez (3)	J M (Jesus Maria)	Guadalupita	Catalina		x	Navajo	y
	Jesus Maria	Conejos CO	Jose Miguel	x			
	Jesus Maria	Conejos CO	Maria Guadalupe		x		
Velasquez	Jose Arcario	Conejos CO	Jose Antonio	x			
Vigil (6)	Agapito	Las Animas CO	Guadalupe		x		
	Agapito	Las Animas CO	Josefa		x	Navajo	
	Agapito	Las Animas CO	Marcelina		x		
	Agapito	Las Animas CO	Maria Francisca		x		
	Agapito	Las Animas CO	Pedro Antonio	x			
	Agapito	Las Animas CO	Ramon	x			
Vigil	Antonio Maria	Conejos CO	Guadalupe		x		
Vigil	(Jose) Eduvigen de Jesus	Coneojs CO	Juan Antonio	x			
Vigil (2)	J. Maria	Canon	Juliana		x	Navajo	y
	J. Maria	Canon	Lucas	x		Navajo	y

LAST NAME	OWNER'S FIRST NAME	RESIDENCE	NAME OF INDIAN	M	F	TRIBE	ON HEAD'S REPORTS?
Vigil (2)	F. (Francisco)	Guadalupe	Maria Rosalia		x	Navajo	y
	Jose Francisco	Huerfano	Vicente	x			
Vigil (3)	Jose Simon	Costilla CO	Ana Maria		x		
		Costilla CO	Maria de la Cruz		x		
		Costilla CO	Jose Santiago	x			
Vigil (3)	(Jose) Tomas	Culebra	Francisco Antonio	x		Navajo	y
	Jose Tomas	Huerfano	Lucas	x			
	J. T.	Cerritos	Vicente	x		Utah	y
Vigil	(Juan de Jesus)	Cerritos	Lucas	x		Utah	y
Vigil (3)	Maria D(olores Vallejos)	Culebra	Jose Antonio	x		Navajo	y
	Maria D(olores Vallejos)	Culebra	Maria Vigil		x	Navajo	y
	Maria D(olores Vallejos)	Culebra	Maria (del) Rosario		x	Navajo	y
Vigil (2)	Maria G(uadalupe) Vallejos	Culebra	Juan Antonio	x		Navajo	y
	Maria G(uadalupe) Vallejos	Culebra	Ma Aleoric (Acaria)		x	Navajo	y
Vigil (3)	Juan M. (Miguel)	Culebra	Juan Antonio	x		Navajo	y
	Juan M. (Miguel)	Culebra	Juliana		x	Navajo	y
	Juan M. (Miguel)	Culebra	Pablo	x		Ute	y
Vigil	Ramon de Jesus	Las Animas CO	Antonia Maria		x	Navajo	
Woodson (3)	(James Bernard)	Guadalupe	Andres	x		Navajo	y
	(James Bernard)	Guadalupe	Gabriel	x		Navajo	y
	(James Bernard)	Guadalupe	Maria Catalina		x	Utah	y

Notes

1. University of California at Berkeley, Bancroft Library, Special Collections, Kit Carson Papers, Bonds of Traders (Vallejo), 1855–1860, BANC MSS P-E 64, reel 11.

2. October 6, 1855, two-month license; June 1, 1856, one-month license; October 23, 1857, one-month license; and January 22, 1858, one-month license. The three-month license issued on March 22, 1858, allowed Beaubien to travel to Fort Laramie, then in New Mexico Territory, and "trade with any Indians found along the way." University of California at Berkeley, Bancroft Library, Special Collections, Kit Carson Papers, Bonds of Traders (Beaubien), 1855–1860, BANC MSS P-E 64, reel 11.

3. University of California at Berkeley, Bancroft Library, Special Collections, Kit Carson Papers, Bonds of Traders (Valdez), 1855–1860, BANC MSS P-E 64, reel 11.

4. These geographic place names are still visible on topographic maps created by the Geological Survey Division of the US Department of the Interior. Ruybal's son, Ramón, said that the raiders went over the Mesa de la Fragua through the Cañada de la Jara; but, considering where they were headed, La Fragua was too far northwest.

5. A cañada may seem like a type of canyon, but actually it is a formally designated easement for driving livestock.

6. The four men from Conejos under Vigil's attack command were Juan Antonio Chaves, (José) Benito Gallegos, José Ignacio Galvis, and Guadalupe Mes. The four men from Conejos, under Martín's command, included Serafín Aragón, Paz Maés, Antonio Sierra, and Pedro Sierra. I am thankful to former New Mexico state historian Robert J. Torres for bringing this document to my attention.

7. University of California at Berkeley, Bancroft Library, Special Collections, Miscellaneous Accounts, 1851–1866, Peonage Contract between Juan Antonio González and Theodore D. Wheaton, March 22, 1851.

8. Juan Miguel Martínez married María Manuela Gallegos in Carnero, Saguache County, on November 6, 1879. They had six known children. He died in Saguache on January 22, 1922 (Family History Library, Film 007833396, Image 33: 55; and FamilySearch, accessed 2016).

9. Four years before her testimony, Margarita Trujillo bore a son, José Irene[o] Trujillo (Salazar 1864, 109).

References

Aitken, Barbara. 1931. "Folk-History and Its Raw Material: White Men's Raids on the Hopi Villages." *New Mexico Historical Review* 6, no. 4 (October): 376–82.

Brigham Young Collection. 1853. "C. A. W. Bowman of Abiquiú, New Mexico." LDS Church History Archives. Salt Lake City, Utah.

Brooks, James F. 2002. *Captives and Cousins: Kinship and Community in the Southwest Borderlands*. Chapel Hill: University of North Carolina Press.

Brugge, David M. 2010. *Navajos in the Catholic Church Records of New Mexico*. 3rd ed. Santa Fe: School for Advanced Research Press.

Cobos, Rubén. 1983. *A Dictionary of New Mexico and Southern Colorado Spanish*. Santa Fe: Museum of New Mexico Press.

Colorado Humanities. 1979a. "Oral History of Max (Melaquias) and Lulu (Leocadia Sandoval) Valdez." Huérfano County Oral History Project. Available at http://www.kmitch.com/Huerfano/oral52.html.

———. 1979b. "Oral History of Sam Vigil." Huérfano County Oral History Project. Available at http://www.kmitch.com/Huerfano/oral151.html.

Colorado State Archives. 1892. "Will Record 20198-M." Huérfano County, 1874–1911, vol. 1, 14–15.

Colorado Tax Schedules. 1863. "1863 Colorado Tax Schedule, Annual Assessment: St. Vrain and Easterday." Available at Ancestry.com.

Colville, Ruth Marie. 1984. "Trails and Wagon Roads of the San Luis Valley." Series, "Mt. Lookout: Where You Can See for Two Days." *Del Norte Prospector*, May 9.

———. 1996. *La Vereda: A Trail through Time*. Alamosa, CO: San Luis Valley Historical Society.

Combs, D. Gene. 1973. "Enslavement of Indians in the San Luis Valley of Colorado." *San Luis Valley Historian* 5, no. 1: 1–28.

Costilla County Records. 1868. Book 1. Costilla County Clerk, San Luis, Colorado.

Downing, Finis E. 1945. "With the Ute Peace Delegation of 1863, across the Plains and at Conejos." *Colorado Magazine* 22, no. 5 (September).

Durán, Eduardo, Bonnie Durán, Maria Yellow Horse Brave Heart, and Susan Yellow Horse-Davis. 1998. "Healing the American Indian Soul Wound." In *International Handbook of Multigenerational Legacies of Trauma*, edited by Yael Danieli, 341–54. New York: Plenum Press. Available at https://www.researchgate.net/publication/232490895_Healing_the_American_Indian_Soul_Wound.

Family History Center. 1860. "No. 16622." Nuestra Señora de los Dolores, Arroyo Hondo, New Mexico.

Gibson, Charles E. ca. 1930. "An Interesting Trip." Colorado Writers Project, 75, 78–79. Denver: Hart Research Library, History Colorado Center.

Haley, J. Evetts. 1935. "The Comanchero Trade." *Southwestern Historical Quarterly* 38, no. 3 (January): 157–76.

Huang, Hsinya. 2006. "Blood/Memory in N. Scott Momaday's *The Names: A Memoir* and Linda Hogan's *The Woman Who Watches over the World: A Native Memoir*." In *Concentric: Literary and Cultural Studies* 32, no. 1 (January): 171–95.

Jefferson, James, Robert W. Delaney, and Gregory C. Thompson. 1972. *The Southern Utes: A Tribal History*. Ignacio, CO: Southern Ute Tribe.

Jones, Sondra. 2000. *The Trial of Don Pedro León Luján: The Attack against Indian Slavery and Mexican Traders in Utah*. Salt Lake City: University of Utah Press.

Kenner, Charles L. 1969. *The Comanchero Frontier: A History of New Mexican–Plains Indian Relations*. Norman: University of Oklahoma Press.

Kraemer, Paul. 2013. *Perfect Crystals and Valuable Ores: Perspectives on New Mexico History*. Los Ranchos, NM: Rio Grande Books.

Lamadrid, Enrique. 2003. *Hermanitos Comanchitos: Indo-Hispano Rituals of Captivity and Redemption*. Albuquerque: University of New Mexico Press.

Lamar, Howard R. 2000. *The Far Southwest, 1846–1912: A Territorial History*. Albuquerque: University of New Mexico Press.

Lecompte, Janet. 1978. "John Lawrence of Saguache." *Colorado Magazine* 52, no. 2 (Summer).

López-Tushar, Olibama. 1997. *The People of El Valle: A History of the Spanish Colonials in the San Luis Valley*. 3rd ed. Pueblo, CO: El Escritorio.

Louis B. Sporleder Collection. Denver Public Library, Western History Department, box 2. Denver, Colorado.

Martin, Bernice. 1990. *Frontier Eyewitness: Diary of John Lawrence, 1867–1908*. Printed by author.

Martínez, Lucas. 2005. *A Translation and Transcription of the Lucas Martínez Journal, 1865 to 1959*. Denver: Hart Research Library, History Colorado Center.

Martínez, María Clara. 2013. "'Un Indito' José Miguel Romero: Los Romeros de Norte Veta." Raíces, *La Sierra* (San Luis, Colorado), April 12.

Meketa, Jacqueline Dorgan. 1986. *Legacy of Honor: The Life of Rafael Chacón, a Nineteenth-Century New Mexican*. Albuquerque: University of New Mexico Press.

National Archives and Records Administration (NARA). 1860. "US to Seledonio Valdes, 1860." Records of the New Mexico Superintendency of Indian Affairs, 1840–1880. August 25.

———. 1865a. "Lafayette Head to Governor Evans." Letters Received, Office of Indian Affairs, 1824–1881, Colorado Superintendency, 1861–1864. July 17.

———. 1865b. "Gov. Evans to Commissioner D. N. Cooley." Letters Received, Office of Indian Affairs, 1824–1881, Colorado Superintendency, 1861–1864. July 29.

———. 1866. "Agent Head to Gov. Cummings." Letters Received, Office of Indian Affairs, 1824–1881, Colorado Superintendency, 1861–1864. February 28.

———. 1867a. "A. B. Norton to N. Taylor." Letters Received, Office of Indian Affairs, 1824–1881, New Mexico Superintendency, 1861–1864. August.

———. 1867b. "John Ward to A. B. Norton." Twenty-One Names of Citizens Reported to Have Participated in a Captive-Taking Raid on the Moqui Pueblos at Oraibi. Letters Received, Office of Indian Affairs, 1824–1881, New Mexico Superintendency, 1861–1864. August 1.

———. 1877. "Irvine to Smith." Letters Received, Office of Indian Affairs, 1824–1881, New Mexico Superintendency, 1861–1864. March 28.
Nuestra Señora de los Siete Dolores. 1885. "Registro de Matrimoniales, 1871–1899." Walsenburg, Colorado.
Pacheco, Nellie. 2014. Interview with the author, Rye, Colorado.
Pfeiffer Papers. 1868–1869. "Head to Pfeiffer." Colorado State Archives. April 1, 1868; February 4, 1869.
Pino, Theresa. 1885. Our Lady of Sorrows/Saint Mary Church, Walsenburg, Colorado, Baptisms, May 15, 1878–April 5, 1886.
Quintana, Frances Leon. 1991. *Pobladores: Hispanic Americans of the Ute Frontier*. Notre Dame, IN: University of Notre Dame Press.
Rael-Gálvez, Estevan. 2002. "Identifying Captivity and Capturing Identity: Narratives of American Indian Slavery in Colorado and New Mexico, 1776–1924." PhD diss., University of Michigan.
Raleigh, Frances. 2011. *Velarde Family History*. Printed by author.
Richeson, A. K. ca. 1930. "Interview with Felix Cordova." Colorado Writers Project. Denver: Hart Research Library, History Colorado Center.
Romero, Brenda. 2002. "The *Indita* Genre of New Mexico: Gender and Cultural Identification." In *Chicana Traditions: Continuity and Change*, edited by Norma E. Cantú and Olga Nájera-Ramírez, 56–80. Urbana: University of Illinois Press.
Salazar, David H. 1864. "Baptism of José Antonio Gómez." Nuestra Señora de Guadalupe Church Baptisms, August 14. Denver, Colorado.
Salazar, Manuel de Jesús. 2017. Interview with the author, Denver, Colorado, March 25.
Sánchez, Joseph P. 2015. *Early Hispanic Colorado, 1678–1900*. Los Ranchos, NM: Río Grande Books.
Sánchez, Virginia. 2010. *Forgotten Cuchareños of the Lower Valley*. 2nd ed. Charleston, SC: History Press.
———. 2011. "Linked by Water, Linked by Blood: Madrid Ditch no. 2 in Cucharas, Colorado, 1884–1903." *New Mexico Historical Review* 86, no. 4 (Fall): 429–59.
Sporleder, Louis B. 1932. "A Day and a Night on Spoon River." *Colorado Magazine* 10, no. 1 (May).
Steinel, Alvin T. and Daniel Webster Working. 1926. *History of Agriculture in Colorado, 1858–1926*. Fort Collins, CO: State Agricultural College.
Thompson, Jerry D. 2015. *A Civil War History of the New Mexico Volunteers and Militia*. Albuquerque: University of New Mexico Press.
Trujillo, José E. 1990. "History of Atanacio Trujillo." *Nuestras Raíces* (Genealogical Society of Hispanic America) 2, no. 1: 55–58.
US Census. 1860. "Culebra Precinct, Taos County, New Mexico, pg. 202, schedule 1, lines 24–25, Household/Dwelling 1800." Available at Ancestry.com.

———. 1870. "Cucharas, Huérfano County, Colorado, pg. 19, schedule 1, line 15, Household 167, Dwelling 171." Available at Ancestry.com.

———. 1880. "Huérfano County, Colorado, pg. 4, ED 60, lines 16–21, Precinct 8, Household/Dwelling 27." Available at Ancestry.com.

———. 1900. "Huérfano County, Colorado, pg. 177, ED 142, B, sheet 11, line 77, Household 276, Dwelling 293." Available at Ancestry.com.

CHAPTER NINE

Genízaro Settlements of the Sierra Sandía
Resilience and Identity in the Land Grants
of San Miguel del Cañón de Carnué
and San Antonio de las Huertas

MOISES GONZALES

The cultural identity of the Genízaro descendent communities in the Sandía Mountains resides in the material and cultural memory of the people who still occupy those lands. The communities of San Miguel de Carnué,[1] San Antonio de Padua, and San Antonio de las Huertas are situated along the base of the Sandía mountain range and were founded as buffer settlements to protect Villa de Alburquerque from raids from the Comanche, Kiowa, and Apache Nations. Many Genízaro families participated in the formation of frontier settlements, as well as in the struggle to maintain them due to frequent attacks. These communities were often temporarily abandoned and reorganized as buffer towns well into the early nineteenth century, precisely why these land grants were often considered for annulment. Francisco Ignacio de Madariaga, assessor for the Mexican government, noted that in order to maintain the necessary population at the three settlements, he would cancel the land rights of the settlers who refused to return, despite their objections (Swadesh 1980a, 44). Many would stay and endure the constant threat of attack to maintain the status of landowners in a community land grant, rather work as indentured servants in the Río Abajo. Although raids would continue well into the 1860s, collective community building led to the resiliency of these communities today. This chapter describes the evolution of Genízaro settlements and identity through historical documents, oral histories, and contemporary

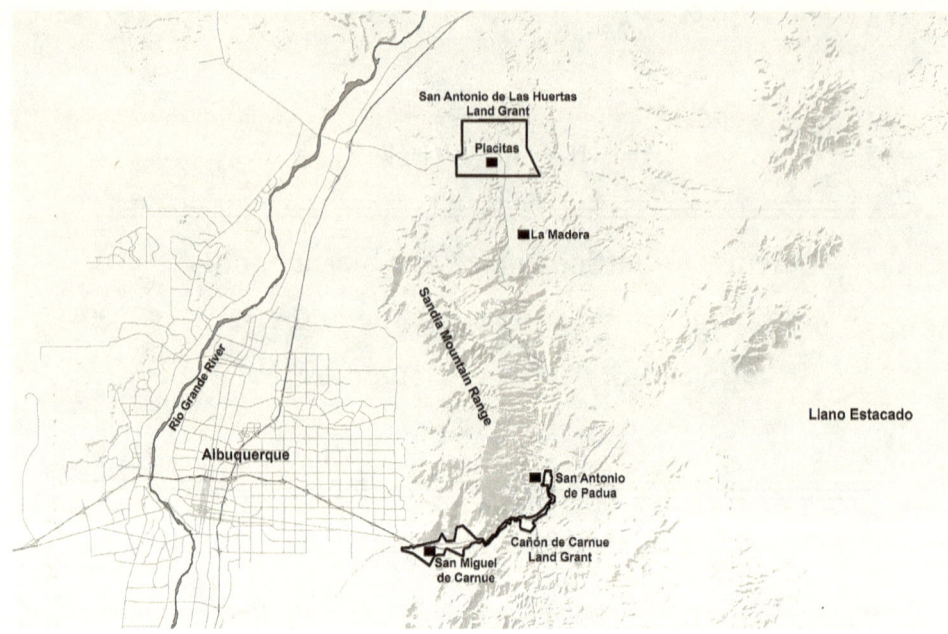

FIGURE 9.1 Plazas de la Sierra Sandía. Courtesy of Moises Gonzales.

cultural rituals such as the dances of the Comanchitos and Matachines. The contexts, adaptations, and evolution of Genízaro identity from the late eighteenth century, up to the contemporary cultural practices and organization of Genízaro settlements in the Sandía Mountains, will emerge.

The formation of Genízaro communities began in the eighteenth century in New Mexico and continued until the end of the colonial period when the Plan de Iguala was created on February 24, 1821, to assert Mexican independence and serve as the guiding principal of law until the Mexican constitution was adopted in 1824. The plan asserted racial equality in Mexican society, and the term "Genízaro," along with caste terms associated with racial classification such as *coyote*, *mestizo*, *mulato*, and *castizo*, were dropped from use in official documents and Catholic Church records. Almost a century earlier, in the mid-1700s, Spanish colonial governor Tomás Vélez Cachupín deployed a plan for New Mexico whereby landless Genízaros and mixed Indian castes could assist in establishing a network of defensible buffer settlements to protect the primary governing centers of Santa Fe, Santa Cruz, and Alburquerque. Beginning with the first Genízaro settlement of Belén, established in 1741,

Cachupín established Genízaro settlements or settlements with enclaves of Genízaros at Las Trampas (1751), Abiquiú (1754), Cañón de Carnué (1763), and San Antonio de las Huertas (1767) (Gonzales 2014, 583–602). The purpose of establishing these communities was to reduce the attacks by Comanches, Utes, Apaches, Kiowas, and Navajos that were threatening the survivability of both the Pueblo and Hispano communities of northern New Mexico (Quintana 1991, 31–33). Cachupín would specify that these communities be established in compliance with the Laws of the Indies, which required the construction of compact, defensible settlements as well as a system of equitable distribution of land and water for both individual and communal use (Ebright 1994, 145–47).

In the 1760s, Villa de Alburquerque, New Mexico's southernmost governmental center, experienced a number of problems that may have motivated Spanish authorities to establish defense settlements in the Sandía Mountains just east of the Río Abajo. More frequent Comanche raids threatened an area from Isleta Pueblo to the south of Alburquerque as far as San Felipe Pueblo to the north. Another challenge was a rapidly growing, floating population of Genízaros and mestizos with no ties to specific settlements in the Río Abajo and without title to farmland or grazing land. Having little or no stake in society made it difficult to fully transition and assimilate into Hispano colonial culture. Governor Cachupín and many other governors and officials saw the permanence of mixed-Native communities in the Sandía Mountains as critical to the sustainability of the settlements along the Río Grande. The Comanche threat was so significant that in 1779 Bernardo de Miera y Pacheco noted on a detailed map of the Alcaldía de la Villa de Alburquerque the *frontera y entrada de los enemigos Cumanchis* (border and entrance of the Comanche enemies) at the edge of the Sandía Mountains, depicting passages into the Río Abajo as well as Carnué and San Antonio de las Huertas (Miera y Pacheco 1779).

The strategic placement of settlements in the Sandía Mountains was driven by the need to defend Cañón de Carnué, also known as Tijeras Canyon, which was the pass between the Sandía Mountains and the Manzano Mountains. The pass was a natural route for trade and warfare, and the Utes, Comanches, and Kiowas conducted many raids in the early 1700s (Simmons 1982, 99–100). The establishment of Villa de Alburquerque in the Provincia del Río Abajo in 1706 only invited more raids on Pueblo and Hispanic settlements. El Cañón de Carnué became an easy entry from the Llano Estacado ("Staked Plains") into the Río Abajo. Secondary passes were also utilized

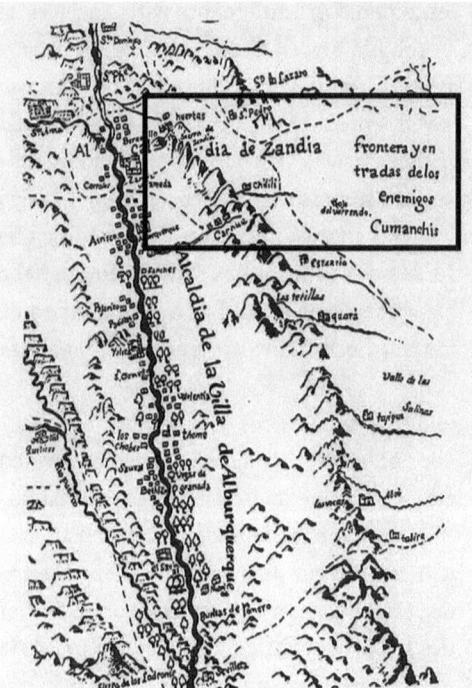

FIGURE 9.2 Detail of map by Bernardo Miera y Pacheco, 1779. Courtesy of New Mexico State Records Center and Archives.

by Plains tribes through Cañón del Comanche and Abó Pass in the Manzanos and on the northern end of the Sandías through Arroyo del Tuerto and Cañón de Agua, which bisected the San Pedro Mountains east of the Sandías. The northern pass into the Río Abajo impacted the settlements of the Tiwa pueblo of Sandía, Bernalillo, and several Keresan pueblos just to the north along the Río Grande. The contested mountain passes on the north and south faces of the Sandías led to a prolonged project by governors and *alcaldes* to settle and sustain more mountain communities. This process of settlement and resettlement of the mixed-caste Genízaro communities of la sierra eventually led to a unique expression of cultural practices that persist today in the cultural landscape of the land grant communities that still occupy these lands.

The Settlement of the Cañón de Carnué Land Grant: A Brief History

In 1754, Tomás Vélez Cachupín stated:

> The capital city of Santa Fe, with its forces, has the responsibility of repelling incursions by Carlana and Natage Apaches and also by the Comanches, that of Santa Cruz [de la Cañada] with its adjacent districts and towns, from attacks by Utes and other allies; and that of Alburquerque against the Faraones and Gileños. Thus each town with its outlying districts has this annoying and difficult situation, its residents living in constant anxiety, they and all their rural property subject to becoming victims of the cruelty and fierceness of those barbarians. (Archibald 1976, 313)

For this reason, Cachupín saw a vision of establishing defensible buffer settlements at Carnué and Las Huertas to protect the Río Abajo. In 1763, the Carnué Land Grant was given to nineteen settlers at the mouth of Tijeras Canyon in which they were directed to construct a compact defensible plaza (Swadesh 1976, 31–44). According to Cachupín, in ordering a defensible plaza, "they should do this in union of its towns and buildings of adobe according to the possibilities and style of the country for there is greater security, strength and maintenance in view of the incursion which the barbarous hostile nations are in the habit of making" (Vélez Cachupín 1773). Ethnically, the settlement was made up of mestizo, Coyote, and Genízaro settlers, and based on close analysis of church marriage records, the Genízaro and Coyote population at Carnué was approximately 47 percent.

From the onset of Carnué's creation, Comanche and Apache raids would render this settlement unsustainable as well as uninhabitable, and by the April 1771, the settlers at Carnué abandoned the town and returned to Villa de Alburquerque and various other communities along the Río Abajo despite being ordered to go back to the settlement by the alcalde, Francisco Trébol Navarro. Navarro attempted to resettle Genízaros from the Río Puerco region west of Alburquerque, but the effort failed when this landless group of mixed Hispanicized Natives realized the constant threat of raids they would face by residing at Cañón de Carnué. The resettlement of Carnué would not occur for another fifty years, when Plains Apaches yet again threatened the grazing lands of the Hispano elites. Increased raids threatened livestock on the *dehesa del llano* (pasture of the plain), Alburquerque's east mesa, in the early 1800s, which served as the commons for both Pueblo and Hispano land grant communities now under siege by the Apaches (Swadesh 1980a, 38). The solution was once again to turn to the landless mixed indigenous populations of the Río Abajo to resettle Carnué and again serve as the protective settlement of Alburquerque, as well as turn to the children and grandchildren of the original 1763 settlers.

By the early 1800s, under pressure from local prominent families of the Río Abajo to protect grazing land as well as from the landless Genízaro, Coyote, and mestizo population who desired to acquire land, authorities once again opened the Carnué Land Grant for settlement. The second land grant community included mixed indigenous populations from Los Padillas, Belén, Atrisco, Los Ranchos de Alburquerque, and Alameda. In many cases, the petitioners for the 1819 land grant were seeking an alternative to the servitude and peonage that was their lot in the irrigated valley of the Alcadía de Alburquerque. And in 1819, a second land grant was established consisting of two settlements within the boundaries of the original land grant. San Miguel de Carnué occupied the site of the 1763 settlement, and the second settlement, San Antonio de Padua, was built on the site of an abandoned Tano-Tiwa pueblo. The pueblo had been abandoned in the early seventeenth century due to nomadic raids, most likely by Apaches. The early 1800s brought freedom and opportunity to the descendants of the 1763 Carnué settlement as well as to the new population. However, constant attacks by the Navajo and Apache as well as campaigns against the Apache by the new settlers created yet another layer of indigenous hybridity that is today evident among the culture and peoples of the Cañón de Carnué Land Grant.

The Settlement of San Antonio de las Huertas: A Brief History

Just as the Cañón de Carnué Land Grant was seen as a key defensible settlement on the south side of the Sandía Mountains, Governor Cachupín envisioned a similar type of community located at the north end to provide protection for Sandía Pueblo, Bernalillo, and other surrounding settlements. In 1765, Juan Gutiérrez, Andrés Aragón, Javier Gutiérrez the Genízaro, José Antonio Archibeque along with his son, Miguel Gallegos, Matías Gonzales, and José Gonzales petitioned for a tract of land known as Las Huertas (J. Gutiérrez et al. 1765). According to Heather Noelle Atherton: "The parcel of land they requested was bordered on the east by the brow or edge of the

San Pedro road (*la ceja del camino de San Pedro*), on the west by some high hills belonging to Las Huertas, on the north by the brow or edge of the Casa Colorada, and on the south by a red hill" (2013, 34). However, Governor Cachupín never acted on the petition because he left office while these families were occupying the settlement and utilizing the lands of Las Huertas as common land. By 1767, the settlement at Las Huertas grew to include twenty-one families, and the new governor of New Mexico, Pedro Fermín de Mendinueta, approved the grant on December 31, 1767 (Mendinueta 1767). At this time, Mendinueta expanded the boundaries to accommodate additional settlers and only approved the grant on the condition that a defensible plaza be constructed under the ordinance of the Laws of the Indies, due to the attacks that the community would need to repel. Las Huertas defended itself against many raids by the Utes and Comanches in the late eighteenth century; however, by the early nineteenth century, San Antonio de las Huertas would also undergo abandonment and resettlement. Just as with Carnué, the settlers were a mixed group, including mestizos, Genízaros, and Coyotes; they included more Indians, as captive Apache and Navajo children were raised by Las Huertas families in the early 1800s.

By then, the middle Río Grande was under tremendous attack by the Navajo and Apache, and the buffer settlements in the Sandía Mountains were subject to extreme stress. According to the 1802 census of Las Huertas, it is clear that many additional families were added to the land grant settlement in order to aid in its defense (New Mexico Census 1802). The census reveals that sixty-two families resided in Las Huertas, and many of them came from well-documented Genízaro families in the Corrales, Alameda, and Los Ranchos de Alburquerque areas. For example, Diego Gurulé, Salvador Gurulé, and Antonio Gurulé were all freed servants from the Elena Gallegos family of Los Ranchos. If fact, José Antonio Genízaro is noted as a head of household living with three of his grandchildren. The 1802 census is one of the only documents in colonial New Mexico in which Genízaro is recorded as a surname. We also know that prominent Genízaros were brought to Las Huertas at this time to assist in its defense, such as Salvador Gurulé, who is believed to be the son of Antonio Gurulé and Teresa Gutiérrez, the Genízaro founders of Belén. Based on the militia muster rolls of Las Huertas, Salvador was one of twenty-three men who had adequate arms, possessing an *escopeta* (flintlock shotgun), *lanza* (lance), and two horses. There were an additional thirty-one men in the muster rolls with inadequate arms, only possessing a *flecha* (arrow) and lanza (New Mexico Military Census 1802). By 1821, at the time of Mexican independence, New Mexico found itself militarily unorganized and under constant attack by the Navajo, who threatened the Sandía settlement.

On April 23, 1823, the alcalde of Alameda sent orders for the resettlement of *vecinos* (neighboring landed residents) at Las Huertas, to take refuge in Algodones due to dangerous attacks by the Apache; they were given temporary land for agricultural purposes there (Forrest 1996, 361). According to Atherton: "At Algodones, situated northwest of Las Huertas on the Río Grande, the displaced families were provisioned with land for agriculture and grazing" (2013, 34). In addition to moving to Algodones, some former Las Huertas settlers found themselves residing in Socorro, Alburquerque, and La Ciénega (south of Santa Fe). Some young *huertanos* went as far as Abiquiú, where they lived and got married, returning to Las Huertas in the late 1830s, such as Baltazar Baca, who later returned to assist in the formation of the La Madera settlement at the eastern edge of the Las Huertas Land Grant. The resettlement of the grant took place in the early 1840s, when additional settlements were established to serve as outlying protective communities, such as Tejón, Chimal, and La Madera. For the next thirty years, communities in the Las Huertas Land Grant, just as those in its sister land grant to the south, conducted counterattacks and raids on the Apache and Navajo in addition to participating in the captive slave trade of the Llano Estacado. In this period, buffalo hunting and trade in captives became the basis of the local economy, furthering the complexity of Genízaro identity in the Sandía mountain communities (Rebolledo and Márquez 2000, 165).

Adaptive Indigenous Origins of the Sandía Mountain Settlements

According to colonial records, Barrio de Analco was the first community to absorb the free Genízaros into the broader population. Then, in later decades, the settlements of Belén and Abiquiú were founded almost entirely by Genízaros. Frances Leon Swadesh argues that there were large numbers of Genízaro communities among the populated settlements throughout New Mexico during the late eighteenth century (1974, 31). Genízaro scholars also agree that by the mid-1700s, the Genízaro population had grown larger than what could be absorbed or sustained in these few settlements as well as in predominately Spanish settlements. Scholars such as Russell Magnaghi (1990,

FIGURES 9.3A, 9.3B
Salvador Gurulé (sixth entry), Military Census of Las Huertas, 1806. Spanish Archives of New Mexico II, Reel 16, frame 188. Courtesy of the Center for Southwest Research, University of New Mexico.

92), Ramón Gutiérrez (1991, 171), and Estevan Rael-Gálvez (2007) agree that Genízaros made up as much as one-third of the total population in New Mexico in the late eighteenth century. For this reason, during the settlement and resettlement of the defensible buffer communities of San Antonio de Padua, Carnué, and Las Huertas well into the early nineteenth century, a significant number of Genízaros and Coyotes became the foundation of indigenous identity. And, although these settlements were not made up of entirely of Genízaros and included many mestizos, the continual infusion of Native captives into these communities as late as the 1860s iteratively added to the evolution of Genízaro cultural practices, with all community members sharing a common cultural narrative.

My investigations in the Sandía settlements have led me to ask the question: if by the late eighteenth century the Genízaro population had expanded to make up a significant percentage of New Mexicans, as scholars suggest, than how much of the Genízaro identity still exists in the present-day settlements of the Sandías? Unlike other Hispano communities in New Mexico that claim Spanish heritage, the people who occupy these communities are always eager to share the story of their Comanche or Apache heritage. My first encounter came as a young boy at the dinner table, where my grandfather Moises would tell us grandchildren that we were Comanches, but later acquired Apache blood from the captive children who had been brought in and raised in the sierra. Although the term "Genízaro" was long forgotten in the vernacular language, such as that spoken by my grandfather, almost all *serreños* (people of the sierra) today acknowledge their indigenous background. To understand contemporary awareness of Genízaro identity, my research approach has been to examine the adaptive indigenous experience in three periods: (1) times prior to the settlement of the Sandías, (2) the first settlement period of the early nineteenth century, and (3) the mid-nineteenth-century period characterized by the infusion of captive children as a result of mutual warfare among bands of Navajo, Apache, and Utes.

Indigenous Identity prior to the Sandía Mountain Settlements of the Late Eighteenth Century

The land grant settlement documents of Cañón de Carnué in 1763 and the Las Huertas Land Grant of 1767 reveal a mixed distribution of españoles, mestizos, Coyotes, and Genízaros. At Carnué, of the original nineteen settlers, five were Genízaros, four were Coyotes, and ten were españoles (García-Luna 1999). Atherton asserts that the landless colonists who established Las Huertas were composed of "families who considered themselves to be culturally Spanish as well as those who were labeled as Genízaros" (2013). Although Coyotes and Genízaros were significantly represented at the foundation of both land grants, it is more likely that the settlers who were identified as españoles were actually mestizos who had already assimilated into Spanish cultural norms. *Mestizaje*, the cultural amalgamation of Spanish and Native Americans, had already been under way in New Mexico during the seventeenth century. Due to the many short periods of abandonment and resettlement of these mountain grants, it is clear that some original settlers may have left and returned, or perhaps their children returned to intermarry with the local population. It is apparent that in both land grant communities, the children of Genízaro and Coyote families did return, and their descendants still occupy grant lands.

In 1763, Gregorio Gutiérrez, a Coyote and one the nineteen petitioners of the Cañón de Carnué Land Grant, settled on the grant and later abandoned it. Gregorio's mother was María Naranjo Hurtado, who was the daughter of Juana Hurtado, a Pueblo woman from Zuni Pueblo who as a child had lived in captivity with the Navajo and been redeemed by her uncle, also of Zuni heritage, in 1692 (Brooks 2002, 196). Gregorio left Carnué when the settlement was abandoned in 1771 and did not return. However, his son, Juan Antonio Gutiérrez, who married in 1781 in Alburquerque, appears to have returned to Carnué during the 1819 resettlement of the grant. Today, the official seal of the Cañón de Carnué Land Grant displays the foundation years of 1763 and 1819 in recognition of the Genízaro and Coyote founders of the first settlement.

Today, many Sandía Genízaro descendent families can trace their direct ancestry to two well-documented Genízaro servants by the name of Rosa and Bernadina, who worked in the household of Santiago Gurulé and Antonia Quintana in Los Ranchos de Alburquerque (Langham Olmsted 1981, 75). Many of Bernadina's grandsons participated in the resettlement of Carnué in 1819, while Rosa's son Antonio Gurulé went on be one of the original twenty-one settlers of the Las Huertas grant in 1767. Las Huertas was very unstable due to devastating Apache raids during the 1820s, and settlers were ordered to retreat to Algodones on April 23, 1823 (Atherton 2013, 38). The heirs of the Las Huertas Land Grant, which extends into the present-day villages of Placitas, La Madera, and San Pedro, still proudly acknowledge their connection to the Genízaro Gurulé founders of the sierra.

The Repopulation of the Sandía Settlements in the Early Nineteenth Century

The resettlement of the two grants in the early 1800s introduced another layer and infusion of indigenous identity. In this period, the Comanche and Kiowa threats had subsided due to a peace treaty between the Spanish and the Comanche; however, raids by the Apache and the Navajo threatened the permanent settlement of the Sandía mountain communities. In 1819, Cañón de Carnué was resettled by some children of the 1763 settlers; however, most of the fifty-two families who resettled the grant were identified as Genízaros or classified as mestizo children of Genízaros. In San Antonio de las Huertas, it is also clear that many additional settlers were added to the settlement in the early nineteenth century who were not part of the original twenty-three petitioners. A major distinction must be made between the mestizo castas of the early 1700s and the mestizos of the late 1700s. Mestizos of the *reconquista* period in New Mexico after 1692 were primarily the offspring of mestizos and Pueblo women, whereas by the late eighteenth century mestizos were primarily the children of Genízaros.

At Las Huertas, these new settlers not in the original petition were recruited and added to assist in sustaining this important protective defense community. According to the Las Huertas 1807 census and the 1802 military census, it is clear that the settlement grew from the original twenty-three families to sixty-two families. The natural increase of the population was augmented by newly recruited landless Genízaro, mestizos, and Coyotes. Landless families such as José Antonio Genízaro (Genízaro), Torbibio Gurulé (mestizo), Pedro Gurulé (Coyote), Antonio Gurulé (mestizo), and Manuel Muñiz (mestizo) were recruited from Los Ranchos de Alburquerque (Langham Olmsted 1975, 1–47).

The resettlement of the 1819 Cañón de Carnué Land Grant constituted a new infusion of landless mixed indigenous populations. According to Swadesh, "[t]he need for a buffer community did not abate, although . . . fifty years passed before there was another settler population at Carnué" (1976). The Alburquerque elites supported the grant not only to provide opportunities to landless and mixed indigenous people but to secure the defense of the Río Abajo. For that reason, the resettlement of the Carnué Land Grant drew from landless peasants from Los Padillas, Los Ranchos, Pajarito, and many other settlements around Villa de Alburquerque. Although the 1819 petition for the Carnué grant doesn't specify ethnic background, a comparison between the list of settlers of the grant and the 1790 Spanish census reveals that peasant children of Genízaros, Coyotes, and Natives participated in the resettlement (Langham Olmsted 1975). At least four Genízaro grandchildren of the Indian servants Rosa and Bernadina, who worked in the household of Santiago Gurulé as mentioned above, settled in the San Antonio settlement of the Carnué Land Grant, including Juan Antonio, Juan Cristóbal, Juan, and Cristóbal, along with mestizo Antonio Tórrez of the same place. A Carnué Genízaro by the name of Pablo Padilla of San Andrés de los Padillas joined the settlement, along with Manuela Padilla, who was the daughter of a well-known Genízaro of the Isleta area known as Estevan Padilla (Sisneros n.d.). Many other Coyotes such as Juan Anzures and his wife, María Guadalupe García, also joined the settlement at Carnué.

By the start of the nineteenth century, the threat of nomadic raids shifted from the Comanche and Kiowa to aggressive bands of Apache and Navajo. This period renewed interest in the resettlement of Carnué as well as Las Huertas, infusing the mountain communities with another generation of indigenous persons, adding to the Native diversity of Sandía communities.

Nineteenth-Century Indigenous Captive Identities

By the early to mid-nineteenth century in New Mexico, indigenous classifications were being eliminated by the church and government records; however, communities in the Sandía settlements continued to see an inflow of Native American captives, further building their indigenous identity. After all but disappearing from vernacular speech, today the word "Genízaro" has made a resurgence as a Native American identity, whereas in communities such as Carnuel, San Antonio, and La Madera, most people refer themselves as Apache or Comanche. Sylvia Rodríguez, in her detailed study of Matachines, cited the ethnographic work of Frances Quintana, stating that "even though San Antonio's settlers came mostly from Barelas, and Alburquerque Barrio, and from the vicinities of Isleta and Sandía Pueblos, the people today seem more conscious and proud of their Apache ancestry. This is not so puzzling in light of the fact that their geographic orientations or watershed faces not toward the Río Grande valley but toward the Plains, from whence came the nomadic tribes" (Rodríguez 1996, 125). At Carnué community events and gatherings, many people engage in conversations about indigenous family origins in the Cañón de Carnué region. This identity still holds today.

The limited amount of productive farmland and the threat of attack on animals grazing on the periphery of settlements in the sierra created an economic incentive to participate in buffalo hunts on the plains, which also brought many captive plains children into local families. During a 1990 interview, Adilia García, age seventy-two, described stories from her youth as told to her by her grandmother. She stated that many Indian children were raised in families in San Antonio de Padua and Carnuel (García 1990). Cultural adaptations over two centuries of Pueblo, Comanche, Ute, Navajo, and Apache contact resulted in unique cultural identities and practices up until the mid- to late nineteenth century. By the late 1860s, relocations to Navajo, Comanche, and Apache reservations at the hands of the US Army impacted lifestyles and cultural exchanges in Sandía mountain communities. By the twentieth century, these communities remained isolated, and many indigenous practices and customs remained unknown outside their communities until scholars in the latter part of the twentieth century undertook detailed and sensitive ethnographic documentation.

Economic Factors That Shaped the Genízaro Culture of La Sierra

In June 2016, a small group of Genízaro scholars met for a writers' seminar at the School for Advanced Research in Santa Fe, and Charles M. Carrillo posed the question: "Do we know or have an understanding of what Genízaros dressed like?" I was taken by his question and wondered what economic and cultural factors determined the dress and appearance of people from the Sandía Mountains. My research had revealed that the annual buffalo hunts of the late eighteenth and early nineteenth centuries shaped the economic conditions and physical material practices of this region. The annual hunting trips to the Llano Estacado, the Staked Plains, departed after the October harvest and returned before Christmas. These expeditions were economically beneficial given the value of tanned hides and the products that were made from them. They also brought a new infusion of Native captives into the community's cultural fabric. The flow of hides and illicit captives took place in the Sandía region, but it also occurred in many other Genízaro mountain settlements of northern New Mexico, such as Abiquiú, Ranchos de Taos, San Miguel del Vado, and Ojo Caliente (Brooks 2002, 237).

The extremely dry conditions of the Sandías as well as the constant threat of attack on livestock such as sheep, cattle, and horses limited agricultural production. Communities came to rely on buffalo hunting as the basis of economic wealth and trade. Swadesh notes that "the growth of San Antonio was linked with the industries that brought in residents, and also caused San Antonio residents to be absent for greater or lesser stretches of time. From the beginning, men customarily were absent were absent for months at a time, hunting buffalo and trading on the plains" (Swadesh 1980a). José Librado Arón Gurulé, during an interview in 1939, recounts family stories from Placitas confirming that buffalo hunts continued until 1865: "Men from Ojo de Las Casa, Placitas, La Madera, Tejón, Algodones, and Bernalillo would make up a hunting party and set out for the Llano Estacado." He goes on to state that "aside from all these labors there was the weaving of wool into cloth and the making of it into garments for the women and children, and into shirts for the men. Many skins of animals tanned to perfection by a member of the great household [were] made into breeches for the men and boys and leggings and *tewas* [moccasins] for the whole clan" (Rebolledo and Márquez 2000, 165). Although the Sandía mountain settlements were originally seen as way to adapt Genízaros to Spanish lifestyles through farming and ranching, the toll of prolonged raids and the very limited farmland created an economic incentive to organize the economy around hunting and the trading of goods and captives.

Since the late eighteenth century, settlers in this region have negotiated, adapted, and emerged from being Genízaro captives or slaves to becoming entrepreneurs of local resources and social organizers.

> Oral histories corroborate this disquiet through narratives of raiding, abduction, slavery, and even death. Nevertheless, a number of these onetime enemies became respected community and family members after being captured and acculturated into the Spanish colonial lifestyle. The production of Genízaro culture was partly created by the ongoing cyclical process of moving from captive servant to full participant as an actor of community survival. For women this was protecting the settlement from raiding during the seasonal hunts. For men, their role was participating in the annual hunts on the plains and engagement in the act of slave trading among friendly nomadic tribes. (Atherton 2013, 346)

Contemporary Cultural Performance and Memory

In existing literature about Genízaros and Genízaro-descended communities, because the term and other caste terms disappeared as ordained in Article 11 of the 1821 Plan de Iguala, scholars seem to assume that culture and identity disappeared as well. In one of the first scholarly articles on Genízaros, Fray Angélico Chávez wrote that "within a relatively short time, those who were assimilated along with the former Genízaros into the Spanish-speaking community, whether through some Hispanic intermarriage or none at all, became 'Mexicans'" (Chávez 1979, 198–200). To some extent, Chávez's statement can be borne out in church and state documentation describing the racial and ethnic makeup of large Hispano towns such as Santa Fe and Alburquerque. However, in communities such as Abiquiú, Alcalde, Ranchos de Taos, Las Huertas, San Antonio, and Carnué, the continuing practice of indigenous dance and ritual remains a marker of indigenous identity. Unlike many historians who argue that Genízaro identity disappeared during the nineteenth century, ethnographic scholars such as Frances Swadesh-Quintana, Sylvia Rodríguez, and Enrique Lamadrid have focused on cultural performance and ritual as a contemporary practice of identity. These important ethnographic studies have documented the Genízaro dances of Abiquiú, Comanche dances in Placitas and Rancho de Taos, and Matachines dances of Taos, the Sandía Mountains, and Alcalde. In the Sandías, the cultural practice and performance of the Comanchitos and Matachines as studied by each of these scholars represent the memory and resiliency of Genízaro culture.

DANZA DE LOS MATACHINES

The Matachines dance-drama of the sierra is also celebrated in many other villages in northern New Mexico in association with Catholic holidays including Christmas, New Year's, and the feast days of San Antonio de Padua and San Lorenzo. Pueblos that celebrate Matachines include Taos, Picurís, Ohkay Owingeh, Santa Clara, San Ildefonso, Jémez, Cochití, and Santo Domingo. Hispano villages or *placitas* celebrating the dance include Arroyo Seco, Alcalde, El Rancho, Bernalillo, and in the Carnué Land Grant of the east Sandía Mountains, San Antonito, San Antonio, Carnuel, and Canoñcito. Matachines are celebrated in the southern New Mexican village of Tortugas as well as Juárez and all over northern Mexico. These dances are presided over by the Monarca, a regal, crowned, and masked figure associated with the Aztec king Moctezuma, and the Malinche, danced by a young girl representing purity and the first Christian convert. The *abuelos*, or grandfather figures, symbolize ancestral order and tradition. Only found in northern New Mexico, the *toro* or bull dancer symbolizes evil and imperial Spain. The danza of the sierra features a male/female abuela called the Perijundia, who is the wife of an abuelo. At the choreographic center are the twelve *danzantes*, spiritual warrior dancers battling evil for the protection and good of the community.

People speculate that the danza may have been introduced to the Carnué communities by a neighboring Pueblo; however, in the sierra, the danza is deeply tied to the history of conflict and intermarriage with the Apache. According to Rodríguez: "[E]ven though San Antonio's settlers came mostly from Barelas, an Alburquerque barrio, and from the vicinities of Isleta and Sandía Pueblos, the people there today seem more conscious and proud of their Apache ancestry. . . . This is not so puzzling in light of the fact that their geographic orientation or watershed faces not toward the Río Grande valley but toward the eastern plains, whence came the nomadic tribes" (1996, 125). Modifications, nuances, and contemporary adaptations in the danza have shifted over time. Originally, the dance was performed in December around Christmas, also coinciding with the return of the buffalo hunters. The Monarca would customarily wear moccasins made specifically for the performance of the Matachines (García 1991). Today, San Antonio's feast day is observed on June 13 in alignment with the Catholic calendar. "The growth of San Antonio was linked with the industries that brought in residents, and also caused San Antonio residents to be absent for greater or lesser stretches of time. From the beginning, men customarily were absent for months at a time, hunting buffalo and trading on the plains" (Swadesh 1980a).

Also embedded in the contemporary practice of the Matachines is the memory of slavery, captivity, and interconnections with the Comanche. According to Enrique Lamadrid, musical elements of the Hispano-Comanche dance tradition were incorporated into the Matachines. "The Matachines dances of the Holy Child Parish in the Sandía Mountains east of Albuquerque have always ended with a movement called 'El Comanche,' in which the abuelos, or ancestral spirit clowns, kill the bull dancer, all to the same tune to which the Comanche lullabies and certain inditas are sung" (Lamadrid 2015, 229–96).

Just as with the Matachines, villagers celebrate the Comanche dance traditions in all the pueblos to honor the peace with their former foes, the

FIGURE 9.4 Los Matachines, San Antonio feast day, June 14, 1935.
Courtesy of the Gonzales family.

Nuhmuhnuh or tribal Comanches of the southern plains. The dance is practiced in pueblos such as Taos, Santa Clara, and Ohkay Owingeh but also in Hispano communities such as Ranchos de Taos, Alcalde, Bernalillo, Placitas, and Atrisco. In a detailed study of Hispano-Comanche dance, Lamadrid observes that in New Mexico, "Hispanos and Pueblo Indians dress, sing, and dance as or about Comanches, creating a dialogue that questions history as it challenges and affirms identity" (Lamadrid 2003, 27–50). In the Sandía mountain community of Placitas, the Comanchitos dance is still performed during Christmas to celebrate the birth of Santo Niño. The dance was also celebrated in the satellite community of La Madera up to the 1940s and is enjoying a contemporary revival through the support of elders and clan relationships from Placitas.

The song for the dance is performed by an elder, accompanied by guitar and *tombé*, a single-headed, southern plains–style drum, with verses sung in Spanish with a vocable chorus. Vocables are nonlexical syllables characteristic of North American indigenous singing (Lamadrid 2003, 165). The dance is performed by children ranging in age from toddlers to young adults in the formation of a line dance with singers, guitarists, and drummers to one side. On Christmas Eve, the dance is preceded by Las Posadas, the ceremonial pre-Christmas procession that makes various stops in the village. Following Las Posadas, the Comanchitos dance is performed in front of a community member's home. The last verse, as performed in Placitas and more recently in La Madera, attests to memory of captive children who were incorporated into the community and the obligation of the community to care for them. Villagers who have moved to larger towns such as Bernalillo have taken the tradition with them (Lamadrid 2003, 127).

Al Santo Niño de Atocha,	Holy Child of Atocha,
le encargamos por favor,	we ask you please,
cuida de sus comanchitos,	take care of the little Comanche children,
que no olvide cuantos son.	don't forget how many they are.

Comanchitos de la Sierra, La Madera, December 17, 2016

The danza enacts and represents the memory and tension of mutual captivity, initiation, and community resilience based on the complex relationship with warring tribes. The dance of the Comanchitos is a symbolic way of coping with and understanding the trauma and complexity of a generative and transformed Genízaro identity. One popular *indita* (little Indian song) from my grandmother, Carmen Chávez Gonzales, "La indita de San Luis Gonzaga," is remembered and sung for the Comanchitos de la Sierra. San Luis has his own feast day on June 21, but whenever there is dancing, his verses are sung. Between the verses, vocables recall the power of a mixed indigenous heritage. Historically, the verses were also sung during the pre-Christmas celebrations that welcomed the *ciboleros* (buffalo hunters) home from the hunt. They often brought back captives for adoption. Child captives are remembered as the little Comanches. "Music forms such as the indita ballads and regional dance/dramas such as the Matachines and the Comanches are sung and celebrated in both Pueblo Indian and Nuevo Mexicano communities across the state. These cultural expressions contain explicit references and implicit structures, which in performance reenact and redefine political and cultural relationships between both groups" (Lamadrid 2002, 164).

San Luis de Gonzaga,	Saint Aloysius Gonzaga,
jey yana . . . jey ya ne yo,	hey yanna . . . hey ya ney yo,
jey yana . . . jey ya ne yo.	hey yanna . . . hey ya ney yo.
Los inditos le cantaban,	The little Indians would sing to him,
los inditos le cantaban,	the little Indians would sing to him,
jey yana . . . jey ya ne yo,	hey yanna . . . hey ya ney yo,
jey yana . . . jey ya ne yo.	hey yanna . . . hey ya ney yo.[2]

Children with roots in Placitas and La Madera were often sung to with *arrullos* (lullabies) whose lyrics reference the pain of the past, the subjective experience of Genízaro history. The implied captivity narrative inspires both fear and security in the mind of a child. No child wants to be captured or sold by Indian raiders, and parents reassure their children that it won't happen to them (if they behave and go to sleep).

El cumanche y la cumancha	The Comanche and his wife
se fueron pa' Santa Fe,	went to Santa Fe,
a vender al cumanchito	to sell their little Comanche
por azúcar y café.	for sugar and coffee.[3]

Bernardo Gallegos affirms that Nuevomexicano identity is rooted in the history of "kidnapping as a cultural form. . . . Indian Slavery in fact was central to the formation of New Mexican culture and identity during the Spanish, Mexican, and early American periods" (Gallegos 2017, 106). Contrary to the claim of Fray Angélico Chávez and other contemporary New Mexican historians that Genízaro identity and cultural practices ended in New Mexico during the early nineteenth century, ethnographic observation of contemporary cultural performances reveals that Genízaro culture has persisted in mountain communities of the Sierra Sandía. Through community rituals, dances, and customs, Genízaro descendants regularly enact and maintain their traditions. And, more important, an understanding of Indo-Hispano identity in New Mexico signifies an acknowledgment of Genízaro subjectivity. Therefore, Genízaro identity is ultimately emblematic of Nuevomexicano identity.

Cultural Landscape Preservation and Genízaro Identity

Through existing connections to ancestral lands and genealogical links to eighteenth-century Genízaro settlers and nineteenth-centuries captives, the placitas of La Sierra Sandía demonstrate the maintenance of Genízaro identity in New Mexico. The experiences of living in a military buffer zone, participating in communal buffalo hunts, and integrating captives engendered a unique Genízaro resiliency and cultural practice that has survived into present times. Traditional governance is articulated through land grant councils and acequia commissions, in their ongoing struggle to preserve the land and water resources of the vecinos and *herederos* (heirs). Today, membership and recognition as heirs in the Cañón de Carnué or San Antonio de las Huertas Land Grants in the Sandías provide Genízaro descendants with a sense of belonging and love of homeland popularly known in New Mexico as *querencia*, derived from the verb *querer*, to love and belong to (Lamadrid 1995). Both community land grants are recognized as local governments by the State of New Mexico (New Mexico Statutes 2016). In this context, the concept of Genízaro Nation for the placitas of the Sierra Sandía means the recognition, protection, and validation of indigenous rights for a community on its land. Recognition as Genízaros is not a movement for the creation of a tribe, but rather acknowledgment of history and cultural identity (Rael-Gálvez 2007).

Stretching from the Santo Niño Church in Carnuel northbound along Highway 14, the villages of San Antonio, Cañoncito, San Antonito, La Madera, San Pedro, and Placitas continue indigenous practices through ceremonial dance, sacred pilgrimages, and the celebration of traditional saint days, as well as the preservation of foodways and traditional medicine and healing. Beginning with the Santo Niño fiesta celebration in May in Carnuel and ending the year with the Noche Buena or Christmas Eve celebration in Placitas, these traditions and customs thrive. Centuries of mestizo historical and cultural memory live on. Ritual characters like the Abuelo and the Malinche of the Matachines are shared by both Hispanos and Pueblos, as is the commemoration of captivity and initiation through the Comanchitos dance. Genízaro identity continues to be practiced and celebrated.

Throughout New Mexico, culturally hybrid practices such as rituals, customs, and foodways are explicitly performed, and they implicitly politicize an identity within an indigenous framework. Pekka Hämäläinen points out that, in order to subvert such Anglo-American constructions of stigmatized racial mixing and impurity, many New Mexicans have attempted to reclaim for themselves a "Spanish" identity. Groups of New Mexican mestizos with links to historically Genízaro communities have actively embraced the hybridity of the Comanchería and the Apachería, those vast cultural territories beyond the control of colonial authorities. They have memorialized their connections in expressive culture, clothing, and oral traditions, and they reenact those linkages in popular local performances of Los Comanches. In doing so, they disassociate themselves from the privileged coalition of Anglo- and Spanish Americans, undermine the hegemonic pretensions of that coalition, and promote a distinctive Chicana/Chicano consciousness that traces its roots to the ethnic melting pot that was Comanchería (Hämäläinen 2008, 360).

FIGURE 9.5 Comanchitos de la Sierra, La Madera, December 17, 2016. Courtesy of Lynn Velarde de Gonzales.

Serreño Genízaro identity has evolved, as in other villages in New Mexico, a pan-indigenous identity (Comanche, Kiowa, Apache, Ute, Navajo, Pawnee, and Pueblo) with its ethnogenesis in the early eighteenth century and subsequent consolidation. After 1821, Mexican national narratives erased Genízaros as a recognizable group, and after 1846, US national narratives either ignored Genízaros or labeled them as Mexican immigrants in order to perpetuate the triumphalist Anglo master narrative of the West. Serreño communities of the Sandía Mountains, along with many other Genízaro communities throughout New Mexico, embody our mixed indigenous heritage as a defiant act in honor of our ancestors and challenge the colonial power of the nation-state to dominate our identity.

Notes

1. Carnué in this chapter refers to the Cañón de Carnué Land Grant, and Carnuel refers to the village of Carnuel.

2. "La Indita de San Luis de Gonzaga" was recorded by the author's aunt, Joanne Gonzales, on February 26, 2016. Moises Gonzales, personal collection.

3. This lullaby was recorded in Ranchos de Taos and published (Lamadrid 1994; Lamadrid 2003). Virginia Sánchez found it in nineteenth-century diaries from southern Colorado (see her chapter in this volume).

References

Archibald, Robert. 1976. "Cañón de Carnué: Settlement of a Grant." *New Mexico Historical Review* 51, 4 (October): 313–28.

Atherton, Heather Noelle. 2013. "Community Formation in the Spanish Colonial Borderlands: San José de las Huertas, New Mexico." PhD diss., Columbia University.

Brooks, James F. 2002. *Captives and Cousins: Kinship and Community in the Southwest Borderlands*. Chapel Hill: University of North Carolina Press.

Chávez, Fray Angelico. 1979. "Genízaros." In *Handbook of North American Indians*, vol. 9, *Southwest*, edited by Alfonso Ortiz and William C. Sturtevant, 198–200. Washington, DC: Smithsonian Institution.

Gonzales, Moises. 2014. "The Genízaro Land Grant Settlements of New Mexico." *Journal of the Southwest* 56, 4 (Winter): 583–602.

Ebright, Malcolm. 1994. *Land Grants and Lawsuits in Northern New Mexico*. Albuquerque: University of New Mexico Press.

Forrest, Suzanne Sims. 1996. "A Trail of Tangled Titles: Mining, Land Speculation, and the Dismemberment of the San Antonio de las Huertas Land Grant." *New Mexico Historical Review* 71, no. 4 (October): 361–93.

Gallegos, Bernardo. 2017. *Postcolonial Indigenous Performances: Coyote Musings on Genízaros, Hybridity, Education, and Slavery*. Rotterdam: Sense Publishers.

García, Adilia. 1990. Interview, East Mountain Oral History Project. Center for Southwest Research, University of New Mexico, October 31.

García-Luna, Jacqueline. 1999. "The San Miguel de Laredo–Carnué Land Grant of 1763, part 1: The History." *New Mexico Genealogist* 38, no. 4: 151–71.

Gutiérrez, Juan, Andrés Aragón, Javier Gutiérrez, José Antonio Archibeque, Miguel Gallegos, Matías Gonzales, and José Gonzales. 1765. Spanish Archives of New Mexico I, SG #144, Roll 26, frames 939–40.

Gutiérrez, Ramón A. 1991. *When Jesus Came, the Corn Mothers Went Away: Marriage, Sexuality, and Power in New Mexico, 1500–1846*. Stanford, CA: Stanford University Press.

Hämäläinen, Pekka. 2008. *The Comanche Empire*. New Haven, CT: Yale University Press.

Lamadrid, Enrique. 1994. *Tesoros del Espíritu: A Portrait in Sound of Hispanic New Mexico*. With Jack Loeffler, recordist, and Miguel Gandert, photographer. Albuquerque: Academia/El Norte Publications.

———. 1995. "La Querencia: Moctezuma and the Landscape of Desire." *Blue Mesa Review* 7 (Spring): 3–8.

———. 2002. "La Indita de San Luis Gonzaga: War with Spain, Faith, and Ethnic Relations in the Evolution of a New Mexican Religious Ballad." In *Recovering the U.S. Hispanic Literary Heritage*, vol. 4, edited by José Aranda Jr. and Silvio Torres-Saillant, 154–71. Houston: Arte Público.

———. 2003. *Hermanitos Comanchitos: Indo-Hispano Rituals of Captivity and Redemption*. Albuquerque: University of New Mexico Press.

———. 2015. "Cautivos y Criados: Cultural Memories of Slavery in New Mexico." In *Linking the Histories of Slavery: North America and Its Borderlands*, edited by Bonnie Martin and James F. Brooks, 229–56. Santa Fe: School for Advanced Research Press.

Langham Olmsted, Virginia. 1975. *New Mexico Spanish and Mexican Colonial Censuses: 1790, 1823, 1845*. Albuquerque: New Mexico Genealogical Society.

———. 1981. *Spanish and Mexican Censuses of New Mexico, 1750–1830*. Albuquerque: New Mexico Genealogical Society.

Magnaghi, Russell M. 1990. "Plains Indians in New Mexico: The Genízaro Experience." *Great Plains Quarterly* 10, no. 2 (Spring): 86–95.

Mendinueta, Pedro Fermín de. 1767. Spanish Archives of New Mexico I, SG #144, Roll 26, frame 940.

Miera y Pacheco, don Bernardo de. 1779. Map of the Internal Province of New México. New Mexico State Records Center and Archives, Drawer 1. Available at http://dev.newmexicohistory.org/filedetails.php? fileID=301.

New Mexico Census. 1802. Spanish Archives of New Mexico, Reel 1, frame 576.

New Mexico Military Census. 1802. Spanish Archives of New Mexico I, 1802 Military Census for Las Huertas.

New Mexico Statutes. 2016. "Management of Spanish and Mexican Grants." Chapter 49, Land Grants; Article 1, General Provisions; Section 49-1-1.

Quintana, Frances Leon. 1991. *Pobladores: Hispanic Americans of the Ute Frontier*. Notre Dame, IN: University of Notre Dame Press.

Rael-Gálvez, Estevan. 2007. "A Memorial Recognizing the Role of Genízaros in New Mexico History and Their Legacy." Forty-Eighth Legislature, House Memorial 40, Senate Memorial 59. Santa Fe: New Mexico State Legislature. Available at https://www.nmlegis.gov/sessions/07%20Regular/memorials/house/HM040.html.

Rebolledo, Tey Diana, and María Teresa Márquez, eds. 2000. *Women's Tales from the New Mexico WPA: La Diabla a Pie*. Houston: Arte Público.

Rodríguez, Sylvia. 1996. *The Matachines Dance: Ritual Symbolism and Interethnic Relations in the Upper Río Grande Valley*. Albuquerque: University of New Mexico Press.

Simmons, Marc. 1982. *Albuquerque: A Narrative History*. Albuquerque: University of New Mexico Press.

Sisneros, Samuel. n.d. "The Life and Times of Esteban Padilla: How the Acquisition of Land Changed His Social Status and Place in the Padilla Family Hierarchy." New Mexico History.org, Office of the State Historian. Available at http://new mexicohistory.org/people/esteban-padilla.

Swadesh, Frances Leon. 1974. *Los Primeros Pobladores: Hispanic Americans of the Ute Frontier*. Notre Dame, IN: University of Notre Dame Press.

———. 1976. "Archeology, Ethnohistory and the first Plaza of Carnuel." *Ethnohistory* 23, no. 1 (Winter): 31–44.

———. 1980a. "Ethnohistory of the Area." In *Archaeological Investigations at San Antonio de Padua, LA 24, Bernalillo County, New Mexico*, edited by Al Dart. Santa Fe: Office of Archaeological Studies, Museum of New Mexico.

———. 1980b. "The Tijeras Canyon Area." Unpublished monograph, Box 1, Center for Southwest Research, University of New Mexico.

Vélez Cachupín, Tomás. 1773. Spanish and Mexican Archives of New Mexico, SG #150, Reel 27, no. 483–44.

CHAPTER TEN

*Huellas de Sangre, Amor,
y Lágrimas: Rescatando a Mis Cautivas*
Trails of Blood, Love, and Tears:
Rescuing My Captives

SUSAN M. GANDERT

That sense of belonging—*querencia*—that I feel for New Mexico is deeply rooted in both the stories I heard growing up and the histories I am just beginning to explore. The storytellers in my family have mostly disappeared, their voices slowly fading, but sometimes a whisper of memory appears in a conversation or in my mind, some story told by my mother, my father, something I overheard as a child. Those glimpses of my family's history have been romanticized in my imagination, and I am oblivious of the hard work, poverty, and suffering that my ancestors must have endured. The men were ranchers, farmers, miners, sheepherders, or day workers. The women were mothers, wives, bootleggers, and heads of family whenever necessary. I see their lives through the prism of my childhood. In the steamy kitchen, my mother would cook and tell me stories of her childhood, which now seem much more colorful than my own childhood in Santa Fe. During summer vacations I would spend a week or two with my grandparents in Mora, New Mexico. The mornings were filled with hard work, but the afternoons were spent visiting with a myriad of *tíos* and *tías*, *primos* and *primas*, and although I can still hear the rhythm of the gossip and stories, I was too young to remember or even understand the details of those stories.

Erased or forgotten from these stories are the Native American ancestors who make up about a third of my DNA. I always knew that as a Nuevomexicana whose lineage goes back countless generations, I had to have some Native American ancestors, but I never questioned their role in the family histories. When my mother was first married and living in Fort Sill, Oklahoma, some Indian ladies at the laundromat would ask her where she found her "good-looking Indian soldier." My father, tall and dark, was not *puro alemán* (pure German), like his Gandert surname. When my oldest brother, Joseph, was born, Uncle Boni (Bonifacio) Gandert commented proudly: "Este, sí, es puro alemán" (This one, yes, is pure German). Ah, the wonders of genetics!

It was not until after my mother had passed away that I began to explore the DNA threads of my family. A colleague and friend, Ángelo Cervantes, persuaded me to participate in the New Mexico DNA Project, which looks into the origins of New Mexico families and their descendants over four centuries by collecting DNA samples. He also told me about a study by Andrew Merriwether of the San Luis Valley that showed Hispanos in the valley to be about 67 percent European and 33 percent Native American; however, the mtDNA (mitochondrial DNA) was about 85 percent Native American. Suddenly, I was possessed by the romantic notion of how ancient Native grandmothers connected me to this vast and beautiful land. It was almost a nineteenth-century vision that I had gleaned from copies of *New Mexico Magazine* of my childhood, with the colorful photo-essays of Indian dances and women wearing colorful costumes, dripping with turquoise jewelry, pots balanced on their heads. I never really thought the lives they lived to be a part of my family history, my DNA. How did these statistics relate to my family? What were their stories? At first, I was reluctant to participate, but finally Cervantes convinced me. As a result of these tests, I began to delve more deeply into my family history, one that included *cautivas* and slave owners.

I had my brother Miguel test for both the mtDNA and the Y chromosome as I began the search for the family's origin. I knew the direct male line would be European, since the first Gandert in New Mexico was William Frederick, father of the aforementioned Uncle Boni. I had no expectations for the mtDNA, which would be the direct female lineage, going back thousands of years. Later, I also tested my father's mitochondrial DNA. In both cases, the markers indicated a New World origin. It was my friend Cervantes who interpreted the results—Pueblo Indian on my mother's side and Apache/Navajo on my father's side. The science was fascinating, but what about the family history?

My mother was the storyteller of my youth. On the day she was born, some

FIGURE 10.1
Lillian P. Mondragón de Gandert, 1949. Born 1930 in Antonito, Colorado; died 2009 in Albuquerque, New Mexico. Courtesy of the Gandert family.

members of her family threatened to kill her and her teenage mother—Josie Valdez—or so the story goes. A young member of the household ran across the field to get the midwife, Emilia Mondragón. He was shouting, "¡Las van a matar! ¡Las van a matar!" (They're going to kill them! They're going to kill them!). Sometimes I think that the screams of childbirth were what frightened the young boy. After my mother was born, Emilia bundled her up and took her home, and Lillian Petra became the youngest child of Emilia and Bernardo Mondragón. In census reports and school diplomas, she is known as Lillian, and that is how family and friends referred to her. Inexplicably, upon marriage to my father her name on later official documents appears as Cecilia. Her new brothers were Maclovio, Lorenzo, and Cleofes. She also had a half-sister, Bernie, short for Bernabe, who was from Bernardo's first marriage. For my mother, her parents would always be Bernardo and Emilia Mondragón from Antonito, Colorado. I cannot imagine how Josie must have felt to have her child taken away. She is said to have left a letter for my mother, but it was destroyed in a house fire.

Not until she was about six or seven years old did my mother discover who her real, biological mother was. Her brother Lorenzo started calling her a little *india*, saying that she was the granddaughter of the *navajosa* (Navajo woman) who cleaned their floors. She cried and told Emilia what Lorenzo had said. Her mother told her a shortened version of the truth. She was adopted, and the woman who cleaned the floors was her grandmother. The part about being Indian never seemed to have much importance when my mother told the story, either for her or for me.

That was one of the many stories my mother told, but it was not until my brother Miguel attended a lecture at the School of American Research in Santa Fe that we learned that my mother's maternal grandmother was a cautiva. When Gertrudes Gallegos, later Valdez, was a young child, she was taken from her family and later exchanged in some form to the Valdez family, for whom she was the *criada* or domestic servant. Later she married Juan, the youngest Valdez brother. My mother remembers her as an old, tiny, bowlegged woman who was very stern and would swat at the boys with whatever was at hand—broom, mop, wet rag—for tracking in on the clean floors. She never said a mean word or raised a hand to my mother when she walked across the newly cleaned floors. My mother was very spoiled, but she said that there was always something about that woman that commanded her respect, even before she knew that the tiny, weathered woman was her grandmother. And although Gertrudes was her grandmother, my mother never tried to get to know her.

My mother possessed a deep hurt about the circumstances of her birth. Josie Valdez was young, single, and pregnant. She was about nineteen when my mother was born, but my mom never knew her. When Josie was about thirteen, she ran away to Walsenburg, Colorado, and married a twenty-one-year-old man. Later she divorced him and returned home, probably pregnant with Armando, my mother's biological brother. After Josie died, Gertrudes raised Armando as her son. One story is that Josie worked in the Mondragón house before her mother did, or maybe in place of her mother. It seemed that the stigma of servitude had followed her into the next generation. Soon she was pregnant again with my mother. After the baby was taken, Josie left Antonito and returned to Walsenburg. Soon after, she was killed in an accident. A car in which she was a passenger was hit by a train. My mother sometimes wondered rather wistfully what was in the letter that was destroyed in the fire. However, she did have a small, black-and-white photograph of Josie, a sad, young, modern-looking woman wearing a cloche-style hat—the daughter of a cautiva.

The story of my mother's cautiva grandmother was confirmed by my mother's real cousin, Isidoro Valdez. I think he was the only Valdez with whom she

FIGURE 10.2 Gertrudes Gallegos de Valdez, ca. 1951. Birthplace unknown, ca. 1862; died 1954 in Salida, Colorado. Courtesy of the Gandert family.

FIGURE 10.3 Josie Valdez, ca. 1931. Birthplace unknown, ca. 1911; died in Walsenburg, Colorado, date unknown. Courtesy of the Gandert family.

kept in touch. We did visit her brother Armando in San Diego when I was six, but she really considered the Mondragóns her family. She adored her father, Bernardo, and her brothers, and they adored her.

When Miguel came home with the news of our cautiva great-grandmother, we thought he must be mistaken. My mother had a fair complexion and hazel-green eyes. She had mentioned that Gertrudes was sometimes referred to as la navajosa, and we knew that she was my mother's grandmother. Still, we were skeptical. Were we part Navajo? The results of the mitochondrial DNA were a surprise and a mystery—haplogroup B4'5? It turns out that Gertrudes was not of Navajo descent but Pueblo. As a cautiva, she must have been taken from her family and maybe bought and sold in someplace like Taos. Gertrudes married the youngest son in the Valdez family. He worked with my mother's father herding sheep. They used to call him Juan Cebo because he liked to eat the fat from the roasted lambs. Although I think the DNA results would have been an interesting detail for my mother, she cared more about the family she loved during her life and was not interested in exploring a past that she had not witnessed.

My father was the one who we were sure had a Native American ancestor or two, because he was so dark and handsome. Had not those Indian women in Fort Sill, Oklahoma, mistaken him for Native American? I do not remember any family stories about Native American ancestors on his side of the family, and although the physical characteristics of my dad and aunts point in that direction, my grandmother would have strongly protested such an idea. I wonder what she would have said if she'd known that she had an Apache ancestor—mtDNA haplogroup C. Apparently, the Jicarilla Apaches were among the first settlers in the Mora Valley. The Comanches drove them off the plains and into the refuge of the mountains.

The Gandert surname was always a source of pride in my family. There was something romantic about the nineteen-year-old William Frederick Gandert leaving Hannover, Prussia, to seek his fortune on the other side of the Atlantic. Whenever we visited my grandparents in Mora, William Frederick was omnipresent. The hand-tinted photograph of this blue-eyed, fair-haired, handsome man with long sideburns, as far as the family was concerned, depicted the original Gandert. Everything Gandert started and stopped with him.

William F. Gandert came from Germany and worked as a muleteer between St. Louis, Missouri, and Santa Fe, New Mexico. Then for ten years he

FIGURE 10.4 William Frederick Gandert, ca. 1863. Born 1832 in Hannover, Prussia; died 1896 in Agua Negra (Holman), Mora, New Mexico Territory. Courtesy of the Gandert family.

worked as a merchant and store clerk around Taos and Santa Fe. He spent those years accumulating some wealth and land. The 1860 US Census shows that at twenty-eight years of age, William was wealthy in comparison to his neighbors. His personal estate was worth $1,300. His occupation was listed as a merchant. Although his residence was San Antonio, Mora, New Mexico Territory, he received mail at the post office in Fernando de Taos. Was it in Taos that he acquired or bought the Indian servant Augustina Gandert? William lived during a turbulent time when it was not uncommon for the Comanches to ride through Hispanic and Pueblo villages kidnapping women and children. Later, some of those captives were sold informally in towns where there had been slave markets in the eighteenth century, places like Taos.

Augustina Gandert first appears in the 1870 census. She was a thirty-year-old Indian woman from Utah. When I discovered this information, I wondered when William had bought her. Was she his companion as he traveled the Santa Fe Trail, trading goods? Maybe she taught him about native healing plants, and with that knowledge he decided to use the title of "doctor." How did her role change when he married the eighteen-year-old María de Jesús Vigil? I do not want to think of him as just a slave owner, with all the negative baggage that carries with it. Although I know that she was sold and traded as property, I want him to be the young European adventurer who had made enough money to settle down and start a family.

William married María de Jesús Vigil of Agua Negra, Mora, New Mexico Territory, and by 1870 had a one-year-old son with her—Andrés. No longer a merchant, he is listed in the 1870 US Census as a farmer with property worth $1,000 and a personal estate of $564. William was a wealthy man in comparison to his Nuevomexicano neighbors, and few of them had domestic servants. Maybe it was during this time that his neighbors began calling him Dr. Gandert. In family stories, he was referred to as "el Papá doctor." He was forty years old, and his young wife María de Jesús was eighteen. I learned that thirty-year-old Augustina was a domestic servant in the Vigil household. I still imagined her to be more than a servant before he married María de Jesús, but this was before I heard from a great-grandson of William, John F. Córdova, that Augustina was part of a dowry from the Vigil family. Still, I think that maybe she was a wedding gift to the new family of María de Jesús. Why did she not live with William, his young wife, and their one-year-old son Andrés? She had the surname Gandert, indicating that she was the property of William, but she was living with the family of María de Jesús. Augustina was baptized on November 22, 1867, around the time that William and María de Jesús were just beginning their new life together.

The family fascination with William Gandert has obscured and erased the Indian woman who was a part of his household during his two marriages. By 1880, Augustina had rejoined the Gandert household. María de Jesús had a child almost every other year and must have needed help. The house was some distance from any neighbors. Today, one can still find the stone foundation of the family homestead, although grazing cattle now overrun it. Augustina continued in the Gandert household after the death of María de Jesús and her only daughter, María Teresa Sofía, both of whom probably passed away during childbirth.

By the 1880 census, Augustina was helping William's new, young wife, María Altagracia, raise the four sons from his first wife—Andrés, Carlos, Daniel, and Frederick. María Altagracia was young, only twenty-four, while William was forty-eight. Augustina was forty, and her Indian identity had all but been erased. On the census, she was identified as white and from New Mexico. The Gandert family was growing. María Altagracia had five children of her own— John, Bonifacio, James, Magdalena, and Regina. I imagine Augustina to be like a second mother to the children of this large family before she passed away. This woman, who had been baptized and given the Gandert name, died in a fire in the back of the Gandert home. According to Córdova, she was using candles in the servant's area of the house, when it caught fire. She died, along with two children. Where they her children or other *criados* bought in Taos?

It is both fascinating and difficult to imagine my great-great-grandfather as a slave owner. I prefer the heroic and kind William Gandert who appears in Taos teacher Josephine Córdova's memoir, *No lloro pero me acuerdo* (I Don't Cry, But I Remember). (Josephine is no relation to John F. Córdova.) During William's life in Mora, the Indian raids were devastating to many families. One neighbor family suffered the tragedy of having their young son stolen by Indian raiders. When little Manuel de Atocha was taken, his mother, Josefa Martínez, was so distraught that she could not take care of her daughter, María de las Nieves. Josephine Córdova tells the story of Dr. Gandert (William) and his wife, who took care of the little girl until her mother was able to recover sufficiently from her grief to once again take care of her.

As was the custom, which continues to this day, promises and threats could be used to coax a saint to act on one's behalf. Sometimes buried, turned to face a wall, or even kept upside down, the statue of a particular saint could be incentivized into action. So, Josefa took her problem directly to the saint who could help her out. She decided that the Blessed Mother would not only understand her suffering but would help her to get her son back, especially if Mary's own son was held captive. Overcome with despair, Josefa went to the church, stole the baby Jesus, and held him hostage until his mother helped her to find little Manuel de Atocha. In her prayer, Josefa pleaded and negotiated not only with the Blessed Virgin but also with the baby Jesus. She even promised to sacrifice a future child to the church to serve the Blessed Mother. Such pathos is only rarely expressed in poetic form, with the stories about cautivos and the slave trade in New Mexico. Josefa's prayer is especially poignant, since her son was the namesake of the child Jesus. Manuel or Emmanuel is the Old Testament name for Christ, and Santo Niño de Atocha continues to be a particularly popular devotion in northern New Mexico.

Virgencita de los campos	Little Virgin of the countryside,
Tráeme a mi hijo Manuel.	Bring back to me my son Manuel.
¡Yo te entregaré al tuyo	I will deliver yours to you
Cuando lo traigas a él!	When you bring me back mine!
Santo Imanuel de Atocha	Blessed Emmanuel de Atocha,
Si me traes a tu tocayo	If you return to me your namesake
Te llevaré muchas flores	I will bring you many flowers
Durante el mes de mayo.	During the month of May.
Si tú, Madre, no me ayudas	If you, Mother, will not help me,
Creo que tengo razón	I believe I have good reason,
También tu hijito estará	For your son will also be
Cautivo en esa prisión.	A captive in that prison.
Si tú me traes a mi hijo	If you return to me my son,
Algún día te he de dar	One day to you I will surrender
A uno de mi familia	One from my family
Que te sirva en tu altar.	To wait upon you at your altar.
Mi gente te ha servido	My people have served you
Con humilde devoción	With humble devotion.
Un muy gran favor te pido	A very great favor I beg of you.
No desprecies mi oración.	Do not spurn my prayer.

Little Manuel de Atocha was never found, and his mother never fully recovered. The cautivas who were a part of my family history, Gertrudes and Augustina, were never reunited with their families, who must have lived with the same profound sorrow and grief that plagued Josefa. Gertrudes created a family with the youngest son of the Valdez family, although her daughter was a thirteen-year-old runaway. The last census information on Gertrudes shows her living with her grandson Armando, who is listed as her son rather than her grandson.

Augustina disappears from the government census documents, as do William and his wife María Altagracia. According to some family stories, William was poisoned by his best friend. In some versions, he is said to have slept with his best friend's wife. However, John F. Córdova relates the version told to him by his mother, Adela Gandert, that both William and Altagracia died in 1896, he of pneumonia and she of influenza. The 1890 US Census documents were burned in a fire, so one of the last records of William's family is from 1900. There were three Gandert households in Agua Negra, Mora, New Mexico Territory. The two oldest sons were married, and another brother was head of a household with four younger siblings. Sometime in that twenty-year gap, Augustina died, although it is not clear if this was before or after the deaths of William and Altagracia. Although she was not a biological ancestor, she is still an integral part of my family history.

The story of the cautivos and slavery in New Mexico is barely a footnote in the history books, but as a result of my research into my own family, I have managed to rescue two cautivas from being forgotten. Whether a part of my DNA or not, they are my family history. Augustina, Gertrudes, and even William, who chose to settle in northern New Mexico after years of traveling and trading along the Santa Fe Trail, are all a part of the profound querencia that transcends the science of DNA.

Reference

Josephine M. Córdova. 1976. *No lloro pero me acuerdo*. Edited by Kathryn Córdova. Dallas: Taylor Publishing.

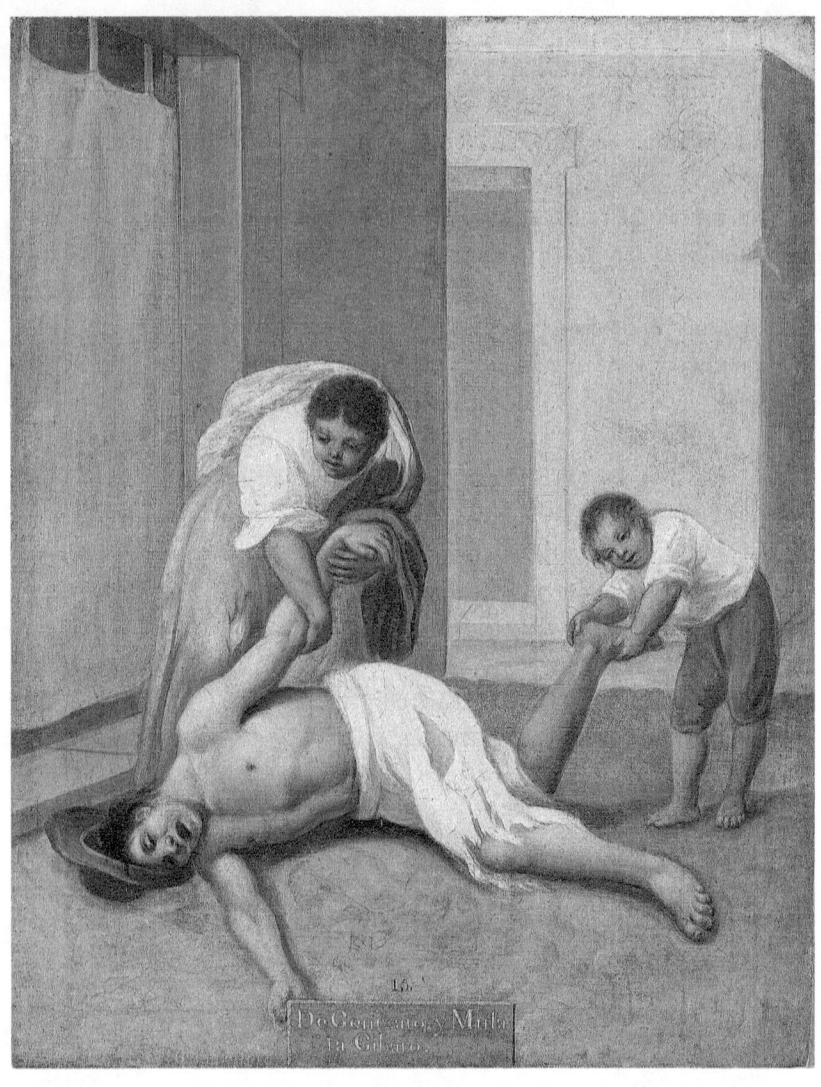

FIGURE 11.1 De Genízaro y Mulata, Gíbaro, ca. 1775. *Casta* painting by Francisco Clapera. Courtesy of the Denver Art Museum. In Nueva España, "Genízaro" was a generic term designating low-caste mestizos, on the lower rungs of the social hierarchy of color and honor. Only in the upper Río Grande does it become an ethnic term of self-designation. Nuevomexicano society was composed of Hispanos, Pueblos, and Genízaros.

CHAPTER ELEVEN

Genízaro Salvation
The Poetics of G. Benito Córdova's
Genízaro Nation

MICHAEL L. TRUJILLO

The anthropologist, fiction writer, and Genízaro intellectual G. Benito Córdova's greatest work, the novel *Big Dreams and Dark Secrets in Chimayó* (2006), ends with the death and rebirth in afterlife of the novel's protagonist, Salvador Cascabel Natividad. Salvador's transformation and the novel's textual form itself are enactments of the author's self-consciously crafted Genízaro poetics. Córdova's "savior" is a middle-aged Nuevomexicano from Chimayó, a custodian at the Los Alamos National Laboratory, and occasional handyman for Anglo-American immigrants to New Mexico like Georgia O'Keeffe. He possesses the most grotesque pathologies of Mexican American manhood and is alcoholic, abusive, absurdly macho, and destructively proud. After his death, Salvador's soul wanders in the afterlife for seven days in an interstitial purgatory. He meets a duende, or dwarf, who guides him by telling him that he, like Salvador, lived life in reverse and informs him of the "Law of Reverse Effects." That duende/dwarf then lists how Salvador's desires have almost always led him to acts that had the opposite of his intended effect. He tells Salvador:

> When you can't swim, you don't insist on walking in seawater or skin diving. You wait until the water freezes, then you walk over the ice. Yeah, Salvador, you love to swim upstream. And different in your case means the opposite. *That's* the solution. That's the answer. You would have been so much happier. (2006, 303)

The duende tells Salvador, "Think in reverse, vato loco. If you think something is good, and it's killing you, think the opposite. Do the reverse" (2006, 304). Following Pedro's directive, Salvador takes a step backward. By his third step, he hits his stride, turns, and flips a backward somersault. He has learned that life, death, and resurrection are the same.

Cordova's Genízaro poetics is, on one horizon, deeply personal in that it emerges from the author's own biography. On another it represents a subjugated knowledge that emerges along the dirt-road byways of northern New Mexican villages and the asphalt streets of New Mexico's cities and towns. Key sources for this chapter include (1) Córdova's creative writings, including the sublimely beautiful novel *Big Dreams and Dark Secrets in Chimayó* and the essay collection *The 3½ Cultures of Española* (1989); (2) Córdova's doctoral dissertation "Missionization and Hispanicization of Santo Thomas Apóstol de Abiquiú, 1750–1770" (1979); and (3) other works, such as an astounding, undated paper clearly intended for public presentation titled "The Genízaro." Córdova explains: "Historians of New Mexico call detribalized Indians 'Genízaros.' In actuality, Genízaros are special individuals with two cultures, Indian and Hispano. More importantly, Genízaros are a living bridge between two people" (n.d.[a], 1). In *Big Dreams and Dark Secrets*, Córdova ultimately crafts an indigenous Genízaro trickster poetics that subverts Eurocentric Nuevomexicano identity and foretells even as he conjures a Genízaro future and Genízaro nation.

Natividad

Born in 1942, G. Benito Córdova died five years after the publication of *Big Dreams and Dark Secrets in Chimayó*. A controversial academic who never gained a tenured position, he remains paradoxically influential among Nuevomexicana/o academics interested in our ethnic/racial identity and ascription. His thinking, if almost always without explicit recognition, has national resonance. He was a key consultant in the creation of the *American Encounters* exhibit at the Smithsonian Institution's National Museum of American History (1992–2004). He appeared as a representative of Genízaros as indigenous people in the documentary *Surviving Columbus: The Story of the Pueblo Peoples* (1992). He was a key interlocutor for University of California, Berkeley, folklorist Charles Briggs and inspired land grant studies scholar Malcolm Ebright and New Mexico state historian Rick Hendricks to write the book *The Witches of Abiquiú: The Governor, the Priest, the Genízaro Indians, and the Devil* (2006).¹ He is the discursive grandfather of an emerging cohort of young Nuevomexicano anthropologists including Ranchos de Taos native Gregorio P. Gonzales and his biological nephew David F. García, of Española. Both García and Gonzales recently completed doctorates at the University of Texas at Austin. This edited volume, *Nación Genízara*, is in large part Córdova's legacy.

Córdova was raised in the overwhelmingly Nuevomexicano communities in the Española Valley during his early childhood, but spent his later high school years in the nearby, largely Anglo-American city of Los Alamos. He earned a doctorate in educational foundations from the University of New Mexico, and a master's in anthropology from the University of Arizona. At Arizona, he studied with a Santa Clara Pueblo native, anthropologist Edward Dozier. Córdova taught at Española Valley High School and married a Paraguayan woman. In the late 1990s and early 2000s, he taught at the University of New Mexico, Gallup. His dissertation remains his most impressive scholarly work and represents the first lengthy academic text to engage Genízaro identity.² Of greatest significance for the edited volume that this chapter forms part of, *Nación Genízara*, is that through his paternal family line he is an heir to the Spanish colonial-era land grant of Abiquiú. This sixteen-thousand-acre land grant is located about twenty-two miles north of Española. Unlike the vast majority of such grants in the US Southwest, Abiquiú remains largely intact and collectively governed by its heirs. More significantly, this land was explicitly granted to Genízaros. Interestingly, Córdova's roots in Abiquiú descend through a father and grandfather also named Benito Córdova.³

In 2002, Córdova applied for tenure at the University of New Mexico's Gallup campus. His application's cover letter further contextualized his scholarship, teaching, and service in the story of his Genízaro ancestry (Córdova 2002). He wrote that he had gone to Gallup to learn about his Genízaro and specifically Navajo ancestry. Gallup borders a Navajo reservation, and the student population is predominately Native American. Córdova wrote on the first page of his application letter: "My grandmother had been captured by the Mexicans in 1854 and purchased by Vicente Córdova as chambermaid to his wife, Gerónima Montoya" (2002, 1). His grandmother was baptized at the "Genízaro Pueblo of Abiquiú" on July 24, 1864. He quotes the baptismal priest's entry in the church documents: "Today, I the curate of Santo Tomás

Apóstol de Abiquiú solemnly anointed with the holy oils of baptism a female from the Nation of Navajo who appears to be seven years of age" (Córdova 2002, 1).

He tells those who were to evaluate his work at the University of New Mexico's branch campus—he was ultimately denied tenure—that this young Navajo girl was given the Spanish and Christian name of María Rita Córdova.

Returning to *Big Dreams and Dark Secrets*, the key to Salvador's promise of redemption is his Genízaro transgression of racial boundaries, which stands in stark contrast to the sterile purity of Spanish American identity as elaborated by mid-twentieth-century figures like folklorist Aurelio Espinosa and essayist and scholar Fray Angélico Chávez. In the novel, readers learn that Salvador's grandmother, like Córdova's, was a Navajo woman who lived in Chimayó and was a Genízara. Her experience stands in for that of Córdova's own family and New Mexico's long and fraught history of ethnic/racial boundary crossing. She is a Genízara, and Salvador, as her descendant, is a Genízaro, too. Moreover, Salvador is at first ashamed of his grandmother, and *Big Dreams and Dark Secrets* may be read as his halting but ultimately successful recuperation of this ethnic/racial ancestry. Córdova himself followed a similar trajectory. In "The Genízaro," Córdova asserts Genízaro identity to a presumably Nuevomexicano audience with a full-throated roar:

> I, Gilberto Benito Córdova, proclaim here before all of you that I will shout it from the mountain tops, "I am Genízaro! I am a Genízaro! Soy lo que soy, I am what I am; I am from the past, heading for the future. Soy Genízaro; I am a Genízaro." And I ask you at this time to proclaim it along with me, "Soy Genízaro; I am a Genízaro and I will keep this beautiful secret a secret no more." (n.d.[a], 20)[4]

It is in this context that the significance, contradiction, and promise of the novel's protagonist's full name, Salvador (Savior) Cascabel (rattle, as in rattlesnake) Natividad (Nativity), takes on its significance and meaning.

We're Not All Happy

In Michel Foucault's terms, Córdova's work may be understood as the excavation of a subjugated knowledge of an already subjugated people (1982). Many of the novel's characters and places are recognizable people and sites from the Española Valley and other northern New Mexican locations such as Española, Chimayó, Alcalde, Los Alamos, Abiquiú, San Juan, and Carson National Forest. The site of Córdova's early childhood and high school teaching career is surrounded by the art-tourism centers of Santa Fe and Taos and the high-tech laboratory town of Los Alamos, where Córdova attended high school and his father worked. Students from Abiquiú and Chimayó attend Española Valley High School, where the adult Córdova taught. Notably, the opposition between Córdova's natal and ancestral communities and the town where he earned his high school education is highlighted by a sports rivalry. In the 1990s and 2000s, the Los Alamos High School Hilltoppers and Española Valley High School Sundevils were fierce competitors.

The Española Valley school district itself is largely populated by descendants from the Spanish and Mexican periods of settlement. Chimayó, in particular, is the site of the Good Friday pilgrimage to the Santuario de Chimayó, a shrine said to contain healing dirt. Abiquiú is nationally known for its beautiful landscape made famous by the artist and Anglo immigrant to New Mexico Georgia O'Keeffe. This geography is also a place of suffering and tragedy. In the late 1990s and early 2000s, a shocking series of newspaper articles and news stories in both the regional and national media described the area's high death rate from overdoses from illegal drugs. Indeed, Española's Río Arriba County had the highest statistical rate of illicit drug overdoses of any county in New Mexico, with New Mexico in turn having the highest rate of overdoses of any state in the country. Moreover, Córdova himself was no stranger to addiction. At the University of New Mexico, Gallup, he was well known as a leader in the university's alcohol recovery community. He judged this work to be among his most important contributions to the campus community.

Córdova explicitly recognizes Salvador's experience as a map for a more general regeneration. Speaking of his then-unfinished novel, Córdova said in an interview: "Salvador is a typical norteño. He wants to be in charge of his house and his woman. When things don't go his way, he drinks and gets in fights with people" (Pacheco 2004, 9). He explains:

> The Indians weren't happy when they had to give up their language and culture, and neither were the Hispanics when the American troops came. . . . Despite popular belief, everything is not hunky-dory. We're not all happy eating McDonald's hamburgers and doing American drugs. (Pacheco 2004, 9)

Córdova continues: "Our people are suffering; we're spiritually dead. We're a conquered people, and we've never come to terms with that" (9). He tells of his project's urgency: "We're drinking and drugging ourselves to death" (9). *Big Dreams and Dark Secrets*' Salvador is a Nuevomexicano from Chimayó, an alcoholic, a former custodian at the Los Alamos National Laboratory, and an impenitent former member of the regional lay Catholic brotherhood popularly known as *penitentes*. He confronts problems immediately recognizable to many of us in the real world such as an unfulfilling job, lost love, alcoholism, and insecurity stemming from oversized machismo. These are familiar problems to Córdova.

Recovery

Córdova's dissertation for his doctorate in education is nominally a study of the Franciscan mission at Abiquiú as a tool for indoctrinating and transforming the Genízaros into Hispanic citizens or *vecinos*. More properly, it is about the recovery of Abiquiú's indigenous history as a Genízaro pueblo. In 1754, Spanish colonial governor Tomás Vélez Cachupín created a town grant operated like an Indian pueblo for Genízaros under the supervision of a Franciscan missionary (Córdova 1979; Quintana 1991, 23; Ebright and Hendricks 2006, 269). Over the years, individual Genízaros changed their status by a process of assimilation that began with the acquisition of worldly possessions, primarily through war booty. Because of the town's ethnic and racial complexity, Ebright and Hendricks describe Abiquiú as a place of uncertainty and ambiguity, or middle ground. They invoke the indigenous concept of *nepantla* to illustrate this idea. Like Córdova, they describe eighteenth-century Abiquiú as a place where the supposedly indigenous and Spanish aspects of Genízaro identity were never fully resolved; "they were neither the Indians that they had been, nor the Spaniards they would become" (2006, 4). Implicit in Córdova's dissertation and explicit in his later work is that Genízaro identity was never fully replaced, as Ebright and Hendricks likewise indicate. We never became fully, or simply, Spanish.

Córdova and other scholars of the Genízaro phenomenon were not the first to delve into the complexities of New Mexico ethnic and racial identity. The literature on this larger subject is broad, and is the subject of my book *The Land of Disenchantment* (2009). In both my own experience and Córdova's, Spanish-dominant and elder Nuevomexicanos would often use the

Spanish-language ethnic term "mexicana/o" as a term of ethnic self-reference. Some would refer to cultural phenomena, others, and occasionally themselves as "indio." Archaeologist and artist Charlie Carrillo's chapter "Oral History-Ethnohistory of the Abiquiú Reservoir Area" (1992) supports that ethnic and racial identity remained an open question in Abiquiú. He writes: "Many elder residents in Abiquiú, Cañones, Coyoté, and Youngsville recall their Indian ancestry. Although they refer to themselves as mexicanos they recall a grandparent who was an Indian. Because of its Genízaro history, Abiquiú residents more readily recall an indio or india ancestor" (1992, 122).

Carrillo notes that some elders recalled being called Genízaros as children. Córdova describes his understanding in similar terms: "Since my youth, I remember being told that I was an Indian and that Abiquiú was an Indian Pueblo" (n.d.[a], 2).

As a child, Córdova knew that there was some truth to Abiquiú's reputation as a Native community. People from the neighboring communities always referred to Abiquiú as "el pueblo" (n.d.[a], 2). His mother, who was Nuevomexicana but not from Abiquiú, would sometimes inadvertently call his father "un indio."[5] The young Córdova would ask his father what sort of Indian he was, and the elder Benito Córdova would respond that he didn't know. If pressed, his father would respond "semos indios," or "we're just plain Indians." He explains a childhood conversation with his uncle Leandro:

> I yearned to be an Indian. And he assured me that I was one, just as all the people from Abiquiú were. "It's just that we don't talk about it," he said. "They are secret Indians, masquerading as mejicanos." . . . The only time I received recognition as an Indian was when people were angry at me; then, they inevitably called me "indio." Paradoxically, this sarcasm made me both proud and ashamed of being an Indian. (n.d.[a], 6–7)

He continues:

> Sometimes out of desperation, when someone called me an indio, I would defend myself by rebutting their attack with a "¿Si soy indio, if I am an Indian, dime de qué clase de indio soy, tell me what type of Indian I am?" and the most I got from them was that I was a "pinche indio." . . . So that meant that I was a wretched, damn Indian. Deep down within me I took comfort, got strength, and even became prouder from these personal attacks. For although they hurt me, they also served to reassure me that I was an Indian. (n.d.[a], 7)

His fictional Genízaro savior named Salvador must also learn that he, and thus we, are Genízaro people.

A Trickster Tale

Like Paul Radin's classic telling of the Winnebago or Ho Chunk trickster cycle, the novel's story follows an overall trajectory of development that includes nineteen episodes of rejection, reversal, and transformation (Babcock-Abrahams 1975, 181; Radin 1956). Córdova's narrative often parallels Radin's tale, as both include episodes of ahistorical, abiological, and asocial acts that culminate in rejections, reversals, and finally transformations (Babcock-Abrahams 1975, 181; Radin 1956). The trajectory is a developmental process: at the beginning of Radin's cycle, his protagonist is so unconscious of himself that his body is not a unity. His two hands fight each other. His sex is ambiguous. He does not even recognize his anus to be a part of himself (Jung 1956, 203). Through his adventures, he gains biological, psychic, and social awareness to the point at which he returns to society and appears socialized and, further, assumes his role and identity as culture-hero.

Big Dreams and Dark Secrets presents a parallel trajectory of development; its nineteen chapters exist in a strange symmetry with Radin's cycle. Through the final pages of the text, Salvador possesses overblown machismo and great, uncontrollable anger, but he often does not know why. Córdova writes: "Anger should have a reason for existing. But in Salvador's case, anger erupts when it chooses, 'cause it exists and has a life of its own. Salvador knows that he has a reason for being angry. Unfortunately, for the moment, he doesn't know why" (2006, 124).

After divorcing his wife, he emerges with an absurd masculinity: "The product of this tragedy was that the walking ghost of Salvador resurrected as a Chimayó super macho, and a macho compounded with machismo, as everyone who has lived with one knows, is a tyranny that darkens the sun. Drinking became Salvador's life dance. Drinking became an outward sign that screamed, 'I want to die and rest in peace, for eternity'" (21).

Salvador's misadventures include accidentally marrying his best friend's bride, doping the food of a gluttonous friend with Ex-Lax, building an adobe wall for Georgia O'Keeffe, dying in a national forest, and having an encounter with heaven's gatekeeper. At key moments in the text, he is inexplicably shadowed by a duende, or goblin, that only he can see, and the narrative moves, sometimes seamlessly, from realistic events to alcohol-induced hallucinations and, finally, mythological truths.

A Spiritual Geography

Salvador's friend Tomás "No Más" Sánchez and his trusty dog Solo Vino often accompany him, and the trio tool around in Sal's beat-up truck, "the Brown Buzzard." Salvador's village antagonists include his ex-wife Blanca Flor, don Wilberto B. C. Ferrán, and the village's Spanish-born priest, Padre Piedra. Salvador also encounters, or reports encounters with, supernatural figures such as Pedro de Urdemalas, Spider-Woman, Saint Peter, a giant serpent that is actually a log and/or the dog Solo Vino, and a dead but supernatural tree. In the racially and class-charged situations that arise throughout the novel, Salvador's Anglo antagonists include Dr. Carlisle Esmithenburgestein Johnson, a counselor at the alcohol treatment facility in Embudo, game warden Billy Bob Buford, the artist Georgia O'Keeffe, and his Los Alamos National Laboratory (LANL) boss, Wilhelm Hightower.

The protagonist also inhabits a spiritual geography that provides a reservoir of traditional knowledge that will, if he heeds it, answer the most painful aspects of his existence (Córdova 2006, 156–58). Chimayó's wise man, Wilberto B. C. Ferrán, tells Salvador that Chimayó's famed chapel, the Santuario de Chimayó, with its *pocito*, or hole containing healing dirt; and the mountain known as El Cerro de los Pedernales near Abiquiú, are actually two parts of a single sacred place.[6] Ferrán explains that it is for this reason that the Genízaros settled Chimayó and Abiquiú. Ferrán tells Salvador: "El Pocito is only half of the shrine. The holiest of all Genízaro shrines exists in two places at the same time, Salvador. They're one and the same, positive, and negative and at the same time both male and female. God, of course, is complete unto Him and Herself. God *is* both Male and Goddess" (156).

The feminine pocito at Chimayó and the masculine peak at Abiquiú are joined by an underground river of brine that connects the two. Córdova writes:

> Don Wilberto B. C. Ferrán goes on to describe the complexity of the mesa vortex. How it connects the feminine pocito at Chimayó with the masculine peak at Abiquiú.
>
> "It's a body of water, an underground river of brine. The flow connects the two. The female pocito and the male Cerro de los Pedernales are like a car

battery," the old man explains. "To be complete, the shrine must have a negative and a positive." (15)

The Loco, the Sinner, the Fool

Guillermo E. Hernández's *Chicano Satire: A Study in Literary Culture* (1991) provides insights that are helpful for understanding *Big Dreams and Dark Secrets* and other Chicana/Chicano uses of the trickster figure as social critique. Hernández states that in the Western tradition, satire is associated with a number of stereotyped figures who are subjected to hostility, humor, or indifference (1991, 2). These negative figures are often ultimately traced to marginal groups or individuals who are frequently subjected to censure or abuse. Thus, stigmatized members of a social group are subjected to the antagonism or even the hatred of majorities who feel threatened. However, a more common response toward the marginal, when not perceived as an immediate threat, is censure, ridicule, or indifference. In this respect, satire fulfills the function of punishing those who, sometimes through no fault of their own, transgress the rules of appropriate social behavior. In Enrique Lamadrid's prior telling of the Pedro de Urdemalas tale (1995, 19–20), from an early age Pedro loses the shame, or

> *vergüenza*, that orders, pacifies, and ultimately limits the lives of the rest of humankind. To be *sin vergüenza* is of particular significance for Nuevomexicanos as it is for Latin Americans; the charge of being without shame or lacking honor or dignity suggests asociality. To be called shameless is an insult and its significance is perhaps best illustrated by the fact Chicana theorists have inverted the insult in their critical engagement with an oppressive patriarchal social order.[7]

In his encounters with Anglo antagonists, our sin vergüenza, Salvador, is often the object of Anglo-American ethnic/racial marginalization and functions as the Chicano negative to the Anglo ideal. These differentials are particularly apt and potent with reference the Los Alamos National Laboratory, an overwhelmingly Anglo institution with an employment hierarchy in which the vast majority of scientists and administrators are Anglos while blue-collar workers such as custodians are often Nuevomexicano. Even if they do not work at Los Alamos themselves, most Española residents count relatives or friends among those who do. Joseph Masco, writing about the 1990s, states:

Within the laboratory, a Hispanic Roundtable took on the issue of a glass ceiling in promotions and began a public discussion of institutional bias against Nuevomexicanos. Nuevomexicano employees argued that LANL was profoundly divided between scientists and management who are largely from out of state, on the one hand, and the support staff, which is made up predominantly of locals, on the other. They pointed out that [of] 2,760 LANL employees making over $60,000 a year, only 110 were Nuevomexicano, and attributed this disparity to a glass ceiling at the laboratory, and specifically to a LANL practice of hiring from outside the state rather than from within. (2006, 206)[8]

In 2006, LANL's longtime governing body, the Regents of the University of California, settled a class-action lawsuit brought by the Hispano Roundtable and other groups for racial and gender discrimination. The regents agreed to pay $12 million to current and former Hispanic and female employees at the laboratory.

Hightower and a Perfect Wall

Of the Anglos at LANL, Salvador complained, "They're really prejudiced *cabrones*" (Córdova 2006, 88); and, "They really hate Chimayosos. Seventeen years, *seventeen years* I worked for the *cabrones* on the 'Hill,' and when I really needed them . . . and needed them bad, they fired my ass! *¡Pinches desgraciados!*" (39). Still, in even such power-laden and unequal interactions, Salvador is not blameless. For instance, it is in his confrontation with Hightower over his excessive use of profanity that he loses his job as a custodian (88–92). Called into Hightower's office, Salvador thinks to himself, "Oh, shit! *¡Me van a chingar!* This Gringo wants to screw my Chimayó *huevos. My miserable broom-pushing jale they call a 'career ladder,' Just 'cause I use a ladder to get supplies from the storage closets*" (89). Relieved that he is not facing accusations of on-the-job drinking, he decides that complete and vehement denial is his smartest course of action. Salvador responds to his boss's accusation of excessive profanity with the assertion, "*Fuck, no!*" He continues, "Absolutely not, Mr. Hightower. I've never used no cuss words at work, Señor. Never! *Fuck~k no! No way sir!* Honest to God, Mr. Hightower!" (90). Not surprisingly, Hightower fires Salvador despite his denial.

The chapter titled "Perfect Wall," which Córdova read aloud at a 2004 reading, is another example of satire. It renders Salvador's machismo even more absurdly. The chapter relates Salvador's drunken hallucination of an encounter between him and New Mexico's most famous artist, Georgia O'Keeffe (1887–1986). For decades and since her definitive relocation to New Mexico in 1945, O'Keeffe lived in a house in the village of Abiquiú. As the ultimate butt of patriarchy's joke, Salvador fails to best O'Keeffe in one of the most basic and base aspects of masculinity, a pissing contest.[9] Upon hearing her compliments of his Chicano artistry, Salvador boasts that he is a man who possesses big balls, while she has none. To show his contempt, he proceeds to unzip his fly in order to urinate on the wall. However, before he can consummate the act, the artist forbids him to urinate on "her" wall. Córdova writes: "The brown emaciated Genízaro faces the Gringa *pintora*. The wily artist smiles at him and in a low hardboiled no-nonsense voice reproaches the waterman from Chima. 'No, no-o, no-o, you don't! Not on my wall,' she reprimands Flaco" (120). Angered, Salvador challenges her to the contest: "'Vieja puta,' Salvador screams, 'When are you going to learn that you're never going to be able to piss like a real Chimayoso. Like an hombre! An hombre con huevos! BALS period'" (120). To Salvador's surprise, the artist questions his masculine superiority, and Salvador, therefore, challenges her to the contest. Their argument continues:

> Her blue eyes are aglow with anticipation. After all, she's as obstinate as Flaco is and has had more practice. Salvador is shocked that a woman would have the audacity to challenge him at anything, much less at a pissing contest. Yet, here she stands before him ready and willing for action. "Yeah, for once and for all, I'm going to teach you the difference between a man and a woman," Flaco snarls at her, and Solo Vino yelps in the background. (120)

Artist and *vato loco* square up for the dual. Despite his confidence, the contest ends badly for him. He "watches in impotent embarrassment as yellow fluid trickles down the front of his pants and onto his rattlesnake Durango boots" (121). The "supermacho" is not only a failure in this test of masculinity—he is also incontinent. At this moment, Flaco awakens from his dream/fantasy to find himself wetting his bed. He realizes that he has soaked his underwear, his blanket, and even his prized, if battered, Tony Lama boots (121). Still, as is already evident in the Hightower/LANL encounter, Salvador's antics are not the chief butt of the novel's joke.

Their Confessions, If You Heard Them

As a Genízaro trickster tale should, Córdova's novel also contains subversive potential. Radin states: "That those who gave the Wakdjunkaga cycle its present form intended . . . to make it a satire on man and on Winnebago society there is little question in my mind" (1956, 151). Such satiric elements include, among others, Wakdjunkaga's absurd war bundle ritual, the trickster's marriage in transsexual disguise to the chief's son, and the trickster's misapprehension of his own tremendous penis and blanket for the chief's banner. The lampooning of the chief's banner is particularly effective. Radin states: "The satire here is directed at one of the most important of the Winnebago feasts, that given by the chief of the tribe once a year, at which he raises his emblem of authority, a long feathered crook. It is his obligation at this feast to deliver long harangues admonishing his people to live up to the ideals of Winnebago society" (1956, 152).

Waking up one morning, Wakdjunkaga sees his blanket suspended high in the air on his own absurdly long and erect penis. Confusing the blanket and penis for the chief's long feather crook, thus rendering chief's authority ridiculous, Wakdjunkaga exclaims: "Aha, Aha! The chiefs have unfurled their banner! The people must be having a great feast!" (Radin 1956, 152). Córdova's trickster narrative similarly renders the representatives of mainstream American culture and society, such as Salvador's Los Alamos boss, ridiculous.

The story of Salvador's firing from his custodial job at Los Alamos reveals that his boss and LANL's crimes are far greater and much worthier of social sanction than Salvador's relatively minor transgressions. Córdova states: "The National Lab perennially contaminates and poisons Mother Earth with its plutonium experiments, all in the belief that bombs and weapons of mass destruction will save and help spread democracy" (2006, 91). Such statements are supported by recent academic texts, such as Myrriah Gómez's dissertation "Nuclear Alienation: A Literary Analysis of Race, Space, and Resistance Surrounding the Nuclear Coloniality of Los Alamos, 1942–2012" (2014), Masco's *The Nuclear Borderlands* (2006), and Jake Kosek's *Understories* (2006); LANL has itself long been actively involved in its own research tracing the spread of toxins produced by the laboratory in the surrounding environment. LANL scientist P. R. Frésquez told Kosek: "There is not a significant animal or plant that we have not tested in the region. I see the plants and animals as a medical researcher might see a petri dish—as a chance to better understand the nature and movement of toxic material in the environment. For us, the lab is everything around us" (Kosek 2006, 265).

The scientist continued: "You find the most interesting things in the strangest places. Some of the highest concentrations of radioactive materials were found in a fruiting apricot tree in the middle of town that has its roots right down into an old landfill. Similarly, you find that even when you think things seem stable and well-contained, you find surprises such as the forest of the Bayo Canyon" (Kosek 2006, 266). Bayo Canyon leads from Los Alamos toward lower-elevation communities such as La Mesilla and Santa Clara, thus justifying the fears of contamination described in length in Myrriah Gómez's dissertation.

In Córdova's novel, the narrator notes that Salvador's transgressions are small in comparison: "Toxic waste, after all, has a life span of more than twenty thousand years. Salvador, by contrast, if he's lucky, might live for fifty years" (2006, 91). The comparative misdemeanor of Salvador's crimes is made even more emphatically clear in Córdova's statement, "In the history of the world, no one has ever been killed by eating badly roasted green chile and refried beans or suffered physical injury by listening to cuss words, including bilingual ones" (92). Córdova satirically notes that Salvador has learned much from working at LANL: "On the positive side, Salvador worked at a very scientific laboratory and had caught on to the 'spirit of science' and elevated nontruths to a new level" (88).

Córdova's description of artist Georgia O'Keeffe in the chapter "Perfect Wall," and by extension the Santa Fe and Taos art communities that idolize her and her aesthetic choices, is even more devastating (107–21). Córdova aptly demonstrates the ridiculousness of Santa Fe style and the art community's desire to consume New Mexico's supposed premodernity. In reference to her desire to witness authentic Native and Latino communities, Córdova's narrator states that O'Keeffe once drove all the way to the "Heart of Indian Country," Gallup, and stayed in a motel owned by a Hindu from India, to purchase a (presumably Navajo) "genuine imitation plastic squash blossom necklace" from an Arab vendor (119). The narrator tells the story of how she contracts a native of the Española Valley village of Alcalde to build a wall around her home. When the contractor builds the wall in exact accordance to her specifications, she is horrified and angered by the wall's straightness and uniformity. She orders the Alcalde man to tear it down and rebuild it. After these events are repeated, the flummoxed and angered contractor recommends the only man desperate and crazy enough to work for her, Salvador.

Although he never arrives at the jobsite, in a drunken delirium Salvador fantasizes about building her a wall that she would like. In this dream, he outdoes New Mexico's most famous Anglo artist, bolstering his supermacho self-image. In a scenario that is perfectly plausible in the context of Santa Fe's and Taos's faux-adobe style, Salvador imagines building the artist the wall she would want—"a wall more crooked and ugly than his mother-in-law." The wall would completely lack utility, varying in height from six inches to taller than Salvador (117). Upon surveying Salvador's handiwork, O'Keeffe states:

> Sal . . . Sal, I'm here to personally congratulate you. . . . You're the only man in the universe to understand, truly understand . . . me. You alone understand that this wall is an aesthetic masterpiece. Art! Chicano art, which cries to blend with the contour of my quinta: it needs to complement my lesser canvas art, which is so esteemed by the world. You're a Genízaro genius. You're one of a kind. Chimayoso! (118)

O'Keeffe is beside herself and cannot hold back her praise: "The splendor of your wall will outlast the fame of all my creations. All of my canvas artwork!" (119). Still, it is important to remember that Salvador is not only a catalyst of jokes; he is also a savior.

A Genízaro Walks in Two Worlds

Tricksters like Córdova's Salvador have the double role of making use of humor and symbolic inversion to illuminate the inevitable contradictions of societies and their institutions. In doing so, they provide the engine for reinventing culture and later revitalizing it (Babcock-Abrahams 1975, 14; Hyde 1998; Spinks 2001). At some moments, when language cannot fully articulate experience, attention shifts to the margins and the possibilities of a new semiotic that produces a satisfactory (or dissatisfactory) match (Spinks 2001, 11). At such moments, trickster narratives proliferate in the form of dreams, hallucinatory voices, neuroses, and psychoses. In the case of *Big Dreams and Dark Secrets*, Córdova posits a new/old Genízaro way that is not bound by exclusionary, one-track thinking.

Córdova draws his hero as scatological, or, in Mikhail Bakhtin's more empathetic terms, carnivalesque (Bakhtin 1984). In Córdova's words, "Flaco

Salvador was skinny piñón size, a little larger than a small jalapeño, but he had a heart the size of a big bushel of small Chimayó red chile" (2006, 14). Here, Bakhtin's vision of the folk as opposed to state-sponsored discourses of appropriate behavior is relevant. Córdova states, "Salvador was *buena gente: Chico pero picoso*, small but snappy as his middle name, Cascabel—rattler—implied" (14). Upon his death, Salvador is honored by his drinking friends, *la plebe* (common folks), for possessing the qualities of a real man.

> "Muy hombre" is La Plebe's technique of incorporating into one man the showmanship of former jailbird Freddy Fender, the sexuality of Don Juan, musical ability of Julio and Enrique Iglesias, and the *cojones* of Pancho Villa. Only one man in the whole world has all of these qualities in him, and that person, as everyone knows, is Flaco Salvador. (Córdova 2006, 270)

Another Genízaro, the older and wiser don Wilberto B. C. Ferrán, provides Salvador with a folkloric and subjugated theory of Nuevomexicano ethnic/racial identity. Córdova states: "Don Wilberto B. C. Ferrán was the acknowledged village elder." Playing on a joke that contends that the Española library only contains one book, Córdova writes that Ferrán gained much of his knowledge from the singular and fabulous text. "The libro brimmed with encyclopedic knowledge, and from it don Wilberto B. C. Ferrán pontificated, philosophized, and solved problems on every aspect of life" (48). We learn that Ferrán is the son of a Navajo captive brought to Chimayó and purchased by the Ortegas, a well-known, real-life family of weavers in Chimayó. Ferrán's father is a mystery. Many villagers suspect that he is really the child of the village priest (48). Through the story of Ferrán's mother, he asserts the reality of Nuevomexicano racial mixture and places it within New Mexico's historical Genízaro specificities of forced incorporation and primal acts of gendered, sexual domination.

Ferrán does not seem to fret over his dual heritage. Rather, he has learned that his Genízaro ancestry gives him the ability to move through multiple subjectivities. Ferrán explains, "Mi madrecita was Navajo. She knew the Goddess and walked with Her to the freshness of the first rays of the morning" (150).[10] He continues, "A Genízaro . . . is a person who walks in beauty in different worlds, in different realities." In contrast, for Férran, "mestiza/o" is an ascribed identity and therefore lacks the choice integral to Genízaro identity. Still, at this point midway in the novel, Salvador cannot yet fully comprehend Ferrán's Genízaro reality:

Salvador thought he understood the significance of his words, before don Wilberto B. C. Ferrán could finish his explanations, the annoying borracho interrupted the old man "But . . . but . . . I'm . . . I'm half Hispanic, half Indian. A mestizo!" The sage shook his head in disgust and replied, "That's what you've *been anointed to be, Salvador.* You can, if you choose, be a Genízaro. That's you're right. You can attempt to forget who you are, but it doesn't work that way. You're a Genízaro! And as long as you live you shall remain a Genízaro." (151)

This Genízaro identity goes beyond mestizaje in another particularly important respect.[11] Where mestizaje speaks of the creation of national and ethnic subjects, Genízaros remain denigrated even within those traditions of national/ethnic identity that celebrate mestizaje (Contreras 2008, 30; Forbes 1973, 149).[12] Ferrán states, "A mestizo surrenders his right to choose. A mestizo throws himself at the mercy of the fry cooks of the world. Just like you, Salvador" (Córdova 2006, 153).

Deep New Mexico

In Miguel Gandert's *Nuevo México Profundo*, Enrique Lamadrid draws explicit connections to the negative, liberating powers of a Genízaro past (Gandert et al. 2000; Lamadrid 2000). This book's publication may have been preceded by Córdova's own thinking on this same subject; he dwells on the exact same performances (n.d.[a], 2–3). Each November, at the time of the feast of Santo Tomás the Apostle, the memory of capture, ransom, and incorporation is enacted by village children dressed in bright red cloth, buckskin, scarves, ribbons, feathers, and Tewa-style face paint (Gandert et al. 2000, 56–60). These dances call to memory the fact that many New Mexican villagers were also the victims of raids and themselves then incorporated into Native societies. Among the songs and dances that speak to these origins is an acting-out of captivity and redemption. In "The Genízaro," Córdova writes that although throughout the year the people of Abiquiú refer to themselves as "mejicanos" and "Spanish Americans," on these same feast days "[a]lmost everyone at Abiquiú went through a strange transformation and started talking about how they were Indian. My uncle Leandro, for example brought out his tombé [an indigenous drum] and drilled the nanillé dancers, on how to dance in the old Indian way" (n.d.[a], 2).

He continues:

> People whooped it up just like at any Indian doings. Occasionally, dancers from San Juan [Pueblo], Taos [Pueblo], and Apaches from Jicarilla reservation at Dulce came and participated in the festivity. People went out of their way to demonstrate and proclaim that they were Indians to anyone who would listen. They were proud of being Indian and on these two days so was I. (3)

On these feast days, the young Córdova was made whole and, thus, found resolution if for only a few days. Such folk performances, however, can also be a form discipline even as they stand apart from the Anglo-dominated modernity of much of twentieth and twenty-first century New Mexico.

Sacred Clowns

Through another ritual dance form, Salvador's friends and kin chastise the overblown macho. Salvador is, after all, a *sinvergüenza* (shameless one) in both Anglo and Nuevomexicano terms. He has lost his way and is ritually castrated at Alcalde's Matachines dance. The Matachines dance, as described in Córdova's chapter 3, "Matachín Magic," is ritually enacted at a village in the Española Valley on the day following Christmas, at Ohkay Owingeh Pueblo on Christmas day, and on other days in numerous other Native American pueblos and Nuevomexicano villages (Romero 1993, 2006, 2007; Rodríguez 1996). At the Alcalde event, figures dressed in distorted buckskin masks enact, among other things, the ritual castration of a dancer known as the "Torito" or little bull.[13] In this act of mock castration, the ritual performers enforce the social mores of their community. However, there is a critical difference between their actions and Salvador's firing by Hightower. In the course of Salvador's conversation with Ferrán, he recognizes the Matachines' origins in other, older social orders. Salvador wonders if the dancers are Old Testament gods or Native American kachinas invading the world of Catholicism, and concludes that they exist in a different reality (Córdova 2006, 50). In other words, Salvador receives his comeuppance at the hands of the other/older ways of being that he has too often forgotten.[14]

While watching the dancers, Salvador's cousin Agustín tells him to be careful because "*They* [the performers] were ordered to even the score" (Córdova 2006, 61). Suffering from a blackout, Salvador does not remember his offense. In the following chapter, Salvador's friend Tomás reminds him that in a drunken stupor he interrupted Christmas Mass at Chimayó's Holy Family Catholic Church. In what can only be described as a Bakhtinian moment, he washed his face and combed his hair with holy water, and then spat in the font (67–70). Just as Padre Piedra was about to consecrate the Eucharist, Salvador grabbed the sacramental bread and wine and gorged on each in succession. He followed these acts with a tremendous fart and burp. Rendering his actions even more ridiculous, he told the Mass-goers that the "wine was 'exquisite'... 'charming'... 'an exceptional month!'" (69).

At Alcalde, just as the Abuelos disciplined wayward unruly children, Salvador must pay for his transgression by being symbolically castrated. The Abuelos and Matachín dancers descend upon him, and he becomes the Torito, the victim of their mock castration. Córdova narrates:

> The twelve angry masked men, the two demented tricksters, the castrated and bleeding little bull, the hordes—the mob—look down and jeer him, Flaco Salvador. His legs are angrily jerked by the Abuelos, and finally he is rolled on his back. He yelps like a puppy that's been kicked by a cruel, unforgiving master. (64)

In this way, the ritual dancers render the self-identified supermacho a eunuch.

In an earlier conversation with Ferrán at the Rock Bottom Bar, Salvador asks the elder about the Matachines: "*Esplain* to me ... those *pinche* masked ones. What are they?" (55). Ferrán replies, "Los Matachines are the laughter of God"; he elaborates: "The Matachines were created at the dawn of time to make men laugh: to make the insolent and arrogant less stubborn. More humble!" (55). The wardens of the dances, the Abuelos, we learn are "roguish pranksters" who pace like "hungry coyotes" among the Matachín dancers to ensure that their costumes are in order and make certain all is as it should be in their "insanity dance" (60). They also jeer and hurl sexual innuendos at the crowd, and carry long buckskin chicotes (whips) to enforce their brand of (dis)order. Córdova further states that they "resemble coyote tricksters from an age when the world was balanced differently" (60).

The Color of the Sun Comes in Many Colors

Years ago, I ran across an extremely disconcerting notebook entry by New Mexico curator Elizabeth Boyd about Córdova. The Philadelphia-born art curator was perhaps one of the most influential experts on New Mexican Spanish art. Indeed, her extensive writings on folk art, such as *Popular Arts of*

Spanish New Mexico (1974), went far to define Nuevomexicano cultural production in a Spanish rather than Mexican context, and elide both indigenous elements and Mexican continuity. Her vision leaves little conceptual space for Genízaro pasts and far less for a Genízaro present. In a note dated November 27, 1970, she records a conversation with an Abiquiú local about Córdova. She writes of the then young man, "[H]e is having a guilt complex thing about his heritage." She notes that his father, if from Abiquiú, never lived there and was instead educated in the largely Anglo and weapons lab–company town of Los Alamos. She notes that "all of his education has been books and not with the local people." While I find the envisioned effort of an Anglo curator to help Córdova recover from a supposed "guilt complex" disturbing and somewhat bizarre, I find that the entries do indicate that the anthropology graduate student in his late twenties was likely troubled and alienated. I suspect that Boyd would have had little to offer, to help Córdova heal. Moreover, her Spanish aesthetics may have been part of the cause of his pain. In his "The Genízaro," he states: "At this time in [the] history of the Genízaro, many Genízaros have aligned themselves to only one culture" (n.d.[a], 16). While some have chosen to be Indian, more have chosen to be "hispanos," and that is "unfortunate." He states that this is why so many "hispanos" are today so culturally confused.

Córdova found help in the guidance of an indigenous anthropologist of mixed ancestry. Upon obtaining his undergraduate degree at New Mexico Highlands University, Córdova wrote to University of Arizona anthropologist Edward P. Dozier. Dozier was an enrolled member of Santa Clara Pueblo and himself of mixed Pueblo and Anglo-American familial lines (Norcini 2007). Dozier helped Córdova to understand his own mixed condition:

> I went to study anthropology with him. From Dr. Dozier, who was a Pueblo Tewa from Santa Clara and who had lived only a few miles from Abiquiú, I learned that it was okay, that it was respectable, to be a Genízaro. In conversation with Dr. Dozier I sometimes suspected that he, too, was a Genízaro, which is why he was so sympathetic and encouraging to my work in this area. (Córdova n.d.[a], 12)

Córdova incorporated such a vision within his own teaching. He wrote in an unpublished letter about teaching at the University of New Mexico, Gallup:

> This and many other experiences have repeatedly forced me to learn and relearn that reality like the color of the sun comes in many colors. Sunlight,

when passed through a prism, clearly demonstrates that what may appear to the human eye as white, is in reality a rainbow or kaleidoscope of colors. In the history of history there are many realities, not just the White man's or the Conquistador's notion quashing the red savage as is so often portrayed in the standard textbook for the advancement of civilization. Likewise, Christianity is not the only religion that is satisfying to God. (2002)

For Boyd and likely some "Hispanos," Córdova's pain was incomprehensible. From the same pain emerged a deeper understanding. Genízaro power is founded in the indigenous experience that remains unarticulated in so-called Anglo, Spanish, or even mestizo ways of being.

You're a Healer, Heal Quickly

In a manner that is indicative of Genízaro experience, Córdova's *Big Dreams and Dark Secrets* follows two tracks. Salvador both wins his way into heaven in a retelling/inversion of the Christian narrative, and he must discover is own indigenous Genízaro center place. Córdova asserts that it is important to learn about Genízaros like Salvador because the majority of the so-called Hispanos in New Mexico come from a Genízaro descent. He warned his presumably Nuevomexicano reader that "you" may be a Genízaro and unaware of it (n.d.[a], 17).

Salvador is a Genízaro savior who always already carries the world and its subversion within him. In his talk and as I consider the novel's exit point, I hear his speech reach a crescendo that is simultaneously the conjuring a Genízaro future: "I am proud of being a Genízaro; and, with the help of God, I will do everything, everything, in my power to proclaim and expand my Genízaro conscientiousness" (n.d.[a], 20). Using the language of indigeneity, Córdova tells his audience:

> The day is coming soon, hermanos and hermanitas, when the great Genízaro people will come together to form a mighty and tremendous Genízaro nation and the children of these formerly tribeless people will walk in pride, knowing, and proclaiming to all what they are, "Genízaro! Genízaro!"

Before these final lines of this speech, he notes the Genízaro's apparent lack of written history and public culture even as he writes it. He, thus, tells the story of people even as he conjures them or us into existence.

In the last chapter of *Big Dreams and Dark Secrets*, Salvador wanders in the afterlife for seven days in an interstitial purgatory. On the seventh day, he meets the duende that has shadowed him throughout his life. The duende tells Salvador that he is the folkloric *pícaro* Pedro de Urdemalas himself. In the course of the conversation, Salvador comes to the realization that the duende/Urdemalas is at the same time Saint Peter, and all (the duende/Urdemalas/Saint Peter) transfigure into Chimayó priest Padre Piedra. In his Pedro apparition, this multifaceted figure guides Salvador by telling him that he, like Salvador, lived life in reverse and informs him of the "Law of Reverse Effects." Pedro then lists how Salvador's desires have almost always led him to acts that had the opposite of his desired intention. Following Pedro's directive, Salvador takes a step backward. By his third step, he hits his stride, turns, and flips a backward somersault. In his death and his understanding of the Law of Reverse Effects, Salvador comes to a transcendent understanding of the universe. Years earlier, in his application cover letter for tenure at the University of New Mexico, Gallup, Córdova described the manuscript that would become the novel: "My novel has to do with spiritual centering and reflects many of the issues that our students and community finds itself floundering through" (2002). In the completed text, Córdova writes: "Yes, in his final adiós, Salvador discovered the hearth of his spiritual center—his inner still-point—solitude and peace—a place of harmony and bliss, where he dreams eternity very much awake" (2006, 307).

Salvador's death, ninety pages prior, contains another resolution of equal significance. We learn that on her deathbed, Salvador's mother, María Guadalupe, explained his name (214). The word "salvador," she told her then seven-year-old son, means more than its English equivalent: "The name is Spanish, *sanador*: healer. A sanador mends. He makes whole" (214). Córdova adds that a sanador is more than a curandero because he liberates, aids the needy, and encourages the spiritually lame to walk in interior freedom (214). María Guadalupe wished the same for her son. "Hijo mío," she said with telling ambiguity, "You're a healer. Heal quickly" (214). Maria's son is a savior who must mend both others and himself. Ferrán offers a different but related view:

> Contesting María Guadalupe's Catholic notion of savior and sin, Ferrán tells Salvador that his name was of Greek origins rather than Spanish. He said, "It comes from *soter*, one who sows seeds in the Earth's womb." He tells Salvador

that, "At Chimayó we don't need to have to be redeemed from sin." Rather, Salvador is to teach the sick to exercise choice. (Córdova 2006, 14)

Similarly, in Salvador's own last hours on El Cerro de los Pedernales, he encounters another woman who pushes him toward assuming agency. As Salvador lies underneath the ocote where he will die, the tree becomes Spider-Woman, the indigenous goddess who taught Navajos how to weave. She tells him, "Hijo, hijo mío, you have misunderstood. If you tangle your yarn, your web will become a trap" (218–19). Determined to reach Salvador, she continues, "Hijo, hijo mío, you are not dependent on the weaver. *You are the weaver*" (218–19). María's son and Ferrán's wayward pupil and others like him are exhorted to become the *subject in* as well as *subject to* history. In this way, a Genízaro nation is born.

Notes

1. Córdova published an article titled "The Witches of Abiquiú" (1997b) in the popular journal *La Herencia de Norte* almost a decade prior to Ebright and Hendricks's publication of their book *The Witches of Abiquiú*.

2. Córdova's dissertation is a direct antecedent to Ebright and Hendricks's *The Witches of Abiquiú* and Bernardo Gallegos's *Postcolonial Indigenous Performances: Coyote Musings on Genízaros, Hybridity, Education, and Slavery* (2017). Historian James F. Brooks cites the dissertation in his highly praised *Captives and Cousins: Slavery, Kinship, and Community in the Southwest Borderlands* (2002). Perhaps most interestingly, the anthropologist Frances Leon Quintana (née Swadesh) acknowledges a great debt to Córdova's dissertation for his inclusion of key documents (Quintana 1991, 24). Her *Primeros Pobladores* (Swadesh 1974) and its revision as *Pobladores* (Quintana 1991) conceptualized northern New Mexico as a place where hybrid identities like Córdova's Genízaros are not a deviation but exemplary of a common condition.

3. G. Benito Córdova was born on October 10, 1943, in Dixon, New Mexico (Córdova n.d.[b]). He states that he was raised in Abiquiú, the Española Valley village of El Guache, the town of Española, and Los Alamos. In a biographical note in his résumé, Córdova states: "During my youthful states in Abiquiú, I loved with my aunt Natividad, who survived to a ripe age of one hundred and one years" (n.d.[b]). New Mexico deputy state historian Rob Martínez found records of Córdova's father and namesake Benito Córdova and grandfather Benito Córdova in US census documents without difficulty. The 1930 US Census records a forty-two-year-old Benito Córdova and his family, including a six-year-old son Benito Córdova, living in Abiquiú. The 1940 census records a now sixteen-year-old Benito Córdova living with his uncle José Martínez and aunt Natividad.

4. Córdova's "The Genízaro" (n.d.[a]) is written in a manner likely intended for the author's personal use. It contains numerous spelling and grammatical errors. It is also written in all capital letters and is thus nonstandard in style. I have edited my quotations of this unpublished manuscript for grammar, punctuation, and style.

5. Charles Carrillo states that while the term "Genízaro" was rarely used by Abiquiú's younger residents, elders would often describe their ancestors as "Genízaros" (1992, 12). He, however, concluded that most would emphasize Spanish ancestry at the expense of Native American ancestry (1992, 124).

6. El Cerro de los Pedernales is best known in the wider American national imagination through its representation in paintings by Georgia O'Keeffe.

7. For further discussion on this topic, see Karen Mary Dávalos (2008) and Edén Torres (2003).

8. One member of the Hispano Roundtable told Masco: "They didn't keep me poor and dumb and ignorant and now I'm saying I want more. I expect to be treated like anybody else that is working up here" (Masco 2006, 207).

9. Salvador also fails to satisfy another major measure of machista masculinity. While engaged in lovemaking with Blanca Flor, she tells him: "You . . . don't . . . you . . . don't satisfy me" (Córdova 2006, 135).

10. Córdova states that anthropologist and Santa Clara native Edward P. Dozier first taught him that it is acceptable to be a Genízaro (n.d.[a], 12).

11. The fictional Wilberto Ferrán's theory of Genízaro identity parallels the views of mestizaje articulated by Chicana feminist theorists such Gloria Anzaldúa (1987) and anthropologist Karen Mary Dávalos (2001). Dávalos writes: "We cannot consider mestiza/o experience from one perspective for it always originates from at least two places. Mestizaje is thus both an expression of affirmation and self-determination and a result of domination" (2001, 27).

12. In *Aztecas del Norte*, Jack Forbes makes the often-quoted claim that "Aztecas del norte . . . compose the largest single tribe or nation of Anishinabeg (Indians) in the United States today" (1973, 30).

13. "Abuelo" is a term of respect for wise elders, but, as Córdova tells us, Matachín Abuelos are wise with a difference. These Abuelos wear distorted buckskin masks. They are borderline senile, which explains why they appear like Coyote tricksters from a "different age" (2006, 60).

14. In a related passage from an earlier article, Córdova writes:

> There comes a time the student of culture must ask the difficult question, "What is the meaning of this comic opera?" Obviously, both the Hispanic and Indian communities look upon the *matachines* with a sense of wonderment, reverence, and awe. Both groups recognize that *matachines* fall into the domain of the holy, and sense that they function in the orb of the ancient sacred, a realm which the Western world seems to have forgotten. (1997a, 15)

References

Anzaldúa, Gloria. 1987. *Borderlands/La Frontera: The New Mestiza*. San Francisco: Aunt Lute Books.

Babcock-Abrahams, Barbara. 1975. "'A Tolerated Margin of Mess': The Trickster and His Tales Reconsidered." *Journal of the Folklore Institute* 11, no. 3 (March): 147–86.

Bakhtin, Mikhail. 1984. *Rabelais and His World*. Translated by Hélène Iswolsky. Bloomington: Indiana University Press.

Boyd, Elizabeth. 1974. *Popular Arts of Spanish New Mexico*. Santa Fe: Museum of New Mexico Press.

Brooks, James F. 2002. *Captives and Cousins: Slavery, Kinship, and Community in the Southwest Borderlands*. Chapel Hill: University of North Carolina Press.

Carrillo, Charles M. 1992. "Oral History-Ethnohistory of the Abiquiú Reservoir Area." In *History and Ethnohistory along the Rio Chama*, edited by Frank J. Wozniak, Meade F. Kemrer, and Charles M. Carrillo. Albuquerque: US Army Corps of Engineers.

Contreras, Sheila Marie. 2008. *Blood Lines: Myth, Indigenism, and Chicana/o Literature*. Austin: University of Texas Press.

Córdova, Gilberto Benito. n.d.(a). "The Genízaro." Unpublished manuscript in the possession of the author.

———. n.d.(b). Résumé of Dr. G. Benito Córdova. Unpublished manuscript in the possession of the author.

———. 1973. *Abiquiú and Don Cacahuate: A Folk History of a New Mexico Village*. Los Cerrillos, NM: San Marcos Press.

———. 1979. "Missionization and Hispanicization of Santo Thomas Apóstol de Abiquiú, 1750–1770." PhD diss., University of New Mexico.

———. 1990. *The 3½ Cultures of Española*. Albuquerque: Academia/El Norte Publications.

———. 1997a. "The Twelve Masked Apostles." *La Herencia del Norte* (Winter): 13–15.

———. 1997b. "The Witches of Abiquiú." *La Herencia del Norte* (Fall): 18–19.

———. 2002. "G. Benito Córdova To Whom It May Concern," November 1. Unpublished letter in the possession of the author.

———. 2006. *Big Dreams and Dark Secrets in Chimayó*. Albuquerque: University of New Mexico Press.

Dávalos, Karen Mary. 2001. *Exhibiting Mestizaje: Mexican (American) Museums in the Diaspora*. Albuquerque: University of New Mexico Press.

———. 2008. "Sin Vergüenza: Chicana Feminist Theorizing." *Feminist Studies* 34, nos. 1–2 (Spring–Summer): 151–71.

Ebright, Malcolm, and Rick Hendricks. 2006. *The Witches of Abiquiú: The Governor, the Priest, the Genízaro Indians, and the Devil.* Albuquerque: University of New Mexico Press.

Forbes, Jack. 1973. *Aztecas del Norte: The Chicanos of Aztlán.* Greenwich, CT: Fawcett.

Foucault, Michel. 1982. *The Archaeology of Knowledge and the Discourse on Language.* New York: Pantheon.

Gallegos, Bernardo. 2017. *Postcolonial Indigenous Performances: Coyote Musings on Genízaros, Hybridity, Education, and Slavery.* Rotterdam: Sense Publishers.

Gandert, Miguel A., Lucy Lippard, Chris Wilson, Enrique Lamadrid, and Ramón Gutiérrez. 2000. *Nuevo México Profundo: Rituals of an Indo-Hispano Homeland.* Santa Fe: Museum of New Mexico Press.

Gómez, Myrriah. 2014. "Nuclear Alienation: A Literary Analysis of Race, Space, and Resistance Surrounding the Nuclear Coloniality of Los Alamos, 1942–2012." PhD diss., University of Texas at San Antonio.

Hernández, Guillermo E. 1991. *Chicano Satire: A Study in Literary Culture.* Austin: University of Texas Press.

Hyde, Lewis. 1998. *Trickster Makes This World: Mischief, Myth, and Art.* New York: Farrar, Straus and Giroux.

Jung, Carl G. 1956. "On the Psychology of the Trickster Figure." In *The Trickster: A Study in American Indian Mythology,* by Paul Radin, 195–211. New York: Schocken Books.

Kosek, Jake. 2006. *Understories: The Political Life of Forests in Northern New Mexico.* Durham, NC: Duke University Press.

Lamadrid, Enrique R. 1995. "The Rogue's Progress: Journeys of the Pícaro from Oral Tradition to Contemporary Chicano Literature of New Mexico." *Melus* 20, no. 2 (Summer): 15–34.

———. 2000. "Abiquiú: Genízaros and the Price of Freedom." In *Nuevo México Profundo: Rituals of an Indo-Hispano Homeland,* by Miguel A. Gandert et al., 57–58. Santa Fe: Museum of New Mexico Press.

Masco, Joseph. 2006. *The Nuclear Borderlands: The Manhattan Project in Post–Cold War New Mexico.* Princeton, NJ: Princeton University Press.

Norcini, Marilyn. 2007. *Edward P. Dozier: The Paradox of the American Indian Anthropologist.* Tucson: University of Arizona Press.

Pacheco, Ana. 2004. "G. Benito Córdova." *La Herencia del Norte* 41 (Spring): 8–9.

Quintana, Frances Leon. 1991. *Pobladores: Hispanic Americans of the Ute Frontier.* Notre Dame, IN: University of Notre Dame Press.

Radin, Paul. 1956. *The Trickster: A Study in American Indian Mythology.* New York: Schocken Books.

Rodríguez, Sylvia. 1996. *The Matachines Dance: Ritual Symbolism and Interethnic Relations in the Upper Río Grande Valley.* Albuquerque: University of New Mexico Press.

Romero, Brenda Mae. 1993. "The Matachines Music and Dance in San Juan Pueblo and Alcalde, New Mexico: Contexts and Meanings." PhD diss., University of California, Los Angeles.

———. 2006. "Sound, Image, and Identity: The Matachines Dance across Borders." In *Transforming Images: New Mexican Santos In-Between Worlds*, edited by Claire Farago and Donna Pierce, 187–91. University Park: Penn State University Press.

———. 2007. "La Danza Matachines as New Mexico Heritage." In *Expressing New Mexico: Nuevomexicano Creativity, Ritual, and Memory*, edited by Phillip B. Gonzales, 61–83. Tucson: University of Arizona Press.

Spinks, C. W. 2001. "Trickster and Duality." In *Trickster and Ambivalence: Dance of Differentiation*, edited by C. W. Spinks, 7–19. Madison, WI: Atwood.

Swadesh, Frances Leon. 1974. *Los Primeros Pobladores: Hispanic Americans of the Ute Frontier*. Notre Dame, IN: University of Notre Dame Press.

Torres, Edén E. 2003. *Chicana without Apology/Chicana sin Vergüenza: The New Chicana Cultural Studies*. New York: Routledge.

Trujillo, Michael L. 2009. *Land of Disenchantment: Latina/o Identities and Transformations in Northern New Mexico*. Albuquerque: University of New Mexico Press.

CHAPTER TWELVE

Sangre de Indio que Corre en Mis Venas
Nativo Poetics and Nuevomexicano Identity

LEVI ROMERO

> Darker than most
> Lighter than others
> Moreno enough not to have
> Made it as an haciendado
> *"El Sol y Los de Abajo," José Montoya (1972)*

In the 1977 film *Águeda Martínez: Our People, Our Country*, the renowned weaver states: "I come from a people who are very old. I have Navajo grandparents on both sides" (Esparza 1977). Proclaiming their Native American heritage, like doña Águeda, is something that many Nuevomexicanos speak of with a sense of *orgullo*, a pride in their *herencia indígena*, their indigenous heritage. But the case has not always been as such. The identity of some Nuevomexicanos is based solely on Spanish heritage, continuing to propagate the myth of a pure European ancestry. The youth engaged in the Chicano movement, the *movimiento* of the 1960s, openly embraced their *mestizaje* and indigenous heritage in a manner that many of their *antepasados* had not. For many, to be *español* implied an upper-class social standing based on European descent. But for young Chicanas and Chicanos, the movement was a *concientización*, a coming to cultural and political consciousness, a recognition of pride in mestizo and indigenous heritage. Famed poet of the people Cleofes Vigil reflected on the melding of the two cultures. Much of his work celebrated the ancestral lineage of the Indio and the Nuevomexicano, one culture born of two through a sharing of language, foods, traditions, customs, and ritual and a mutual respect for *la tierra sagrada*. He reminded his audiences of the interrelationships that bore a new Indo-Hispano mestizaje:[1]

> Si va uno a la historia pa' atrás, de los primeros españoles que vinieron al Mundo Nuevo, no trajieron españolas, beautiful Spanish señoritas de la España (If one looks back to history, to the first Spaniards that came to the New World, they did not bring women, beautiful Spanish señoritas from Spain). They found beautiful Indian girls and they married Indian girls, and there is where this new race came from. (Lamadrid 1994, 34)

Vigil, ever the cultural troubadour and manito warrior, wrote a new *indita* for the 1976 Bicentennial to inform America what New Mexico was doing in 1776—negotiating a lasting peace with the Comanches. His "Himno de la nacioncita de la sangre de Cristo" is a love song to a new people, in the register of what Tomás Atencio called "Genízaro Consciousness" (1985, 16):

Vinieron los españoles	The Spanish came
de la España a esta tierra,	from Spain to this land,
donde hallaron sus querencias	where they found their heart's desire
y hermosas indias morenas.	and beautiful dark Indian women.
jeyá, jeyá, jeyá, ja . . .	heya, heya, heya, ha . . .
Aquellas indias hermosas,	Those beautiful Indian women,
virtuosos, llenas de gracia,	virtuous, full of grace,
escogieron para esposas	they chose as wives
donde nació linda raza,	and bore a handsome new race,
jeyá, jeyá, jeyá, ja . . .	heya, heya, heya, ha . . .
Raza buena y amorosa,	A good and loving race,
color bronce de mestizo,	bronze-colored mestizos,
mezcla del indio del pueblo	mixture of the Pueblo Indian
donde salió un genízaro.	from where the janissary came.
jeyá, jeyá, jeyá, ja . . .	heya, heya, heya, ha . . .
Con sus cantos penetrantes	With their penetrating songs
y sus cuadros espirituales,	and their spiritual paintings,
alaban la Santa Tierra	they praise the Holy Earth
que para todos es la madre.	who for all is the mother.
jeyá, jeyá, jeyá, ja . . .	heya, heya, heya, ha . . .
Ya se oía en los campos	In the countryside could be heard
aquel canto, aquella danza,	that song, that dance,

retumbaba en la montaña	echoing in the mountains
que Sangre de Cristo llamaban.	they called the Blood of Christ.
jeyá, jeyá, jeyá, ja . . .	heya, heya, heya, ha . . .
Españoles y cumanches	Spanish and Comanches
todos en armonía,	all in harmony,
se juntaban a cantar	would gather to sing
y a bailar con alegría,	and dance with gladness,
jeyá, jeyá, jeyá, ja . . .	heya, heya, heya, ha . . .
Comiendo elotes tostados	Eating roasted corn
que la tierra producía,	that the earth produced,
machucando carne seca	pounding dried meat
de cíbolo que había,	from the buffalo,
jeyá, jeyá, jeyá, ja . . .	heya, heya, heya, ha . . .
(Lamadrid 1994, 37–38)	

Traditional forms of song, music, and dance also depicted a bicultural assimilation. A newfound appreciation arose for traditional indita ballads and Indo-Hispano ritual dances like the Comanches, the Matachines, and the Nanillé (Lamadrid 2003). In contemporary music, 1970s hit songs on the radio such as "Sangre de Indio" (Ramírez 1970) proclaimed a lover's affection for his "indita querida" while also acknowledging his indigenous heritage.[2]

Sangre de indio	Indian blood
que corre en mis venas	that runs in my veins
como tinta que no ha de borrarse,	like indelible ink,
así son mis recuerdos de ti.	so are my memories of you.
Si supieras indita querida	If you knew, beloved Indian woman
lo que sufro por ti en esta vida,	what I suffer for you in this life,
si supieras lo mucho que te amo,	if you knew how much I love you,
que hasta lágrimas lloro por ti.	even tears I cry for you.
Esta sangre que corre en mis venas	This blood that runs in my veins
sangre de indio que te ama, que te ama,	Indian blood that loves you, loves you,
esta sangre que corre en mis venas	this blood that runs in my veins
sangre de indio que corre por ti.	Indian blood that runs for you.
(Ramírez 1970)	

This is, of course, ultimately a love song, but it also denotes a strong sense of cultural heritage emblematic of a mestizaje born and nurtured over hundreds of years through a symbiotic relationship between the Indio and the Hispano peoples. Ramírez's remembrance of the one he loves so dearly is undeniably as strong and enduring as the Indian blood that runs through his veins. Another hit song of the period made popular by the same artist, Tiny Morrie's "Mi Prieta Linda" also proclaims a lover's affection toward a dark-skinned girl. Not a light-skinned Spanish girl, but a *prieta linda* mestiza.

> Por ahi viene mi prieta linda
> es la dueña de mi querer,
> en mis ojos la miro preciosa
> como un lirio al amanecer.
>
> Estas soguillas de oro que traigo
> a mi prieta se las voy a dar,
> con el retrato de ella y el mío
> pa' que nunca me vaya a olvidar.
>
> Cuatrocientas cuidades anduve
> cuatrocientas más las andaré,
> pero amor como mi prieta linda
> nunca, nunca lo encontraré . . .
> (Sánchez 1971)

> There comes my lovely dark girl
> who is the owner of my love,
> in my eyes I see her so precious
> like an iris at the break of dawn.
>
> These golden cords that I bring
> to my dark one I will give,
> with the picture of her and me
> so that she'll never forget me.
>
> I traveled four hundred cities,
> four hundred more will I roam,
> but love like my lovely dark one
> never, never will I find . . .

Songs like these affirmed and celebrated the indigenous heritage of the Nuevomexicano, el Indio-Hispano, and the love and affection that he held for his *herencia y su sangre indígena*. These songs were not cultural testaments reproduced in scholarly journals by researchers and academics. They became part of the popular culture lexicon of the period expressing mestizaje through song, art, dance, *teatro*, film, and oral history documentation. Many periodicals and publications began to print materials that revealed a history that had been subjugated by mainstream print and other forms of media, including standardized education and curriculum at all levels. These attitudes and perspectives emerged with a determined conviction. One such publication was *Ceremony of Brotherhood: A Commemorative Anthology of the Pueblo Revolt* (1981), edited by Rudolfo Anaya and Simon Ortiz. In the book's introduction,

Anaya writes of the symbiotic relationship that was forged through initial conflict and turmoil but evolved into a harmonious coexistence:

> In that year of 1680 the land and the survival of a native culture were at stake, and those who would oppress sought to use these elements to turn the people against each other. But in spite of the tyrants, a group of people emerged who had the wisdom to create a new harmony from both world views. They learned to live together and to share the precious earth and water of the Río Grande Valley and the mountains of the Sangre de Cristo. These people were the farmers from both cultures, they were the seekers after peace and harmony, the common people of the land. Together they created a life which was a living example of the ideal that people from different cultures can live side by side in peace. They can learn from each other, they can share their ways, and they can create a better future. (1981, 2–3)

And, indeed, these two cultures created a model of coexistence that can serve as an example for cultures across the world today. The book's contributors consisted of more than seventy Native and Chicano writers and artists from New Mexico and other parts of the Southwest whose poetry, art, photography, essays, and oral history created a volume that brought together the two cultures to present, as Anaya expressed, a new harmony from both world views. Alfonso Ortiz's essay "The Pueblo Revolt of 1680: In Commemoration," in the same collection, captures the symbiotic nature of this coexistence and stresses those enduring connections:

> A final example of the kind of society we have in New Mexico, at least as regards Pueblo and Hispano peoples, is much more personal, but I feel it proper to relate here because it is itself a ceremony of brotherhood. On the last day of January 1975, my Tewa grandmother passed on after having just completed her ninety-first year of life. That night, at the beginning of the first rosary being recited for her in a mortuary in nearby Española, my grieving relatives and I looked up to see that a column of Hermanos were filing in along the central aisle between the benches and proceeding to kneel down by the rail near the casket. They had come to lead the prayers that night because they felt the passing of such an old and good friend and neighbor could not fail to be noted in this way by the Hermanos. Some of them had actually only known my grandfather, who passed on twenty-nine years earlier, but they felt they had to accord my grandmother the same respect they had accorded him. I should like to

believe, in any case, that these and other examples of cooperation, respect, and brotherhood which can be cited have occurred because Hispano and Pueblo peoples have long since become brothers and sisters and good neighbors who respect one another. Yet, this kind of story is never told by those who prefer to emphasize differences rather than similarities, barriers rather than bonds. (Anaya and Ortiz 1981, 16–17)

The works in *Ceremony of Brotherhood* are worthy of citing and sharing because they present a unique and rare account of the interrelations between Native and Indio-Hispano peoples as presented by members of both communities in an artistic and creative collaboration. Cleofes Vigil's verse comes to mind again:

Vinieron los españoles	The Spanish came
de la España a esta tierra	from Spain to this land
donde hallaron sus querencias	where they found their heart's desire
y hermosas indias morenas.	and beautiful dark Indian women.
jeyá, jeyá, jeyá, ja . . .	heya, heya, heya, ha . . .
(Lamadrid 1994, 37)	

Alejandro López's profoundly insightful oral history documentation also included in the *Ceremony* anthology. "Memorias de Mana Felipita" is an account by a woman from Arroyo Hondo, a town just a few miles from San Cristóbal, where Cleofes lived, sharing her village's ancestral history.

Muchos de estos [Indios] se quedaron en 'onde yo vivía en el Arroyo Hondo, se hicieron como los mejicanos. Estos indios se mezclaron con los mejicanos, ellos no se casaban, ellos se llevaban las mujeres que querían, No había, decía mi *agüelita*, padres, no había jueces; antes que entraran los españoles no había nada. Allí está una iglesia que se tardaron siete años haciéndola. Todavía está. Los indios vivían allí pero cuando pelearon, ellos se *rendieron*, se quedaron con los españoles y se hicieron mejicanos. Hay muchos indios, yo los conocí, pero allí se nombraron mejicanos porque nomas votaban y ya eran mejicanos. Ellos hablaban en español. Ya hay muy poca gente de sangre española pura y hay indios que tenían sangre española.

Su papa de mi *agüelito* vino de España, se llamaba Francisco Quintana. Él entró en esa conquista cuando pelearon allí en el Arroyo Hondo. *Antonces* él se casó con una nativa de allí, seguro que era india y de allí era mi *agüelito*. Yo tengo que tener sangre de indio también. Su mama era de Santa Fe. Aquí no sé cómo estaría la gente pero allá [en Arroyo Hondo] sí toda la gente estaba mezclada con indio y español.

Todos eran un solo pueblo. Estos indios que se fueron con los españoles se mezclaron y ellos ya no eran indios, eran mexicanos.[3]

Many of these [Indians] stayed over where I lived in Arroyo Hondo; they became like the [New] Mexicans. These Indians mixed with the [New] Mexicans, they didn't marry, they took the women that they wanted. There were no, what my grandma called, priests, no judges; before the Spanish came there was nothing. Over there is a church that they took seven years in making. It is still there. The Indians lived there but when they fought, they surrendered, they stayed with the Spanish and became [New] Mexicans. There are many Indians, I knew them, but there they called themselves [New] Mexicans because as soon as they voted they were [Mexicans]. They spoke in Spanish. There are now only few people of pure Spanish blood and there are Indians that had Spanish blood.

My grandfather's father came from Spain, he was named Francisco Quintana. He joined that conquest when they fought over there in Arroyo Hondo. Then he got married with a native from there, for sure she was Indian, and my grandfather was from there. I must have Indian blood too. His mother was from Santa Fe. I don't know about those people, but there [in Arroyo Hondo] the people were all mixed with Indian and Spanish

They were all one people. These Indians that went with the Spanish and mixed were no longer Indians, they were [New] Mexicans. (Anaya and Ortiz 1981, 60–61)

The "Estos Indios" that mana Felipita refers to are Hispanicized Indians, the Genízaros. It is the indigenous legacy that Cleofes sings about in "Himno de la Nacioncita":

Raza buena y amorosa,	A good and loving race,
color bronce de mestizo,	bronze-colored mestizos,
mezcla del indio del pueblo	mixture of the Pueblo Indian
donde salió un genízaro.	from where the janissary came.
jeyá, jeyá, jeyá, ja . . .	heya, heya, heya, ha . . .
(Lamadrid 1994, 38)	

Unlike many people who denied their indigenous ancestry, doña Águeda did not negate *nuestra sangre indígena*. She states: "Estamos al estilo indio. Ya sea que *séanos* mexicanos. Ya sea que *séanos* hispanos. Lo que quieran. Pero *semos* más indios" (We are of Indian lifestyle. Even though we are [New] Mexicans. Even though we are Hispanos. Whatever they want. But we are more Indian) (Esparza 1977). But finding pride, beauty, and relevance to personal identity in one's indigenous history has not always been for everyone. Personal accounts like this one, shared by a woman who recalls the shame surrounding a person's indigenous heritage, are not uncommon in some people's families: "My dad was always so proud of how fair and light skinned my mom was. She could pass for white. He saw that as like a badge of honor that he landed a light-skinned woman. My grandma on my dad's side once told me, 'Ay, mi 'jita, estuvieras tan linda si no estuvieras tan negra, que lástima' [Oh, my little daughter, you would be so beautiful if not for your dark complexion, how sad]." But the writers and artists of the movimiento period began to challenge these stereotypes. An intimate sense of Indio-Hispano consciousness began to emerge in their narratives, poetry, songs, and films. Nuevomexicano-born poet, painter, writer, and musician José Montoya, who lived and worked as a professor of art at California State University, Sacramento, was the founder of a group of artists known as the Royal Chicano Air Force. He was also a founding member of the musical group Trío Casindio (Almost Indian). Montoya was born and partly raised east of Albuquerque in the mountain village of Escabosa. The area has a strong historical connection to its indigenous past, and his upbringing amid the East Mountain communities' feast days, observed with Matachines and Comanche dances and other rituals, undoubtedly influenced his world view. Montoya's linguistic and cultural perspectives in his writing evoked Nuevomexicano colloquialisms. In his poem "Chicanos en Korea," Montoya questions the plight of the American soldier who upon his return home after having served his country in military duty is poorly treated because of his ethnicity. This type of cultural juxtaposition was prevalent and often a subject addressed in Montoya's and other Chicana/Chicano works that arose out of the Chicano movement.

Ay, Aztlán del Corazón	Oh, Aztlán of the Heart,
Tierra de mi gente	Land of my people,
Por qué nos tratan tan mal	Why do they treat us so bad
Como hijos desobedientes.	Like disobedient children.
Somos Indios Mexicanos,	We are Mexican Indians,
Sin embargo somos gente.	Nevertheless we are people

In many of his poems, Montoya celebrated hometown heroes and social misfits from within the Chicano barrios whose herencia indígena persisted through their personal and social proprieties. In his poem "El Tirilongo," Montoya again presents a portrait of a Chicano who defiantly expresses his indigeneity in spite of the social norms imposed upon him.

Le decían el Tirilongo	They called him Tirilongo,
Cholo Apache hijo del sol	Cholo Apache son of the sun.
Le gustaba borlotear	He liked to mix it up,
Le gustaba tamborear	He liked to drum,
Le gustaba ver el sol	He liked to see the sun
En el Sun Dance y en los Pow-Wows	In the Sun Dance and the Pow-Wows,
Danzas Azteca y el patín	Aztec Dances and the skate.
Al Tirilongo Tirili	They called this Tirilongo Tirili,
Le decian El Matachín.	They called him the Matachíne.

(Montoya 1992, 248–49)

Montoya's poem "Hispanic Nightlife at Lunas Café" magnifies the dilemma of almostindianness—the struggle or *joda* of being almost Indian. Casi-indio. Neither wholly accepted by the Indio nor celebrated by the Hispano. In this cultural stratum, the individual who claims his indigenous heritage struggles for acceptance and recognition but cannot find either beyond his own affirmation.

It is a well known fact	
That in the education we got	
From the Chicano movement	
We discovered, affirmed	
Confirmed and reaffirmed	
Our "Indianness"	
No sooner had our indigenismo[4]	(Indianness)
Emerged fuerte y sano	(strong and healthy)
From healing enjuagadas	rinses)
Cleansing and re-cleansing y más	(and more)
Que fue reviviendo la	(That it was revived the)
Consencia Europa—that same	(European consciousness)
Conquista attitude que	(Conquest . . . that)

Habéamos mandado a la madre	(We had sent to hell)
Con Cortez y los Malinchistas	(With Cortez and the traitors)
¡Pero la mera madre nos / los	(But in mother truth we / they were)
Rechazó!	(Rejected!)
So today the struggle within	
Our Mejicanidad es una	(Mexicanness)
Lucha Antigua entre lo Indio	(Ancient struggle between the Indian)
Y lo Europeo—and from	(And the European)
There the struggle / joda	(struggle)
Vacillates entre Chicano / Hispano	
Mejicano / Indio y hasta Latino	(and even Latino)
¡Eres tú, bruto!	(You are it, brute!)
¿Quo Vadis, Chicano?	(Where are you going?)
Me pregunta un cuate firme	(A firm dude asks me)
De Tepito	(From Tepito)
Y le digo al Chilango de	(And I tell the D. F. dude)
La capirucha, que that's what	(with the hood, that)
The Chicano needs to know	
In Tewa or Apache	
O hasta Azteca—a dilemma?	(Or even Aztec)
Tú dile, ma!	(You tell him, ma!)
So the lines are drawn	
And it's not an Apache	
Or even an imperious Aztec	
Or a Tewa or two against	
Some Moor in Spain from Africa	
Or Visgoth from up North.	
It is about those of us	
Who are neither from	
Mayan splendor nor Iberian	
Gypsy—We who didn't	
Make it whole almost,	
Casi-were not ni Moros	(Almost . . . nor)
Ni Negros, ni Blancos,	(Nor Blacks, nor Whites)
Somos más, Casi!	(We're more, Almost!)
So the Casis, then, are	(the Almosts)
The ones on the line—	

Casindios on one side	(Almost Indians)
Casispanos on the other	(Almost Hispanos)
Los Casindios in their struggle	(The Almost Indians)
Siguen al Masindio Masiso	(Follow the Firm MoreIndian)
Y su Masisa de maíz . . .	(And his Firmness from corn . . .)
(Montoya 1992, 232–33)	

So the Casis then are the ones, as Montoya's poem stresses, straddling the line. *Casi si, casi no.* Almost Indian, but not quite. The Xicanindio, as the iconic Chicano poet and Native rights activist raúlrsalinas (Raúl R. Salinas) self-identified, continued to exist on the margins, but with a reinvigorated and transformative conviction forged of the struggle for self-determination. This *nuevo* Mexicano identity reached back to its ancestral lineage as it moved forward with a raised fist, proclaiming "una mezcla del indio donde salió un genízaro" (a mixture with the Indian from where the janissary came).

The geographic distance to Mexico and the cultural, social, and political disjunctions from Spain and Western culture helped the *nuevomexicano del norte de más allá* create a stronger bond to his *nativo vecinos*. The spiritual reverence for the earth, Nuestra Madre Tierra, is a shared regard, although the ritual and ceremony might differ between the Native peoples and their mestizo neighbors. Tomás Atencio's beautiful and redolent contemplations on this shared love for *la tierra sagrada* is another *testimonio* captured in Tesoros del Espíritu:

> *Y creo que el pensamiento que tenía la gente indígena entonces los indios, era de que la tierra era sagrada. Entonces hacía este paisaje ser sagrado . . . La creencia en Chimayó, dígase, es el símbolo más importante porque es que la tierra es sagrada. Y todos creemos eso, y ese es el símbolo, ¿verdad? Y es indio, y es indio, pues indo-hispano, ¿verdad? porque los hispanos también lo creen. Pero en dónde es, en dónde está el sipapú ese de la tierra sagrada, en una capilla católica que es española, ¿verdad?*

> And I think that the philosophy that the indigenous people, the Indians, had was that the land was sacred. Then it made the landscape sacred. . . . The belief in Chimayó, you could say, is the most important symbol why the land is sacred. And we all believe that, and that is the symbol, right? Because the Hispanos also believe it. But where is that *sipapú* of sacred earth, in a Catholic chapel that is Spanish, right? (Lamadrid 1994, 40)

In the religious and spiritual practices of the Hermanos Penitentes, the Native influence in the rhythms and syncopations in many of the alabados, including the use of the *tombé* (Indian drum) and *pito* (flute), can be heard. In alabados to La Virgen de Guadalupe, the Indio pastor Juan Diego holds a significant and important role.

Se fue el Indio al mandado	The Indian went on his errand,
luego a la cuidad bajó.	then went down to the city.
Entró en casa del obispo	He entered the house of the bishop
y sus embajadas le dio.	and gave him his message.
O, Guadalupe dichosa,	Oh, fortunate Guadalupe,
de los Indios el consuelo,	of the Indians consolation,
Protectora Mejicana	Mexican Protectoress
y embajadora del Cielo.	and ambassador of Heaven.

(Hermandad de Nuestro Padre Jesús Nazareno)

In other religious practices and feast day celebrations, indita ballads and Matachines and Comanche dance rituals are still observed in many Indio-Hispano villages such as Ranchos de Taos, Abiquiú, and the Albuquerque East Mountain communities of Carnué, San Antonio, Chililí, and others. The December 16, 2017, ritual procession and Comanchitos dance was celebrated on the site of the former plaza of La Madera, a once populous village on the San Antonio de las Huertas land grant. A new generation of East Mountain men, women, and children have successfully revived traditions and customs that celebrate their indigenous heritage. Traditionally, the date is the first day of the Novena de Noche Buena, when Posadas processions and Comanchitos dances are held (Lamadrid 2003, 80–134). Nineteenth-century *ciboleros* (hunters) from these communities made every effort to be home by Christmas, when dances were celebrated in thanksgiving for their safe return and the bounty of the *carne seca* they brought with them. A traditional Hispano Comanche *arrullo* (lullaby) was sung, along with *versos* from the Comanchitos celebration and the "Indita de San Luis Gonzaga," which is accompanied with Native-style syllable singing and the steps of a sacred healing dance:

De mi casa he venido	From my house I have come
a pasear este lugar,	to visit this place,
denme razón de San Luis	let me know of Saint Aloysius

que le prometí bailar.	for I promised to dance for him.
Yana jeya jo,	Yana heya ho,
yana jeya jo,	yana heya ho,
yana jeya jo.	yana heya ho.
Yana jeya jo,	Yana heya ho,
yana jeya ho.	yana heya ho.
(Lamadrid 2002, 180)	

The complexity of claiming a Nuevomexicano indigenous heritage lies within the dark history of colonialism. To move forward, there must be a form of truth and reconciliation that does not quell previous conflicts with a self-induced glorification to claims of indigeneity without acknowledging the wrongs of the past. But we should also honor the symbiotic relationships that Alfonso Ortiz spoke about in his introduction to *Ceremony of Brotherhood*: "[E]xamples of cooperation, respect, and brotherhood which can be cited have occurred because Hispano and Pueblo peoples have long since become brothers and sisters and good neighbors who respect one another" (Anaya and Ortiz 1981, 17). The Indio-Hispano may not have been raised in the Indian way, but his heart beats with the rhythms of his ancestral past.

May the earth wind clouds
snow rain all plants
animals las estrellas el sol el cielo
Nuestra Señora la Virgen María
and the spirit of our antepasados
be a blessing upon us
as we journey forward.

Taos Nicho

¿tus santos y tus velas	(your saints and candles
qué me salvarán?	what, will they save me?)
sin la cruz	(without the cross
no hay gloria	there is no glory)
pero como dice mi Hermano Juan	(but as my Brother Juan says
todos quieren la gloria	everyone wants the glory
pero nadien quiere la cruz	but nobody wants the cross)
indigenous mother	
encased in the dead dust	

of permanence
how fast the world
goes us by
shadowy and flapping
like the clothes on the line
in the backyard
off a backroad
in Ranchos
the sky darkening
along the edge of the mountain
autumn storm clouds approaching
slowly
as if set and framed within
a landscape interpretation
of an oil or pastel
to what direction
should i cast out my prayers?
the sun comes up still
to the east
but my life is disoriented
my feet are fast and swift
but with no direction
no intent, other than
in the getting there
i feel like the Indian dancer
in the painting
whose head dress and plumes
are frozen
and whose gaze
has been blushed out
by a well applied
brush stroke
it is in the what
is not there
that one can find what is
on this day, *en este día*
el Día de La Asunción de Nuestra Señora   (the day of the Assumption of Our Lady)

i watched footage
of last summer's parade
on the local TV station
watched the young fiesta queen
white gloved and crowned
waving her hand
flicking her wrist
in perfect motion
to the crowd along
the procession
as they do
in events and places like Macy's
or Pasadena
and the young caballeros
in their stout horses
trailed behind
yelling through perfect teeth
¡Que Viva la Fiesta! (Long live the Fiesta!)
dressed as Conquistadores
wearing their new grown beards
and the latest style of sunglasses
and i thought of the Pueblo down road
and what its people
must feel for this
reenactment
and i am everything at that point
and nothing
for i feel joyous and celebratory
for we have endured
my people
mi raza (my race/people)
los manitos (northern New Mexico people/culture)
la huerfandad (orphanhood)
the orphaned ones
whom Spain abandoned
Mexico did not adopt
and the U.S. never wanted

and i feel the sorrow of the *Indio*
because of that
enduring
and my heart
if it could be captured
painted and displayed
exhibited in the finest gallery
where the locals do not enter
would be earthen, grayed
and splintered
a tinge of red perhaps
colors of
the wooden crosses
tilting in their final balance
in the *camposantos*   (holy ground—cemeteries)
among the ruins
of those first *iglesias*
destroyed in the Pueblo Revolt
of that not
so long
ago

(Romero 2008, 140–43)

Notes

1. Aural histories, music, and narratives on mestizaje in New Mexico were compiled by Enrique Lamadrid and recorded by Jack Loeffler in *Tesoros del Espíritu: A Portrait in Sound of Hispanic New Mexico* (1994). Cleofes Vigil is one of the key and most original voices in this discourse.

2. Amador Sánchez, known by his stage name Tiny Morrie, popularized "Sangre de Indio" in New Mexico, covering the song composed by Tejano singer and composer Agustín V. Ramírez. The theme of indigenous heritage continues to be popular in Mexico and the United States. Banda Machos and Jenni Rivera have recorded different songs with the same title.

3. The term *mexicano*, when used in New Mexico, refers to Nuevomexicanos. When used to reference Mexicans from Old Mexico, people say "mexicanos de México" for clarification.

4. Spanish words in the bilingual lines are translated in right-hand column.

5. In Puebloan theology, the *sipapú* is the passageway through which people emerged into the present world. It is represented by a small hole in the center of the *kiva* (subterranean chapel or meeting house).

References

Anaya, Rudolfo A., and Simon J. Ortiz, eds. 1981. *Ceremony of Brotherhood: A Commemorative Anthology of the Pueblo Revolt*. Albuquerque: Academia.

Atencio, Tomás. 1985. "The Old Town Liquor Dispute: Social Change and Conflict in New Mexico." Southwest Hispanic Research Institute Working Papers, no. 112. University of New Mexico, Albuquerque.

Esparza, Moctesuma, prod., and Esperanza Vásquez, dir. 1977. *Águeda Martínez: Our People, Our Country*. Los Angeles: National Latino Communications Center.

Lamadrid, Enrique. 1994. *Tesoros del Espíritu: A Portrait in Sound of Hispanic New Mexico*. With Jack Loeffler, recordist, and Miguel Gandert, photographer. Albuquerque: Academia/El Norte Publications.

———. 2002. "La Indita de San Luis Gonzaga: War with Spain, Faith, and Ethnic Relations in the Evolution of a New Mexican Religious Ballad." In *Recovering the U.S. Hispanic Literary Heritage*, vol. 4, edited by José Aranda Jr. and Silvio Torres-Saillant, 154–71. Houston: Arte Público.

———. 2003. *Hermanitos Comanchitos: Indo-Hispano Rituals of Captivity and Redemption*. Albuquerque: University of New Mexico Press.

Montoya, José. 1992. *In Formation: 20 Years of Joda*. San Jose, CA: Chusma House. Used with permission.

Ramírez, Agustín V. 1970. "Sangre de Indio." © San Antonio: San Antonio Music Publishing. Used with permission, translation by the author.

Romero, Levi. 2008. *A Poetry of Remembrance: New and Rejected Works*. Albuquerque: University of New Mexico Press.

Sánchez, Amador "Tiny Morrie." 1971. "Mi Prieta Linda." Words and music © Albuquerque: Striking Music Publishing LLC. Used with permission, translation by the author.

CHAPTER THIRTEEN

Genízaro Identity and DNA
The Helix of Our Native American Genetic History

MIGUEL A. TÓRREZ

Genetic testing for genealogical and anthropological research is an ever-growing science and a passionate pursuit for many Nuevomexicanos, from cultural historians to curious individuals and families interested in their hidden history. Genetic genealogy blends traditional genealogy with a scientific approach. The deep roots and migration patterns of population groups can be ascertained from Y-DNA (direct paternal) and mtDNA (direct maternal) testing. The genetic genealogy of New Mexico is the focus of this inquiry. The work is defined by a specific geographic region and timeline in history, and has been an ongoing effort for over ten years. DNA testing has answered many questions regarding family lineages such as surname links and distinctions among those who settled the upper Río Grande. In addition, it provides contemporary New Mexicans with a view into their genetic ancestry.

This population as well as those abroad with New Mexican genealogical connections are tracing their roots to the early colonial settlers who descended upon La Nueva México[1] during various waves of settlement in the sixteenth and seventeenth centuries. Notable among them are the families who came during the first colonization of the don Juan de Oñate expedition, and later, both returning and new families from the era of reconquest led by don Diego de Vargas. Accompanying these colonists were *indios mexicanos* (Mexican Indians), freemen as well as servants from central and northern New Spain. In succeeding centuries, indigenous peoples from various groups became an integral part of the *mestizaje*, which developed from a mixing of cultures and biological affiliations.

As noted throughout *Nación Genízara*, the classification of indigenous groups and their presence among the "Spanish" or "New Mexican" communities and households are what we seek to define and better appreciate. This pursuit is based on curiosity and longing for an understanding of our roots and our place in history, even more so as social issues concerning race take center stage in today's society. Some seek to distinguish categories of race, while others focus on equality and limiting racial division. Ironically, it is the classification of race that assists in DNA testing. As Kim TallBear states, "The historical constitution of continental spaces and concomitant grouping of humans into 'races' is the macro frame of reference for the human-genome-diversity researcher" (2013, 5). Social and cultural topics are magnified by DNA testing, which offers a mechanism for investigating origins and interrogating the identity that so many individuals seek.

Since around the turn of the twenty-first century, the commercial accessibility of DNA testing has opened a new avenue for genealogical research, which is widely profiled in social media, television, magazines, and advertising. DNA testing has become the tool of choice for those seeking a more intimate understanding of their identity. According to TallBear:

> For twenty-first-century researchers, including genealogists, indigenous DNA is part modern humans' inheritance and a mechanism through which whites can both claim continuity with an aboriginal past and produce knowledge that is ultimately of benefit to all humankind. DNA research and other forms of scientific knowledge production are the twenty-first-century civilizing and development project. (2013, 137–38)

The ability to understand our genealogical past from the perspective of genetic inheritance is awakening a suppressed mestizo/Genízaro identity among Nuevomexicanos and paving a way for a cultural emergence.

I, like many others, have answered the call for a more thorough understanding of who I am and where I come from through genetic genealogy. My interest in my cultural identity has led me to my current position as chair and administrator of the New Mexico Genealogical Society's DNA Project (NMGS DNA Project). During my genealogical and DNA consultation during the past decade, I have heard many accounts of why this quest to know our roots is important. I can attest that my personal experience and reasons echo those of many who seek knowledge of their cultural identity through genealogy and DNA.

Growing up in the 1980s when television, video games, and many other technological distractions were all-consuming, I had a grandfather who told stories of his youth in Chimayó, his World War II experiences, and so much more. His storytelling sessions were frequent in his home, no matter the time of day. The time to sit and listen was always "now." My grandfather, Juan Bautista Baca, was born in 1915 in Chimayó, a centuries-old community nestled in the Cañada de Santa Cruz. He gave me a perspective of a time and place much different from what I was experiencing in my youth. He recalled accompanying his father on a horse-drawn wagon to sell produce in distant villages such as Mora. He described how his family farmed as a way of life and survival. His experiences were so far removed from my understanding of life, they played like a movie in my mind, awakening a love of history for me.

Although I had the luxury to experience such stories, my knowledge of New Mexico's history, its people, place, and time, is due to my own personal search for identity. To write names on paper that displayed my ancestry was not enough for me. I wanted to experience their time and place through history, and to do so I needed to learn as much about New Mexico's past as possible. It was during my early twenties that I really began to reflect on my existence, reaching for a bigger purpose. Who was I? Where had I come from? What was it that made me who I am, and where do I want to go in life? To answer these questions, I sought to understand those who came before me. My quest for knowledge of my race, ethnicity, and identity was coupled with social issues regarding Mexican immigration that at that time were actively being discussed. I felt sympathetic to these issues but wasn't quite sure why. As I pondered this sympathy, I began to realize that I had something in common with the immigrants. Despite a common language origin and many common cultural aspects, we were still different. What did it mean to be Mexican versus New Mexican? Many of my elders said that they spoke Mexicano as opposed to Spanish, which complicated the matter even further. I was only then gaining an understanding of the complexity of race and culture, all the while learning that it was though our genetic and historical past that we were connected.

Sadly, the public education system's presentation of New Mexico history taught me very little about the real context and details of our history. The limited information in New Mexico history classes didn't prepare me to answer my own questions. I began to rely on family history and higher education to give me insight.

I grew up in a small community that was known historically as Los

Ranchitos de San Juan, or Los Ranchitos de Chinagos. It is situated on the north end of what is today known as Española, near the pueblo of Ohkay Owingeh (San Juan Pueblo). As a child, I built many friendships with my Native American neighbors that continue to the present. Many children from the pueblo of Santa Clara also attended the schools in Española, and thus I was lucky to have friends from both of these surrounding pueblos. Through these friendships, I was fortunate enough to share in their culture—feast days, back-road drives, late-night bonfires near the river, traveling up Santa Clara Canyon, camping trips—and also a little understanding of their language. For some unknown reason, they seemed more like kin than just friends. Their language and practices resonated within me and made me feel content, although it wasn't until later in life that I reflected on these feelings and connections. Many of the elders I grew up around distinguished between "us" (the Spanish) and "them" (the Native Americans). I learned about the early twentieth-century movement in New Mexico to suppress mestizo heritage for the betterment and advancement of its people in the eyes of Anglo America. By 1907, politicians, clergy, educators, and scholars, including Aurelio M. Espinosa, fueled and dramatized this notion:

> Nuevomexicanos possessed a language and folklore rich in Castilian archaisms that dated to the fifteenth and sixteenth centuries; Nuevomexicanos' geographic isolation, combined with their long occupation of the land and resistance to Indian linguistic and cultural influences, had perpetrated those archaisms; and while the Nuevomexicanos' Spanish contained few Indian elements, it had adopted many English words. (Nieto-Phillips 2004, 180)

I began to discover that many in my own family were invested in these ideas and had benefited from them. With a deeper understanding of the complexities of New Mexico history, I began to understand that it was the bond that weaves through us in our concealed genetic helix of DNA that made me feel comfortable among *mis vecinos indios* (my Native neighbors).

At this time of self-reflection, the positive changes in my life—marriage, children, and the exploration of self-identity—inspired me to pursue my genealogical research. My grandmother, Isabel Madrid-Baca, told me that her father mentioned that he had a Navajo grandmother in his lineage. Family lore also held that through our grandmother Adelina Medina's side, we had a connection to Picurís Pueblo. My great aunt, Amalia Medina, looked very Native American, and grandma Delfinia López was short, dark, and wore her hair in braids, much like the *tsa'yass* (elderly village grandmothers) I was familiar with in the Tewa pueblos.

In historical context, New Mexico's people are truly a blend of many different origins. Iberia, the land of our Spanish European roots, had been occupied by the Moors for over seven hundred years and was also home to the Sephardic Jews before they fled to North Africa and the Middle East during the Spanish Inquisition. There was also an earlier presence of northern European people who had a taste for conquest, such as the Visigoths and Vandals, among many others such as the Phoenicians and the Greeks. The Ibero-American intermixture of our ancestors occurred even before the first contact with Hernán Cortés and his armies during their invasion of Mexico in 1518. Iberian men then fathered the forthcoming generations with Native Mexican women, producing the first mestizo generations. The men who traveled to Mexico during the sixteenth and seventeenth centuries were of many backgrounds and cultures, and greatly diversified the gene pool. Many of these first-, second-, and third-generation mestizos became the colonial settlers of New Mexico, ancestors of the Nuevomexicanos.

Genealogical research has been a compelling and controversial topic for many years. In 2000, Family Tree DNA (FTDNA) began offering DNA tests to the public and gave birth to a new vogue for genetic genealogy. Other testing services followed, such as National Geographic's Genographic Project, with its emphasis on cultural geography, and 23andMe, whose data is compiled into databases on health and disease.

We should establish some fundamental definitions to help us understand an emerging discipline. Genetic genealogy is the application of genetic testing to paper-trail family trees. Y-DNA, mtDNA, and atDNA tests are the three common tests that can be taken. The first is gender specific, and has different objectives and correlations to ancestral lineages.

Y-DNA test: Since only males carry the Y chromosome, this test relates to a direct paternal lineage. The results can be compared to other males with the same surname. It can also link males to others with different surnames, to establish a link to a genetic population group with a common ancestral line, also known as a haplogroup. The male Y-DNA haplogroup can define a male's paternal racial or ethnic origins.

Mitochondrial DNA (mtDNA) test: Mitochondrial DNA is inherited by a son or daughter from a mother. Since males and females both inherit their mother's mtDNA, both males and females can test their direct maternal lineage. However, when men procreate, their children will inherit the mtDNA of their mother, and their own mtDNA is not passed on. A female will pass her mtDNA to her children, both sons and daughters, but it will only continue further through her daughters. Mitochondrial DNA will establish a haplogroup for the direct maternal lineage. The mtDNA haplogroup can also define a person's maternal racial or ethnic origins for both males and females.

Autosomal DNA (atDNA) test: This DNA is inherited from both the mother and the father, and gives a wider view of the genetic family tree. Autosomal DNA recombines as it is passed from a mother and father to a child, and thus it is unique to the individual. Due to the unique and random nature of inheritance, contributing DNA from a particular ancestor or ancestors may not reveal any particular ethnicities. That is to say, if we have a Native American ancestor in our recent past, such as a grandparent, we traditionally think that means that we are one-quarter Native American; however, atDNA may not reflect heritage as such. Autosomal DNA gives a personal perspective of ethnic percentages referenced to world population data. My atDNA indicates that I am 54% European, 31% New World (an accumulation of various Native American tribes over the centuries), 8% Middle Eastern, 3% Jewish diaspora, 1% South Central African, 1% West African, and 2% Siberian. These population groups can be further broken down into subcategories. Although we can learn a lot from an atDNA test, it is not representative of a person's entire past.

The combination of DNA results relative to specific branches and their association to a paper-trail genealogy is referred to as genetic genealogy. Traditional genealogical paper-trail research consists of constructing a pedigree that outlines or traces a person's ancestral lineages, starting from that person and working backward in time as far as possible. In traditional genealogy, investigating documents that name and confirm ancestors is key to continuing that ancestral line. There is a multitude of records one can research to accomplish this task: family, sacramental, civil, land, military, and many others. With a good idea of what genetic genealogy entails, let's define the goal of the New Mexico Genealogical Society's DNA Project.

The project's goals are to validate genealogies tracing back to their known origin in New Mexico using Y-DNA and mtDNA testing. Autosomal DNA is not used to accomplish these goals. As described above, atDNA is a tool that does not answer the questions related to specific lines but rather provides a personal experience of inherited ethnic percentages. Many of the test takers in our project do have atDNA results, so the analysis of their data will be presented in the context of percentage of ethnic inheritance among Nuevomexicanos.

To understand who the Nuevomexicano is, we need to understand who the people that settled New Mexico were. Settlements were established in different waves, sometimes in large groups and other times with smaller families, and groups came at different times. Tracing family lines to these settlers is often quite difficult. Some genealogies have paper-trail roadblocks. Some are traceable all the way back to the 1598 Oñate settlement, while others can only trace back to the *reconquista*, or the Mexican or territorial periods. Some lineages are also traceable to known Native American ancestors and are labeled as such in the historical record (Esquibel 1998; D. Snow 1998).

Y-DNA and mtDNA testing are tools that can help confirm or distinguish branches of the same surname and help to paper-trail roadblocks by possibly linking them to surname lineages or family branches confirmed by DNA to compare to the paper trail. The NMGS DNA Project requires that a participant submit a genealogy for the lineage tested, be it Y-DNA or mtDNA, or both. The project collaborates with well-known genealogists and volunteers who assist in researching and validating genealogies. The completed genealogies and their associated DNA results are reviewed to determine what the ancestral lines are telling us about their historical origin.

Nuevomexicanos in the context of this work are defined as persons who can trace either their direct paternal (Y-DNA) line, direct maternal (mtDNA) line, or the majority of their collateral lineages to colonial New Mexico (1598–1821). This era begins with the first settlement of New Mexico in 1598 with the Oñate expedition and ends with Mexican independence from Spain in 1821. A person who can trace both paternal and maternal lineages to colonial New Mexico or any of the periods mentioned above is defined as a classic Nuevomexicano. This does not exclude those whose family tree is only partially traceable to colonial New Mexico, but it does place them in subcategories when analyzing atDNA. For Y-DNA (direct paternal) or mtDNA (direct maternal), the lineage must trace to colonial New Mexico to qualify for project membership.

New Mexico genealogical research is an ongoing process, and no person has a 100 percent complete family tree on all branches, since not all family lines that trace to colonial New Mexico have been genetically tested. We can only analyze the data we have to date. But since the pursuit of genetic genealogy continues to expand, the potential for continued success exists.

Data Section

The data presented is representative of NMGS DNA Project participants and was compiled in September 2017. Similar data is found in the New Mexico DNA Project, which is another DNA project related to the geography of colonial New Mexico. Many of the NMGS DNA Project participants also belong to the New Mexico DNA Project, and thus much of the data is overlapping.

Figures 13.1 and 13.2 represent the distribution of mtDNA haplogroups for participants in the NMGS DNA Project. MtDNA haplogroups, A, B, C, D, and X are known haplogroups found among Native Americans. As detailed in table 13.2, each haplogroup contains subgroups, and in most cases the subgroups are a result of more precise levels of testing, which may range and vary among participants. Higher-level testing refines or narrows a position on the phylogenetic tree. Among Nuevomexicanos, it can be stated with relative confidence that mtDNA resulting in haplogroups, A, B, C, D, or X have an extremely high probability of descent from a Native American foremother. Haplogroup designations to tribal affiliations are not well established due to the limits of control region sequencing as well as the historical fluidity of Native American tribes, and the absorption and amalgamation between

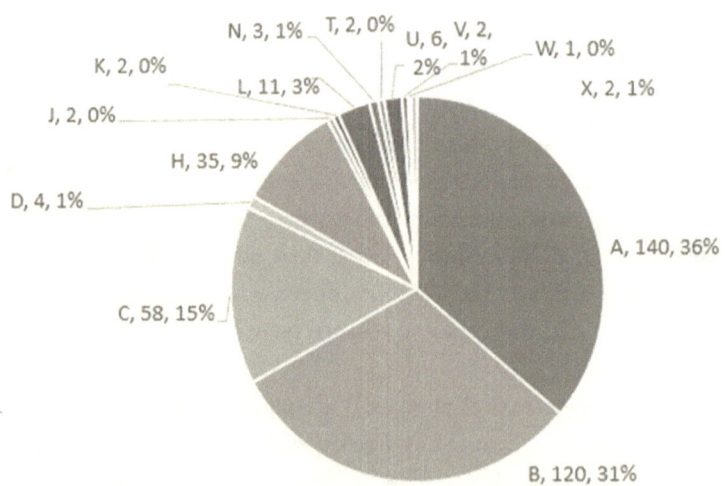

FIGURE 13.1 MtDNA haplogroup distributions in New Mexico genetic genealogy. Courtesy of the NMGS DNA Project.

SNP	Cnt	SNP	Cnt	SNP	Cnt	SNP	Cnt	SNP	Cnt
SNP	Cnt	A2v1-T152C!!!	6	B2x	1	H1c1a	1	L3e2b	1
A	73	A2w	1	B2y1	4	H1j	1	L3f	1
A2	6	B	2	B4'5	57	H24	1	M	1
A2a	3	B2	10	C	28	H2a1	5	N9a	1
A2a4	1	B2a	3	C1b	3	H3aa	1	T1a1	1
A2a5	1	B2a1	3	C1b11	16	H3c2a	2	T2b21	1
A2c	1	B2a1a	4	C1c	4	H5a3a	1	U3	1
A2d1a	1	B2a1b	4	C1c1b	1	H5g	2	U3a1	1
A2e	2	B2a2	18	C1c5	1	H82	4	U4	1
A2g	1	B2a4a	2	C1c6	1	H8c	1	U5a1a1	1
A2g1	6	B2a5	1	C1c7	1	J	2	U5a2-T16362C	1
A2-G153A!	5	B2b	1	C1c-T195C!	1	K	2	U5b1b1a1a	1
A2h1	20	B2c	1	C4c2	2	K1b2a	1	V	1
A2j	1	B2-C16278T!	2	D	1	L1c2	1	V7	1
A2n	1	B2c2a	1	D1c	1	L1c2b1a1	1	W1g	1
A2q1	4	B2f	1	D1i2	2	L2a	4	X2a1b	2
A2v	1	B2g1	1	H	14	L2a1b1	1	Grand Total	388
A2v1	1	B2o	3	H10e	1	L2b	1		
A2v1b	5	B2t	1	H1a1	1	L2b1a	1		

FIGURE 13.2 MtDNA SNP (single nucleotide polymorphism), also known as a "snip," is a location where a chemical at an individual ladder rung has mutated. This allows for a timeline for the variations among the haplogroup mutations. Depicted are the distributions in New Mexico genetic genealogy. Courtesy of the NMGS DNA Project.

different tribal groups. Among New Mexico cases, the correlation of haplogroup association is done by comparing genealogies of family lines with known tribal connections. NMGS DNA Project data demonstrates that the three largest haplogroups found in New Mexico mtDNA are A, B, and C. Haplogroups D and X occur at 1 percent frequency. MtDNA research conducted among North American and Mesoamerican population groups has provided haplogroup frequencies between the two regions that can be used to perform comparative analysis. Samples from the American Southwest have shown high levels of haplogroup B and moderate levels of haplogroup C, with haplogroups A, D, and X occurring at lower frequencies. Frequencies among Mesoamerican populations show similar trends; however, haplogroup A appears at a higher frequency than does haplogroup B. This comparative analysis suggests that the two regional areas have differing population histories

(M. Snow, Durand, and Smith 2010, 3). Further scholarly research on mtDNA, and the work of New Mexico genetic genealogy, will advance our understanding of associations between mtDNA haplogroups and tribal groups.

The genealogical trail of an individual's maternal line, together with an analysis of that person's mtDNA matches, can support or redirect the possible origins of the given mtDNA lineage. The 1824 marriage record of María Miquela Quintana (Christmas and Sánchez Rau 2002, 143) is an example of how a genealogy and mtDNA lineage work together in understanding haplogroup origins. In this case, if an mtDNA sample is taken from a direct female descendant of Quintana, originally defined as an Indian of the Ute Nation, we would gather insight on a Native American tribal group and its correlation to an mtDNA haplogroup designation. Genealogical research indicates that there are many families with roots to Miquela still living in Santa Cruz de la Cañada, and thus a connection to Ute history exists among them.

A higher-profile mtDNA example is that of María de la Cruz, wife of Juan Pérez de Bustillo. Bustillo was an Oñate-period settler, and his lineage traces to seventeenth-century Mexico City. There are over one hundred matching mtDNA samples with a direct link to María de la Cruz. A mapping of their genealogies has provided a solid analysis of her mtDNA haplogroup A. Some within the match list can be further categorized into subgroup A2h1. The defining of Cruz's mtDNA sequence and haplogroup gives us insight into a Native American female ancestor of seventeenth-century Mexico.

María Magdalena Leyba (fig. 13.3) and Amelia George (fig. 13.4) are ancestors of two individuals with matching mtDNA, among a larger group of Nuevomexicanos matching the same B2 mtDNA haplogroup sequence. María Magdalena Leyba was born in 1927 in Truchas, New Mexico. Her direct mtDNA lineage traces back to María Bárbara Anaya of Santa Fe, born around the 1750s–1760s. Amelia George, born circa 1888 at Red Valley, New Mexico, was raised among the Navajo, specifically the Kinlichiinii, Red House Clan. Family oral history recalls that Amelia was the daughter of a Pueblo or Hopi woman by the name of Lady Redhouse. A genealogical connection between these two women and those who match their mtDNA sequence is being investigated. Many of these matches show roots to Abiquiú and Santa Cruz de la Cañada. From these historical connections, we hypothesize that the link among this sequence is the Tano tribe. The history and movement of the Tano people are consistent with the migration of the ancestors in question.

The mtDNA perspective that New Mexico's genetic genealogy provides

FIGURE 13.3 María Magdalena Leyba.
Courtesy of Daniel D. Romero.

FIGURE 13.4 Amelia George.
Courtesy of Mr. Francis

allows a large percentage of the state's population a glimpse of their Native American foremothers. New Mexico's genetic genealogy is continually uncovering and validating these types of histories.

Y-DNA haplogroups Q and C are known Native American groups and contain SNP subgroups. Most New Mexico cases that result in haplogroups Q or C are of Native American origin; typical subgroups are Q-M3, Q-M242, and C-P39. Within these subgroups are the further refined C-M216, C-M217, and C-Z30747, to name a few. These refinements are typically accomplished by additional SNP testing. Some of the subgroups developed prior to migration from Europe and Asia. In a Y-DNA study that investigated the origin of Native American paternal lineages, researchers reported: "According to our present data, the Native American population system had two major founding haplogroups (Q = 76.4% ; C = 5.8%), which together account for 82.2% of the 588 Native American Y chromosomes in this study" (Zegura et al. 2004, 170). The remainder fell under the European haplogroup R and was reported to likely be the result of admixture in recent times. Figure 13.5 shows that haplogroup Q occurs in 10 percent of the samples and haplogroup C in 1 percent of the samples in the NMGS DNA Project. Subgroup occurrence

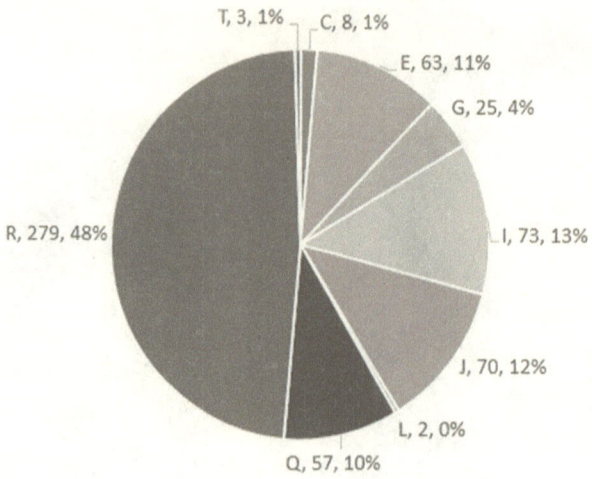

FIGURE 13.5 Y-DNA haplogroup distributions in New Mexico genetic genealogy. Courtesy of the NMGS DNA Project.

SNP	Cnt	SNP	Cnt	SNP	Cnt	SNP	Cnt
		G-Z726	1	J-M67	1	R-M513	1
C-M216	2	I-A7134	1	J-PF7415	1	R-M173	1
C-M217	2	I-BY13531	1	J-Z467	1	R-M198	3
C-P39	3	I-BY13534	1	J-ZS1682	1	R-M222	1
C-Z30747	1	I-BY138	1	L-M20	2	R-M269	240
E-BY6865	1	I-M170	1	Q-L766	1	R-M512	1
E-L117	26	I-M223	8	Q-M242	21	R-P25	2
E-M183	2	I-M253	41	Q-M3	21	R-P312	4
E-M2	2	I-M423	1	Q-M902	7	R-SRY2627	2
E-M35	27	I-P37	15	Q-Y4276	1	R-Y14468	2
E-PF2546	1	I-S2078	2	Q-YP1095	1	R-Z253	1
E-V12	1	I-Z63	1	Q-YP1107	1	R-Z279	4
E-V13	1	J-CTS1460	1	Q-Z780	4	R-Z283	1
E-V22	1	J-FGC15865	1	R-BY770	1	R-Z381	1
E-Z5013	1	J-L243	1	R-CTS9053	1	R-Z49	2
G-L13	2	J-L70	1	R-DF27	3	R-ZZ12_1	1
G-L78	1	J-L823	1	R-DF83	1	T-CTS6280	1
G-M201	19	J-M172	38	R-L1	1	T-M70	1
G-P15	1	J-M241	1	R-L2	1	T-Y3782	1
G-Z40548	1	J-M267	22	R-L21	4	Grand Total	580

FIGURE 13.6 Y-DNA SNP distributions in New Mexico genetic genealogy. Courtesy of the NMGS DNA Project.

can be tabulated from figure 13.6. When a sample results in these haplogroups, Family Tree DNA (FTDNA) connects the sequence to known SNPs within their database and confirms whether or not the results are of Native American origin. As an example, subgroup Q-M3 is defined as strictly found in American Indian populations, but Q-M242 is found among many Native American populations as well as some Middle Eastern and European populations. FTDNA indicates that among the European populations, Q-M242 is mostly found in northern Eurasia and Scandinavia. Additional SNPs from Q-M242 results may be required to distinguish between Native American and non–Native American origins. In my experience with Q-M242 results, I have only had one case in which a Q-M242 result needed extensive SNP clarification to distinguish between European and Native American origin. In that case, several of the matches had eastern European surnames, but it was only when the sample was upgraded to the Big Y test, which tests for all known SNPs of a given haplogroup, that the Q-YP1095 haplogroup designation was confirmed, establishing a Middle Eastern origin. Comparative genealogies and geographical origins among matches provide clues to determine Native American origin. Those with confirmed Native American origin or oral histories of Native American ancestors have been crucial in establishing Y-DNA sequence origins. In New Mexican cases, many confirmations have resulted from Genízaro paper trails.

A notable example of a Y-DNA study confirming a New Mexican family lineage with direct Native American paternal descent is that of the Espinosa/Espinoza family, tracing back to colonial settler Nicolás de Espinosa. Nicolás was listed in the 1695 muster roll of the Juan Páez Hurtado expedition as a Coyote (offspring of a mestizo and an Indian) and native of Los Lagos, Mexico. Later sacramental records identify him as a mestizo. Y-DNA results for a cluster of contemporary Espinosa/Espinoza families tracing their genealogy to Nicolás result in haplogroup Q-M3, positive of the Q-L663 branch. Among the matches of these samples are men who still live in northern central Mexico or men whose recent ancestry traces to northern central Mexico. A geographic origin analysis of the sample set of these matches indicates that all had historical connections to regions within an approximate thousand-mile radius of Zacatecas, suggesting that the matches all descend from a common tribal group. Many contemporary New Mexicans have a genealogical connection to Nicolás, and via this study we have defined a Mesoamerican Native contribution to our genetic inheritance.

A case study on the Juan Felipe García lineage yielded a paternal link to a Native American origin. Haplogroup frequencies studies such as that by Stephen L. Zegura and colleagues (2004) show a high frequency of haplogroup C among Apache populations. A Big Y DNA test was conducted for Juan Felipe's great-grandson, resulting in C-Z30747. This García lineage ends at Juan Felipe, who was born around 1820. His father has yet to be uncovered in the historical record. His marriage record to Martína Archuleta indicates that his mother was Ana María de los Reyes Gallegos, and in some records she is listed as Ana María de los Reyes García. Juan Felipe's marriage record also indicates that he was from Santa Cruz, but by 1850 he was living in the San Ildefonso Pueblo area. During initial investigation of his origin, researchers assumed that he was from Santa Cruz de la Cañada, but Y-DNA matches to a family with origins in Ojo Caliente, New Mexico (traditionally known as Santa Cruz de Ojo Caliente) indicate that he may actually have migrated from Ojo Caliente rather than Santa Cruz de la Cañada. Although his paternal genealogy ends with his generation, his Y-DNA gives us insight into his paternal origin. As previously stated, the García Y-DNA resulted in Y-DNA haplogroup C-Z30747, a confirmed Native American haplogroup. Prior to obtaining the Big Y results, researchers confirmed his haplogroup as C-P39. Shortly after receiving the results, they added the sample to the C-P39 FTDNA Haplogroup Project, administered by Marie Rundquist, Roberta Estes, and David Pike. The C-P39 project funded the Big Y DNA test, and the outcome was a new subgroup, C-Z30747. Among the García Y-DNA matches are a group of men who do not have a history linked to colonial New Mexico but who show geographical histories in Appalachia and Canada (Estes and Rundquist 2017). Amazing and new discoveries are continually being made by the C-P39 Project. News and updates can be found at the FTDNA C-P39 Project web page.[2] The Juan Felipe García case is another example of how Y-DNA is uncovering histories that had previously been lost.

MtDNA results indicate that 84 percent of Nuevomexicano samples result in Native American haplogroups, and 11 percent of Y-DNA samples. When referenced to a traditional genealogy, we get an indication of what contributes to Nuevomexicano atDNA. Analyzing atDNA statistical data for participants in New Mexican genetic genealogy is not as straightforward as Y-DNA and mtDNA. As described earlier, atDNA reflects the unique inheritance of each individual. AtDNA samples within New Mexican genetic genealogy indicate that the average percentage of Native American genetic inheritance

FIGURE 13.7 *left* Juan Felipe García, born July 1, 1907. Courtesy of Robert F. García Sr.
FIGURE 13.8 *right* Juan Felipe García, later in life. Courtesy of Robert F. García Sr.

among classic Nuevomexicanos is 32 percent. There are outliers above and below these ranges. An analysis of the genealogies of these outliers indicates that those under the average have lineages in which there is pedigree collapse or a relatively small number of distinct ancestors, or that some of the family branches do not trace back to colonial New Mexico. In cases near or above the average, researchers have observed that genealogies for these samples have a higher occurrence of family branches validated by other testers resulting in Y-DNA haplogroups Q or C. In addition, many of the individuals above the 32 percent range have genealogies showing geographical histories related to known Genízaro communities or areas in close proximity to them.

In analyzing what atDNA is telling us about Native American genetic inheritance contributions, we rely on what we already know about those who settled colonial New Mexico. As discussed in earlier chapters, Native American auxiliaries played major roles in the settlement of New Mexico, as demonstrated by the examples of María de la Cruz and Nicolás de Espinosa. However, the most impactful contributions came from the incorporation of detribalized Native Americans into New Mexican society households. These people were integral members of family units and became ancestors of Nuevomexicanos. Indio, Genízaro, *color quebrado* (broken color), Coyote, mestizo, and *lobo* (wolf or quarter-breed) were some of the common classifications for them.

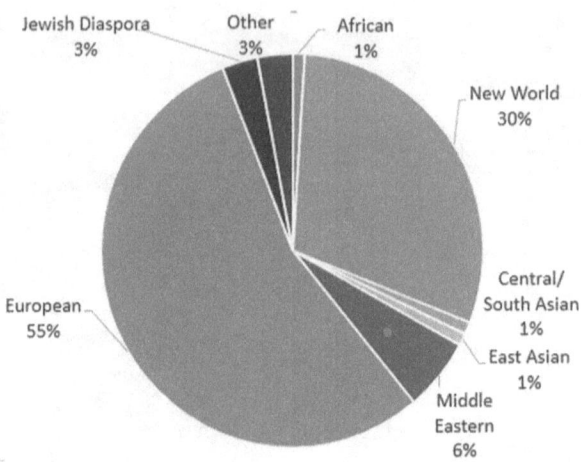

FIGURE 13.9 The charts represent a sample set of fifty randomly chosen participants with atDNA results that can be defined as classic Nuevomexicano. "New World" indicates native to the Americas. The "East Asian" and "Central/South Asian" categories contain population data found among Native Americans. Also included are other world population categories. Due to the isolation of New Mexican people since around 1600, we can assume that any East Asian or Central/South Asian percentage is also inherited from Native American, such as Athabascan, groups. The sum of these three categories equals the average. Courtesy of the NMGS DNA Project.

Oral histories tell us about these ancestors, and historical records support their stories. Supporting documents are found within Catholic sacramental records in the Archives of the Archdiocese of Santa Fe. Most if not all are on microfilm, and many have been extracted and translated into books published by genealogical centers and societies such as the Hispanic Genealogical Research Center and the New Mexico Genealogical Society.

Below are some extracted and translated records from various regions in New Mexico. They show the use of social classifications and how these were distributed across time and place.[3]

1772, Nov. 29 (no. 43), Belén. Juan García (20), español, son of Toribio García and Antonia Teresa Gutiérrez, deceased, and Juana María Andrea Baca (25), d. of Domingo Baca and Juana Chaves, deceased.—Witnesses: Julian Sánchez, notary; Felipe Silva (80), Tomás Chaves (40). Declaration made that the groom's maternal grandmother, Antonia, the daughter of Catarina, was an

Isleta Indian who wore the mantas of the pueblo when she married Juan Gutiérrez, español of Bernalillo, on April 14, 1728. (Chávez 1983, 4:601)

1776, May 18 (no. 17), Belén. Juan Simón Silva (24), genízaro, son of Francisco Silva and Petra Chaves, deceased, and María Ursula Gonzales (20), d. of Antonio Gonzales and Juana María Jaramillo.—Witnesses: Cristóbal María Larrañaga, notary; Juan Crisóstomo Urribalí (36 plus), Pedro Ignacio Barreras (36 plus). (Chávez 1983, 10:1830)

1776, Sept. 25 (no. 8), Belén. Vicente Rael de Aguilar (50), widower, indio genízaro of the Guampe Nation, and María Joséfa García, widow.—Witnesses: Don José Marcelo Gallegos, notary at El Puesto de N. Sra. de Guadalupe; Miguel Barreras (50), Pedro García (40 plus), Gerónimo Martín Silva (39) of Belén, Antonio Tiburcio García (50). (Chávez 1983, 8:1527)

1788, May 21—José Torres, genízaro, single, nat. s/ Rita Torres genízara, & unknown father, m. Ma. De la Luz Mestas, single, d/ Manuel Mestas & Micaela Mestas, genízaros, all of la plaza de la Purísima Concepción of this jurisdiction. Wit: Nicolás Mestas, Antonio Naranjo, and Mariano Truxillo. (Arellanes, Baca, and Windham 1998, 78)

Rivera, Manuel Rafael, Genízaro, baptized 20 Nov. 1779, born 11 day of said month and year; s/ Diego (n.s.), native de San Yldefonso, & Josefa Rivera of the villa of Santa Fe; god mother/María Antonia Mirabal, single, citizen of this pueblo; witnesses/Juaquín Aragón & Juan Domingo. (Baca et al. 2004, 33)

Today the 30th of January of 1891, in the Church of San José in Parkview, I married and veiled Antonio Mestas {XE "Mestas: Antonio"} (Navajo), single adoptive son of Juan Pablo Mestas with Cruz Martínez {XE Martínez Cruz} widow of Urban Mutos. Witnesses, Jesús Molina and Guadalupe Durán. (Padilla y Baca 2004, 33)

In this Church of San Juan on the 14th of January of 1875, I joined in matrimony José Antonio Aragón {XE "Aragón: Antonio"} Indian from San Rafael, single, raised by Vicente Aragón and María Teodora Sisneros with Marina Biareal {XE "Biareal: Marina"} from San Antonio, single, legitimate daughter of Facio Biareal and of María Soledad Salazar. Padrinos, Jésus Ruival and Petra Advinula Aragón. (Padilla y Baca 2002, 48)

Martínez, José Federico, of Abiquiú. Bap on 15 Jun 1876. Between 18 and 20 years old Indio of the Ute Tribe, servant of Cruz Martín. Pads: Juan Andrés Martínez y María Dionides Quintana. Page 61 (Off: Ramón Medina). (Padilla y Baca 1998, 29)

Valdez, Marcelina, of Tierra Azul. Bap on 27 Aug 1877. Adult female of about 25 years of age, una India Navajosa, servant of José Isabel Martín y Catalina Chávez. Pads: Francisco Valdez y Soledad Martín. Page 8 (Off: Ramón Medina). (Padilla y Baca 1998, 39)

In this Church of Abiquiú, today the 28th of November of 1878, I married and veiled Melitón Montaño {XE Montaño: Meliton"} Indian, raised by the Priest Father Salazar with María Dolores Montoya {XE "Montoya: Maria Dolores} single, legitimate daughter of Juan Montoya and of Rafaela Abeytia. Witnesses, Francisco Trugio and Justo Martín. (Padilla y Baca 2003, 38)

In this Church of Abiquiú, today the 7th of October of 1881, I married and veiled José Antonio Vigil {XE "Vigil: Jose Antonio} Navajo raised by Ricardo Vigil and Dolores Vallejos with María Dolores Roybal {XE "Roybal: Maria Dolores"} single, legitimate daughter of Juan Roybal and of Nicolasa Vallejos. Witnesses, Nicanor Via and Benito Sánchez. (Padilla y Baca 2003, 41)

November 18, 1785, 4th degree consanguinity on an equal line for which they were dispensed as they complied with the requirements, Luis Archuleta, Indian, s/ María Guadalupe (n.s.), Indian from this parish, with Francisca de la Luz Montoya, d/ Juan José Montoya and Luisa Vegil, españoles from this parish, Wit: Joaquin Valencia and José Valencia, españoles from this parish. (Christmas and Sánchez Rau 2002, 53)

The sample set of caste identifications in the above records is a small fraction of what can be found among sacramental records. The written history of how Native Americans became incorporated into New Mexican households and social networks is supported by genetic genealogy. When the historical record is referenced with DNA evidence and investigated simultaneously, it becomes apparent that contemporary Nuevomexicanos have diverse backgrounds, including a significant Native American inheritance.

While ethnic DNA testing is growing in popularity, it has also come under critical scrutiny by scholars such as Kim TallBear, author of *Native American DNA: Tribal Belonging and the False Promise of Genetic Science*, in which she argues that DNA testing cannot prove tribal affinity because that is solely a cultural process. TallBear states: "Without ethnography, what indigenous peoples' own transitions from blood to DNA talk mean for indigenous ontologies or for citizenship practices is difficult to pin down" (2013, 9).

I also agree and would argue that genetic testing alone does not prove any tribal affiliation. However, given the ethnographies, stories, and personal testimonials put forward in this anthology, the corroboration of DNA testing of Nuevomexicanos can provide scientific evidence for our shared narratives of slavery, captivity, and indigenous cultural production. TallBear's study is a great contribution toward understanding these issues within the English colonial context of the United States. Spanish colonial indigenous policy, on the other hand, was distinct, with complexities stemming from inclusivity and cultural transformation rather than tribal genocide and removal.

Genetic genealogy investigations provide us with a better grasp on the identity of Nuevomexicanos, namely how various ancestral origins, such as Native American origins, are key components of that identity. From the late nineteenth century into the early twentieth century, Nuevomexicanos gravitated toward the ideology that they were descendants of "pure Spanish" lineages, of "chivalric conquistadores," and that their white European ancestry placed them on the same social level as the Anglo-Americans who had begun to rule New Mexico. The strategy behind these cultural fantasies was successful. In the nineteenth century, Nuevomexicano legislators worked hard to create a legal category of "whiteness" that secured not only prestige but the vote, and eventually statehood (Gómez 2008). These ideologies were not instilled in every Nuevomexicano family but were at the forefront for those who represented New Mexico through politics and education, thus creating a "Spanish fantasy heritage" for Nuevomexicanos in the same way it was invented in California (McWilliams 1990, 35–47). Ethnonyms like Hispano-Americano and Spanish American seemingly created prestige for families. Subsequently, a widespread suppression and denial of Native American identity began and has continued into contemporary times.

Analogous projects such as the Caribbean Indigenous Legacy Project focus on the indigenous peoples of the Caribbean, revealing that the Native American legacy of the Taíno, Kalinago, and Garifuna peoples is alive and has been an integral part of the region since European contact. As with the case of New Mexico, the indigenous history and genetics are present in contemporary people, and some aspects of culture have survived as well. Ranald Woodaman, the project's principal investigator states:

> Native peoples have a long history in the Caribbean that continues into the present.... They were not entirely wiped out within the first hundred years of Spanish colonization, and as cultural ancestors, Native peoples have influenced the art, history, culture, and identity of the entire region. (Smithsonian n.d., par. 5)

In present-day New Mexico, the search for identity has led to the discovery of cultural, historical, and genetic origins. Genetic genealogy is a tool that has allowed us, the Nuevomexicanos, a scientific pathway to honor our Native heritage by not allowing erasure or suppression any longer. A new opportunity has been forged for the rediscovery of indigenous identity through the cultural practices, customs, spirituality, and even foodways that our ancestors have bequeathed us.

Neither authenticity nor cultural authority can be legislated or proclaimed. A well-informed process of self-discovery allows us to hear and appreciate the echoes and resonance of our mestizo and Genízaro past that we embody. The Nuevomexicano identity is complex and defies compartmentalization. The Indo-Hispano rituals, music, and dance that survive in mestizo communities like Abiquiú, Alcalde, and Ranchos de Taos are an inspiration. I feel my own heart beat to the rhythms of their drums.

Notes

1. The feminine gender assigned to the kingdom, or Reino de la Nueva México, expresses the hope that another fabulously wealthy Mexico City might be found there among its many pueblos. City, *una ciudad*, is feminine.

2. The project's web page can be found at https://www.familytreedna.com/groups/ydna-c-p39/about/background.

3. These extracted passages are direct transcriptions and translations, using modern orthography for the names.

References

Arellanes, Eloise M., Evelyn Luján Baca, and Margaret Leonard Windham. 1998. *Santa Clara Marriages, 27 Jan. 1726–27 Dec. 1832*. Albuquerque: New Mexico Genealogical Society.

Baca, Evelyn Luján, Donald Dresson, Amelia García, Lila Armijo Pfeufer, and Margaret Leonard Windham. 2004. *Taos Baptisms*. Vol. 1, *19 June 1701–8 October 1826*. Albuquerque: New Mexico Genealogical Society.

Chávez, Fray Angélico. 1983. *New Mexico Roots Ltd.: A Demographic Perspective from Genealogical, Historical, and Geographical Data Found in the Diligencias Matrimoniales or Pre-nuptial Investigations (1678–1869) of the Archives of the Archdiocese of Santa Fe*. 11 vols. Albuquerque: University of New Mexico General Library, Copy/Media Center. Available at https://digitalrepository.unm.edu/cswr_reference/5.

Christmas, Henrietta Martínez, and Patricia Sánchez Rau. 2002. *Santa Cruz de la Cañada Marriages: 100 Years of Marriages, 1726–1826*. Albuquerque: New Mexico Genealogical Society.

Esquibel, José Antonio. 1998. "The People of the Camino Real: A Genealogical Appendix." In *The Royal Road: El Camino Real from Mexico City to Santa Fe*, by Douglas Preston, José Antonio Esquibel, and Christine Preston, 145–76. Albuquerque: University of New Mexico Press.

Estes, Roberta, and Marie Rundquist. 2017. "Native American Y Haplogroup C-P39 Sprouts Branches!" DNAeXplained. Available at https://dna-explained.com/2015/03/11/new-haplogroup-c-native-american-subgroups/.

Gómez, Laura E. 2008. *Manifest Destinies: The Making of the Mexican American Race*. New York: New York University Press.

McWilliams, Carey. 1990. *North from Mexico: The Spanish-Speaking People of the United States*. Westport, CT: Praeger.

Nieto-Phillips, John M. 2004. *The Language of Blood: The Making of Spanish-American Identity in New Mexico, 1880s–1930s*. Albuquerque: University of New Mexico Press.

Padilla y Baca, Luis Gilberto. 1998. *Abiquiú Baptisms, 1869–1900*. Albuquerque: Hispanic Genealogical Research Center.

———. 2002. *San Juan de los Caballeros Marriages, August 6, 1857–December 18, 1900*. Albuquerque: Hispanic Genealogical Research Center.

———. 2003. *Abiquiú Marriages, 1854–1910*. Albuquerque: Hispanic Genealogical Research Center.

———. 2004. *Parkview Marriages, 1883–1920*. Albuquerque: Hispanic Genealogical Research Center.

Smithsonian Institution. N.d. "Reclaiming Identity: Are the Taíno, the First Native People to Make Contact with Christopher Columbus in 1492, Really Extinct?" Smithsonian Consortia. Available at http://consortia.si.edu/story/feature-story/reclaiming-identity.

Snow, David H. 1998. *New Mexico's First Colonists: The 1597–1600 Enlistments for New Mexico under Juan de Oñate, Adelantado and Gobernador*. Albuquerque: Hispanic Genealogical Research Center of New Mexico.

Snow, Meradeth H., Kathy R. Durand, and David Glenn Smith. 2010. "Ancestral Puebloan mtDNA in Context of the Greater Southwest." *Journal of Archaeological Science* 37, no. 7 (July): 1635–45.

TallBear, Kim. 2013. *Native American DNA: Tribal Belonging and the False Promise of Genetic Science*. Minneapolis: University of Minnesota Press.

Zegura, Stephen L., Lev Zhivotovsky, Tatiana M. Karafet, and Michael Hammer. 2004. "High-Resolution SNPs and Microsatellite Haplotypes Point to a Single, Recent Entry of Native American Y Chromosomes into the Americas." *Molecular Biology and Evolution* 21, no. 1 (February): 164–75.

CHAPTER FOURTEEN

Epilogue
Persistence and Resistance in Genízaro Identity

TERESA CÓRDOVA

The historical and anthropological excavation by the authors in this collection retrieves the cultural memory of generations of "indigenous people of mixed tribal origins living among the Hispano population" in New Mexico and southern Colorado. The result will be a further awakening of what Tomás Atencio referred to as "Genízaro Consciousness" (1985), including an affirmation for many whose historical memory has been deeply embedded in their psyches and a recalibration for those whose identities have been tied to the victors of conquest. The implications are enormous, as the connections to the past bring forth directions for the future, particularly in defense of spirit, place, and cultural survival.

Nación Genízara (*NG* 2020) is testimony that the cultural memory of the people who made up as much as a third of the population of New Mexico by 1790 has not been erased over time, as many historians have assumed (Schroeder 1975, 62; G. Gonzales 2017, 6). This volume describes documents, cultural practices, material relics, and generational knowledge. As long-time Ácoma Pueblo activist Petuuche Gilbert responded when I asked him what he thought of this project: "The evidence is there . . . it's in the historical record," adding that "culture is not lost"; more scholarship can unveil it further (personal conversation, July 22, 2017).[1] This volume of Genízaro scholarship builds and strengthens that literature and opens the way for more. Aware of the impact of the colonizing process on his people, Gilbert expressed the value of decolonizing values and instead embracing cultural roots that have been buried and denied.

We recalled a controversy during New Mexico's Cuartocentenario Celebration (1598–1998) when statues were proposed to honor our first governor, don Juan de Oñate. The debate had largely been framed as Pueblos versus Hispanos, those who identified with Spanish *pobladores* (settlers). The intervention of Chicanos against the Hispanos was especially significant. We affirmed our solidarity and our connections to each other as brown people from the region. As a Bernalillo County commissioner, listening to public testimony, I remembered a time, years earlier, when I spoke passionately against the proposed statue of Oñate before the Albuquerque City Council, proclaiming, "We will not be divided on this issue."

The "we" to which I referred are the pueblos and tribes in the region, including Ácoma, whose objections to the statue stemmed from the painful memories of Oñate's brutality[2]—and the Chicanos, who acknowledged and embraced, though not necessarily with any detail, their transnational indigenous roots. Twenty years after this battle, Petuuche and I reaffirmed our connection to the larger struggle against the multiple expressions of colonial domination and spoke of several examples, including a ritual at the Santa Fe Fiesta. At the heart of the protest is yet another divisive civic spectacle, the entrada or militarized equestrian entry, evincing that every male settler in the original colony was also in the militia. Santa Fe's entrada celebrated the *reconquista*, the so-called bloodless reconquest of New Mexico of 1696 and the return of the Spanish Mexican settlers into the region. The entrada pageant was finally abolished in 2018.

We spoke of the power of the Chicano identity, which recognizes its indigenous roots. It is this indigeneity, or Indianness, that is retrieved and strengthened through the rising Genízaro consciousness for so many mestizos from Nuevo México. For the activist, and for the warrior, the scholarship in this volume fortifies the strands of historical memory and buttresses fights for the future, including the very fight for survival. The cultural, political, and personal recalibrations that will follow from this book will themselves be objects of study. For many, it has the potential for much more. The deep love of place—*querencia*—of Nuevomexicanos is merged with the search for Aztlán (Levin Rojo 2014; Anaya, Lomelí, and Lamadrid 2017), and as the identities of Chicanos are more firmly enmeshed with their indigenous roots, the coalescence among the people of the Americas is made stronger. *Somos un pueblo* (We are one people), and the "sacred *maíz* is our mother" (Rodriguez 2014).[3]

I write the epilogue to this volume, not because I am a scholar of Genízaros but because I am a daughter of their homeland whose long-standing identity as a *warrior woman* is strengthened by the scholarship in *Nación Genízara*. It is an honor to be asked, "How is your identity positioned in this project?" To answer this question, of course, involves more than just my scholarly reaction, but a delving into my own story—and that of my mother—of indigenous connections. It is at once fearful and empowering—a common response when divulging family secrets and previously unspoken appearances in nighttime dreams of mid-nineteenth-century memories.

Although I had never lived in New Mexico before late 1991, my southern Colorado roots originate in Mora and Río Arriba Counties with great-grandparents and grandparents who migrated to the coal-mining region of southern Colorado in the 1860 and 1870s. The story of José Darío Córdova, my father's father, for example, is the story of a ten-year-old boy leaving La Villa de San Antonio, County of Mora, New Mexico, to work in those coal fields, spawning a legacy of four generations who worked in either the coal mines or the fracking fields that followed. I was too young to know him well, although I remember the old *penitente alabado* hymns that my dad would sing as he spoke of his father's time as a member of the Brotherhood.[4]

My maternal great-grandfather, Manuel Pacheco, also moved from the Mora Valley in the 1860s to southern Colorado and settled just west of Trinidad. The historic Pacheco School was built on land that he donated and named after him.[5] My mother, born in 1910, was sent away at the age of five after her mother died. I learned from my mother's older sister, who died in 2003 at the age of ninety-six, that when she went to visit, she realized that my mother had been placed as a servant into that household. I always wondered why the family had not taken her in or given her their name. Only later did I consider that it might have something to do with who her father was. By the time she was fourteen, my mother was on her own, cleaning houses to make a living, just as captive *criada* ancestors had done in the past.

I always felt, ideologically, spiritually, and through my dreams connected to my indigenous roots; all I had to do was look in the mirror to see them. When I went away to a university that was overwhelmingly white, I always got the puzzled look and question: "What are you? Are you Indian or something?" Many of my fellow students, isolated in their experiences and new to the region, it seems, had never seen brown people before. It was later in my life that I learned from my mother that her father was an Apache. It was only through the process of the unfolding of this volume and the subsequent

FIGURE 14.1 Teresa Córdova with her mother, Nora Hawks Córdova (right), and her aunt, Gertrudes González (left), August 22, 1987, at the Ave María Shrine in Trinidad, Colorado. Courtesy of Teresa Córdova.

reimagination that historical accounts make possible, that I saw my mother's birth and her life—in a different way. It was a way that, in my heart and mind, coalesced and helped me feel, even more deeply, the depths of connection to my matriarchal lineage, reinforcing my power as a woman and as a daughter of the region.

In late 2003, with a small inheritance that my Aunt Gertrudes had left me, I purchased Manuel and his wife Filomena's adobe house, which was registered in Manuel's name in 1867 and then recorded in Filomena's in 1913, after her husband died. Purchasing the Pacheco house was a chance to spiritually and physically reclaim my mother's—and her sister's—place in this family as well as their place in the history of the region.

It is with this family background that I respond to *Nación Genízara*, although it is not the only part of me that informs this epilogue. It is also my nearly fifty years of explicit identification with the Chicano movement and my consciousness as a Chicana. For me, being a Chicana means that I have found Aztlán and am connected to the indigenous peoples of the Americas, especially greater Mexico. My querencia has motivated me to always fight for people and place.

The notion of Aztlán, as complex as it might be, is a profound mechanism through which Chicanos make explicit connections to indigenous affinity while also connecting to place. Names in books and journals, subjects of manifestos, and cultural expressions stem from a Chicano concept of Aztlán. Tied also to a concept of place,

> [t]he Aztlán of the Chicano artist is, like La Mancha of Cervantes, the Macondo of García Márquez, the Troy of Homer, or the Omeyocan and Yóllotl of Netzahualcóyotl, a mythic place in time, a mythic timespace, a symbolic elaboration of a basic human relationship. (Gustavo Segade, cited in Anaya, Lomelí, and Lamadrid 2017, 1)

Francisco Lomelí, in the introduction to the revised and expanded edition of *Aztlán: Essays on the Chicano Homeland*, states:

> During the Chicano Movement of the 1960s and 1970s, the idea of a historic-geographic Aztlán served as the most unifying force in the emerging cultural renaissance. Although the place could be many things to many people, it mainly served to help us better understand our pre-history—that is, our roots and origins as part of a collective thought—and, in more modern times, our reaffirmed ethnicity. (Anaya, Lomelí, and Lamadrid 2017, 2)

The concept is not uncontested, and over the years its continued significance has been debated and debunked, as is more generally the role of myth in constructing identity. Nonetheless, there are many who find the most powerful utility not toward the path of cultural nationalism but in the formation of Chicanos, who have indigenous roots, as "a social group occupied within U.S. Society" (Anaya, Lomelí, and Lamadrid 2017, 10). The concept of Aztlán became a basis from which to argue for the socioeconomic and political rights of Chicanos living in *Occupied America* (Acuña 1972).

Nación Genízara adds both complexity and clarity to the New Mexico identity particularly and the Chicano identity more generally, giving more specificity to the origins of the indigenous roots of many Chicanos and an affirmation that the search for Aztlán has not been futile. The lessons from *Nación Genízara* have the potential to transcend Aztlán, to bridge across the Americas and serve as the basis for alliances with indigenous communities throughout the globe seeking to hold on to their place of origin in the face of forced displacement and forced servitude, which remain tragic by-products of globalized capital formation. Before returning to the relevance of my personal story, there are certain elements of these Genízaro accounts worth highlighting in this epilogue.

My introduction to Genízaro identity and scholarship came to me through Genízaro-descended scholar Bernardo Gallegos, who like most of the authors in this volume was introduced to Genízaros through the work of Benito Córdova (1979). I first met Gallegos in 1991 and benefited immensely from our conversations about his research on Genízaros. Since then, he has published several essays on the topic and, more recently, compiled them in the book *Postcolonial Indigenous Performances: Coyote Musings on Genízaros, Hybridity, Education, and Slavery* (2017).[6] In those same conversations, Bernardo instilled in me that a Genízara identity was relevant to me as well.

Gallegos, in his book, informs us that after a "long discussion" about "Genízaros, Pueblos and Indigenous mixed bloods" with Governor Regis Pecos of Cochití Pueblo, the governor proposed that they move state legislation during the 2007 session that would recognize the "role of Genízaros in New Mexico history and their legacy." Pecos, at the time, was chief of staff for Ben Luján, then Speaker of the New Mexico House of Representatives. Eliciting the involvement of Estevan Rael-Gálvez, state historian and Genízaro scholar (and an author in this volume), they drafted a legislative memorial that made its way to and passed both the House (sponsored by Luján) and Senate (sponsored by Senator Richard Martínez) declaring the "existence and importance of the indigenous group and the presence and importance of their descendants today." The text of these memorials is in Rael-Gálvez's foreword to this volume and provides a summary of some key findings from previous research, including that of pioneer Genízaro descendant and scholar Benito Córdova. The state has now officially recognized Genízaros and mixed-blood indigenous people. Important as it is, this recognition comes after years, if not centuries, of denial and erasure. The pressures to deny indigeneity can be replaced by the "prestige and freedom" that Lozen, the Apache woman warrior, enjoyed while she fought with her people for survival (Buchanan 1986).

Unlike several of the authors in this collection, I cannot produce documentation of multigeneration lineage showing my Genízaro roots, but I don't think that whether one can is the only point. With so much historical documentation in this volume on the region, one is left with the question: what makes more sense—to identify with the Spanish entrada and colonial relations of domination, or to identify with resistance to the appropriation and exploitation of the labor and resources of communities across the Americas, including New Mexico and southern Colorado? How then, we might ask, does Genízaro consciousness influence our "identities towards power" (T. Córdova 1998, 19). Gallegos provides a hint toward an answer, citing a 1979 observation by Fray Angélico Chávez, a noted historian and genealogist:

> The people of full or major Genízaro descent and upbringing are definitely more Indianic in their outlook. . . . Significantly in current revolutionary social movements, they are the ones who join the agrarian and urban Mexicans or Mexican-Americans in the social protest, and consequently like to be called "Chicano" along with them. (Gallegos 2017, 270)

By accepting the invitation to write this epilogue, I must think through how Genízaro consciousness affects the view of myself and, more important to me, how it affects my political work. An explicit Chicana identity has been comfortable for me for nearly fifty years. If I add Genízara, what changes? Is it more than just an affirmation of what I have always known? The detail and documentation of these chapters relay knowledge about cultural practices both historical and contemporary, and stories of captivity and enslavement, survival, and resistance. Filling in the blanks of historical memory, at the very least, makes this volume worthwhile. But in my own musings on the topic, I hope to offer further thoughts on what makes *Nación Genízara*, the first book "solely dedicated to the detribalized Native experience in New Mexico," such an important contribution to the movement for Genízaro consciousness.

The term "la nación genízara" is found in colonial documents as a term of collective self-reference (Rael-Gálvez, foreword, *NG*). The term's resurrection points to a persistence of the Genízaro identity, literally over centuries. Similarly, as stated in the introduction, "Today, the persistence of Genízaro identity blurs the lines of distinction between Native and Hispanic frameworks of race and cultural affiliation" (Lamadrid and Gonzales, introduction, *NG*). In these accounts of "conquest, transculturation, and resilience" that span generations, what might we highlight that equips us to survive for several more generations? I offer six highlights drawn from these incredibly rich portrayals of Genízaros and their descendants in New Mexico and southern Colorado. Within each of them, we see what Petuuche Gilbert pointed out to me—that indigenous culture within us is not lost. This volume represents acts of retrieval.

1. Searching for Aztlán: Technology, Trade, New Settlements, and Cultural Survival

Mythic accounts describe Aztecs as having originated in what is today the US Southwest, moving south and eventually attempting to make their way back to their homelands (Rodríguez 2014; Levin Rojo 2014). In chapter 2, Tomás Martínez Saldaña, Enrique Lamadrid, and José Rivera state: "The desire to return to the place of origin remained a spiritual motivation" and pushed indigenous groups from as far south as Mesoamerica in search of the mythic homeland. Returning with "colonizing expeditions," many joined groups of Spanish, indigenous, and mestizo soldiers, farmers, and cowboys who, in turn "mixed with other Indians already in the north."

> Free Mexican Indians participated in the exploration of northern New Spain in the sixteenth century and in its settlement thereafter. Highly motivated by their own origin myths and by the opportunity to return to the northern lands of Aztlán, they volunteered in large numbers to participate in these projects. (Saldaña, Lamadrid, and Rivera, chap. 2, *NG*).

Through historical documents, the authors describe Tlaxcalan trade and migration patterns based on a "social nexus" of cultural organization and agricultural production, which attest to the complex strategies Native people deployed to survive and to negotiate colonialism. By the mid-eighteenth century, Mexican Indians were replaced by Genízaros at Analco, who were given *mercedes* or land grants and who established settlements, adapted a form of economy and trade, and reinvented their indigenous identity on their own terms.

What is particularly striking in this account is the sophistication that characterized the settlements and the various trade relationships, hydraulic technologies, "intricate" agricultural systems, and religious and cultural practices the settlers established. Spanish accounts did not distinguish among the various indigenous Mexicano groups, but further investigations uncovered the depth of complexity in this social nexus. It is this kind of historical excavation that makes this volume so compelling. Complex societies characterized early Genízaro settlements.

2. Stigmas of Captivity, Slavery, and Anti-Genízaro Racism

The practice of slavery among Native Americans was a widespread institution whereby "[s]ettler colonialism intensified Indian slavery as an institution of labor appropriation and as a means of social and sexual reproduction" (Gutiérrez, chap. 5, *NG*). Forms of slavery and captivity are both described in *Nación Genízara*. Genízaros have endured an untold history of slavery and servitude, along with subsequent attitudes translated as a "deep-seated racism" attached to being "Indian like" (Rael-Gálvez, foreword, *NG*) and a pervasive rejection of Genízaros.

Chapters in this volume make clear that the complex Genízaro societies described are changed by experiences of captivity (Saldaña, Lamadrid, and Rivera, chap. 2, *NG*). William Kiser, for example, affirms: "Servants and slaves made up a significant percentage of New Mexico's colonial-era population," adding to "New Mexico's distinctive systems of servitude" (chap. 3, *NG*). Cristina Durán speaks to the experience of Genízara women who were "brought into Spanish households, initially as servants":

> Most sources agree that Genízaros were Indians from various tribes, primarily Plains, who were ransomed from Indian captors by Spanish/mestizo settlers in the eighteenth century, and who then became Hispanicized (and therefore detribalized) through years of servitude in Spanish households. (chap. 4, *NG*)

And while there were "clusters" of slaves and servants, there were also isolated individuals who also experienced forms of captivity and servitude. It is their records and histories that, despite being prevalent, are more difficult to retrieve. Virginia Sánchez speaks to the forgotten histories of southern Colorado, also vividly expressing

> the historical trauma the captured and enslaved endured, their embedded memory of witnessing their family members murdered in raids, and the pain and suffering they endured when their owners imprisoned, beat, starved, raped, or maimed them into submission. (chap. 8, *NG*)

While Sánchez in her research works to "identify, acknowledge, and give voice to the gender and culture of a forgotten and untold history of southern Colorado," she also acknowledges that we do not have the answers, posing several interesting questions regarding those who experienced captivity.

Removed from the protection of family and community . . . how were their bicultural children perceived and treated within Anglo and Hispano communities? Did their daughters fare better than their sons? What historical trauma did they pass on to their descendants? (chap. 8, *NG*)

We learn from Genízaro scholarship that, with "the enormous extent of this slavery and its consequences of displacement,"

[t]here is no way . . . to fully measure . . . the depth of the cultural wound left upon communities enduring these losses which is at the heart of what it means to inherit this legacy. . . . [T]he story of enslaved Indians has been quieted over the years by whispers as much as by silence, hushed aside even by those who have inherited it—carrying if not its geography in their faces and hands, then certainly its memory in an aching consciousness. (Rael-Gálvez, foreword, *NG*)

Susan Gandert writes that her "mother possessed a deep hurt about the circumstances of her birth," and that "it seemed that the stigma of servitude had followed her into the next generation." Gandert proudly manages through her research to "rescue two cautivas from being forgotten." Descendants from Mora, she adds, should be reminded: "Apparently, the Jicarilla Apaches were among the first settlers in the Mora Valley" (chap. 10, *NG*).

It is a significant point of this volume that the experiences of captivity and enslavement are reinforced today through language (e.g., *criado* and *malcriado*) and attitudes (stigmatization), and remain alive in the deep consciousness and historical memories of descendants. Patterns of servitude continued across generations—especially if one is seen as Indian—forcing us to come to terms with the racism and dominance that pervades the Spanish-identified cultures of the region. In reality, hybrid identities more accurately reflect the complexity of Nuevomexicanos.

3. The Complex Nuevomexicano Identity: Spanish, Indian, Indo-Hispano?

The rich scholarship on the region suggests both its historical complexities and the unending desire of its people to maintain historical connections that are deeply rooted. Miguel Tórrez, for example, shares the range of questions that he has asked of himself: "Who was I? Where had I come from? . . . To answer these questions, I sought to understand those who came before me" (chap. 13, *NG*).

This volume is exceedingly rich, with each chapter offering yet more details and documentation. Ironically, the scholarship does not often make its way into the public school system, as pointed by Tórrez: "Sadly, the public education system's presentation of New Mexico history taught me very little about the real context and details of our history. The limited information in New Mexico history cases didn't prepare me to answer my own questions" (chap. 13, *NG*). This volume will surely inspire more stories of family and community histories. Tórrez, like so many others, has sought an understanding of his roots through genetic testing. The results vary, but not dramatically. Besides the various indigenous identifiers, there is also evidence of both Iberian Peninsula and African ancestry, the latter most likely being a function of the centuries that the Moors were in southern Spain. Others find answers in genealogy, successfully finding their ancestors in historical documents such as church records. Yet for so many others, the lineage is more difficult to trace, particularly given the burning of churches in northern New Mexico and elsewhere, purportedly to destroy the records of land ownership typically stored in churches. These people will never know of their ancestry. This volume, however, contains within it the documents not just of individuals and their families but of a region and its people.

4. Genízaro Cultural Practices

"The cultural identity of the Genízaro descendent communities . . . resides in the material and cultural memory of the people who still occupy those lands" (Gonzales, chap. 9, *NG*). How is it that so many of the cultural practices of today among so many Nuevomexicanos are variations of indigenous practices in the Southwest, Mexico, and other parts of Latin America? Most notable are the dances of the Comanchitos and Matachines, but indigenous and mestizo heritage is also reflected in other rituals, symbols, and vestiges of language.

All of this points to the endurance and adaptation of cultural practices. Moises Gonzales, in this volume, makes the further point that "the continuing practice of indigenous dance and ritual remains a marker of indigenous identity" (chap. 9, *NG*). Through historical documents, oral histories, and contemporary cultural rituals, scholars in this volume represent the memory and resiliency of Genízaro culture. Charles Carrillo asks whether the "social cultural transformation" of the process of ethnogenesis was "a strategy for survival" (chap. 7, *NG*). In the village of Abiquiú, for example, the fact that residents "still self-identify as Genízaro, and still maintain their Genízaro dances and vocalizations, is a testament to the fact that the colonial process of acculturation was incomplete" (chap. 7, *NG*).

In the chapter by Michael Trujillo, in which he examines the writing of Gilberto Benito Córdova and others, we get a closer look at an identity that emerged from the Abiquiú context that Carrillo describes. Quoting Córdova, Trujillo reiterates the proclamations of a self-identified Genízaro: "And I ask you at this time to proclaim along with me, 'Soy Genízaro; I am a Genízaro and I will keep this beautiful secret a secret no more'" (chap. 11, *NG*).

While some New Mexico historians might say that Genízaro identity and practices have not endured, the chapters in this volume that highlight contemporary cultural practices clearly make the point that, indeed, contemporary cultural practices reflect an enduring memory. Moises Gonzales documents Genízaro ritual in the Sierra Sandía:

> Contrary to the claim of Fray Angélico Chávez and other contemporary New Mexican historians that Genízaro identity and cultural practices ended in New Mexico during the early nineteenth century, ethnographic observation of contemporary cultural performances reveals that Genízaro culture has persisted in mountain communities of the Sierra Sandía. Through community rituals, dances, and customs, Genízaro descendants regularly enact and maintain their traditions. And, more important, an understanding of Indo-Hispano identity in New Mexico signifies an acknowledgment of Genízaro subjectivity. Therefore, Genízaro identity is ultimately emblematic of Nuevomexicano identity. (chap. 9, *NG*)

Genízaro identity and cultural practices have not remained static but have adapted and evolved over time, in accordance with prevailing needs. Often established as "buffer settlements," Genízaro communities formed collective strategies of self-governance, which in turn led to the resiliency and enduring historical memory that Genízaro scholars can celebrate today.

Noteworthy in *Nación Genízara* is the authors' creative use of various sources to bring forth knowledge about Genízaro life, values, and beliefs. By analyzing songs, poems, ballads, rituals, ceremonies, and other written expression, for example, Levi Romero reveals an endless array of insights and examples of indigenous heritage and connections, all emerging "with a determined conviction." Romero uses these narratives to describe centuries of "coexistence" among "good neighbors" and "harmony" among Native and Indio-Hispano peoples, reinforcing not only the endurance of cultural memory but deep interconnections with it. "The Indio-Hispano may not have been raised in the Indian way, but his heart beats with the rhythms of his ancestral past" (chap. 12, *NG*).

5. Genízaro Scholarship: The Depths and Endurance of Historical Memory

The concept of historical memory is a deep one and is iterated throughout this book. The following statement from the foreword is reinforced in this epilogue:

> Memory sits in places and people, and even if believed to have disappeared, it endures through the generations. Sometimes it resembles a precious seed that has lain for centuries in sacred spaces, shut up airtight and yet still retaining its germinative power. (Rael-Gálvez, foreword, *NG*)

This book speaks to the amazing endurance of memory—and should be respected accordingly. There is legitimacy in historical memory that is passed through the generations. Our task is to hear it—and perhaps even heed it. The question, then, is what do we do with this historical memory? We can take the narratives and traditions from past generations and bring them forward to "reimagine" our present and our future. But then we must ask, reimagine for what purpose?

6. *Nación Genízara*: History of Resistance and Liberation

While we may learn about the legacies of captivity and servitude, we also learn about escape and resettlement—and survival, reflecting agency and self-determination. Benito Córdova, in his novel *Big Dreams and Dark Secrets in Chimayó* (2006), depicts the words of an indigenous goddess speaking to the novel's protagonist: "Hijo, hijo mío, you are not dependent on the weaver. *You are the weaver*" (cited in Trujillo, chap. 11, *NG*). As Cristina Durán, Samuel Sisneros, and others point out, examples of resistance include stories of Genízaras who took "direct action" on their own behalf. This volume is rich on this point alone.

It is important to highlight a key message of this volume, that the "hybrid culture of Genízaros" (Kiser, chap. 3, *NG*), while reflecting the legacy of captivity, also reflects a "distinct oppositional consciousness" (Gutiérrez, chap. 5, *NG*). Resistance is embodied in Genízaro identities and in these chapters; we see an array of strategies that have been employed to express this struggle against forces of domination.

> By the time Mexico achieved independence from Spain in 1821, Genízaros had forged a distinct ethnic and cultural identify for themselves, acquired limited rights to judicial redress, and occupied an important place in local society in spite of their ongoing stigmatization as servile bondpeople. (Kiser, chap. 3, *NG*)

Kiser adds that Genízaro oppositional identity extended to have a wider impact on democracy:

> Also important to this evolution of American democracy, however, was the role that peons, captives, and Genízaros played in promulgating the legal and political revolutions that helped to end most forms of coercive labor in the United States. . . . But an equally significant aspect of Genízaro history involves its contribution to the emergence of free labor ideology and the concomitant abolition of slavery and involuntary servitude in nineteenth-century America, a movement that had far-reaching implications for the future of the democratic nation. (chap. 3, *NG*).

Ramón Gutiérrez poses a connection between the emergence of Genízaro identity and the rise of the Penitente Brotherhood, connecting its "distinct oppositional consciousness" with the "emergence of a distinct ethnic identity with religious and political dimensions" (chap. 5, *NG*). We see evidence of these same connections through the cultural artifacts shared by Levi Romero (chap. 12, *NG*). Durán, in her chapter, rescues the prowess of Genízaras as warriors in taking actions to defend themselves (chap. 4, *NG*).

The complexity of claiming a Nuevomexicano indigenous heritage lies within the dark history of colonialism. Levi Romero writes:

> To move forward, there must be a form of truth and reconciliation that does not quell previous conflicts with a self-induced glorification to claims of indigeneity without acknowledging the wrongs of the past. But we should also honor the symbiotic relationships that Alfonso Ortiz spoke about in his introduction to *Ceremony of Brotherhood*:[7] "[E]xamples of cooperation, respect, and

brotherhood which can be cited have occurred because Hispano and Pueblo peoples have long since become brothers and sisters and good neighbors who respect one another.".... The Indio-Hispano may not have been raised in the Indian way, but his heart beats with the rhythms of his ancestral past. (chap. 12, *ND*)

Concluding Thoughts: Impacts of *Nación Genízara*

This volume, without doubt, conveys the necessity of recognizing Genízaros as important to the history of New Mexico and southern Colorado, while adding to the documentation. *Nación Genízara* responds to the "imperative" to awaken the stories and affirm the deep-seated connections to indigeneity.

It is important to highlight that the concept of *Nación Genízara*, when applied to Genízaro settlements, "means the recognition, protection, and validation of indigenous rights for a community on its land"; it is an "acknowledgment of history and cultural identity," but it "is not a movement for the creation of a tribe" (Gonzales, chap. 9, *NG*). Bernardo Gallegos draws similar conclusions (2017). As he conducted further research and embraced his Genízaro identity, Gallegos describes moments when he realized "that the category 'Indian,' was surrounded by a wall of sorts.... It has become clear to me that any attempt to connect with a specific contemporary Native Nation was a futile effort." He stresses that Genízaros "were more of an economic group than an Indian nation" (2017, 17). He posits:

> Genízaro descendants exist discursively somewhere in the intersection of African Americans due to the slave experience, Native Americans from proximity and genealogy, and Mexican Americans/Chicanos from shared historical experiences. (17)

The process of detribalization meant that indigenous culture was denied to Genízaros. "Since most of them had been sold into slavery at very young ages it would have been near impossible for their descendants to maintain any form of ethnic/tribal identity over the centuries" (Gallegos 2017, 17). But despite being "removed" from indigenous culture, it is still "in the DNA." The many cultural practices that remain as described in this volume are important and vibrant remnants, but they do not fully make up for the extent to which indigenous practices have been submerged for the majority of Genízaro descendants. Similarly, while Genízaro consciousness is not a movement for the creation of a tribe, neither does it replicate restrictive boundaries of formalized memberships. The power of the Genízaro concept is the room that it makes for the detribalized experience, inviting the sons and daughters of the region to reclaim their connections to their indigenous past even when they cannot provide written proof of their heritage, and despite any forces that may seek to deny those connections.

A significant contribution of Genízaro scholarship is its potential to remove barriers and borders that have been erected by centuries of colonization. It is possible, however, to reject colonial constructs and embrace a complex legacy that enables Genízaros to both respect and move past the confines of categorized racial identity while opening pathways to connections with others in the Americas whose ancestors also experienced enslavement, including Afro-Latinos. The "reimagination" that must occur, however, involves rejecting the dynamics of domination and, along with it, identification with the colonizer (T. Córdova 1998). Moises Gonzales urges Genízaros to "disassociate themselves from the privileged coalition of Anglo- and Spanish Americans"; he states that Genízaro communities "embody our mixed indigenous heritage as a defiant act in honor of our captive ancestors, as well as challenge the colonial power of the nation-state to dominate our identity" (chap. 9, NG).

What difference does it make, therefore, to add "Genízara" to my Chicana identity? Romero argues the Genízaro identity gives rise to a distinctive Chicana/Chicano consciousness. The various indigenous symbols adopted by Chicanos, including Aztlán, while somewhat mythologized, not only represent a cultural connection to ancestry but have also become symbols of insistence and resistance—insistence on the deep historical connection to the hemisphere and resistance to the forces that would deny, or attempt to erase, those connections. Genízaro scholarship gives greater credence to these mythologized and documented affiliations and also provides more details and possibilities. *Nación Genízara* helps explain why, for so many, the connection to indigeneity is so deep in our psyches and our souls. As Moises Gonzales reminded me in an email exchange, "Genízaro identity goes beyond a colonial experience and ties all 'Manitos' from Colorado and New Mexico to our indigenous roots."[8]

The quest for indigenous connections lies deep, as this volume teaches us, in the psyche and in the nighttime dreams of the descendants of detribalized Natives. This collection of research essays unveils the persistence of cultural identity, and contained within it is an embedded resistance—both of which can be built upon to assert the legitimacy and authority of indigenous presence in the Americas. Most importantly, the connection to indigeneity and the retrieval of historical memories expand our alliances across the borders of nations and tribes to ensure that our survival in this hemisphere extends to generations to come. As we embrace our mother, the sacred *maíz*, we embrace also the power of the feminine spirit. The persistence and resistance of Genízaro consciousness is powerful, as is the India, Chicana, Genízara who carries with her the "prowess of a warrior" that allows her to reclaim, for her mother, her rightful place in making history, while simultaneously rejecting legacies of servitude and compliance.

Notes

1. Petuuche Gilbert (born 1944), a lifelong resident of Ácoma Pueblo and Native activist, decolonized his name from Gilbert Ortiz in 1992 as a protest during the Columbus Quincentennial. With a bachelor's degree from the University of New Mexico and a master's in political science from the University of Arizona, he has worked over three decades for the Ácoma tribal government. He was a founding member of both the Indigenous World Association, an NGO at the United Nations, and the Native Organizers Alliance. In later years, he has worked against the expansion of uranium mining near his pueblo in environmental organizations, including the Ácoma and Laguna Coalition for a Safe Environment.

2. The website New Mexico History.org relates the story as follows: "In December 1598, on their way to Zuni, Capt. Juan de Zaldívar and his soldiers stopped at Acoma for provisions. While there the Acomas accused one of Zaldívar's soldiers of stealing, and violating an Acoma woman. The Acomas proceeded to kill Zaldívar and nearly a dozen of his men, later claiming that the soldiers had demanded excessive amounts of provisions. A Spanish punitive expedition ascended on Acoma resulting in a three-day battle. When the fighting ended, several hundred Indians were dead, and hundreds of surviving Acomas were held prisoner and taken to Santo Domingo Pueblo to stand trial. Oñate severely punished the people of Acoma. Men over twenty-five had one foot cut off and were sentenced to twenty years of personal servitude to the Spanish colonists; young men between the ages of twelve and twenty-five received twenty years of personal servitude; young women over twelve years of age were given twenty years of servitude; sixty young girls were sent to Mexico City to serve in the convents there, never to see their homeland again" (New Mexico History.org n.d.).

3. The work of Roberto Rodríguez (2014) is a powerful treatise on the indigenous connections across the Americas over centuries as seen by tracing transgeographic cultural expressions around maíz.

4. La Hermandad de Nuestro Padre Jesús Nazareno (The Brotherhood of Our Father Jesus the Nazarene) is a religious fraternity to which most men in the villages of greater New Mexico belonged. Members were nicknamed Hermanos Penitentes in reference to their penitential devotions.

5. An unknown arsonist burned the Pacheco School in the 1990s.

6. Bernardo Gallegos was invited to contribute to this volume, but he was hard at work finalizing his book.

7. Extensively quoted by Romero in his chapter in this volume, *Ceremony of Brotherhood* is an anthology of Native and Hispano poetry, prose, and oral history, edited by Rudolfo A. Anaya and Simon J. Ortiz (1981), in celebration of the cultural legacy of the 1680 Pueblo Revolt; it was published for the revolt's tricentennial, together with other diverse events that were held during 1980.

8. *Manitos* (little brothers) is a nickname used for New Mexicans, both in northern Mexico and in southern Colorado.

References

Acuña, Rodolfo. 1972. *Occupied America: The Chicano's Struggle toward Liberation*. San Francisco: Canfield Press.

Anaya, Rudolfo A., Francisco A. Lomelí, and Enrique R. Lamadrid, eds. 2017. *Aztlán: Essays on the Chicano Homeland*. Albuquerque: University of New Mexico Press.

Anaya, Rudolfo A., and Simon J. Ortiz, eds. 1981. *Ceremony of Brotherhood: A Commemorative Anthology of the Pueblo Revolt*. Albuquerque: Academia.

Atencio, Tomás. 1985. "The Old Town Liquor Dispute: Social Change and Conflict in New Mexico." Southwest Hispanic Research Institute Working Papers, no. 112. University of New Mexico, Albuquerque.

Buchanan, Kimberly Moore. 1986. *Apache Women Warriors*. El Paso: Texas Western Press.

Córdova, Gilberto Benito. 1979. "Missionization and Hispanicization of Santo Tomás Apóstol de Abiquiú, 1750–1770." PhD diss., University of New Mexico.

Córdova, Teresa. 1998. "Power and Knowledge: Colonialism in the Academy." In *Living Chicana Theory*, edited by Carla Trujillo, 17–45. Berkeley, CA: Third Woman Press.

Gallegos, Bernardo. 2017. *Postcolonial Indigenous Performances: Coyote Musings on Genízaros, Hybridity, Education, and Slavery*. Rotterdam: Sense Publishers.

Gonzales, Gregorio P. 2017. "Si Eres Genízaro: Race, Indigeneity, and Belonging in Northern New Mexico." PhD diss., University of Texas.

Gonzales, Phillip B. 2007. "History Hits the Heart: Albuquerque's Great Cuartocentenario Controversy, 1997–2005." In *Expressing New Mexico: Nuevomexicano*

Creativity, Ritual, and Memory, edited by Phillip B. Gonzales, 207–32. Tucson: University of Arizona Press.

Levin Rojo, Danna. 2014. *Return to Aztlán: Indians, Spaniards, and the Invention of Nuevo México*. Norman, University of Oklahoma Press.

New Mexico History.org. N.d. "Juan de Oñate." Office of the State Historian. Available at http://newmexicohistory.org/people/juan-de-onate.

Rodríguez, Roberto Cintli. 2014. *Our Sacred Maíz Is Our Mother: Indigeneity and Belonging in the Americas*. Tucson: University of Arizona Press.

Schroeder, Albert. 1975. "Río Grande Ethnohistory." In *New Perspectives on the Pueblos*, edited by Alfonso Ortiz, 41–70. Albuquerque: University of New Mexico Press.

CONTRIBUTORS

CHARLES M. CARRILLO studied in the University of New Mexico's Department of Anthropology, where his research focused on Hispano material culture (pottery) of the seventeenth and eighteenth centuries. He is currently finishing a book on the origins and history of El Santuario de Nuestro Señor de Esquipulas with Felipe Mirabal. Carrillo has written extensively about the Santero traditions of New Mexico, and he works as a contemporary *santero*. His wife, Debbie Trujillo Carrillo, is a direct descendent of the original Hopi-Tewas who were settled at Santo Tomás Apóstol de los Genízaros de Abiquiú in 1754.

TERESA CÓRDOVA is a Native of Southern Colorado and is the director of the University of Illinois at Chicago's Great Cities Institute. A professor of urban planning and policy in the College of Urban Planning and Public Affairs, Córdova received her PhD from the University of California, Berkeley. As an applied theorist, political economist, and community-based planner, Córdova approaches her work as scholarship of engagement, in which research, pedagogy, and service are integrated. Her analysis of global/local dynamics, including impacts of globalization on Latino communities, informs her publications in community development, Latino, and Chican@ studies.

CRISTINA DURÁN is the dean of the Facundo Valdez School of Social Work at New Mexico Highlands University. She earned a Master of Social Welfare degree at the University of California, Los Angeles, and a PhD in American studies at the University of New Mexico. Before becoming a social-work educator, Durán's professional experiences included positions at La Clínica de la Raza in Oakland, California, and with the Albuquerque Public Schools. Durán's dissertation explored and documented how the cultural landscape in Albuquerque was transformed as a result of the growth of Mexican immigrant entrepreneurship and the built environment of small, immigrant-owned businesses.

MIGUEL A. GANDERT is an award-winning documentary and fine-art photographer and filmmaker. A Distinguished Professor of Communication and Journalism at the University of New Mexico, he teaches courses in photography, multimedia journalism, ethnography, media theory, and intercultural communications. His work explores contrasts between Hispanic life in Spain, Latin America, and Old and New Mexico. He works primarily in black and white and sees documentary photography as both a form of art and a way of understanding complex cultural relationships. A primary focus of those stories is Gandert's mestizo heritage and the fusion and tension of the relationship between Spanish and Native cultures of the Americas.

SUSAN M. GANDERT is a native Nuevomexicana from too many generations back to count. She has taught and traveled extensively in Latin America, and she recently retired from Albuquerque Public Schools. In addition to her BA and MA from the University of New Mexico, she has studied at the Universidad de Alcalá in Spain, pursuing graduate studies in Spanish and Latin American literature, art, and history. She has presented at many academic conferences and consulted on several art exhibitions on Latin American colonial art. She is currently writing *Recuerdos de mis padres / "Memories of my parents,"* a collection of stories about her parents' childhood and youth in Northern New Mexico and Southern Colorado.

DAVID F. GARCÍA, "El Poeta de Abiquiú," earned his PhD in anthropology from the University of Texas at Austin in 2015. His dissertation, "*La Resolana*: A Communicative Cartography of Gathering Spaces in North Central New Mexico," charts local knowledge systems and practices in northern New Mexico. His interests include acequias, foodways, religion, spirituality, folkloristics, Indo-Hispano drama, and dance and music as they relate to sustainability and cultural survival of Indo-Hispano communities. García is an acclaimed traditional poet, singer, and multi-instrumentalist who has mastered the *copla*—the building block of corridos, canciones, sacred music, and the most complex form of all, the *décima*.

MOISES GONZALES is an associate professor of urban design in community and regional planning at the School of Architecture and Planning at the University of New Mexico. He is a Genízaro heir of both the Cañón de Carnué

Land Grant and the San Antonio de Las Huertas land grant by way of Bernadina India, a well-known Genízara servant in the house of Antonio Gurulé of Los Ranchos de Alburquerque. He is a *danzante* (dancer) of the Matachín and Comanche traditions of the Sandía mountain communities. He currently serves on the board of trustees of the Carnué Land Grant and has written various academic articles on the history and culture of Genízaro settlements.

RAMÓN A. GUTIÉRREZ is the Preston and Sterling Morton Distinguished Service Professor of History at the University of Chicago. With a PhD in colonial Latin American history from the University of Wisconsin, Madison, he has also taught at Pomona College; the University of California, San Diego, where he founded the Ethnic Studies Department; and Université Paris Diderot. His works include *When Jesus Came, the Corn Mothers Went Away: Marriage, Sexuality, and Power in New Mexico, 1500–1846*, *Festivals and Celebrations in North American Ethnic Communities*, and *Mexicans in California: Transformations and Challenges*. His many honors include the MacArthur Prize Fellowship.

WILLIAM S. KISER was born and raised in Las Cruces, New Mexico, and specializes in nineteenth-century US-Mexico borderlands history. He earned his PhD at Arizona State University and is currently an assistant professor of history at Texas A&M University–San Antonio and the director of the university's Global Borders and Borderlands History Program. He has published four books: *Coast-to-Coast Empire: Manifest Destiny in the New Mexico Borderlands*, *Borderlands of Slavery: The Struggle over Captivity and Peonage in the American Southwest*, *Dragoons in Apacheland: Conquest and Resistance in Southern New Mexico, 1846–1861*, and *Turmoil on the Rio Grande: The Territorial History of the Mesilla Valley, 1846–1865*.

ENRIQUE R. LAMADRID is a distinguished professor emeritus of Spanish from the University of New Mexico, who taught folklore, literature, and cultural history there since 1985. His research interests include traditional culture and bioregionalism, ethnopoetics, and folklore. His book *Hermanitos Comanchitos: Indo-Hispano Rituals of Captivity and Redemption* won the Chicago Folklore prize, and he now edits the *Querencias* series at the University of New Mexico Press.

TOMÁS MARTÍNEZ SALDAÑA is a professor of anthropology at Colegio de Postgraduados, Texcoco, Mexico, and he is a member of the Consejo Nacional de Ciencia y Tecnología (CONACYT). He is the author of *La Diáspora Tlaxcalteca-Colonización Agrícola del Norte Mexicano*, the classic work on the Tlaxcaltecas and the role they played in the expansion of Mesoamerican agriculture into the northern provinces of Mexico during the Spanish colonial period. He also edited a series on *El Pequeño Riego de México*.

ESTEVAN RAEL-GÁLVEZ is a writer, scholar, and creative strategist, experienced in the executive management of cultural-based organizations. His career in cultural and educational institutions and government agencies includes service as the senior vice president of historic sites at the National Trust for Historic Preservation, the executive director of the National Hispanic Cultural Center, and the state historian of New Mexico. His doctoral dissertation at the University of Michigan at Ann Arbor, "Identifying Captivity and Capturing Identity: Narratives of American Indian Slavery," focuses on the meanings of American Indian slavery and a unique legacy and identity in northern New Mexico and southern Colorado. His book in progress is titled, *The Silence of Slavery*. Estevan was raised on and learned to work a farm/ranch that has been stewarded by his family in Questa, New Mexico, for multiple generations.

JOSÉ A. RIVERA is a research scholar at the Center for Regional Studies at the University of New Mexico, and he is a professor of planning in the School of Architecture and Planning. His research and teaching interests include rural-community development, policy analysis, and water-resources management. He is the author of *Acequia Culture: Water, Land, and Community in the Southwest* and *La Sociedad: Guardians of Hispanic Culture Along the Rio Grande*.

LEVI ROMERO is a *nativo* of the Embudo Valley who rose to become New Mexico's Centennial Poet in 2012. He is an assistant professor of Chicana/o studies at the University of New Mexico and the director of the New Mexico Cultural Landscapes Certificate Program in the School of Community and Regional Planning. His bilingual poetry is a tapestry woven from a palette of Nuevomexicano colloquialisms from the regional *manito* dialect of northern New Mexico, rich with seventeenth-century archaisms and melodic registers. Romero's prize-winning books include *Sagrado: A Photopoetics Across the*

Chicano Homeland, co-authored with Spencer Herrera and photographer Robert Kaiser, and two collections of poems, *A Poetry of Remembrance: New and Rejected Works* and *In the Gathering of Silence*.

VIRGINIA SÁNCHEZ is an independent Colorado historian with an MA from the University of Colorado at Denver. Her book, *Pleas and Petitions: Hispano Life and Conflict in Territorial Colorado, 1861–1876*, is forthcoming from the University of Colorado Press. She has two articles with the *New Mexico Historical Review*, the first coauthored with Phillip B. Gonzales, "Displaced in Place: Nuevomexicanos on the Northern Side of the Colorado–New Mexico Border, 1850–1875," 93, no. 3 (Summer 2018), and "Linked by Water, Linked by Blood: Madrid Ditch No. 2 in Cucharas, Colorado, 1884–1903," 86, no. 4 (Fall 2011). Her book, *Forgotten Cuchareños of the Lower Valley*, is a history of a Hispano-Indo settlement, and it received the 2011 Miles History Award.

SAMUEL E. SISNEROS is a native "Nuevomechicano" from Alburquerque with paternal roots in Anton Chico, San Miguel del Vado, Santa Fe, and Abiquiú and maternal ancestry from Bernalillo, Alburquerque, Los Padillas, and Belén. He earned his MA in borderlands history at the University of Texas at El Paso. Since receiving his MA he has worked as an archivist for over twelve years, first at the National Hispanic Cultural Center and then at the New Mexico State Records Center and Archives. He is currently at the Center for Southwest Research at the University of New Mexico.

MIGUEL A. TÓRREZ is a research technologist at Los Alamos National Laboratory working in material science. He holds a BS in environmental science from Northern New Mexico College. Tórrez is the New Mexico Genealogical Society's DNA Project administrator. He was the project leader of *La Iglesia de Santa Cruz de la Cañada, 1695–2015: Celebrating 320 Years of Parish History*, and he has authored and coauthored many articles on genetic genealogy. He has served on the board for the Chimayó Cultural Preservation Association. In 2012 Tórrez was chosen as an emerging historian by the New Mexico State Records Center and Archives, and he presented his genetic study on the Espinosa clan of New Mexico.

MICHAEL L. TRUJILLO is an associate professor at the University of New Mexico with a joint appointment in American studies and Chicana/o studies.

He earned his doctorate in anthropology from the University of Texas at Austin. He authored *Land of Disenchantment: Latina/o Identities and Transformations in Northern New Mexico*, and his research has been published in *Aztlán: A Journal of Chicano Studies*, *Cultural Dynamics*, and *Oxford Latino Bibliographies*. He is currently writing *Dialectical Americas: American Studies and Compelling Symmetries in New Mexico and Latin America*, which includes a series of case studies of New Mexican cultural assemblages and symmetric phenomena in Latin America. A second book is tentatively titled *City of Violence: Ciudad Juárez in the Mexican and American Imagination after 1993*.

INDEX

Aa Indians, 50, 57n11, 121
Abeyta, Amador, 144
Abeyta, Bernardo, 108
Abeyta, Norberto, 144
Abiquiú, NM, xxv, 1, 3, 6, 13, 19, 31, 65, 75, 105–7, 109, 111, 135, 137–38, 139, 175, 226, 232, 239, 240, 263–67, 272, 277, 283n3, 299, 314, 324, 337; emancipation at, 91; genízaros at, 47, 165–68; population of, 144
abolition: of Indian slavery, 193–95; in Mexico, 4, 49, 52–54; in New Spain, 2; in United States, 8, 48, 54–56, 183, 185
abolitionists, 49, 55–56. *See also* radical Republicans
Abó Pass, NM, 228
Acequia Madre del Analco, 35
acequias, 8, 32, 34, 42
Ácoma Pueblo, 86–87, 143, 326, 342n2
activism. *See* Chicano movement
Age of Revolution, 49, 53
agriculture, 28, 29–31, 33–37, 43. *See also* irrigation; water rights
Aguascalientes, Mexico, 29
Aguilar, Alfonso Rael de, 71
Aguilera y Roche, Teresa de, 87
Alameda, NM, 230, 231
Alburquerque, NM, xviii, 12, 31, 85, 95, 134, 138, 225, 226, 229–32, 235–37, 240; city council of, 327; Franciscans at, 103–11
Alcalde, NM, 23, 240, 242, 265, 274, 278, 324

Alcina, Teodoro, 166
alcohol, 185
Algodones, NM, 232, 235, 239
Alianza Federal de Mercedes, 5
Altagracia, María, 257, 259
Alvarez del Castillo, Juan Miguel, 129
Amazon, 88
Anaya, María Bárbara, 314
Anton Chico, NM, 51
Antonio, Manuel, 112
Antonito, CO, 252
Anza, Juan Bautista de, 78, 142
Anzures, Juan, 237
Apaches, 1, 3, 12, 23, 28, 31, 50, 51, 57n11, 65, 81–82, 89–91, 94, 106, 111–12, 119, 121–22, 125, 129–30, 135, 138, 166–67, 175, 193, 225, 229–32, 234, 237–38, 241, 246, 318, 331; Chiricahua subgroup, 49; Jicarilla subgroup, 191, 255, 278; Mescalero subgroup, 177; raids by, 235–36
Apodaca, Rosalía, 138
Aragón, Andrés, 230
Arapahoes, 175, 195
archaeology, 168–71
Archibeque, José Antonio, 230
Archuleta, Martína, 318
Arizona, 110, 179; District Court of, 182–83
Arizpe, Mexico, 71
Arkansas River, 177
Arroyo Hondo, NM, 183, 293–94

Arroyo Seco, NM, 182, 240
assimilation, 2, 8, 47, 50, 65–67, 92, 106–7, 118, 122, 135, 144, 168, 175, 183–84, 187, 196, 240
Atanasio, José, 130
Athabascans, 171
Atocha, Manuel de, 257
Atrisco, NM, 3, 25, 43, 230, 242
Aztecs, 28, 33, 38, 69, 241, 333
Aztlán, 27, 31, 38, 295, 327, 329–30, 341

Baca, Baltazar, 232
Baca, Bernabé, 129
Baca, Jacinta, 124, 134
Baca, Josefa, 141
Baca, Juan Bautista, 307
Baca, Lucas, 129
Baca, María de la Luz, 141
Baca, María Josefa, 138
Baca, María Rosa, 133
Baca, Miguel Antonio, 133
Baca, Rita Quiteria, 140
Banda Machos, 303n2
Banning, CA, 110
Bañuelos, Baltazar de, 38
baptism, 2, 38, 41, 50, 52, 65, 91–92, 122–23, 137, 139, 141, 142, 144, 147, 183–84, 187; of captives, 194–95, 263–64; statistics on, 90. *See also* Catholicism
Bárbara (captive), 93
Barelas, NM, 237, 241
Barreiro, Antonio, 107
Barrio de Analco, NM, 3, 8, 27, 31, 33, 35, 39, 43, 65, 71, 232, 333; population of, 28
Barrio de San Juan Bautista de Analco, Mexico, 34
Bazán Brothers, 40
Beaubien, Charles, 177, 220n2
Becker, John, 119
Belén, NM, 3, 8, 10, 31, 64, 65, 107, 111, 226, 230–32; demographics of, 138–39; genízaros at, 47, 94–95, 122–25, 137, 165; land grant at, 71, 125; mission church at, 137, 138, 141, 143; population of, 130, 133, 135, 137, 138, 144. *See also* Nuestra Señora de los Dolores de los Genízaros
Benavides, Alonso de, 28, 35, 39, 101
Benedict, Kirby, 57n16
Bernal, Cayetano José, 103, 137–39
Bernalillo, NM, 25, 76, 122–23, 228, 230, 239, 240, 242–43
Bible, 85
Bosque Redondo Reservation, 56, 192–93, 196
Bourbon Reforms, 41
Boyd, Elizabeth, 279–81
Brito, Juan de Leon, 35
buffalo hunting, 238–39
Bureau of Indian Affairs, 56
Bustamante, Rosa, 107
Bustamante, Ventura, 71
Bustillo, Juan Pérez de, 314

California, 102, 323
Camino de Galisteo, 34
Camino de la Cañada, 34
Camino del Alamo, 34
Camino de Pecos, 34
Camino Real de Tierra Adentro, 29, 32, 36, 84, 119
Cañada del Ojo de la Cueva, NM, 179
Canatlán, Mexico, 32
Cañoncito, NM, 240, 245
Canon City, CO, 185
Cañón de Carnué, NM. *See* Carnué, NM
Cañones, NM, 267
Capilla de Nuestra Señora de la Luz, 34
capitalism, 85

Capitulaciones (1591), 28–29
captives/captivity, 1, 8, 11–13, 23, 47–55, 82, 93–94, 112, 118, 125, 143, 173, 177, 180–82, 187–88, 232, 234, 238–39, 243–44, 253–54, 256, 335; baptism of, 194–95; emancipation of, 65–66, 88; murder of, 71; names of, 197–219; outlawed in US, 55–56, 193–95; statistics on, 57n16, 87–88, 90–91. See also *rescate*; slaves/slavery
captivity songs, 188–92
Caraquis, Cristóbal, 126, 128
Caribbean, 88
Caribbean Indigenous Legacy Project, 323
Carmelite Order of New Spain, 105
Carnué, NM, 3, 12, 23, 65, 225, 227, 234, 237–38, 240, 299; land grant at, 229–30, 235–37, 240, 245
Carros, Buenaventura de los, 39
Carson, Christopher, 175, 176
Carson National Forest, 265
Casa Colorada, NM, 231
Casa del Gobernador, 34
Casados, Antonio, 71, 126–28
Castaño de Sosa, Gaspar, xxii
caste system, xvi, 1, 2, 3, 66–67, 118, 128, 134, 137, 167, 175, 236, 322; abolished, 4, 52–54, 139–40, 226. See also Coyotes; *limpieza de sangre*; mestizo(s)
Castillo, Joaquín, 141
Castillo, José Antonio, 141
Catholicism, 6, 9–10, 29–30, 38, 39, 47, 50, 52, 83–84, 96–100, 118, 121, 144, 168, 183, 188, 194, 226, 240–41, 278–79, 320; rituals of, 100–11. See also baptism; Franciscans; missions; *penitentes*
Caxcanes, 27
Cellano, Tommaso de, 96
Cerro, NM, 47

Cerro de la Bufa, Mexico, 38
Cerro de Tepeyac, 38
Cerro Gordo, Mexico, 32
Cervantes, María Cruz, 141
Chacón, Fernando, 105
Chalchihuites, Mexico, 32, 33, 36
Chama River Valley, 175, 181
Chapel of San Miguel, 105
Chávez, Domingo, 75
Chávez, Fray Angélico, 5, 63, 83–85, 111, 166, 244, 264
Chávez, Isabel, 75, 77, 134
Chávez, Manuel A., 92
Chávez, Tomás, 77
Chávez Gonzales, Carmen, 243
Cheyennes, 195
Chicano movement, 5, 14, 288, 295, 327, 329–30
Chichimeca War, 29, 31–32
Chihuahua, Mexico, 29, 42, 84, 89, 143
Chile, 88
Chililí, NM, 101, 299
Chimal, NM, 232
Chimayó, NM, 107–08, 265, 307
Chimayó Rebellion, 4
Christianity, 2, 21, 28, 38–40, 69, 81, 88, 99, 106–07. See also Catholicism; Protestants
churches, 107–8, 147. See also Catholicism; missions
Cíbola, 31
Cinco Señores, Mexico, 32
Ciudad Juárez, Mexico, 42, 240
Civil Rights Act (1866), 185
Civil War, 49, 55, 193
Coahuila, Mexico, 37
Cochití Pueblo, xxi, 166, 240
Codallos y Rabal, Joaquín, 71, 126
Cofradía de Nuestro Padre Jesús Nazareno. See *penitentes*

colonialism, xvi, xix, 7, 19, 28–33, 48, 86–90, 169, 246, 292, 300, 339; British, 50, 81–82; French, 50, 81–82. *See also* settler colonialism; Spain; United States

Colorado, 11, 80, 84, 100, 108, 110, 173–74, 179, 328, 332; Indian slavery in, 184–88; territorial period, 192–96

Colorado River, 177–78

Colotlán, Mexico, 8, 31

Columbian exchange, 39–40, 43

Columbus Quincentennial, 63

Comancheros, 72, 179, 181, 187, 192–94, 232, 238

Comanches, 1, 3, 12, 28, 31, 40–41, 65, 78, 81–82, 89–91, 94, 106, 111, 122, 125, 130, 135, 175, 177, 179, 191, 225, 227, 229, 231, 234, 237–38, 246, 255–56; as genízaros, 141–43; treaty with Spanish, 236, 289

Comanches de la Serna, 191

Comanchitos. See *Los Comanches*

compadrazgo, 123, 139, 141, 187

concubinage, 52

Conejos, CO, 177, 182

Conejos County, CO, 182, 189–90, 193, 195

Confraternity of Our Lady of Carmel, 106

Confraternity of Our Lady of the Light, 104–6

Confraternity of Our Lady of the Rosary, 104

Confraternity of the Blessed Sacrament, 98, 102, 104

Confraternity of the Blessed Souls of Purgatory, 139

Confraternity of the Immaculate Conception, 102

Confraternity of the Poor Souls, 104, 105

Congress (US), 55, 173, 179, 185, 193

Connelly, Henry, 57n16

conquistadores, 28–29, 34, 323

Convento Grande de Francisco, 39

Cooley, Dennis N., 185

Córdova, Gilberto Benito, 5–6, 13, 52, 63–64, 166, 168, 171, 277–78, 280–81, 331, 337, 338; background, 261–64, 283n3

Córdova, Higinio, 187

Córdova, John F., 256, 259

Córdova, José Darío, 328

Córdova, Josephine M., 13, 257

Córdova, María Rita, 264

Córdova, Vicente, 52, 263

Coronado, Francisco Vásquez de, 31

Corrales, NM, 231

Cortés, Hernán, 28, 31, 33, 38–40, 309

Costal, Joseph, 123

Costilla, CO, 183, 189

Costilla County, CO, 180, 187, 189–90, 195

court cases. *See* genízaro(s), rights of

Coyoté, NM, 267

Coyotes, 4, 53, 124, 128, 134–35, 149, 158n13, 162n68, 226, 229–31, 234–36, 317, 319

criado. *See* captives/captivity; slaves/slavery

Croix, Teodoro de, 166–67

Cruzat y Góngora, Gervasio, 120

Cuba, 2, 48, 88, 90

Cucharas, CO, 186, 192

Cuéllar, Gertrude, 75

Cuerno Verde, 23, 142

Cummings, Alexander, 185–86

Curac, NM, 101

Curuna, Antonio, 122, 138

Custody of the Conversion of Saint Paul, 106

dances. *See Los Comanches*; Matachines; rituals

decolonization, xvii, 15, 326

De La Cruz, Manuel, 126
De La Cruz, María, 314, 319
De La Cruz, María Bárbara, 134
Delgado, Carlos, 91, 96, 111
Denver, CO, xviii
Department of the Interior, 56
Díaz, Porfirio, 42
Diego, Juan, 299
diplomacy, 51
DNA data, 312–24
DNA services, 309
Domínguez, Francisco Atanasio, 47, 50, 65, 83–84, 94, 103–7, 112, 130, 143
Domínguez de Mendoza, Gaspar, 3
Doña Inés, xxii
Dozier, Edward, 263, 280
Dred Scott Case, 53
Dulce, NM, 180, 181, 278
Durango, Mexico, 8, 29, 34, 71, 83, 84, 86, 99, 105, 109, 131

Easterday, Harvey E., 189
El Alemán, NM, 130
El Casco San Luis, Mexico, 32, 33
El Cerrito, NM, 51
El Cuajo (genízaro), 129, 143
El Gallo, Mexico, 32
El Paso, TX, 100
El Paso del Norte, Mexico, 10, 29, 42, 84, 107, 118, 120, 124, 126, 129–30, 134
El Pelón (genízaro), 129, 143
El Rito, NM, 176, 182
El Vado, NM, 107
emancipation. *See* abolition
Emancipation Proclamation, 183, 193
Encinillas, Mexico, 127
encomienda, 1–2, 49, 86–88, 91
Escabosa, NM, 295
Española, NM, 270, 292, 308
Española Valley, NM, 263, 265, 278

Esparza, Moctesuma, 14
Espinosa, Nicolás de, 317, 319
estancias, 119
ethnogenesis, 165
Eulate, Juan de, 102
Evans, John, 193

Feliciana, Pascuala, 122
Fernández, Carlos, 70, 125, 142
Fernández, Sebastián, 109
fictive kinship, 2, 48, 52, 92
flora, 37, 39–40
Fort Laramie, WY, 220n2
Fort Sill, OK, 251, 255
Franciscan Province of the Holy Gospel, 106
Franciscans, 9, 47, 64, 86, 96–100, 103, 119, 137, 165, 266. *See also* baptism; Catholicism; missions
French Revolution, 41
Frésquez, Matías, 132
fur trapping, 175–76

Gadsden Purchase, 54
Gallego, Joseph, 93
Gallego, Teresa, 122
Gallegos, Ana María de los Reyes, 318
Gallegos, Elena, 231
Gallegos, Gertrudes, 253–54, 259
Gallegos, José Francisco, 189
Gallegos, Miguel, 230
Gallup, NM, 263
Gálvez, José de, 82
gambling, 192
Gandert, Adela, 259
Gandert, Augustina, 256
Gandert, Bonifacio, 251
Gandert, William Frederick, 251, 255–59
García, Adilia, 238
García, David F., xxv

García, Delfinia, 145
García, José, 134, 145, 147
García, José de Gracia, 187
García, José Ignacio, 182
García, Juan Felipe, 318
García, María Antonio, 138, 145
García, María Guadalupe, 237
García, Miguel P., xix, xxi
García, Pedro, 71
García-O'Neal, Manuel, 145, 147
Gaspar, James L., 190
genízara(s), 64, 71–77, 122, 128, 137–38, 141, 239, 264, 331–32, 341
genízaro(s), 23, 53, 82, 105, 108–9, 159n30, 184, 284n5, 294, 319; citizenship of, 51–52, 53; court cases, 127–29; defined, xv–xvii, xxii, 1, 5, 8, 65–66, 90–91, 167, 174–75; demographics of, 134–35; described, 2, 238; emancipation of, 2–3; ethnogenesis, 3; family units of, 122–25, 132–35; identity, xviii, 4, 6–7, 10–12, 15–16, 19, 21, 50–53, 56, 80, 82–83, 85–86, 111–13, 119, 125, 137, 139, 143–44, 167–68, 225–26, 232, 234–35, 237–38, 240, 243–46, 264, 266, 276–77, 284n11, 306, 332, 337; legislative memorial (2007), xix–xxi, 58n17, 77–78, 331; marriages of, 122–25, 129–30, 132; material culture, 10–11; oral traditions of, 72–74; origins of, 49, 65, 93–96, 111, 150, 226; petitions of, 150–57, 230–31; poetics, 261–62; political roles, 27; punishment of, 75–77, 91–93; relation to *penitentes*, 111–13; religion of, 41; rights of, 3, 9, 43, 48, 64–65, 67–71, 120–22, 126–28; rituals of, 19–20, 23–24, 28, 40–41, 50–52, 56, 144–45, 167–68, 240–44, 277; roles of, 2–3, 31, 48, 51, 111–12, 167; scholarship on, 63–64, 81; as slaves, 16, 86–93, 334; statistics on, 2, 28, 47, 49–50, 56n1, 57n7, 57n11, 57n16, 63–64, 82, 91, 121, 125, 128, 131, 138–39, 229, 232–34; stereotypes of, 94–96, 111–13; treatment of, 127. *See also* baptism; captives/captivity; Catholicism; *Los Comanches*
Genízaro, José Antonio, 231, 236
genocide, 88, 323
George, Amelia, 314
Gilbert, Petuuche, 326–29, 332, 342n2
Gilpin, William, 177
Globe, AZ, 147–48
Gómez, José Antonio, 194, 196
Gómez, Juan de Jesus, 194
Gonzales, Agustín, 141
Gonzales, Concepción, 141
Gonzales, José, 230
Gonzales, José Angel, 4, 78
Gonzales, Matías, 230
González, José María, 189
González, Juan Antonio, 189
Grolet, Jacques, 122–23
Guadalajara, Mexico, 8, 34
Guadiana, Mexico, 32–35
Guanajuato, Mexico, 32
Guerra, Salvador de, 101–2
Guerro, José Cristobal, 71
Gurulé, Antonio, 122–24, 132, 140, 231, 235, 236
Gurulé, Diego, 231
Gurulé, José Librado Arón, 239
Gurulé, José Manuel, 124, 141
Gurulé, Juana María, 141
Gurulé, María Gertrudes, 141
Gurulé, Pedro, 136
Gurulé, Rafael, 140
Gurulé, Salvador, 231
Gurulé, Santiago, 235, 236
Gurulé, Toribio, 236
Gutiérrez, Antonio, 235
Gutiérrez, Bartolomé, 137–38

Gutiérrez, Francisco, 71
Gutiérrez, Gregorio, 235
Gutiérrez, Javier, 230
Gutiérrez, Juan, 230

Harris, Edward R., 187, 193
Head, Lafayette, xviii, 11, 177, 186, 189, 193
Head Downing, Eliza Jane, 186
Hermandad de Nuestro Padre Jesús Nazareno. See *penitentes*
Hilario, José, 187
Hispaniola, 88
Hispano Roundtable, 271, 284n8
Hispanos. See Nuevomexicanos
Holy Office of the Crusade, 98
Hopis, 3, 101, 166, 180–82, 314
Hopi-Tewas, 1, 6, 165, 167
Huachichiles, 27
Huérfano County, CO, 182, 187, 195
Hurtado, Juana, 235
Hurtado, Juan Páez, 317
Hurtado, María Naranjo, 235

Ibarra, Diego de, 38
Ibarra, Francisco de, 32, 35–36
Iberian Peninsula, 40
Iglesia de San Miguel, 34
Iglesia y Convento de San Francisco, 34
immigration, 28, 29
imperialism. See colonialism
Incas, 69
Indé, Mexico, 36
Indians, 30, 32; in California, 102; DNA data on, 312–24; federal recognition of, xix, xxi; labor of, 34; of Mexico, 27–28, 39; origin stories of, 38; raiding by, 1, 11–12, 48, 54–55, 65, 82, 106, 111, 119, 142, 186, 225, 227, 229–30, 237, 257; religious conversion of, 31–33; as slaves, xvi, xxii, 12–13, 35, 48–55, 67–68, 71, 88–90, 93, 122, 133–35, 141, 145, 173, 175–76, 184–88; trade with, 175–77. See *also specific tribes*
indita ballads, 144–45, 190
Indo-Hispano culture. See Genízaro(s)
involuntary servitude. See captives/captivity; peonage; slaves/slavery
irrigation, 36–37, 42. See *also* agriculture
Irvine, Alexander G., 196
Isleta Pueblo, 10, 101–2, 118–19, 122–23, 125, 129, 142, 162n68, 166, 227, 237, 241
Italian Mafia, 111

Jacobs, Abrana, 195, 196
Jacobs, Albert G. T., 195
Janissaries, xvi, 1, 2, 111
Janos Santo Niño, Mexico, 32
Jarales, NM, 124, 134–35, 139, 165
Jémez Pueblo, 144, 240
Jerusalem, 97
Jesus Christ, 41, 96–98, 108, 113
Johnson, Andrew, 56
Jójola, Juan Pedro, 123, 132
Jójola, María Magdalena, 132
Jójola, Reymundo, 123–24, 132, 158n10
Jójola, Tomás, 123, 132
Jójola, Ventura, 132, 134
Jójola Family, 123–24, 132
Juana (genízara), 76
Jumanos, 50, 57n11, 121
just-war doctrine, 8–90
Juzgado General de Indios, 69

Kansas, 173
Keresan Pueblos, 228
King Philip II, 85
King Xicoténcatl, 38
Kiowas, 1, 12, 23, 28, 50, 57n11, 65, 121, 125, 166, 167, 175, 177, 225, 227, 236, 237, 246
Korean War, 295

labor. *See* captives/captivity; encomienda; peonage; slavery
La Ciénega, NM, 232
Lady Redhouse (Hopi), 314
Laguna Pueblo, 126
La Indita, 145
La Madera, NM, 25, 232, 236, 237, 239, 242–45, 299
Lamy, Jean-Baptiste, 9–10, 109–10
land grants, 3–6, 12, 19, 23, 28, 35, 51–52, 65, 71, 78, 125–28, 132, 177, 228–30, 234–37, 245, 263
language, 2, 6, 28, 43, 65, 94, 126, 167, 174, 183–84, 234, 267
La Petaca Creek, 176
La Salle Expedition, 122
Las Animas County, CO, 187, 195
Las Casas, Bartolomé de, 69, 88
Las Huertas Land Grant, 232, 234–36
Las Trampas, NM, 3, 8, 31, 227
Latin America, 1, 2, 69
La Villa de San Antonio, NM, 328
Law of the Indies, 2, 4, 88, 157n1, 227, 231. *See also* Recopilación
Lawrence, John, 184–85
Lente, Andrés, 123
Lente, Salvador Matías, 138
Leyba, María Magdalena, 314
limpieza de sangre, xviii, 66. *See also* caste system
Lincoln, Abraham, 183
Llano Estacado, 3, 227, 232, 238–39
Lomawikvaya (Hopi), 181
López, Delfina, 308–9
López, Linda M., xx, xxi
Los Alamos, NM, 263, 265, 270–71, 273–74
Los Angeles, CA, xviii, 148
Los Bacas, NM, 133, 139, 141
Los Cerritos Largos, CO, 176

Los Chávez, NM, 124
Los Comanches, 2, 14, 19, 21, 23, 142, 225, 240–45, 290, 295, 299–300, 336. *See also* rituals
Los Conejos, CO, 176
Los Garcías, NM, 139
Los Janchis, NM, 139–43
Los Jarales, NM, 47
Los Lagos, Mexico, 317
Los Lentes, NM, 132
Los Lunas, NM, 120
Los Padillas, NM, 119–20, 230, 237
Los Ranchitos de San Juan, NM, 308
Los Ranchos de Alburquerque. *See* Alburquerque, NM
Los Rincones, CO, 176
Los Trujillos, NM, 134, 139
Lozen (Apache), 331
Luján, Ben, xix, xxi, 331
Luján, Juana, 52

Machismo, 266–67, 271–72, 278
Madariaga, Francisco Ignacio de, 12, 225
Madrid-Baca, Isabel, 308
Maés, Romancita, 72–73
Malinche, 21, 38, 241, 245
Manchego, Juan, 138
Manuela (genízara), 75–76
Manzanares, María Regina, 190
Manzano Mountains, 119, 227–28
Marín del Valle, Francisco, 104
marriage, 2, 28, 41, 96, 122–25, 129–30, 139, 187, 229, 240–41
Martín, Bárbara, 137–38
Martín, José, 105, 138
Martín, Manuel, 71
Martín, Manuel Gregorio, 181
Martínez, Josefa, 257
Martínez, Juan Miguel, 190
Martínez, María, 186, 190

Martínez, Richard C., xix–xxi, 331
Martínez, Salvador, 95
Martínez Ranch, 180
Mason-Dixon Line, 55
Matachines, 12, 14, 19–20, 23, 40–41, 225, 237, 240, 245, 278–79, 290, 295, 299, 336
Mayas, 69
Medina, Adela, 308
memory, xv, xviii, xxi–xxii, 28, 40, 56, 72, 145, 161n55, 167, 190, 225, 240, 326–27, 338
Menchero, Miguel de, 66, 125
Mendinueta, Pedro Fermín de, 51, 112, 231
Mendizábal, Bernardo López de, 87, 102
Mendoza, Gaspar Domínguez de, 125
Mesoamerica, 30, 36, 38, 39, 43, 317, 333
Mestas, Ventura, 125
mestizaje, 12, 15, 63, 96, 144, 161n52, 235, 277, 284n11, 289, 291, 305
mestizo(s), 1, 2, 5, 7, 19, 28, 30, 32, 35, 40, 43, 53, 63–64, 72, 111, 119, 133, 137, 226, 229–31, 234, 236, 245, 291, 306, 308–9, 317, 319, 324, 327, 336
Mexican-American War, 54, 109, 143
Mexican Revolution, 42
Mexicas, 27, 35
Mexico, xvi, 2, 19, 29, 35, 40, 42, 54, 81, 240, 298, 309; abolition in, 4, 49, 52–54; American conquest of, xvii; Constitution of, 53, 226; independence of, 1, 4, 28, 41–42, 48, 49, 52, 54, 63, 112, 139, 174–75, 226, 232, 311; mining in, 84–85; politics of, 4; Spanish conquest of, 28–29, 40. *See also* Mexican-American War
Mexico City, 3, 29, 39, 64, 84, 119, 126–28, 342n2
Miera y Pacheco, Bernardo de, 227
militias, 2, 4, 54, 174, 231–32, 327
mining, 2, 32, 33, 38–39, 49, 84–85, 175

Miranda, Juan Durán de, 39
Miranda, María Rosa, 138
missions, 9, 29, 30, 37, 96–100, 106–8, 119, 122, 124, 130, 137, 266. *See also* baptism; Catholicism; Franciscans
Mixtón Mesa, 32
Moctezuma, 21, 33, 241
Mondragón, Bernardo, 252
Mondragón, Emilia, 252
Mondragón, Lillian, 251–53
Montaño, Bartolo, 147
Montaño, Bernabé, 134
Montaño, Joseph María, 75
Montaño, José Victorio, 147
Montaño, Juan Bautista, 75
Montaño, María Petra, 145, 147
Montaño, Matías, 134, 147
Monterrey, Mexico, 8
Montoya, Antonio, 105
Montoya, Gerónima, 263
Montoya, José, 14, 295
Montoya, Pedro Antonio, 141
Moors, 21, 36, 40, 309
Moquis. *See* Hopis
Mora, Alejandro, 76
Mora, NM, 256, 257, 259, 307
Mora County, NM, 328
Mora Valley, NM, 72, 255
Moreno, Juan Felipe, 141
Moreno, Santiago, 141
Morfí, José Agustín, 90, 94, 111–12, 130, 166
Morismas, 21, 40–41
Morrie, Tiny, 291, 303n2
Morrison, Robert A., 185
mulattos, 226
Muñiz, Manuel, 236
Murillo, Isidro, 130
music, 14, 23, 303n2. *See also* captivity songs; *indita* ballads

Nahuas, 38
Namiquipa, Mexico, 32
Nanillé, 14, 19, 290
Navajos, 1, 14, 23, 28, 31, 56, 57n16, 65, 89–91, 125, 130, 134, 144, 166, 167, 174–76, 180, 184, 186, 192–96, 227, 230, 231–32, 234–38, 246, 308; as captives, 187–90, 252–53, 263–64; in Colorado, 193, 196; Long Walk of, 192–93; Red House Clan, 314; reservation of, 263
Navarro, Francisco Trébol, 229
Nebraska, 173
New Galicia, 32, 33
New Mexico, xvi, 1, 88, 119, 173; annexed by US, 80, 83; Catholicism in, 103–13; chattel slavery in, 57n16; colonization of, 9, 27, 29–31, 33–35, 63, 84–90, 311; Cuartocentennial of, 34–35, 327; demographics of, 128–29; described, 107; District Court of, 182; DNA data, 312–24; economy of, 4–5, 53–54, 85, 175, 232; master-servant statute, 55; missionization in, 96–100, 106–8; modernization of, 19; occupied by US, 54, 109; as province of Mexico, 139–40; slave codes, 55; slave population of, 47–48; slave trade in, 258; state legislature, xix–xxi, 58n17, 77–78, 331; statehood, 5, 15, 42, 323; statistics on, 90; Territorial Assembly, 189; territorial period, 5, 13, 42, 55, 143–44
New Mexico DNA Project, 251, 306, 310, 312
New Spain, 1, 27, 31, 32, 41, 42, 47, 96, 98, 122, 139, 305; governance of, 29–30; laws of, 65, 68–71, 81–82, 92; slave raids in, 49–50
Nieves, Josefa María de las, 257
Nombre de Dios, Mexico, 35
Norton, A. Baldwin, 182

Nuestra Señora de Guadalupe Church, 124
Nuestra Señora de los Dolores de la Joya de Sevilleta, 138
Nuestra Señora de los Dolores de los Genízaros, 133–34. *See also* Belén, NM
Nuestra Señora del Pilar de los Garcías, 134
Nueva Vizcaya, 32, 35
Nuevomexicanos, 42, 48, 55, 188–89, 192, 227, 229, 234, 251, 270–71, 293, 303n3, 305, 309, 311, 322–23, 335; culture of, 15; folk art of, 279–80; folk rituals of, xxv, 144–45, 171, 242–45, 290, 324; identity, 5, 13, 15, 112, 262, 276, 288–89, 298, 300, 307–9, 324; slave raids by, 89, 173–74, 180–82, 193–94; trade with Indians, 175–77. *See also* Chicano movement

Oaxaca, Mexico, 34
obrajes, 2
O'Conor, Hugo, 143
Ohkay Owingeh Pueblo. *See* San Juan Pueblo
Ojo Caliente, NM, 31, 51, 65, 111, 135, 182, 239, 318
Ojo de Las Casa, NM, 239
O'Keeffe, Georgia, 261, 265, 272, 274–75, 284n6
Oñate, Juan de, 7, 15, 28, 29, 33, 35–36, 40, 48, 49, 78, 86–87, 100–101, 119, 305, 311, 327. *See also* colonialism
Oñate Cristóbal, 33, 38
O'Neal, Charles, 147–49
Oraibi, 180–82
oral tradition. *See* memory
Order of Friars Minor, 97
Order of Saint Clare, 97
Ortega, Antonio de, 76
Ortíz, Antonio José, 107

Otero, María de la Luz, 140
Ottoman Empire, xvi, 1, 2, 111

Pacheco, Juana María, 190
Pacheco, Manuel, 328
Pacheco School, 328
Pachuca, Mexico, 32
Padilla, Estevan, 237
Padilla, Francisco, 126–28
Padilla, Juan Jose, 129
Padilla, Manuela, 237
Padilla, Miguel, 129
Padilla, Pablo, 237
Paiutes, 1, 28, 166, 167
Pajarito, NM, 237
Paraguay, 88
Parral, Mexico, 29, 32, 84
Parras, Mexico, 8, 31, 36
Partideros, 56n1
Pawnees, 1, 28, 31, 50, 57n11, 65, 89, 121, 126, 167, 246; as genízaros, 128
Pecos, Regis, xxi, 331
Pecos Pueblo, 89, 144
Pecos River, 3
Peñalosa, Francisco Sosa, 33, 87
penitentes, 6, 9, 41, 42, 80, 266, 299, 328, 339, 343n4; origin of term, 100; rituals of, 109; scholarship on, 83–86
peonage, 3, 8, 48, 49, 53–56, 112, 189–90; statistics on, 57n16
Pérez, Albino, 4
Picurís Pueblo, 89, 240, 308
Piño, Pedro Bautista, 108, 139
Piros, 119, 132, 135
Placitas, NM, 23, 236, 239–40, 242, 245
Plains Indians, 66, 121, 129, 229
Plan de Iguala, 4, 52, 175, 226, 240
Plaza de Francisco Chávez, 139
Plaza de los Genízaros, 124, 134–35, 139–41, 143, 147

plazas, 4
Pope Leo XIII, 110
popular sovereignty, 55
presidios, 29, 35, 37, 112
Protector de Indios, 9, 69–71
Protestants, 80, 83
Provencias Internas, 82
Prussia, 255
Puebla, Mexico, 40
Pueblo de Abiquiú. *See* Abiquiú, NM
Pueblo Indians, xviii, 1, 4, 5, 9, 23, 28, 31, 49, 70–71, 74, 86, 88–89, 91, 97, 100–101, 107, 108, 112, 121, 126–28, 130, 135, 143–44, 166, 171, 227, 230, 235, 240, 243, 245–46, 293, 300, 327; as genízaros, 66–67, 124; theology of, 304n5
Pueblo Quemado, NM, 3
Pueblo Revolt, 3, 39, 49, 69, 70, 82, 84, 86, 91, 98, 102, 105, 120, 123, 292

Querétaro, Mexico, 8, 31, 32
Quetzalcóatl, 38
Quinn, Charles, 148
Quintana, Antonio, 235
Quintana, Luis, 127–28
Quintana, María Miquela, 314
Quivira, 31

racism. *See* caste system
radical Republicans, 55–56. *See also* abolitionists
Rael, Antonia, 145, 147
Rael, María Josefa, 129
Rael-Gálvez, Estevan, sponsors legislative memorial, xx–xxi
Ramírez, Agustín V., 303n2
Ramos, Juan, 123–24, 138
Ranchos de Taos, NM, 3, 21, 179, 239, 240, 242, 299
ransoms. See *rescate*

Reaño, Joseph, 89–90
reconquista, 49, 91, 98, 103, 236, 311, 327
Reconstruction, 49
Recopilación, 69, 88, 89
Redondo Beach, CA, 148
Red Valley, NM, 314
Reform Laws, 42
religion, 42, 50, 65, 191. *See also* baptism; Catholicism; Christianity; Franciscans; missions
repartimiento, 2, 66, 91
rescate, 2, 3, 19, 65, 66, 69, 71, 72, 82, 90, 94, 95, 235
Río Abajo, 10, 12, 108, 119–22, 125, 142–43, 225, 227–29, 236–37
Río Arriba, 8, 108, 121, 128, 142–43
Rio Arriba County, NM, 182, 265, 328
Río Bravo. *See* Río Grande
Río Chama, 33
Río Conchos, 29
Río de San Juan de Dios, 34
Río de Santa Fe, 8, 31, 34, 35
Río Grande, 1, 29, 32–33, 36, 39, 42, 47, 231, 292
Río Puerco, 229
rituals, 14, 19, 25–26, 38, 39–40, 240. *See also Los Comanches*; Matachines; Nanillé; Santo Tomás Apóstol
Rivera, Jenni, 303n2
Rivera, Josefa, 124
Romero, Felipa, 141
Romero, José Gerónimo, 186
Romero, José Miguel, 186
Romero, Juan de Jesús, 186
Romero, María Soledad, 187
Royal Chicano Air Force, 195
Roybal, Juana María, 138
Roybal, Juan de Dios, 180
Ruiz, Joaquín de Jesus, 135
Ruta de la Plata, 8

Sabinal, NM, 123, 130–34, 143
Saguache, CO, 184, 195
Saint Bonaventure, 96
Saint Francis of Assisi, 96–97, 102–4
Saint Louis, Missouri, 255
Saíz, Felipe, 89
Salazar, Agustín, 126
Salazar, Antonio, 119, 126, 127
Salinas, NM, 119
Salinas, Raúl R., 198
Salpointe, John Baptist, 110
Saltillo, Mexico, 8, 31, 37, 40
San Agustín de Isleta Church, 123
San Antonio de las Huertas, NM, 3, 12, 225, 227, 230–32, 234, 236–37, 240, 245, 299
San Antonio de Padua, NM, 12, 225, 230, 234, 237–39
San Antonio Mountains, 176
San Antonito, NM, 240, 245
San Buenaventura, Mexico, 32
Sanches, Gertrudis, 141
Sánchez, Diego Antonio, 133
Sánchez, Marcos, 113
San Clemente, NM, 129
San Cristóbal Pueblo, xxii
Sand Creek Massacre, 195
Sandía Mountains, 6, 12, 21, 23, 25, 225–27, 238–41, 246
Sandía Pueblo, 102, 120–23, 130, 228, 230, 232, 237, 241; land grant of, 3, 51
San Eleazario, Mexico, 36
San Esteban de la Nueva Tlaxcala-Saltillo, Mexico, 34, 36–37
San Felipe el Real de Chihuahua, 127
San Felipe Pueblo, 227
San Francisco de los Conchos, Mexico, 32
San Gabriel Yunque Owingeh, NM, 33
Sangre de Cristo Land Grant, 177

Sangre de Cristo Mountains, 51, 292
San Ildefonso Pueblo, 240, 318
San José, NM, 37
San José de Las Trampas, NM. *See* Las Trampas, NM
San José del Vado, NM, 111
San Juan, Manuel de, 127
San Juan del Río, Mexico, 32
San Juan de Nepomuceno, CO, 179–80
San Juan Pueblo, 23, 29, 107, 191, 240, 242, 278, 308
San Luis Gonzaga, 25
San Luis Potosí, Mexico, 8, 32
San Luis Valley, CO, xvii, 251
San Miguel de Carnué. *See* Carnué, NM
San Miguel de la Puente, NM, 52
San Miguel del Vado, NM, 3, 8, 31, 51, 65, 71, 111, 239
San Pedro, NM, 236, 245
San Pedro Mountains, 228
Santa Ana, NM, 37
Santa Bárbara, Mexico, 33
Santa Clara Pueblo, 240, 242, 280, 308
Santa Cruz, NM, 3, 4, 52, 103–11, 125, 127, 226, 314, 318
Santa Fe, NM, 3, 27–28, 29, 37, 39, 78, 84, 85, 86, 110, 127–28, 130, 182, 226, 240, 255–56, 265, 274; establishment of, 8, 33–35; fiesta at, 327; Franciscans at, 103–11; genízaros at, 47, 57n16, 71, 105; occupied by US troops, 141; population of, 87; presidio at, 112. *See also* Barrio de Analco, NM
Santa Fe Ring, 5
Santa Fe Trail, 53, 256, 259
Santa María de la Paz, Mexico, 33, 36
Santo Cristo de Esquipulas, 108
Santo Domingo Pueblo, 240, 342n2
Santo Niño Church, 245
Santo Niño de Atocha, 25, 108, 144, 258
Santo Niño fiesta, 245
Santo Tomás Apóstol, 19
Santo Tomás de Abiquiú, NM. *See* Abiquiú, NM
Santuario de Chimayó, 107–8, 265, 269
Sarita (genízara), 72–74
Senecú, 125
Sephardic Jews, 309
Serrano, Pedro, 89, 91
servants. *See* captives/captivity; slaves/slavery
settler colonialism, 87
Seven Caves of Chicomóstoc, 38
Sherman, William T., 56
Sierra, Antonio, 182
Sierra, José Antonio, 138
Sierra Blanca, TX, 130
Sierra Lanterna, CO, 179
Siete Partidas, 70
Silva, Juana María, 134, 147
Silva, Luis, 138
slave codes, 55
slaves/slavery, xvi, xix, 8, 19, 193; abolished, 2; chattel system, 48, 53–56, 57n16, 87; murder of, 93; statistics on, xvii, 47, 56, 57n16, 87–88; in the US South, xvii, 87. *See also* captives/captivity; encomienda; Indians, as slaves; peonage; *repartimiento*
Smithsonian Folklife Festival, 63
Smithsonian National Museum, 63, 262
Socorro, TX, 65, 134, 135
songs. *See* music; rituals
Sonora, Mexico, 134, 143
Spain, xvi, 1, 21, 36, 42, 49, 88, 139, 241, 298, 309; colonialism by, xxii, 15, 29, 69, 86–90, 118–20, 130–31, 331, 342n2; conquest of Mexico, 27, 38; laws of, 9; policy of, 50, 106–7, 323. *See also* New Spain

Spanish Inquisition, 309
Sporleder, Louis B., 185–86
Stations of the Cross, 97–98, 103
St. Vrain, Ceran, 189
Suazo, Francisco, 134
Suchíl Valley, Mexico, 32

Tafoya, Felipe, 70
Tafoya, Juan de, 127
Tajique, NM, 101
Talpa, NM, 21
Tamarón y Romeral, Pedro, 84, 103
Taney, Roger, 53
Tanos, xxii, 50, 57n11, 121, 230, 314
Taos, NM, 4, 73, 84, 89, 107, 182, 183, 240, 254, 256, 257, 265, 274; genízaros at, 128
Taos County, NM, 189
Taos Pueblo, 125, 240, 242, 278
Tarascos, 27
Tejón, NM, 232, 239
Tenochas, 27
Tenochtitlán, Mexico, 28
Texas, 81–82, 122
Texcocanos, 27
Third Order of Saint Francis, 84, 85, 97, 103–10
Thirteenth Amendment, 55
Tiburcio, Isabel, 141
Tierra Amarilla, NM, 182
Tijeras Canyon. *See* Carnué, NM
Tijerina, Reies López, 5
Tiwas, 3, 10, 118–19, 122–24, 135, 228, 230, 292, 309
Tlaloc, 38
Tlatelolcos, 27
Tlaxcalan Diaspora, 29, 31, 36
Tlaxcalans, 7–8, 27–43; agriculture of, 35–37, 43; material culture of, 40–41; religion of, 38–39
Tolosa, Isabel de, 33

Tolosa, Juan de, 38
Tomé, NM, 3, 47, 65, 95, 107, 112, 120, 125, 131, 142
Tompiro Pueblos, 87, 101, 119
Torres, Diego, 119, 124–25, 127, 132, 134
Torres, Gregorio, 134
Torres, Joaquín, 134
Torres, Josef, 132
Torres, María, 126
Torres, Nicolás, 134
Torres, Salvador, 71
Tórrez, Antonio, 237
Tortugas, NM, 240
trade licenses, 175
Treaty of Córdova, 4
Treaty of Guadalupe Hidalgo, 5, 42, 49, 54, 81, 109
Tres Piedras, NM, 176
Trinidad, CO, 195
Trío Casindio, 295
Truchas, NM, 314
Trujillo, Andrés, 122
Trujillo, Atanacio, 176
Trujillo, María Antonia, 190
Trujillo, Mariano, 138
Trujillo, Santiago, 134
Trujillo, Vicente, 138
Turkey, xvi

United States, 29, 42; abolition in, 48, 54–56, 183, 185; annexation of New Mexico, 80, 83; bicentennial of, 14, 289; Constitution of, 55–56; expansion of, 5, 81–82; independence of, 47; sectionalism in, 49, 54–55; slavery in, 53, 87
University of California, 271
University of New Mexico–Gallup, 263, 265, 280–82
Urrutia, José de, 8, 31, 34

Ussel, Gabriel, 187
Utah, 173, 179
Utes, 1, 3, 23, 28, 31, 50, 57n11, 65, 89–91, 121, 125, 166, 167, 174–76, 184, 227, 231, 234, 246, 314; Muache band, 176–77; slave raids by, 192–94

Valdez, Isidoro, 253–54
Valdez, José Celedonio, 177
Valdez, Josie, 252–54
Valdez, Luis, xvii
Valencia, NM, 3, 47, 65, 120
Valle de San Bartolomé, Mexico, 32, 36
Vallejos, Antonio José, 176, 187
Vallejos, María Dolores, 187, 196
Vargas, Diego de, 15, 305
Vaughn, NM, 186
Velarde, José Desiderio, 188
Velarde, Teresa, 188
Velarde, Victoria, 188
Velasco II, Luis de, 29, 87
Velásquez, Marcos, 133
Vélez Cachupin, Tomás, 3, 4, 28, 75, 78, 89, 93, 168, 226, 229, 230–31, 266
Vigil, Cleofes, 14, 288, 293
Vigil, José, 142
Vigil, José Francisco, 175–76
Vigil, Juan, 181
Vigil, María de Jesus, 256
Vigil, Pascual, 129–30

Vigil, Soledad, 142
Villa Alta, Mexico, 34
Villagrá, Gaspar Pérez de, 100
Virgen de Guadalupe, 38–39
Virgen de la Macana, 39
Virgen de la Sacristía de Toledo, 39
Virginia, 48

Walsenburg, CO, 185, 187, 253
Ward, John, 143–44, 182
water rights, 42
Wheaton, Theodore, 189
Wichitas, 65
women, xvii, 21, 38–39, 47, 50, 54–55, 66, 91, 95–96, 177, 183, 186, 191, 236, 239, 329; as captives, 193–94. *See also* genízara(s)
Woodson, Gabriel, 184–85
Woodson, James Bernard, 184–85, 189

Youngsville, NM, 267
Yucatán, 90

Zacatecas, Mexico, 8, 29, 32, 33, 38–39, 84, 85, 122, 317
Zaldívar, Juan de, 86–87, 342n2
Zárate Salmerón, Jerónimo, 87
Zubiría y Escalante, José Antonio Laureano de, 84, 108–9
Zuñi Pueblo, 86, 126, 235

www.ingramcontent.com/pod-product-compliance
Lightning Source LLC
Chambersburg PA
CBHW030517230426
43665CB00010B/647